Dedicated to the memory of Leo Baxendale

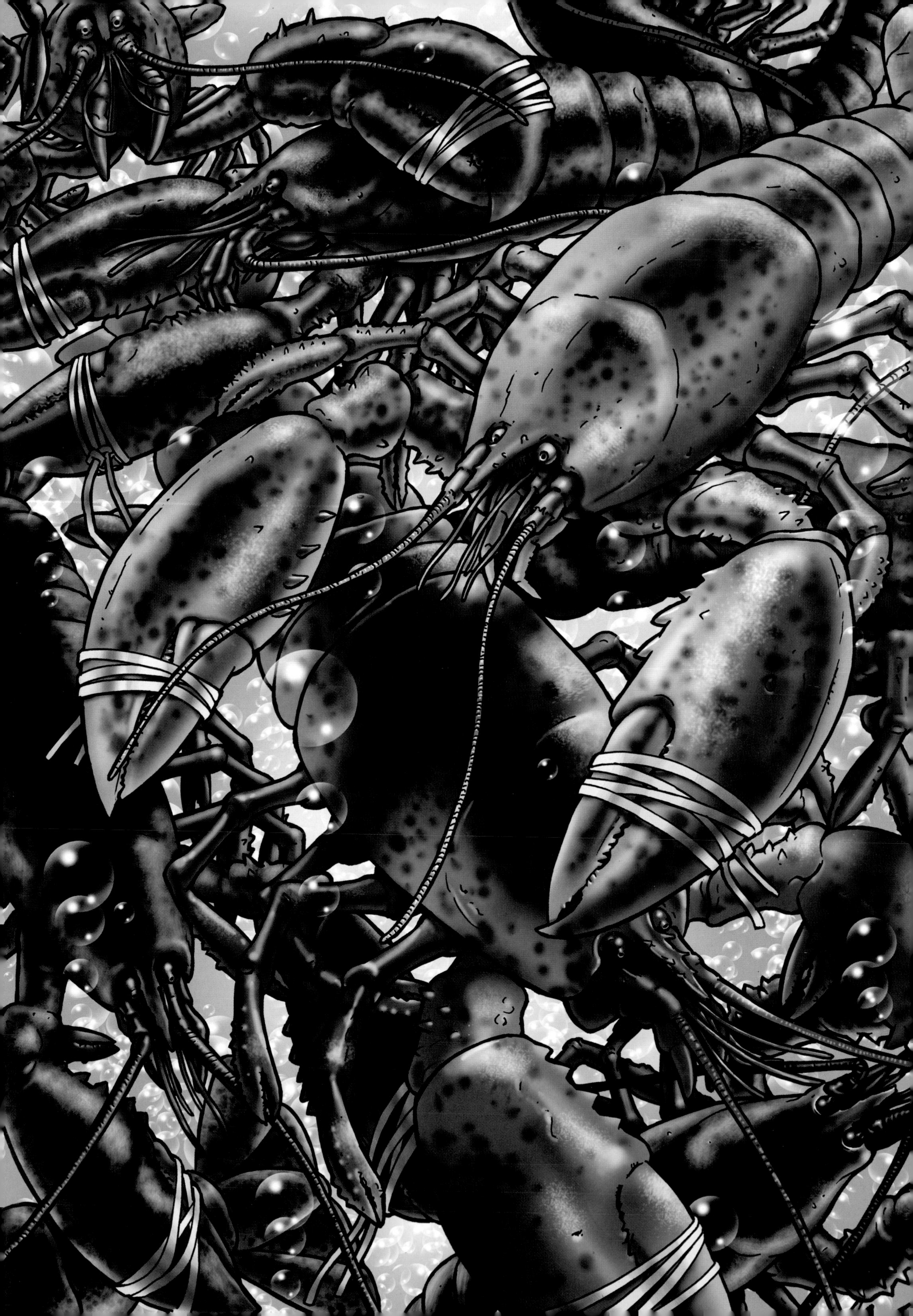

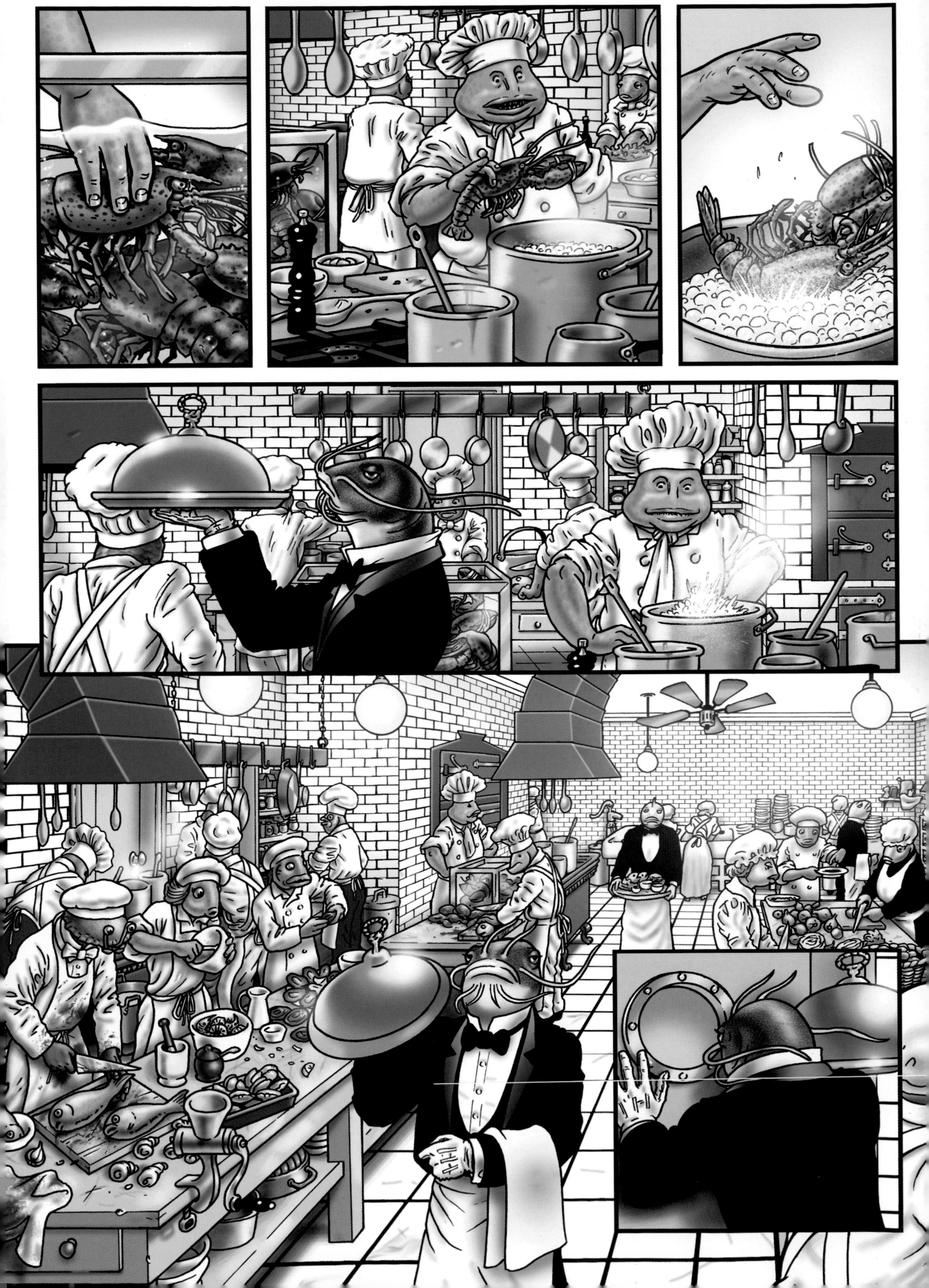

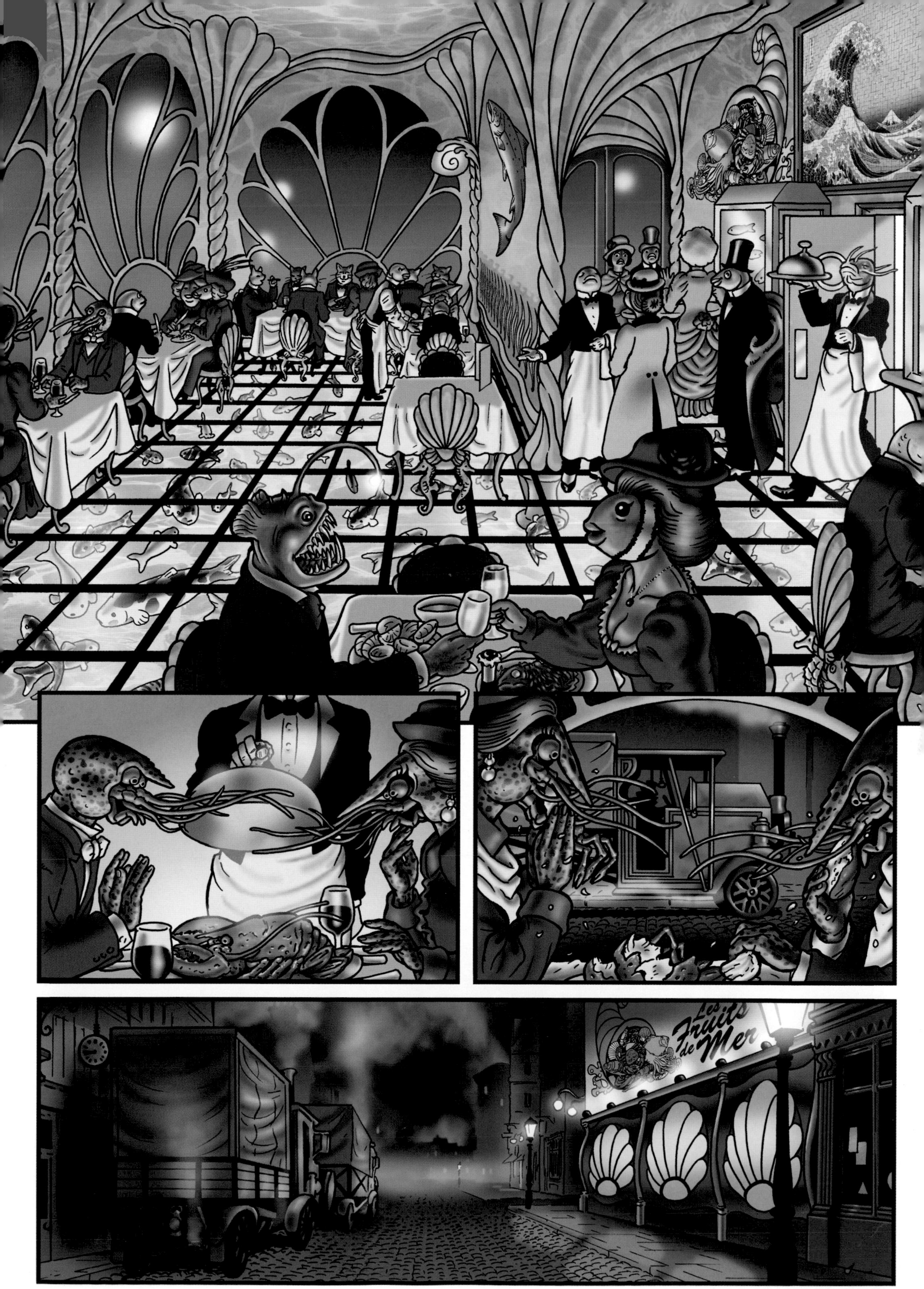
Les Fruits de Mer

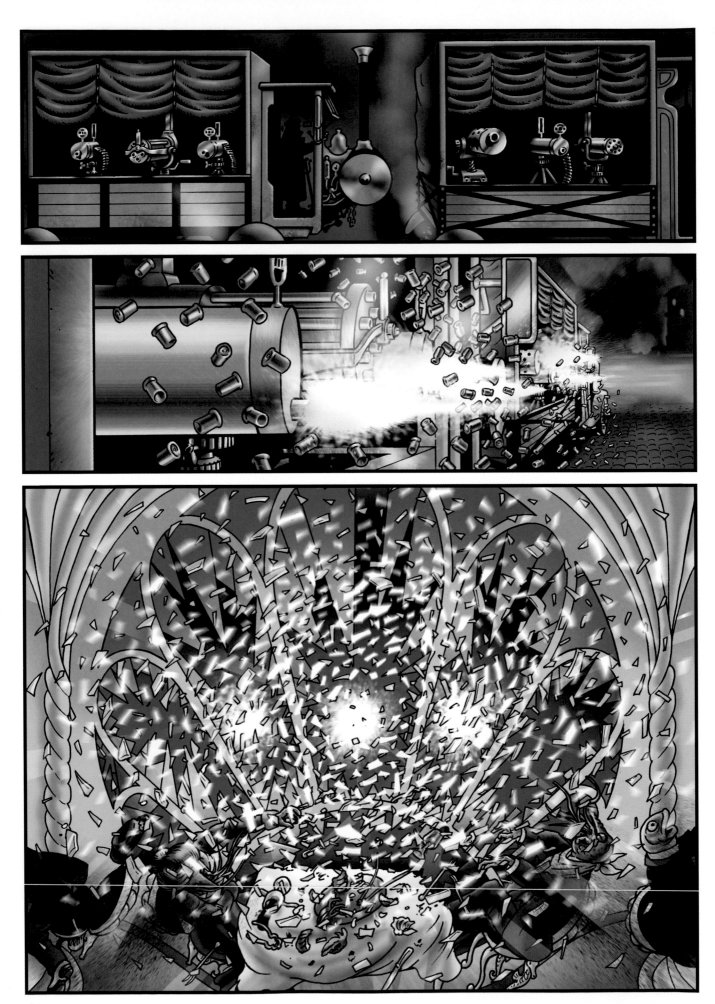

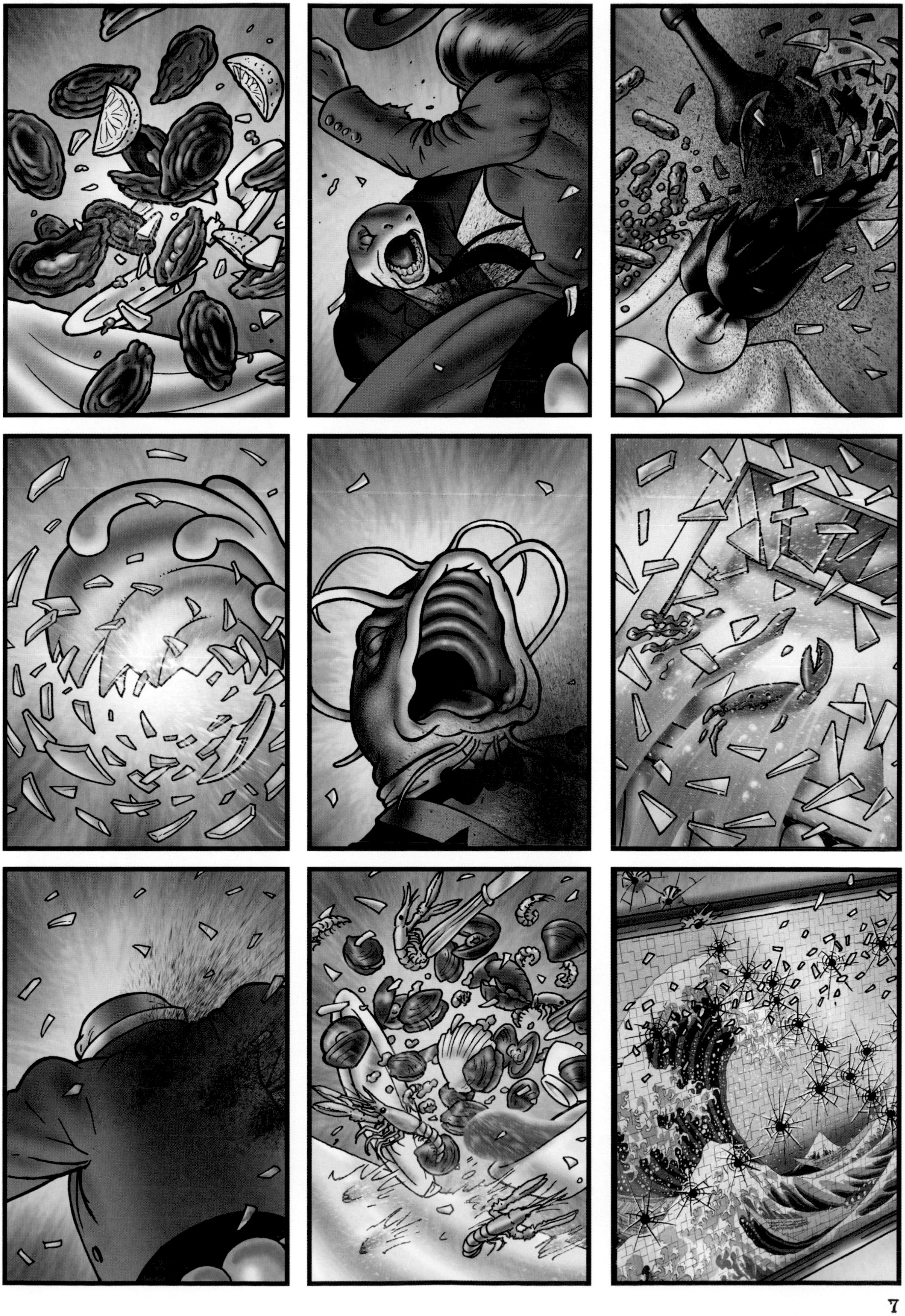

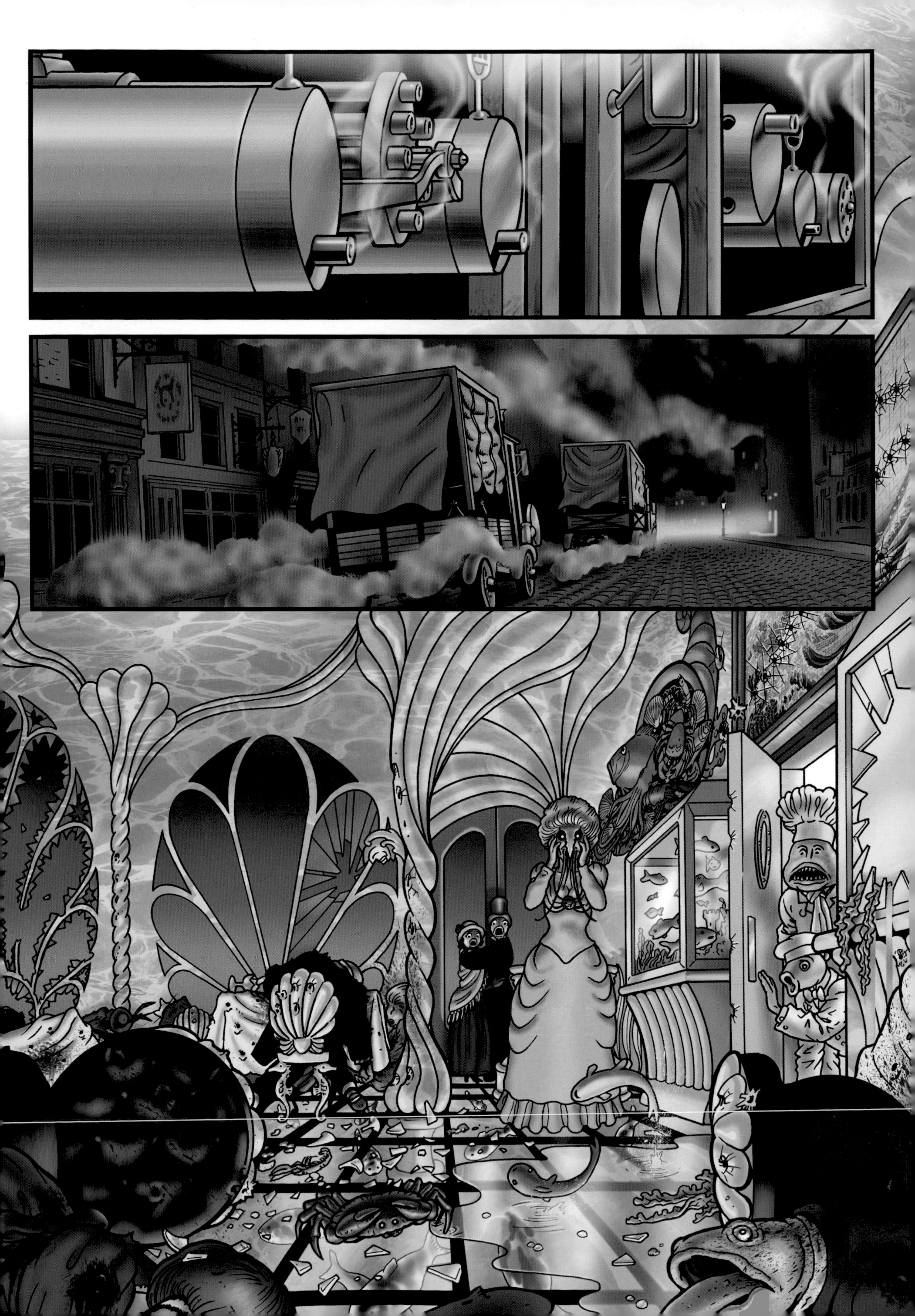

Grandville
Force Majeure

A Fantasy

by

Bryan Talbot

Script, art & book design: Bryan Talbot

Dedicated to the memory of Leo Baxendale

Partial preliminary colouring: Alwyn Talbot, Angus McKie and Jordan Smith
Bryan Talbot hand lettering font available from Comicraft
Colour flats: Jesse Kindzierski

Art Nouveau steampunk pattern by Bryan Talbot,
based on the endpapers of "Dampf und Elektricität:
die Technik im Anfange des XX Jahrhunderts."
Berlin: W. Herlet. [c.1900]

Sincere acknowledgements for proof-reading,
comments on the work-in-progress and other important help to
Mario Benenati, Hannah Berry, Eric Bufkens, Lawrence Dean,
Dan Franklin, Stephen Holland, Dr Mel Gibson, Angus McKie,
Helena Nash, Julie Tait, Dr Mary Talbot, Chris Warner
and the crew of the Steam Yacht Gondola, Coniston.

"Keep clear of the badger; for he bites."
Sir Arthur Conan Doyle, *The Sign of Four*

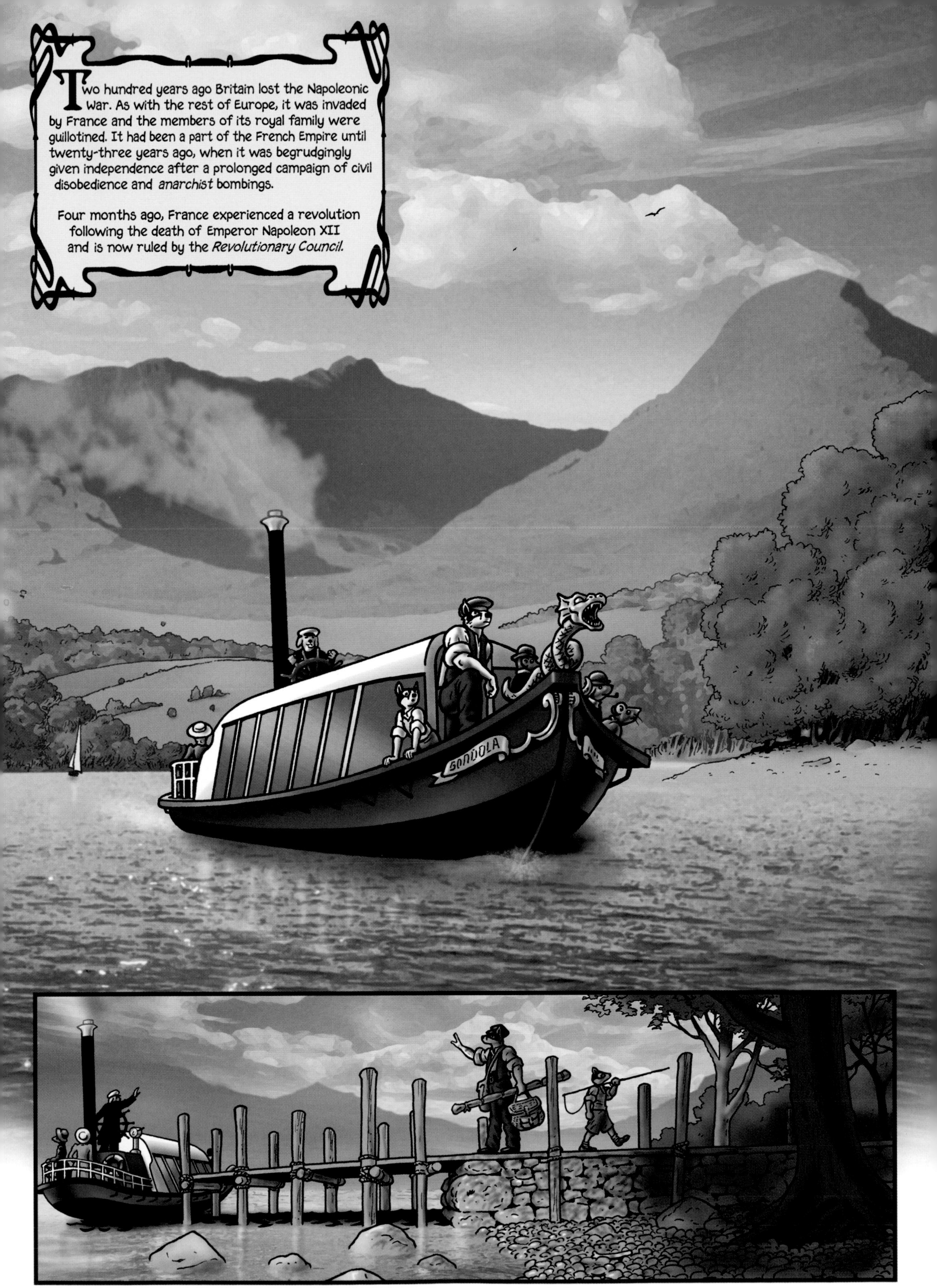
Two hundred years ago Britain lost the Napoleonic War. As with the rest of Europe, it was invaded by France and the members of its royal family were guillotined. It had been a part of the French Empire until twenty-three years ago, when it was begrudgingly given independence after a prolonged campaign of civil disobedience and *anarchist* bombings.
Four months ago, France experienced a revolution following the death of Emperor Napoleon XII and is now ruled by the *Revolutionary Council.*

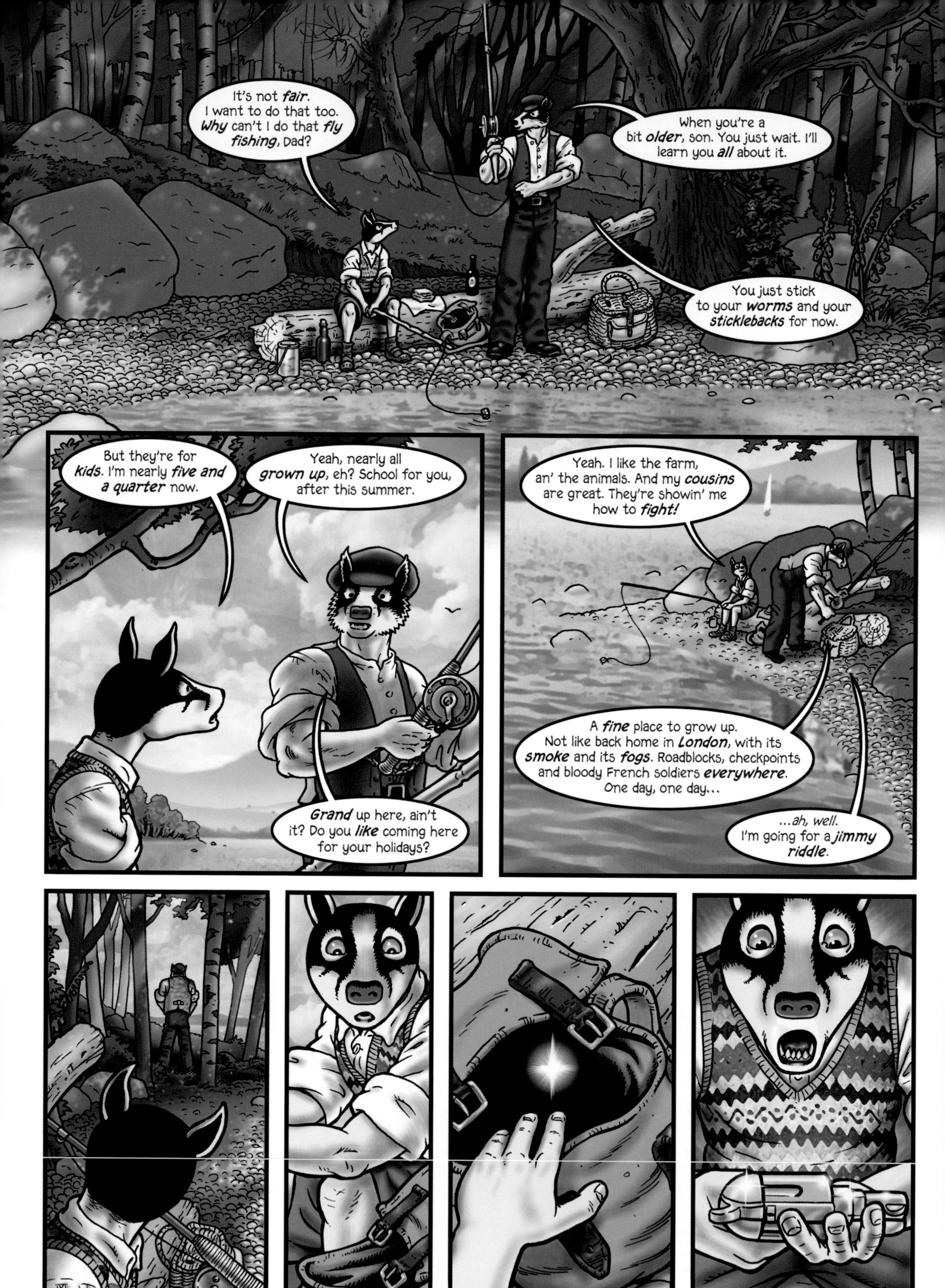
It's not fair. I want to do that too. Why can't I do that fly fishing, Dad?
When you're a bit older, son. You just wait. I'll learn you all about it.
You just stick to your worms and your sticklebacks for now.
But they're for kids. I'm nearly five and a quarter now.
Yeah, nearly all grown up, eh? School for you, after this summer.
Grand up here, ain't it? Do you like coming here for your holidays?
Yeah. I like the farm, an' the animals. And my cousins are great. They're showin' me how to fight!
A fine place to grow up. Not like back home in London, with its smoke and its fogs. Roadblocks, checkpoints and bloody French soldiers everywhere. One day, one day...
...ah, well. I'm going for a jimmy riddle.

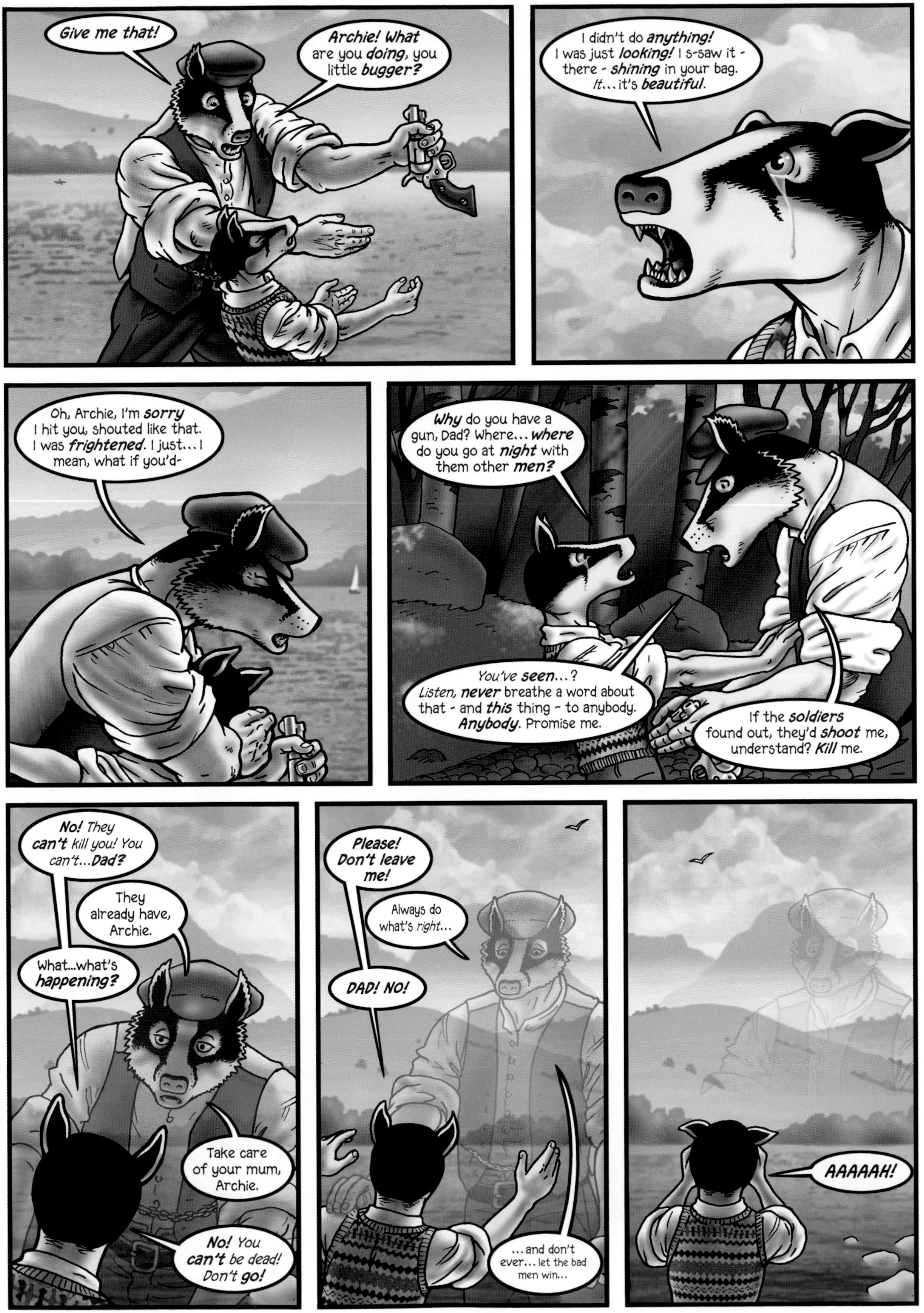

Give me that!
Archie! What are you doing, you little bugger?
I didn't do anything! I was just looking! I s-saw it there - shining in your bag. It... it's beautiful.
Oh, Archie, I'm sorry I hit you, shouted like that. I was frightened. I just... I mean, what if you'd-
Why do you have a gun, Dad? Where... where do you go at night with them other men?
You've seen...? Listen, never breathe a word about that - and this thing - to anybody. Anybody. Promise me.
If the soldiers found out, they'd shoot me, understand? Kill me.
No! They can't kill you! You can't...Dad?
They already have, Archie.
What...what's happening?
Take care of your mum, Archie.
No! You can't be dead! Don't go!
Please! Don't leave me!
Always do what's right...
DAD! NO!
...and don't ever... let the bad men win...
AAAAAH!

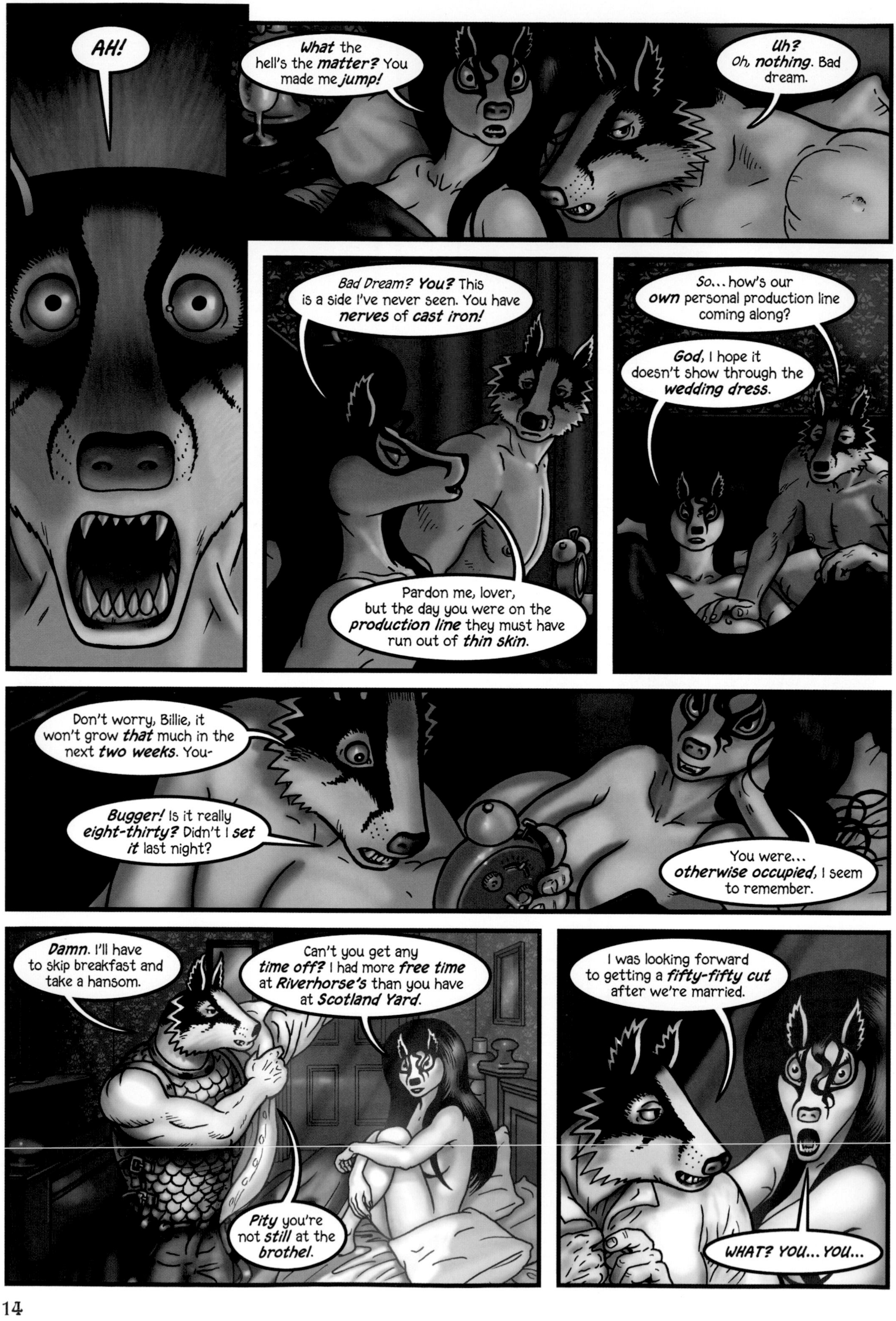
AH!
What the hell's the matter? You made me jump!
Uh? Oh, nothing. Bad dream.
Bad Dream? You? This is a side I've never seen. You have nerves of cast iron!
Pardon me, lover, but the day you were on the production line they must have run out of thin skin.
So... how's our own personal production line coming along?
God, I hope it doesn't show through the wedding dress.
Don't worry, Billie, it won't grow that much in the next two weeks. You-
Bugger! Is it really eight-thirty? Didn't I set it last night?
You were... otherwise occupied, I seem to remember.
Damn. I'll have to skip breakfast and take a hansom.
Can't you get any time off? I had more free time at Riverhorse's than you have at Scotland Yard.
Pity you're not still at the brothel.
I was looking forward to getting a fifty-fifty cut after we're married.
WHAT? YOU... YOU...

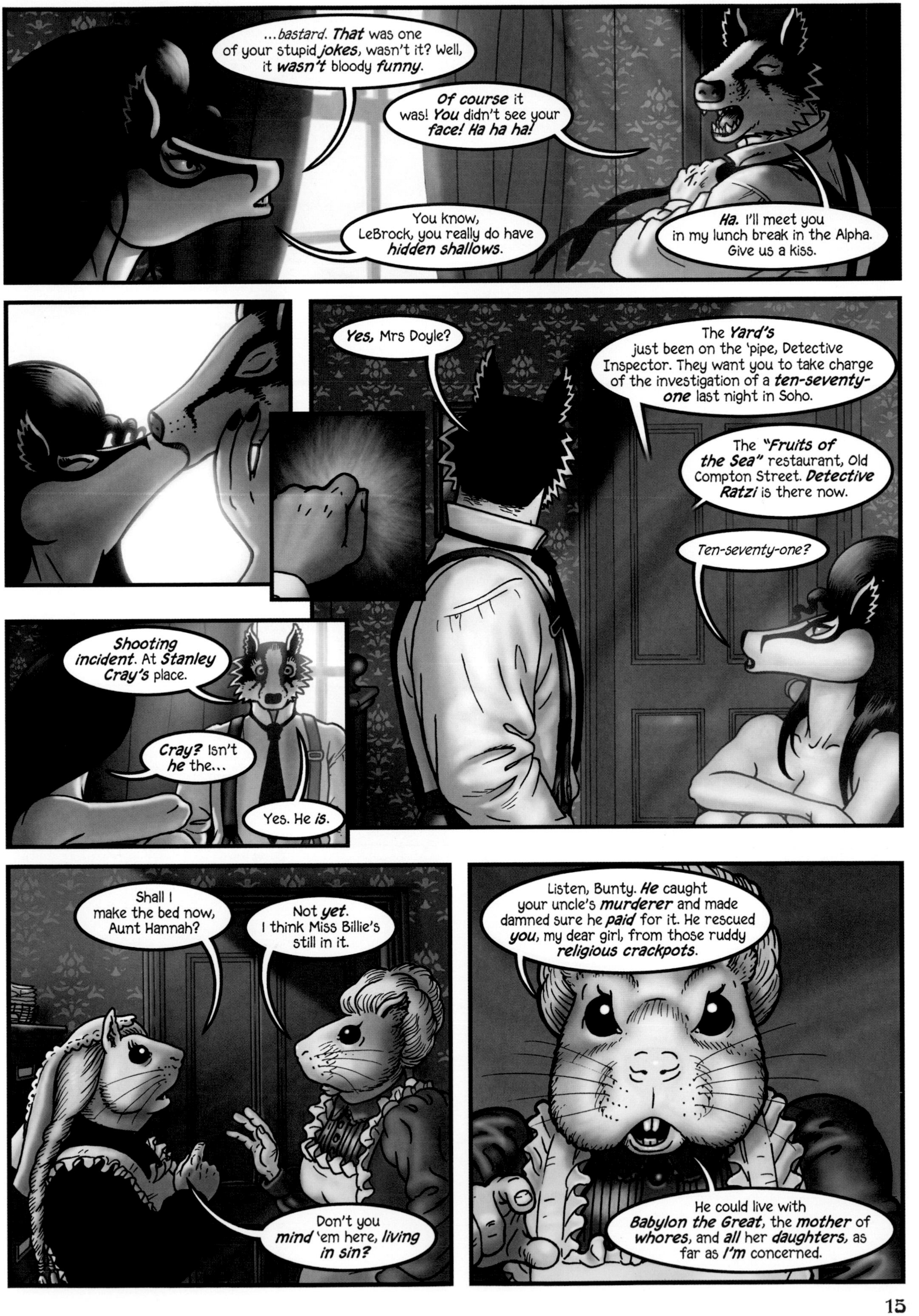
...bastard. That was one of your stupid jokes, wasn't it? Well, it wasn't bloody funny.
Of course it was! You didn't see your face! Ha ha ha!
You know, LeBrock, you really do have hidden shallows.
Ha. I'll meet you in my lunch break in the Alpha. Give us a kiss.
Yes, Mrs Doyle?
The Yard's just been on the 'pipe, Detective Inspector. They want you to take charge of the investigation of a ten-seventy-one last night in Soho.
The "Fruits of the Sea" restaurant, Old Compton Street. Detective Ratzi is there now.
Ten-seventy-one?
Shooting incident. At Stanley Cray's place.
Cray? Isn't he the...
Yes. He is.
Shall I make the bed now, Aunt Hannah?
Not yet. I think Miss Billie's still in it.
Don't you mind 'em here, living in sin?
Listen, Bunty. He caught your uncle's murderer and made damned sure he paid for it. He rescued you, my dear girl, from those ruddy religious crackpots.
He could live with Babylon the Great, the mother of whores, and all her daughters, as far as I'm concerned.

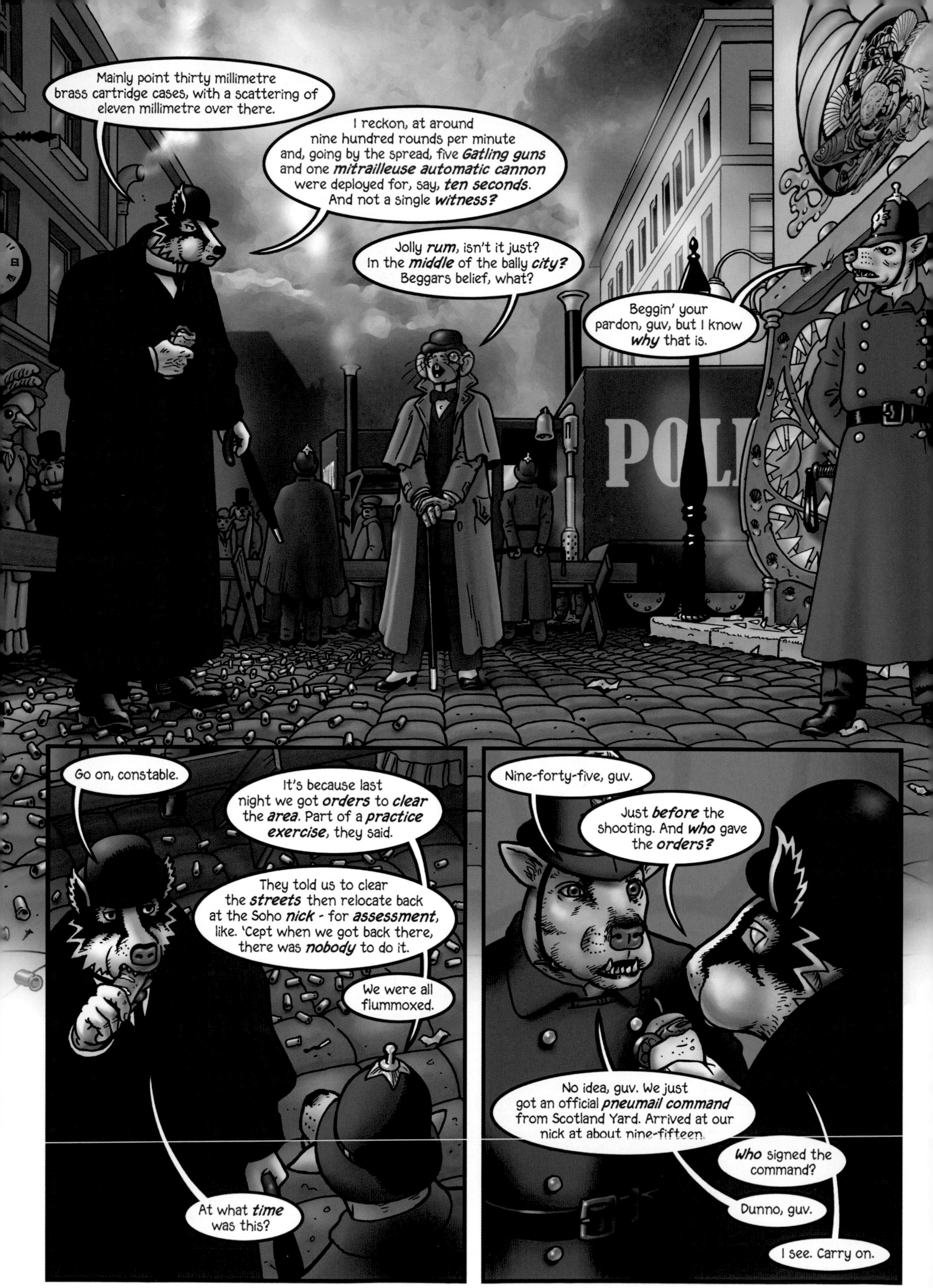
Mainly point thirty millimetre brass cartridge cases, with a scattering of eleven millimetre over there.
I reckon, at around nine hundred rounds per minute and, going by the spread, five Gatling guns and one mitrailleuse automatic cannon were deployed for, say, ten seconds. And not a single witness?
Jolly rum, isn't it just? In the middle of the bally city? Beggars belief, what?
Beggin' your pardon, guv, but I know why that is.
POLI
Go on, constable.
It's because last night we got orders to clear the area. Part of a practice exercise, they said.
They told us to clear the streets then relocate back at the Soho nick - for assessment, like. 'Cept when we got back there, there was nobody to do it.
We were all flummoxed.
At what time was this?
Nine-forty-five, guv.
Just before the shooting. And who gave the orders?
No idea, guv. We just got an official pneumail command from Scotland Yard. Arrived at our nick at about nine-fifteen.
Who signed the command?
Dunno, guv.
I see. Carry on.

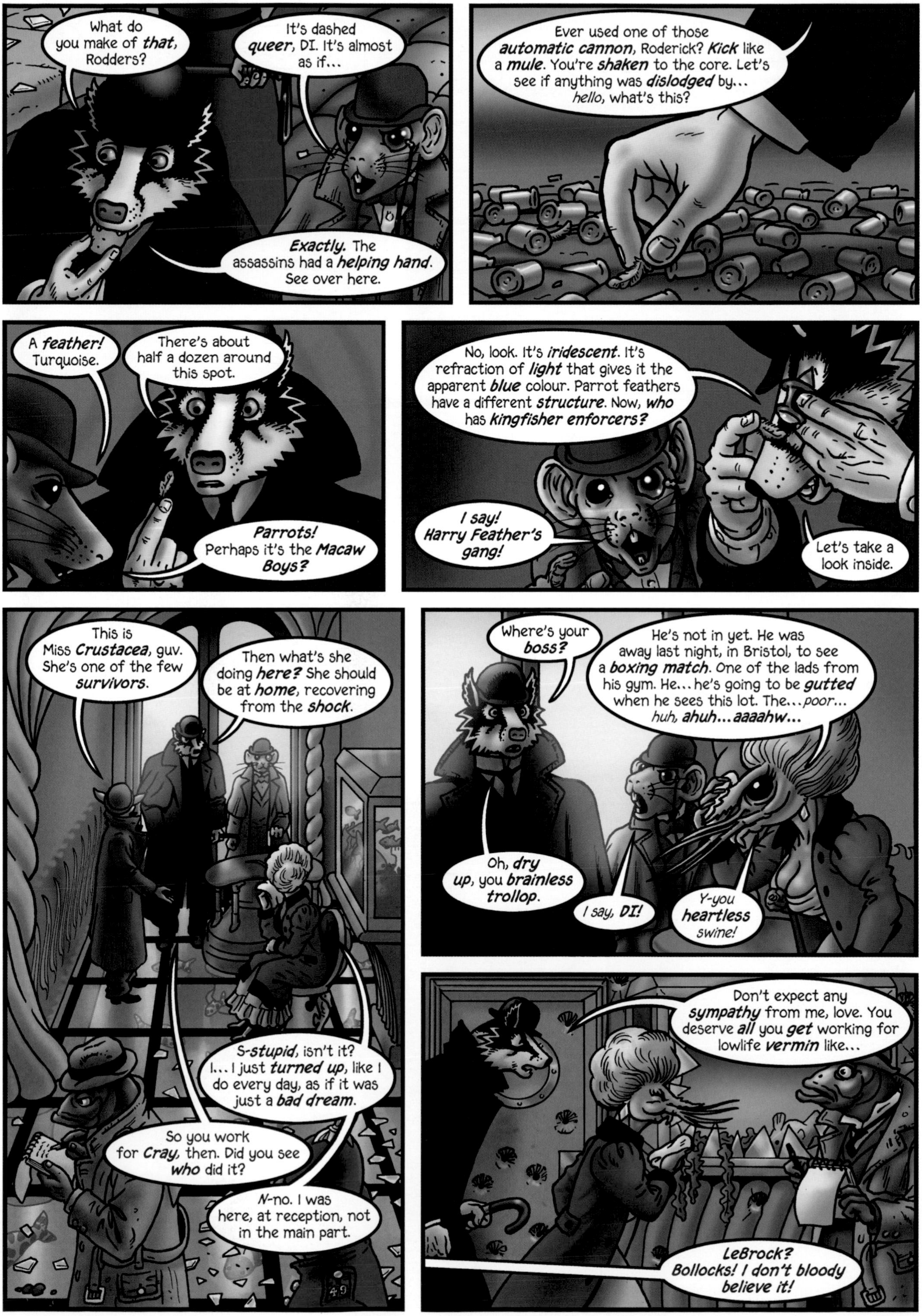

What do you make of *that*, Rodders?
It's dashed *queer*, DI. It's almost as if...
Exactly. The assassins had a *helping hand*. See over here.
Ever used one of those *automatic cannon*, Roderick? *Kick* like a *mule*. You're *shaken* to the core. Let's see if anything was *dislodged* by... *hello*, what's this?
A *feather!* Turquoise.
There's about half a dozen around this spot.
Parrots! Perhaps it's the *Macaw Boys?*
No, look. It's *iridescent*. It's refraction of *light* that gives it the apparent *blue* colour. Parrot feathers have a different *structure*. Now, *who* has *kingfisher enforcers?*
I say! Harry Feather's gang!
Let's take a look inside.
This is Miss *Crustacea*, guv. She's one of the few *survivors*.
Then what's she doing *here?* She should be at *home*, recovering from the *shock*.
S-*stupid*, isn't it? I... I just *turned up*, like I do every day, as if it was just a *bad dream*.
So you work for *Cray*, then. Did you see *who* did it?
N-no. I was here, at reception, not in the main part.
Where's your *boss?*
He's not in yet. He was away last night, in Bristol, to see a *boxing match*. One of the lads from his gym. He... he's going to be *gutted* when he sees this lot. The... *poor*... *huh*, *ahuh...aaaahw...*
Oh, *dry up*, you *brainless trollop*.
I say, DI!
Y-you heartless swine!
Don't expect any *sympathy* from me, love. You deserve *all* you *get* working for lowlife *vermin* like...
LeBrock? Bollocks! I don't bloody believe it!

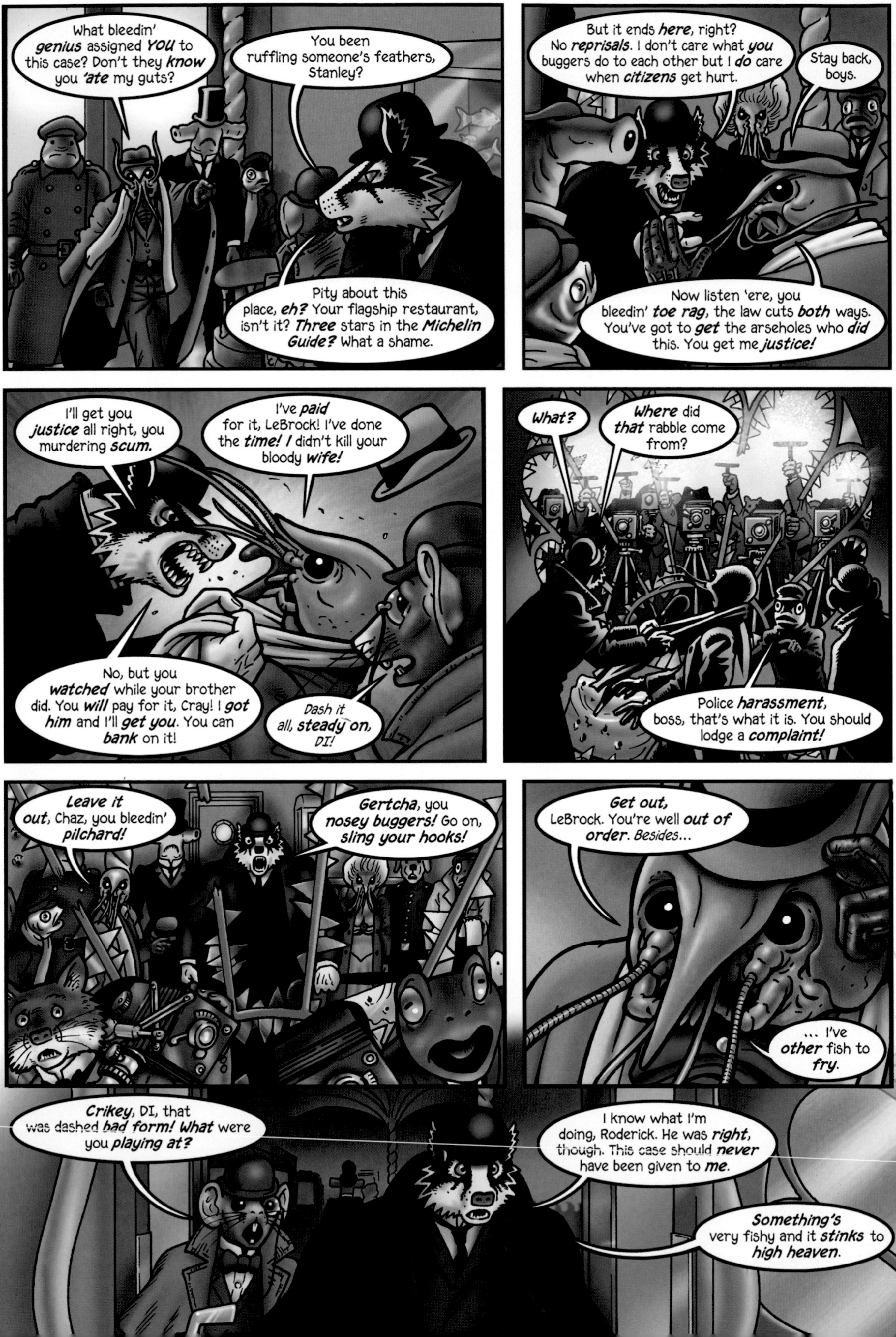
What bleedin' *genius* assigned *YOU* to this case? Don't they *know* you *'ate* my guts?
You been ruffling someone's feathers, Stanley?
Pity about this place, *eh?* Your flagship restaurant, isn't it? *Three* stars in the *Michelin Guide?* What a shame.
But it ends *here*, right? No *reprisals*. I don't care what *you* buggers do to each other but I *do* care when *citizens* get hurt.
Stay back, boys.
Now listen 'ere, you bleedin' *toe rag*, the law cuts *both* ways. You've got to *get* the arseholes who *did* this. You get me *justice!*
I'll get you *justice* all right, you murdering *scum.*
I've *paid* for it, LeBrock! I've done the *time! I* didn't kill your bloody *wife!*
No, but you *watched* while your brother did. You *will* pay for it, Cray! I *got him* and I'll *get you*. You can *bank* on it!
Dash it all, *steady on,* DI!
What?
Where did *that* rabble come from?
Police *harassment*, boss, that's what it is. You should lodge a *complaint!*
Leave it out, Chaz, you bleedin' *pilchard!*
Gertcha, you *nosey buggers!* Go on, *sling your hooks!*
Get out, LeBrock. You're well *out of order*. *Besides...*
... I've *other* fish to *fry*.
Crikey, DI, that was dashed *bad form! What* were you *playing at?*
I know what I'm doing, Roderick. He was *right*, though. This case should *never* have been given to *me*.
Something's very fishy and it *stinks* to *high heaven*.

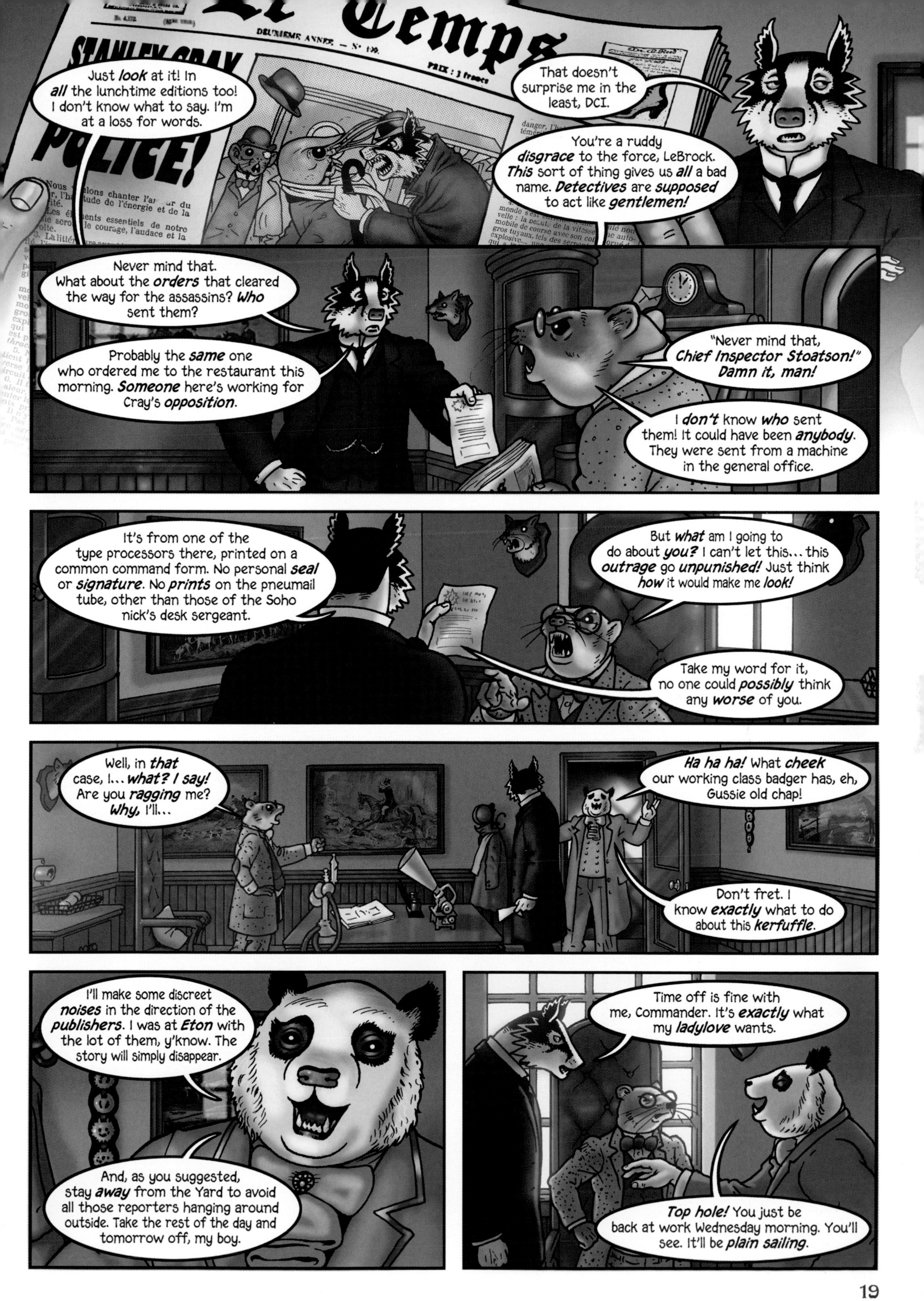

Just *look* at it! In *all* the lunchtime editions too! I don't know what to say. I'm at a loss for words.
That doesn't surprise me in the least, DCI.
You're a ruddy *disgrace* to the force, LeBrock. *This* sort of thing gives us *all* a bad name. *Detectives* are *supposed* to act like *gentlemen!*
Never mind that. What about the *orders* that cleared the way for the assassins? *Who* sent them?
Probably the *same* one who ordered me to the restaurant this morning. *Someone* here's working for Cray's *opposition*.
"Never mind that, *Chief Inspector Stoatson!*" *Damn it, man!*
I *don't* know *who* sent them! It could have been *anybody*. They were sent from a machine in the general office.
It's from one of the type processors there, printed on a common command form. No personal *seal* or *signature*. No *prints* on the pneumail tube, other than those of the Soho nick's desk sergeant.
But *what* am I going to do about *you?* I can't let this... this *outrage* go *unpunished!* Just think *how* it would make me *look!*
Take my word for it, no one could *possibly* think any *worse* of you.
Well, in *that* case, I... *what? I say!* Are you *ragging* me? *Why,* I'll...
Ha ha ha! What *cheek* our working class badger has, eh, Gussie old chap!
Don't fret. I know *exactly* what to do about this *kerfuffle*.
I'll make some discreet *noises* in the direction of the *publishers*. I was at *Eton* with the lot of them, y'know. The story will simply disappear.
And, as you suggested, stay *away* from the Yard to avoid all those reporters hanging around outside. Take the rest of the day and tomorrow off, my boy.
Time off is fine with me, Commander. It's *exactly* what my *ladylove* wants.
Top hole! You just be back at work Wednesday morning. You'll see. It'll be *plain sailing*.

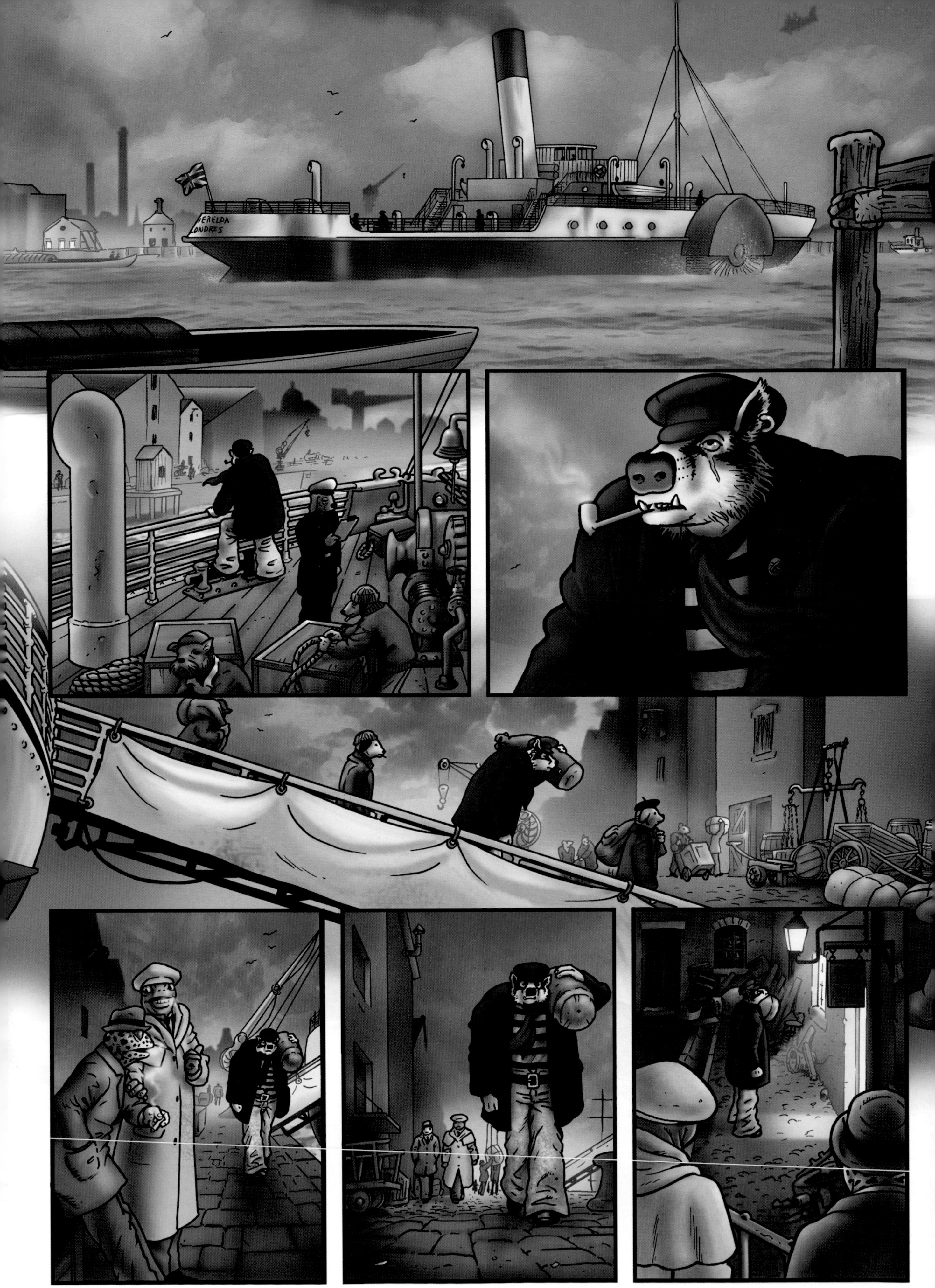

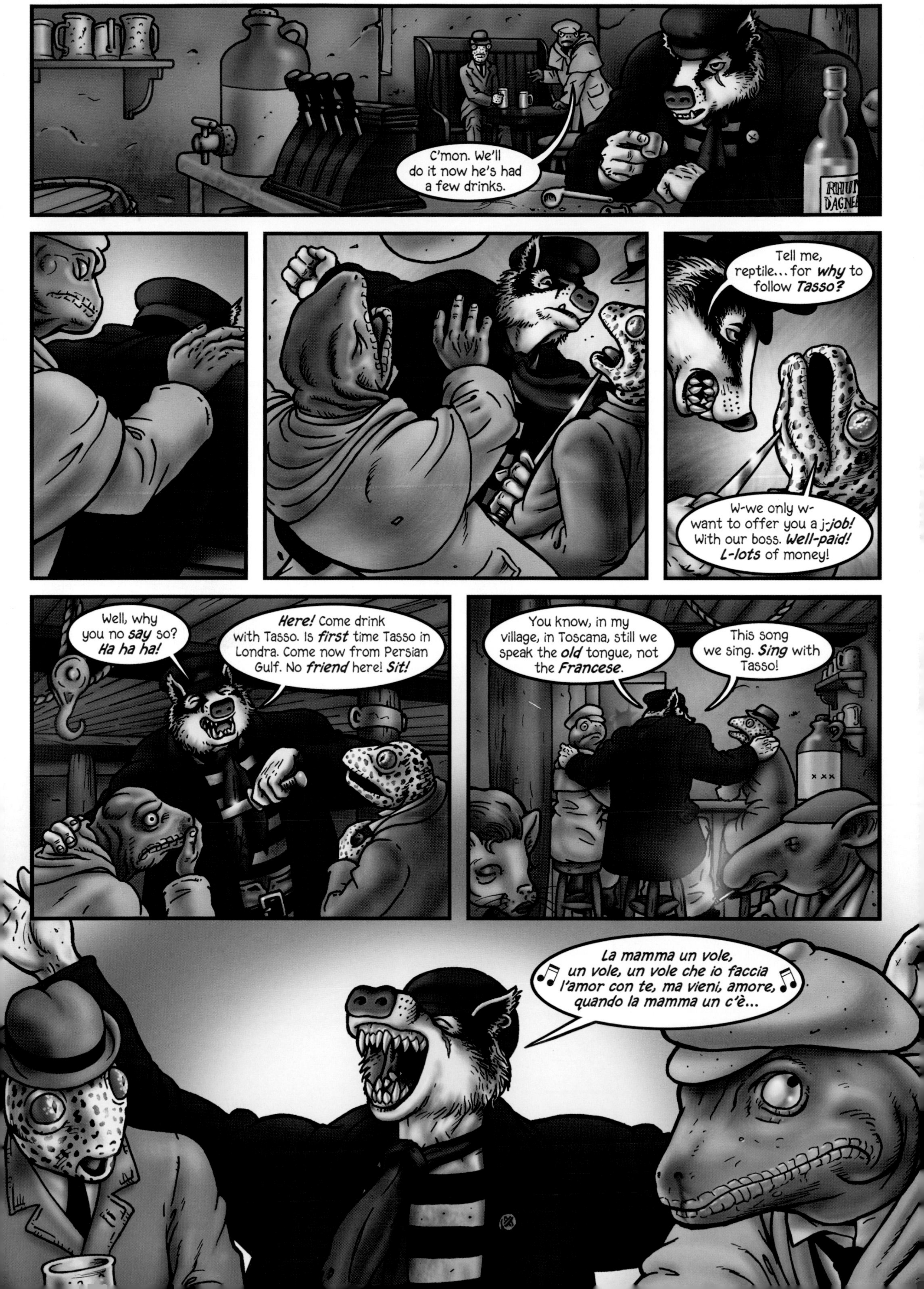
C'mon. We'll do it now he's had a few drinks.
RHUM D'AGNEL
Tell me, reptile... for *why* to follow *Tasso?*
W-we only w-want to offer you a j-*job!* With our boss. *Well-paid! L-lots* of money!
Well, why you no *say* so? *Ha ha ha!*
Here! Come drink with Tasso. Is *first* time Tasso in Londra. Come now from Persian Gulf. No *friend* here! *Sit!*
You know, in my village, in Toscana, still we speak the *old* tongue, not the *Francese*.
This song we sing. *Sing* with Tasso!
La mamma un vole, un vole, un vole che io faccia l'amor con te, ma vieni, amore, quando la mamma un c'è...

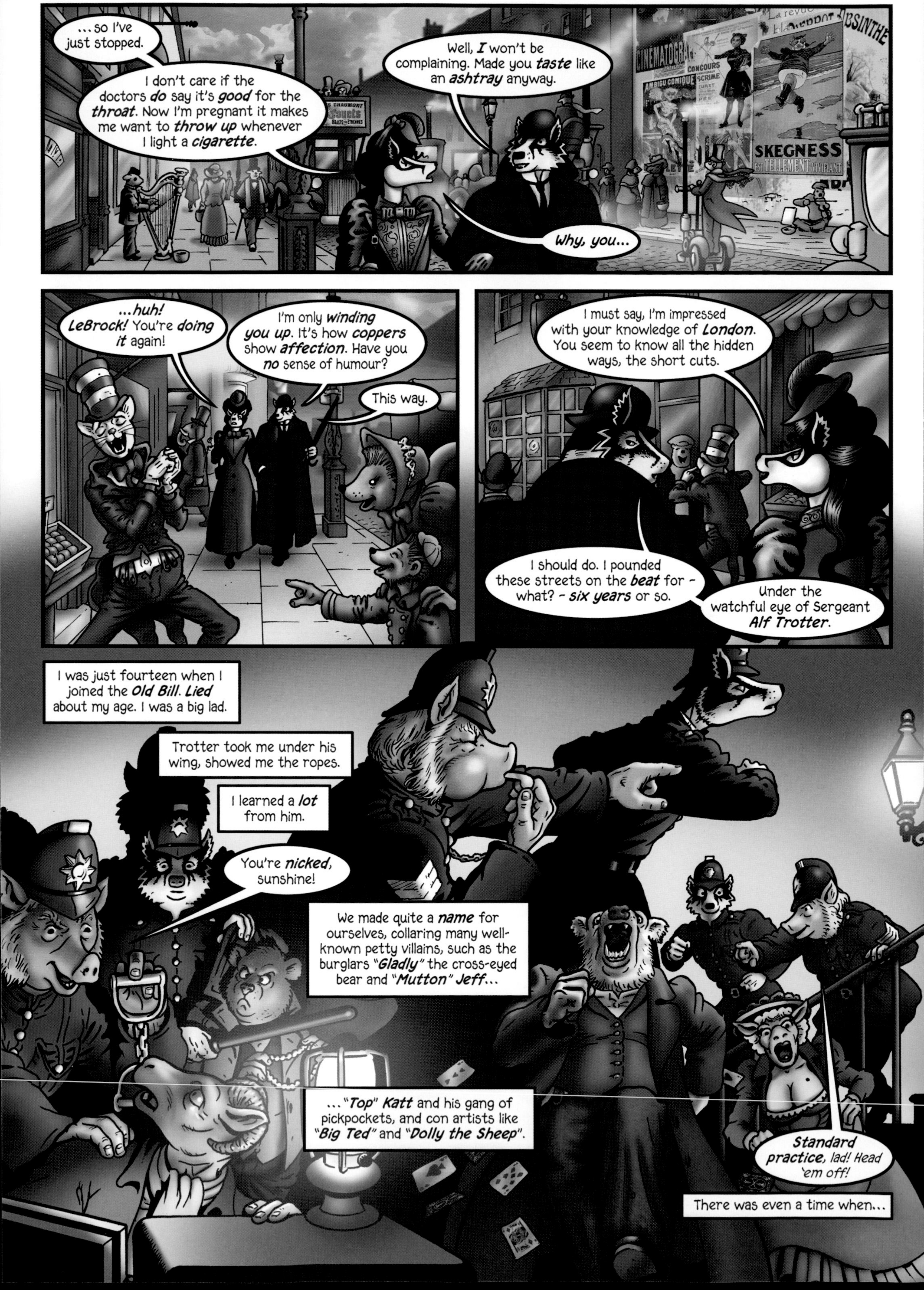
...so I've just stopped.
I don't care if the doctors do say it's good for the throat. Now I'm pregnant it makes me want to throw up whenever I light a cigarette.
Well, I won't be complaining. Made you taste like an ashtray anyway.
Why, you...
CINEMATOGRA
CONCOURS
SKEGNESS
EST TELLEMENT VIVIFIANT
ABSINTHE
...huh! LeBrock! You're doing it again!
I'm only winding you up. It's how coppers show affection. Have you no sense of humour?
This way.
I must say, I'm impressed with your knowledge of London. You seem to know all the hidden ways, the short cuts.
I should do. I pounded these streets on the beat for - what? - six years or so.
Under the watchful eye of Sergeant Alf Trotter.
I was just fourteen when I joined the Old Bill. Lied about my age. I was a big lad.
Trotter took me under his wing, showed me the ropes.
I learned a lot from him.
You're nicked, sunshine!
We made quite a name for ourselves, collaring many well-known petty villains, such as the burglars "Gladly" the cross-eyed bear and "Mutton" Jeff...
..."Top" Katt and his gang of pickpockets, and con artists like "Big Ted" and "Dolly the Sheep".
Standard practice, lad! Head 'em off!
There was even a time when...

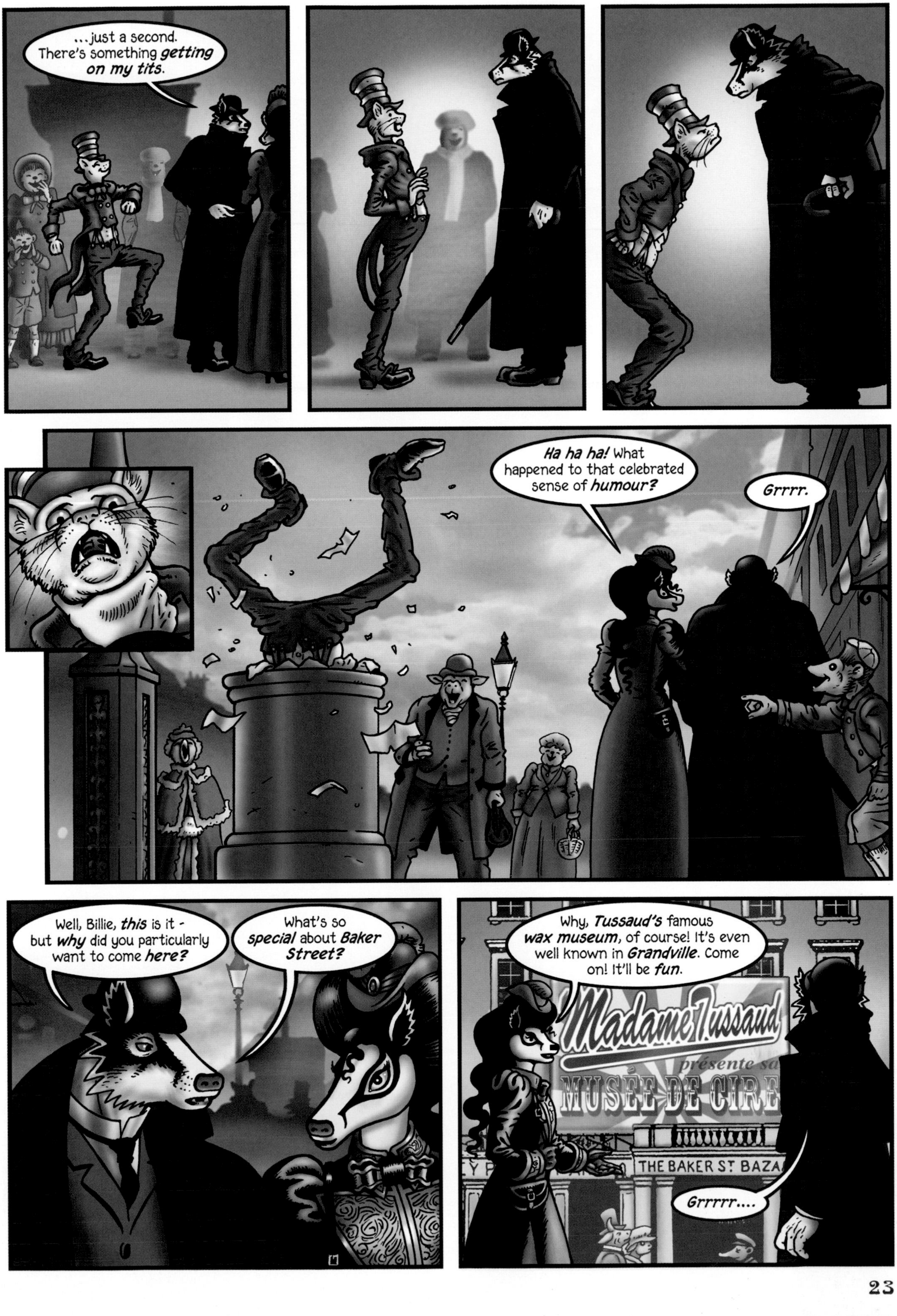
...just a second. There's something getting on my tits.
Ha ha ha! What happened to that celebrated sense of humour?
Grrrr.
Well, Billie, this is it - but why did you particularly want to come here?
What's so special about Baker Street?
Why, Tussaud's famous wax museum, of course! It's even well known in Grandville. Come on! It'll be fun.
Madame Tussaud
présente sa
MUSÉE DE CIRE
THE BAKER ST. BAZA
Grrrrr....

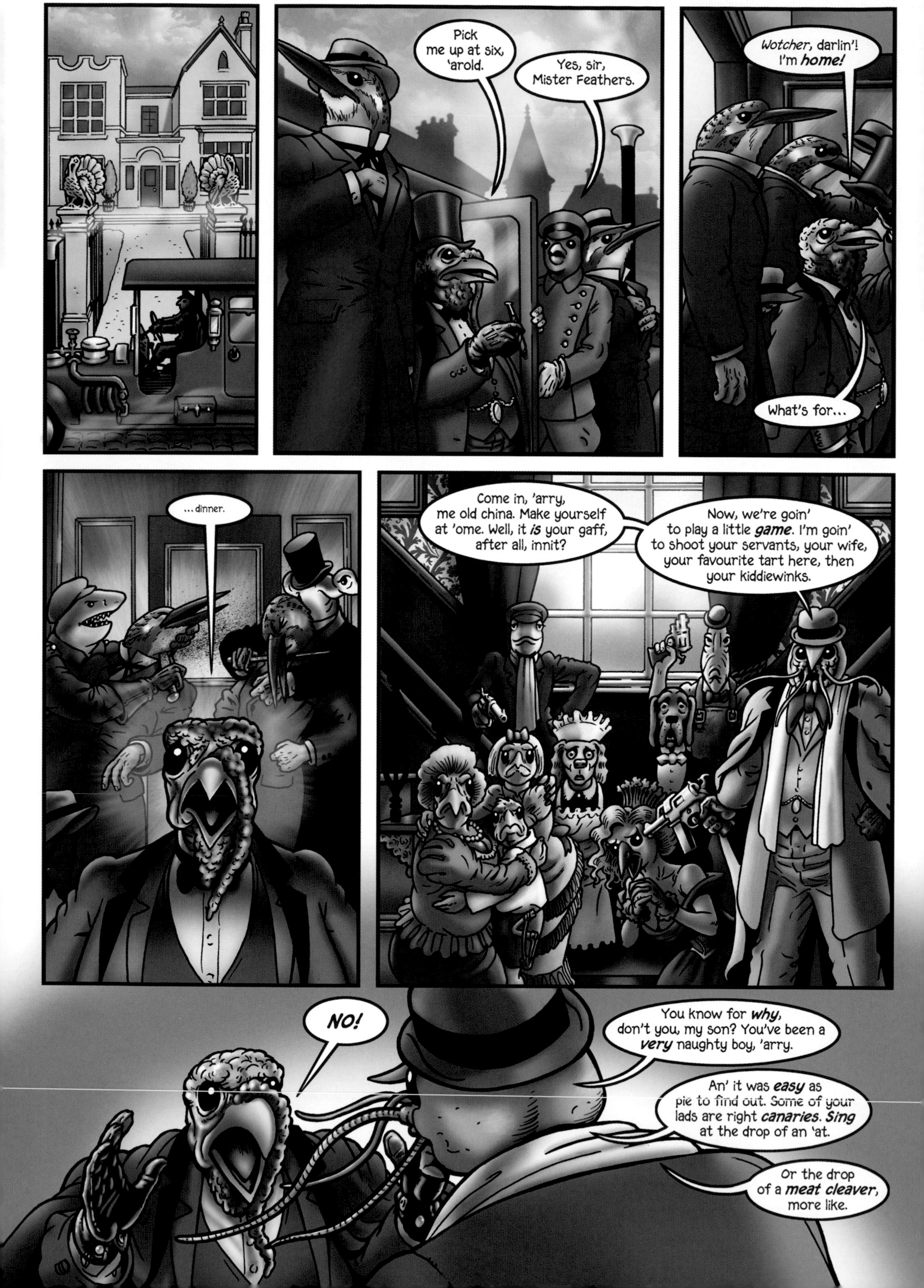
Pick me up at six, 'arold.
Yes, sir, Mister Feathers.
Wotcher, darlin'! I'm ***home!***
What's for...
...dinner.
Come in, 'arry, me old china. Make yourself at 'ome. Well, it *is* your gaff, after all, innit?
Now, we're goin' to play a little ***game***. I'm goin' to shoot your servants, your wife, your favourite tart here, then your kiddiewinks.
NO!
You know for ***why***, don't you, my son? You've been a ***very*** naughty boy, 'arry.
An' it was ***easy*** as pie to find out. Some of your lads are right ***canaries. Sing*** at the drop of an 'at.
Or the drop of a ***meat cleaver***, more like.

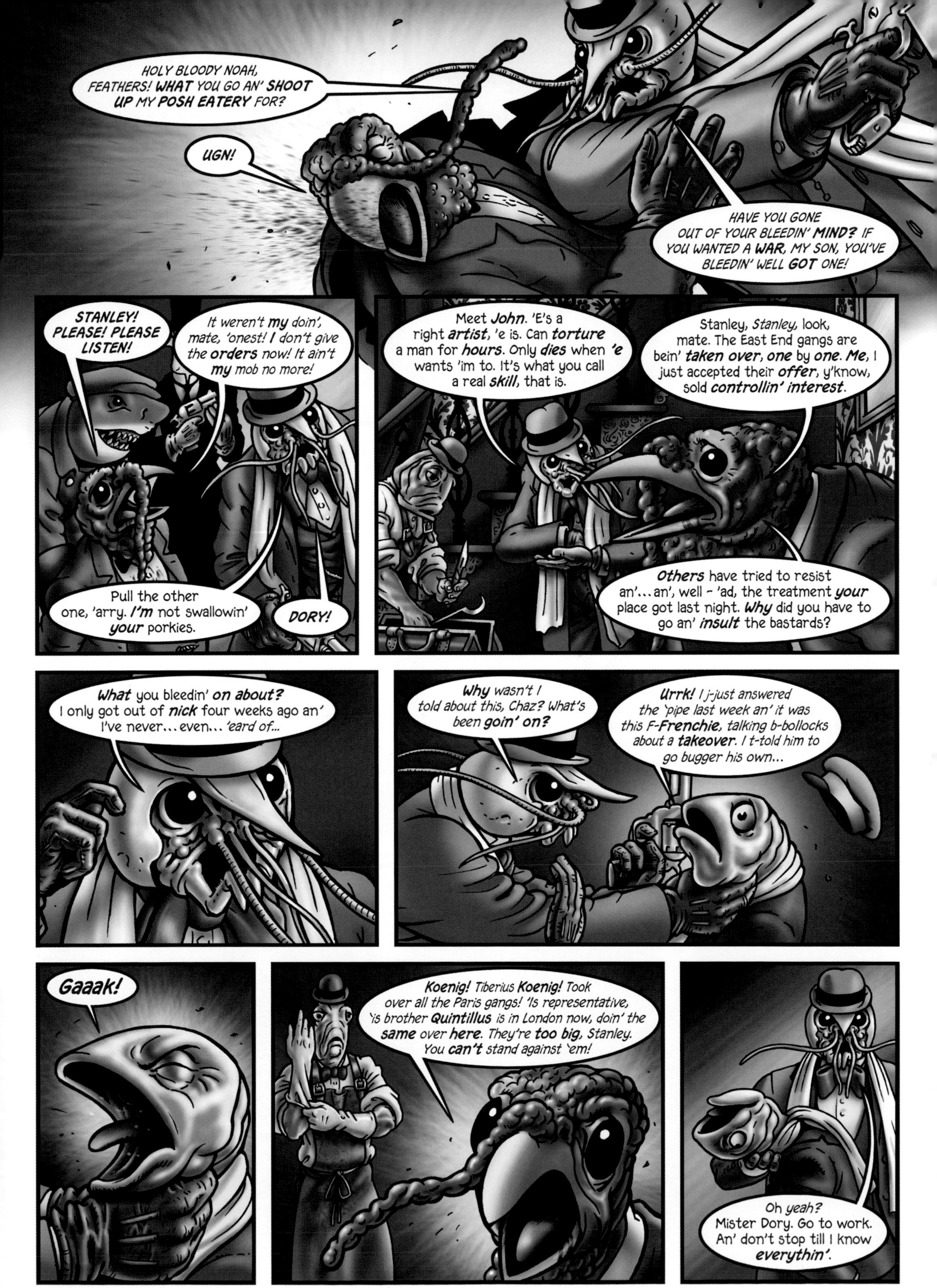
HOLY BLOODY NOAH, FEATHERS! WHAT YOU GO AN' SHOOT UP MY POSH EATERY FOR?
UGN!
HAVE YOU GONE OUT OF YOUR BLEEDIN' MIND? IF YOU WANTED A WAR, MY SON, YOU'VE BLEEDIN' WELL GOT ONE!
STANLEY! PLEASE! PLEASE LISTEN!
It weren't my doin', mate, 'onest! I don't give the orders now! It ain't my mob no more!
Pull the other one, 'arry. I'm not swallowin' your porkies.
DORY!
Meet John. 'E's a right artist, 'e is. Can torture a man for hours. Only dies when 'e wants 'im to. It's what you call a real skill, that is.
Stanley, Stanley, look, mate. The East End gangs are bein' taken over, one by one. Me, I just accepted their offer, y'know, sold controllin' interest.
Others have tried to resist an'... an', well - 'ad, the treatment your place got last night. Why did you have to go an' insult the bastards?
What you bleedin' on about? I only got out of nick four weeks ago an' I've never... even... 'eard of...
Why wasn't I told about this, Chaz? What's been goin' on?
Urrk! I j-just answered the 'pipe last week an' it was this F-Frenchie, talking b-bollocks about a takeover. I t-told him to go bugger his own...
Gaaak!
Koenig! Tiberius Koenig! Took over all the Paris gangs! 'Is representative, 'is brother Quintillus is in London now, doin' the same over here. They're too big, Stanley. You can't stand against 'em!
Oh yeah? Mister Dory. Go to work. An' don't stop till I know everythin'.

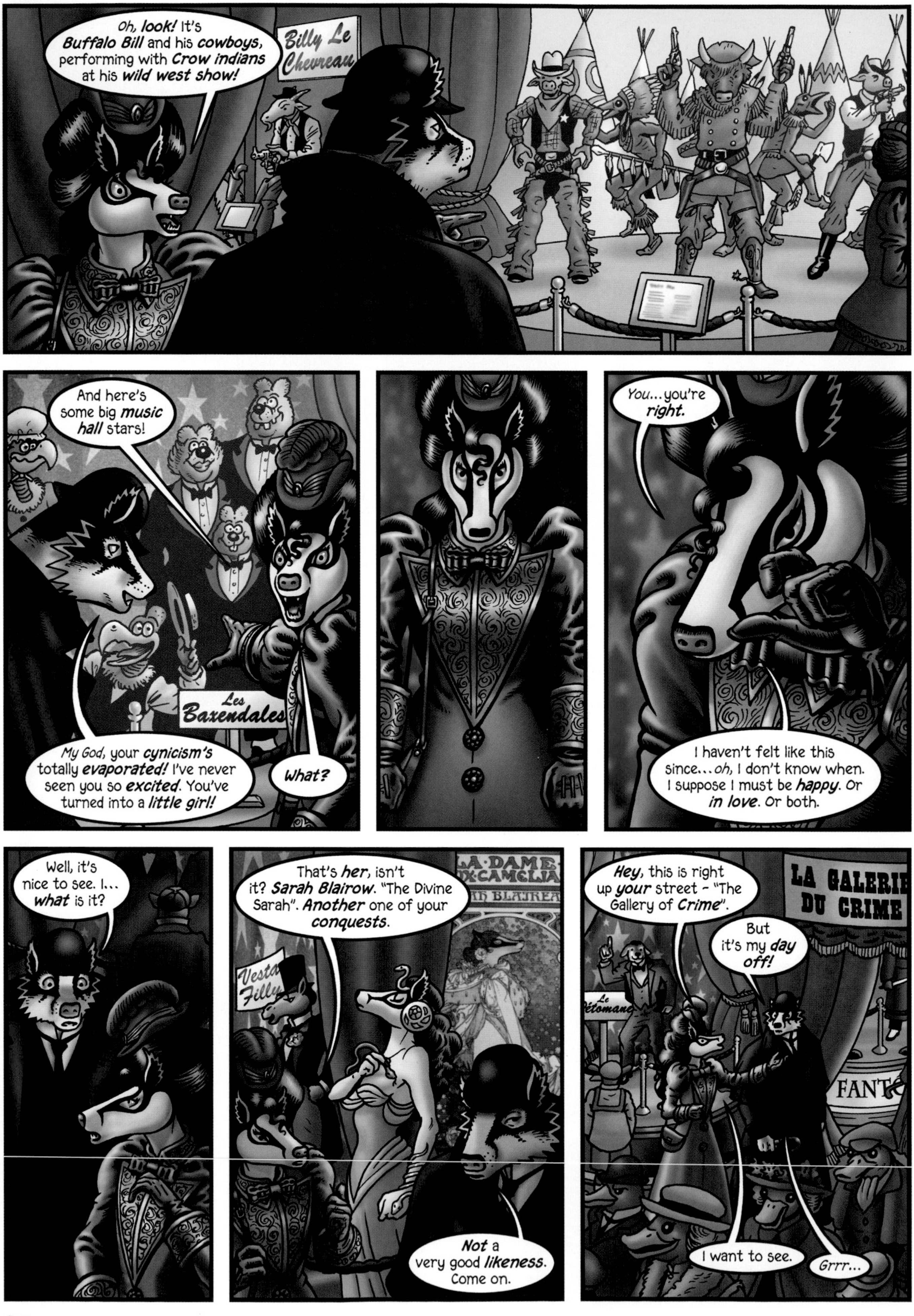
Oh, look! It's Buffalo Bill and his cowboys, performing with Crow indians at his wild west show!
Billy Le Chevreau
And here's some big music hall stars!
Les Baxendales
My God, your cynicism's totally evaporated! I've never seen you so excited. You've turned into a little girl!
What?
You... you're right.
I haven't felt like this since... oh, I don't know when. I suppose I must be happy. Or in love. Or both.
Well, it's nice to see. I... what is it?
That's her, isn't it? Sarah Blairow. "The Divine Sarah". Another one of your conquests.
Vesta Filly
Not a very good likeness. Come on.
LA GALERIE DU CRIME
Hey, this is right up your street – "The Gallery of Crime".
But it's my day off!
I want to see.
Grrr...

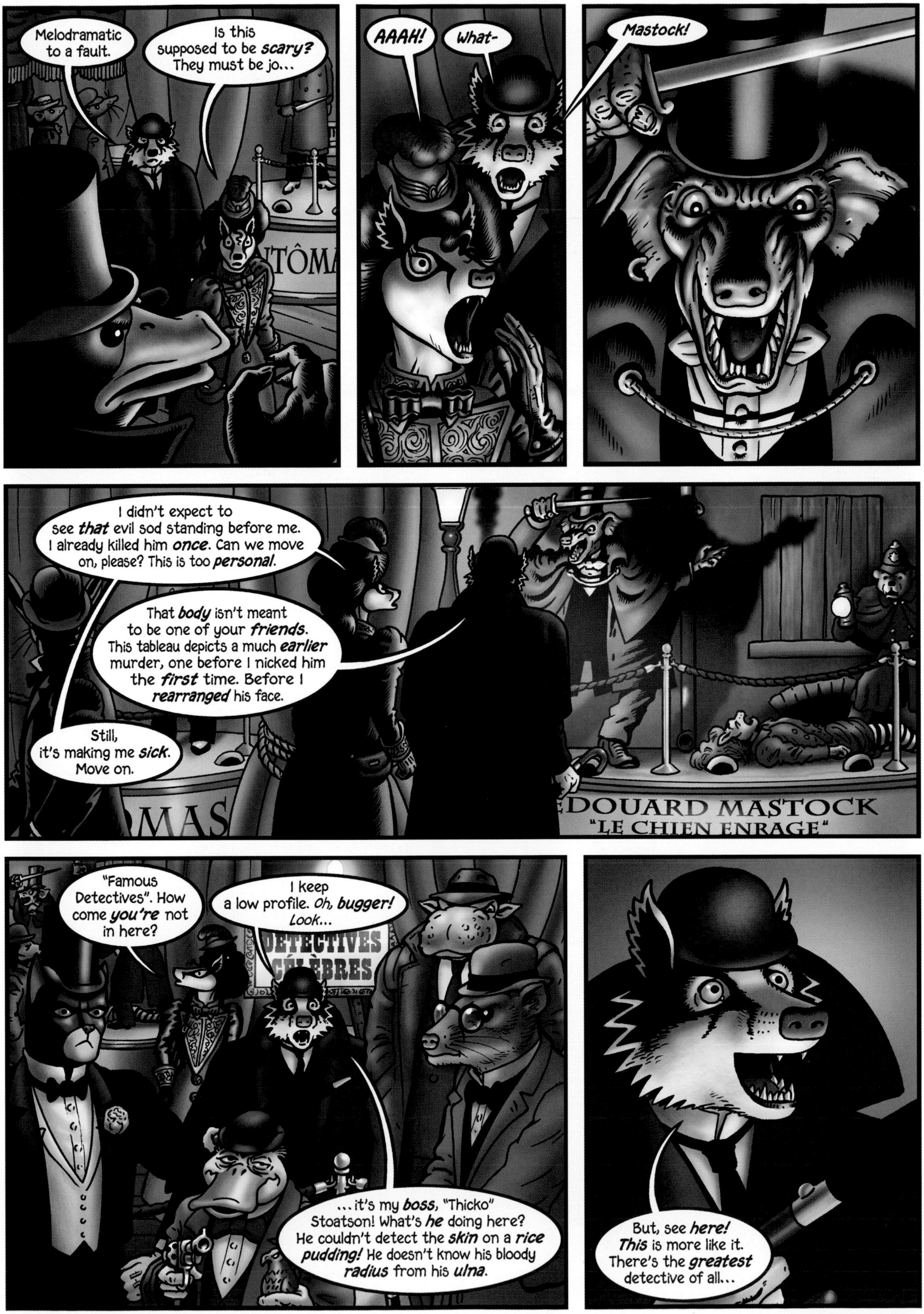
Melodramatic to a fault.
Is this supposed to be *scary?* They must be jo...
AAAH!
What-
Mastock!
I didn't expect to see *that* evil sod standing before me. I already killed him *once*. Can we move on, please? This is too *personal*.
That *body* isn't meant to be one of your *friends*. This tableau depicts a much *earlier* murder, one before I nicked him the *first* time. Before I *rearranged* his face.
Still, it's making me *sick*. Move on.
EDOUARD MASTOCK
"LE CHIEN ENRAGE"
"Famous Detectives". How come *you're* not in here?
I keep a low profile. *Oh, bugger! Look...*
DETECTIVES CÉLÈBRES
...it's my *boss*, "Thicko" Stoatson! What's *he* doing here? He couldn't detect the *skin* on a *rice pudding!* He doesn't know his bloody *radius* from his *ulna*.
But, see *here! This* is more like it. There's the *greatest* detective of all...

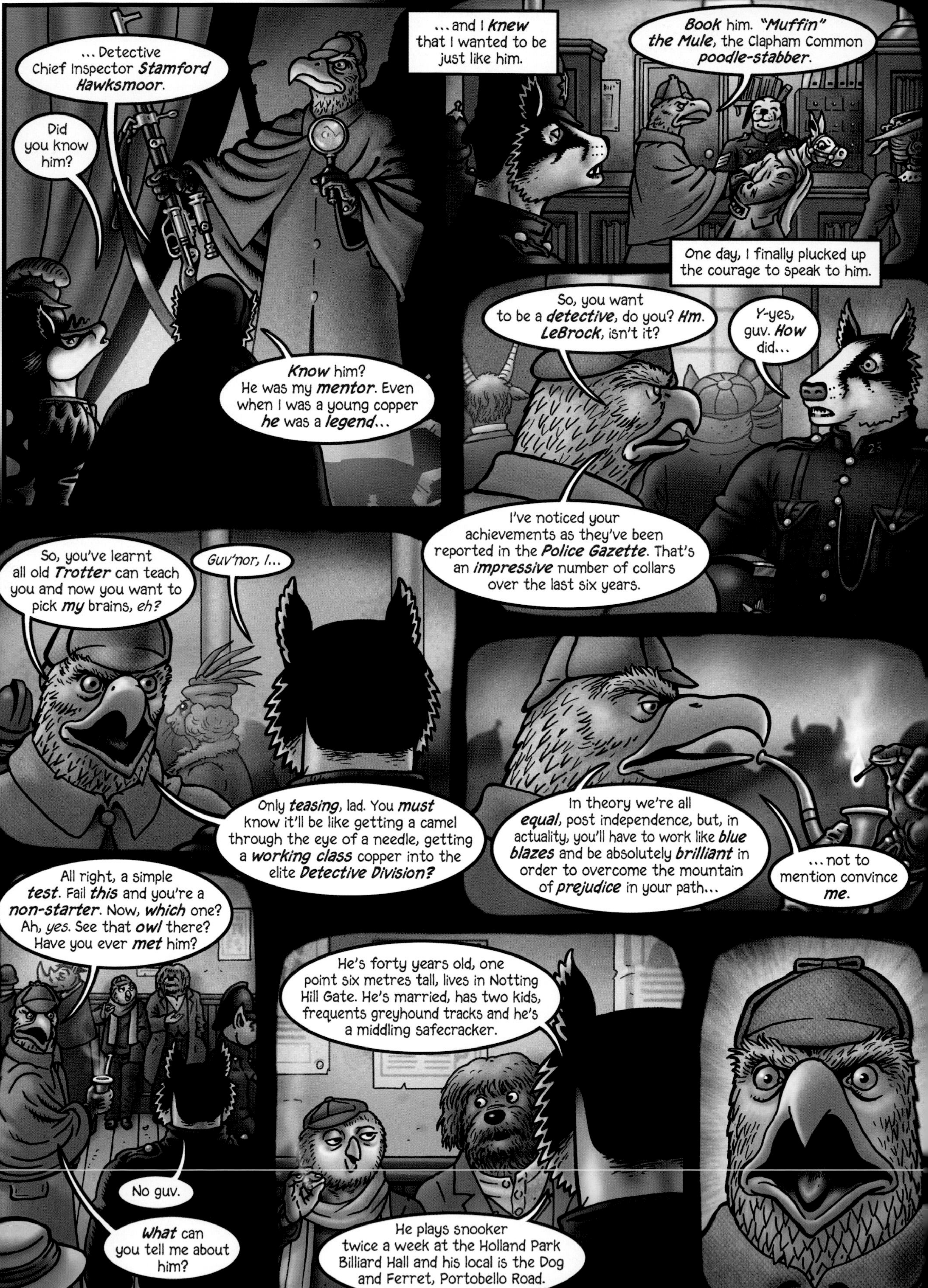
...Detective Chief Inspector Stamford Hawksmoor.
Did you know him?
Know him? He was my mentor. Even when I was a young copper he was a legend...
...and I knew that I wanted to be just like him.
Book him. "Muffin" the Mule, the Clapham Common poodle-stabber.
One day, I finally plucked up the courage to speak to him.
So, you want to be a detective, do you? Hm. LeBrock, isn't it?
Y-yes, guv. How did...
I've noticed your achievements as they've been reported in the Police Gazette. That's an impressive number of collars over the last six years.
So, you've learnt all old Trotter can teach you and now you want to pick my brains, eh?
Guv'nor, I...
Only teasing, lad. You must know it'll be like getting a camel through the eye of a needle, getting a working class copper into the elite Detective Division?
In theory we're all equal, post independence, but, in actuality, you'll have to work like blue blazes and be absolutely brilliant in order to overcome the mountain of prejudice in your path...
...not to mention convince me.
All right, a simple test. Fail this and you're a non-starter. Now, which one? Ah, yes. See that owl there? Have you ever met him?
No guv.
What can you tell me about him?
He's forty years old, one point six metres tall, lives in Notting Hill Gate. He's married, has two kids, frequents greyhound tracks and he's a middling safecracker.
He plays snooker twice a week at the Holland Park Billiard Hall and his local is the Dog and Ferret, Portobello Road.

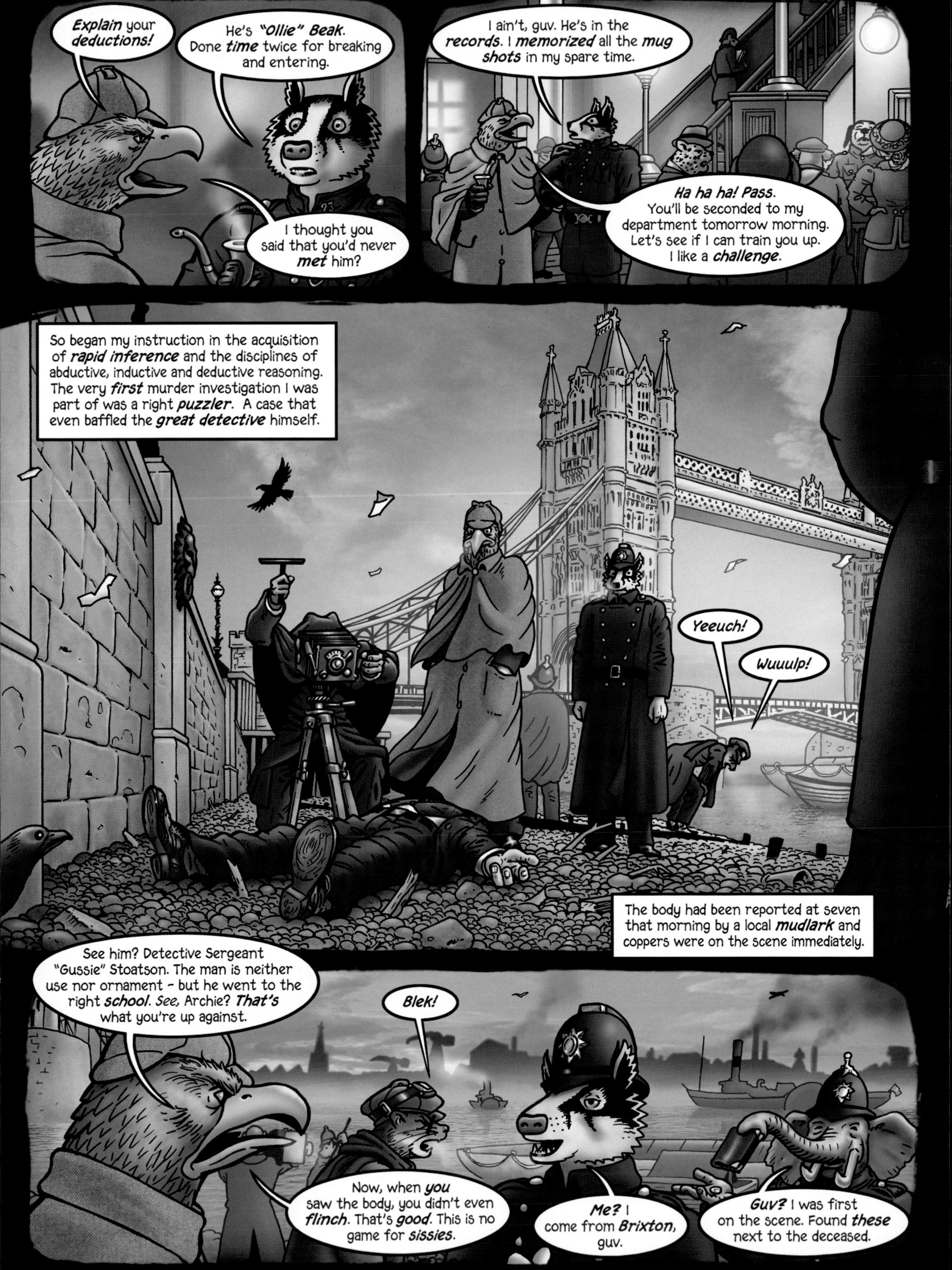

Explain your deductions!
He's "Ollie" Beak. Done time twice for breaking and entering.
I thought you said that you'd never met him?
I ain't, guv. He's in the records. I memorized all the mug shots in my spare time.
Ha ha ha! Pass. You'll be seconded to my department tomorrow morning. Let's see if I can train you up. I like a challenge.
So began my instruction in the acquisition of rapid inference and the disciplines of abductive, inductive and deductive reasoning. The very first murder investigation I was part of was a right puzzler. A case that even baffled the great detective himself.
Yeeuch!
Wuuulp!
The body had been reported at seven that morning by a local mudlark and coppers were on the scene immediately.
See him? Detective Sergeant "Gussie" Stoatson. The man is neither use nor ornament - but he went to the right school. See, Archie? That's what you're up against.
Blek!
Now, when you saw the body, you didn't even flinch. That's good. This is no game for sissies.
Me? I come from Brixton, guv.
Guv? I was first on the scene. Found these next to the deceased.

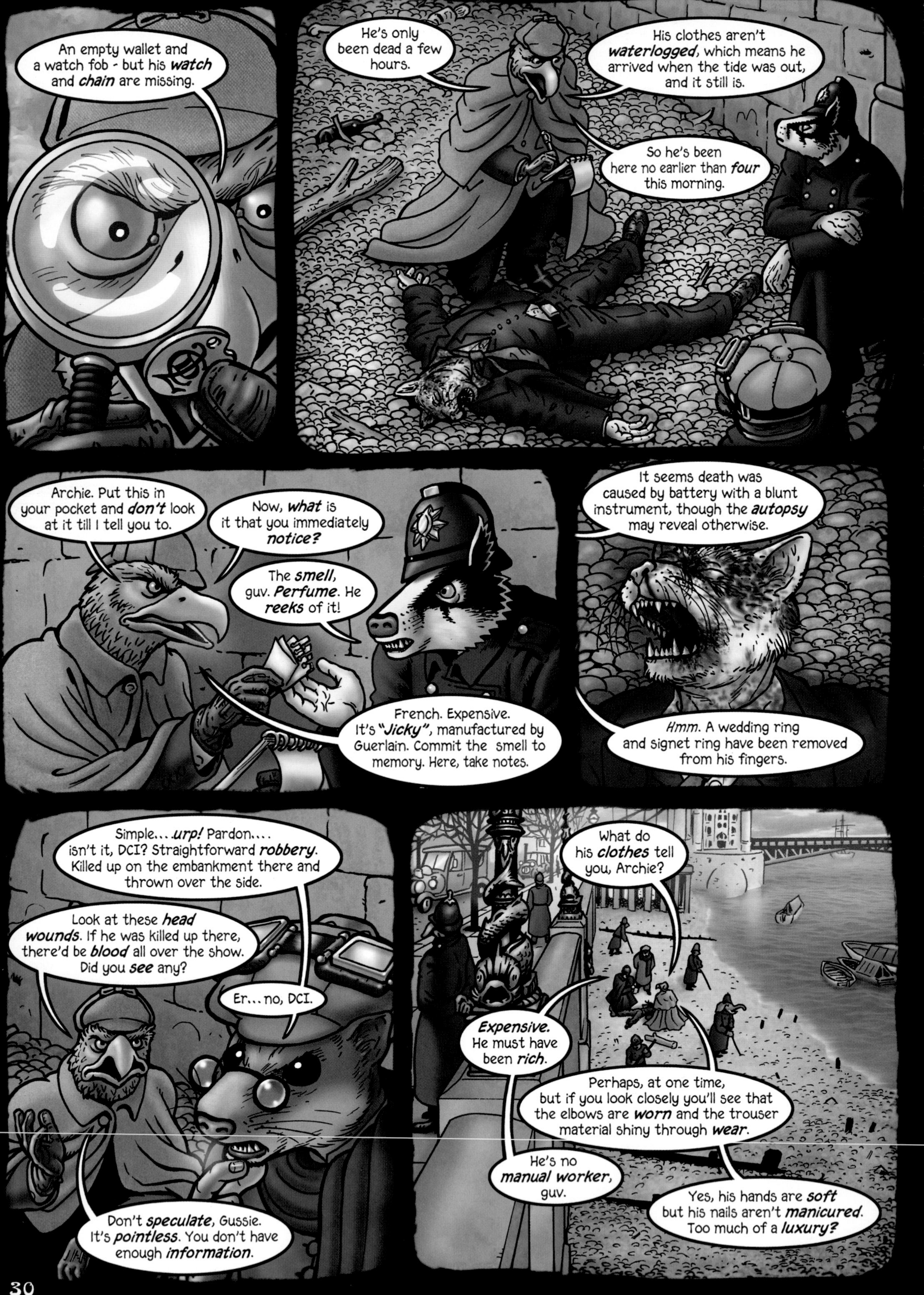

An empty wallet and a watch fob - but his *watch* and *chain* are missing.
He's only been dead a few hours.
His clothes aren't *waterlogged*, which means he arrived when the tide was out, and it still is.
So he's been here no earlier than *four* this morning.
Archie. Put this in your pocket and *don't* look at it till I tell you to.
Now, *what* is it that you immediately *notice?*
The *smell*, guv. *Perfume*. He *reeks* of it!
French. Expensive. It's *"Jicky"*, manufactured by Guerlain. Commit the smell to memory. Here, take notes.
It seems death was caused by battery with a blunt instrument, though the *autopsy* may reveal otherwise.
Hmm. A wedding ring and signet ring have been removed from his fingers.
Simple... *urp!* Pardon.... isn't it, DCI? Straightforward *robbery*. Killed up on the embankment there and thrown over the side.
Look at these *head wounds*. If he was killed up there, there'd be *blood* all over the show. Did you *see* any?
Er... no, DCI.
Don't *speculate*, Gussie. It's *pointless*. You don't have enough *information*.
What do his *clothes* tell you, Archie?
Expensive. He must have been *rich*.
Perhaps, at one time, but if you look closely you'll see that the elbows are *worn* and the trouser material shiny through *wear*.
He's no *manual worker*, guv.
Yes, his hands are *soft* but his nails aren't *manicured*. Too much of a *luxury?*

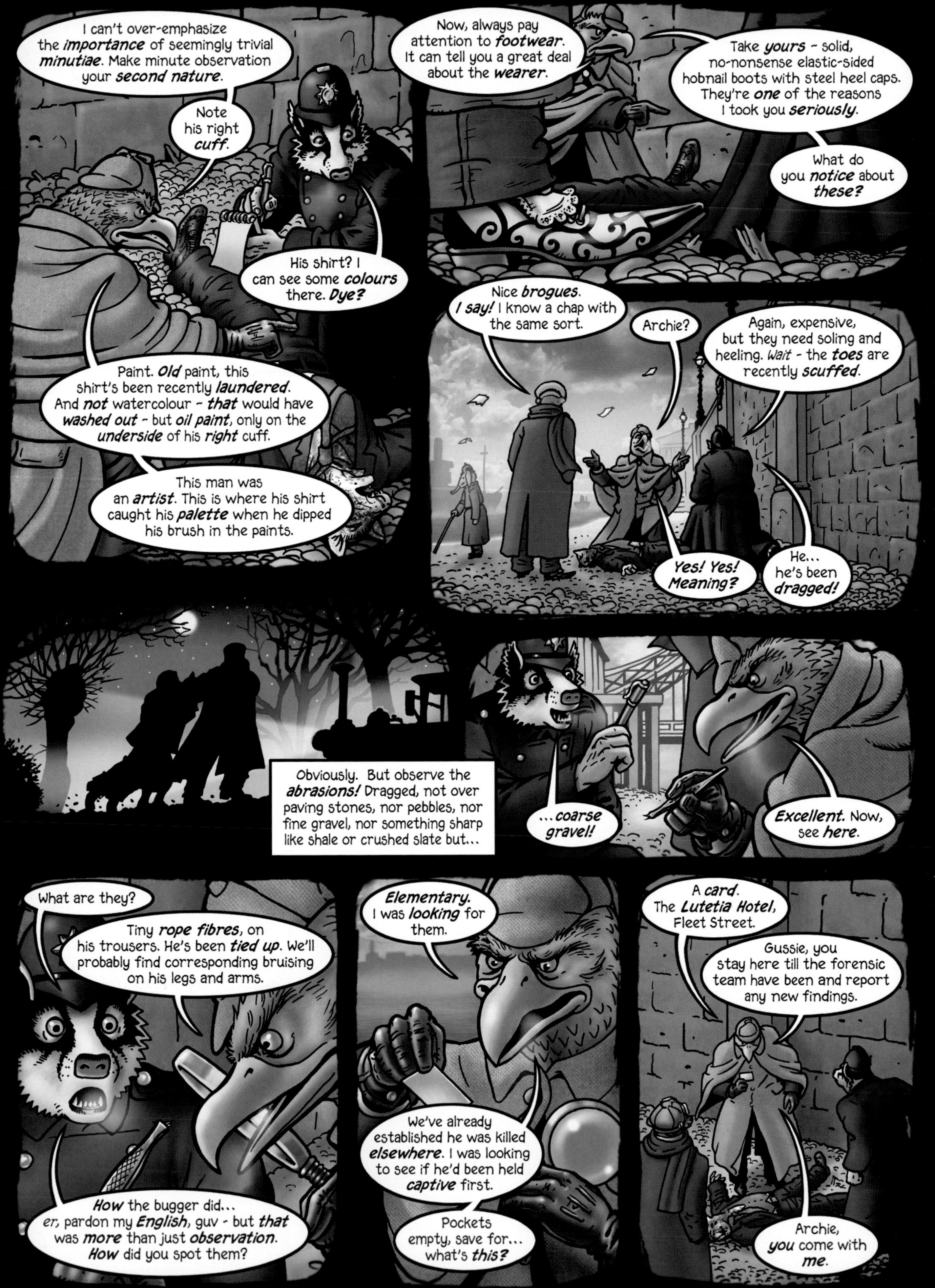
I can't over-emphasize the *importance* of seemingly trivial *minutiae*. Make minute observation your *second nature*.
Note his right *cuff*.
His shirt? I can see some *colours* there. *Dye?*
Paint. *Old* paint, this shirt's been recently *laundered*. And *not* watercolour - *that* would have *washed out* - but *oil paint*, only on the *underside* of his *right* cuff.
This man was an *artist*. This is where his shirt caught his *palette* when he dipped his brush in the paints.
Now, always pay attention to *footwear*. It can tell you a great deal about the *wearer*.
Take *yours* - solid, no-nonsense elastic-sided hobnail boots with steel heel caps. They're *one* of the reasons I took you *seriously*.
What do you *notice* about *these?*
Nice *brogues*. *I say!* I know a chap with the same sort.
Archie?
Again, expensive, but they need soling and heeling. *Wait* - the *toes* are recently *scuffed*.
Yes! Yes! Meaning?
He... he's been *dragged!*
Obviously. But observe the *abrasions!* Dragged, not over paving stones, nor pebbles, nor fine gravel, nor something sharp like shale or crushed slate but...
...*coarse gravel!*
Excellent. Now, see *here*.
What are they?
Tiny *rope fibres*, on his trousers. He's been *tied up*. We'll probably find corresponding bruising on his legs and arms.
How the bugger did... *er*, pardon my *English*, guv - but *that* was *more* than just *observation*. *How* did you spot them?
Elementary. I was *looking* for them.
We've already established he was killed *elsewhere*. I was looking to see if he'd been held *captive* first.
Pockets empty, save for... what's *this?*
A *card*. The *Lutetia Hotel*, Fleet Street.
Gussie, you stay here till the forensic team have been and report any new findings.
Archie, *you* come with *me*.

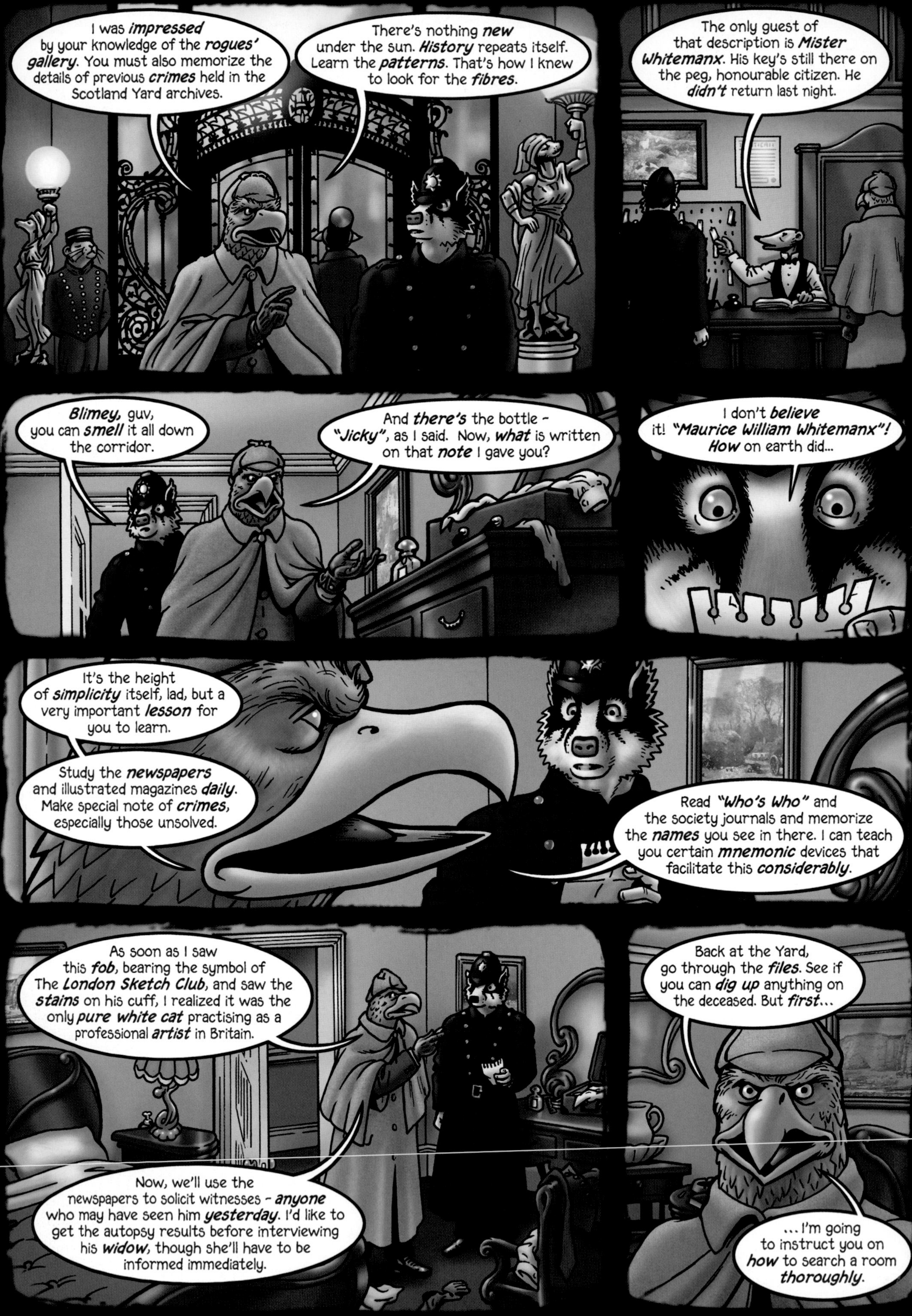
I was impressed by your knowledge of the rogues' gallery. You must also memorize the details of previous crimes held in the Scotland Yard archives.
There's nothing new under the sun. History repeats itself. Learn the patterns. That's how I knew to look for the fibres.
The only guest of that description is Mister Whitemanx. His key's still there on the peg, honourable citizen. He didn't return last night.
Blimey, guv, you can smell it all down the corridor.
And there's the bottle - "Jicky", as I said. Now, what is written on that note I gave you?
I don't believe it! "Maurice William Whitemanx"! How on earth did...
It's the height of simplicity itself, lad, but a very important lesson for you to learn.
Study the newspapers and illustrated magazines daily. Make special note of crimes, especially those unsolved.
Read "Who's Who" and the society journals and memorize the names you see in there. I can teach you certain mnemonic devices that facilitate this considerably.
As soon as I saw this fob, bearing the symbol of The London Sketch Club, and saw the stains on his cuff, I realized it was the only pure white cat practising as a professional artist in Britain.
Now, we'll use the newspapers to solicit witnesses - anyone who may have seen him yesterday. I'd like to get the autopsy results before interviewing his widow, though she'll have to be informed immediately.
Back at the Yard, go through the files. See if you can dig up anything on the deceased. But first...
...I'm going to instruct you on how to search a room thoroughly.

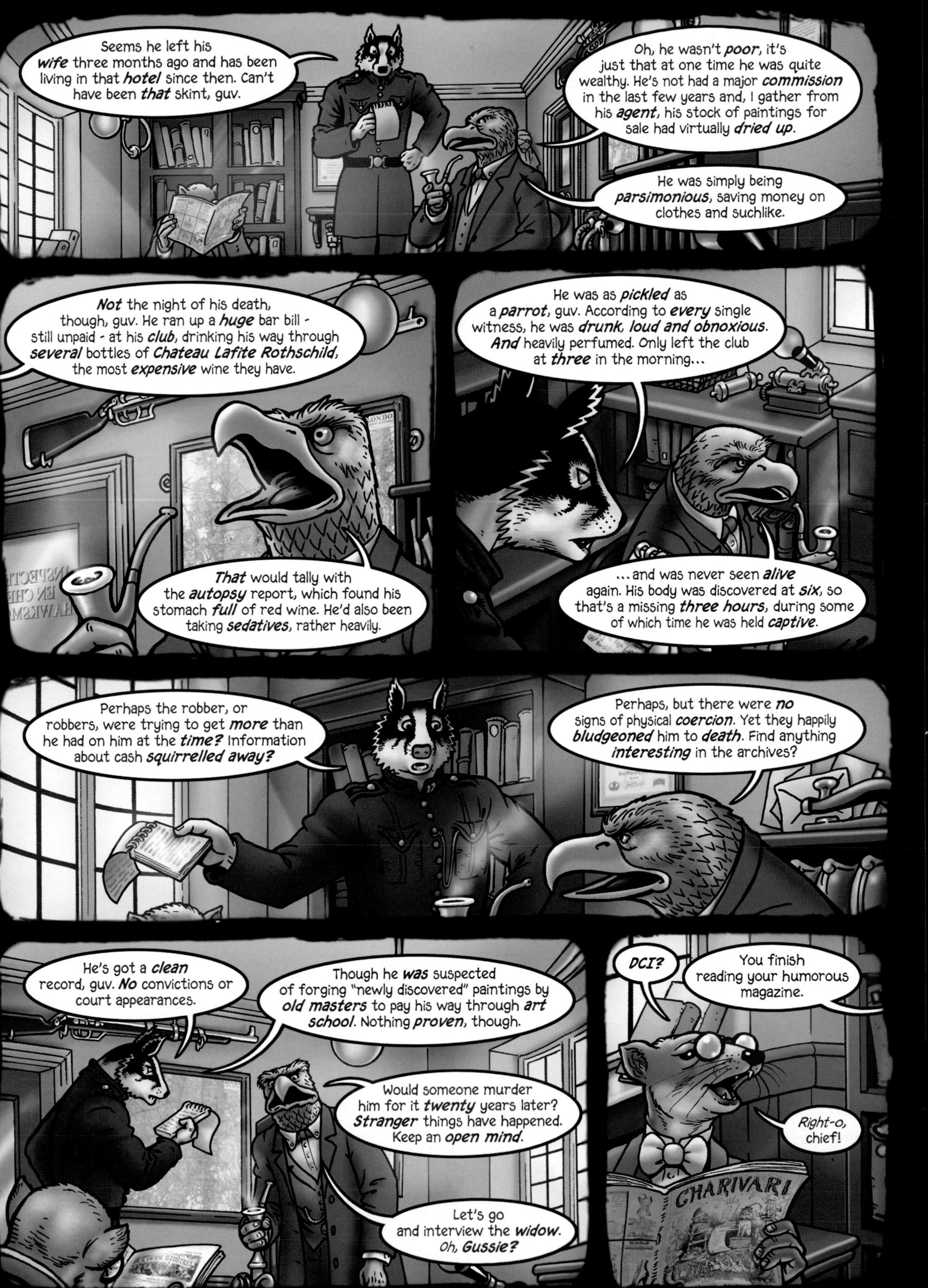

Seems he left his wife three months ago and has been living in that hotel since then. Can't have been that skint, guv.
Oh, he wasn't poor, it's just that at one time he was quite wealthy. He's not had a major commission in the last few years and, I gather from his agent, his stock of paintings for sale had virtually dried up.
He was simply being parsimonious, saving money on clothes and suchlike.
Not the night of his death, though, guv. He ran up a huge bar bill - still unpaid - at his club, drinking his way through several bottles of Chateau Lafite Rothschild, the most expensive wine they have.
That would tally with the autopsy report, which found his stomach full of red wine. He'd also been taking sedatives, rather heavily.
He was as pickled as a parrot, guv. According to every single witness, he was drunk, loud and obnoxious. And heavily perfumed. Only left the club at three in the morning...
...and was never seen alive again. His body was discovered at six, so that's a missing three hours, during some of which time he was held captive.
Perhaps the robber, or robbers, were trying to get more than he had on him at the time? Information about cash squirrelled away?
Perhaps, but there were no signs of physical coercion. Yet they happily bludgeoned him to death. Find anything interesting in the archives?
He's got a clean record, guv. No convictions or court appearances.
Though he was suspected of forging "newly discovered" paintings by old masters to pay his way through art school. Nothing proven, though.
Would someone murder him for it twenty years later? Stranger things have happened. Keep an open mind.
Let's go and interview the widow. Oh, Gussie?
DCI?
You finish reading your humorous magazine.
Right-o, chief!
CHARIVARI

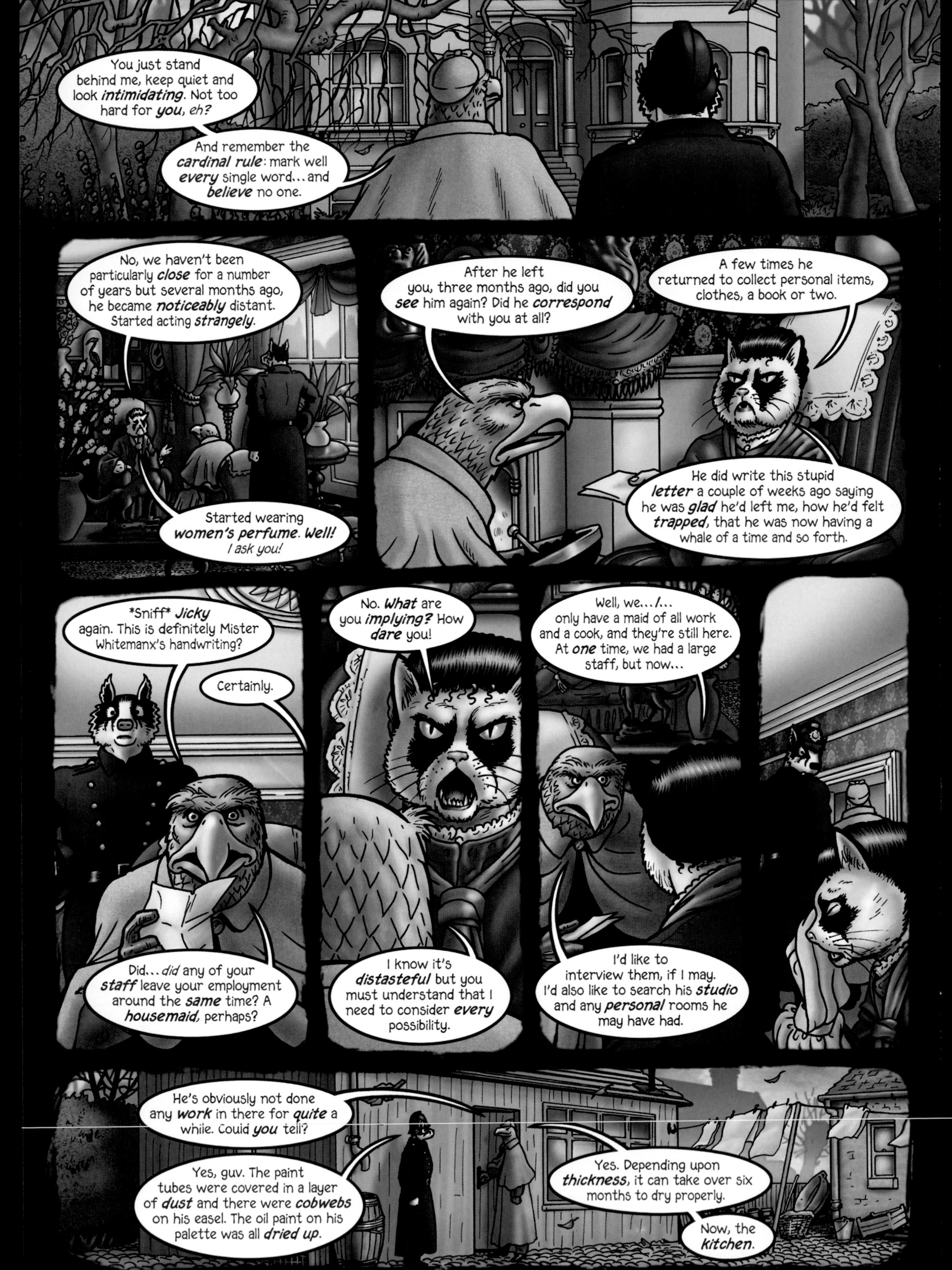

You just stand behind me, keep quiet and look *intimidating*. Not too hard for *you*, *eh?*
And remember the *cardinal rule*: mark well *every* single word... and *believe* no one.
No, we haven't been particularly *close* for a number of years but several months ago, he became *noticeably* distant. Started acting *strangely*.
Started wearing *women's perfume*. *Well!* *I ask you!*
After he left you, three months ago, did you *see* him again? Did he *correspond* with you at all?
A few times he returned to collect personal items, clothes, a book or two.
He did write this stupid *letter* a couple of weeks ago saying he was *glad* he'd left me, how he'd felt *trapped*, that he was now having a whale of a time and so forth.
Sniff *Jicky* again. This is definitely Mister Whitemanx's handwriting?
Certainly.
Did... *did* any of your *staff* leave your employment around the *same* time? A *housemaid*, perhaps?
No. *What* are you *implying?* How *dare* you!
I know it's *distasteful* but you must understand that I need to consider *every* possibility.
Well, we... *I*... only have a maid of all work and a cook, and they're still here. At *one* time, we had a large staff, but now...
I'd like to interview them, if I may. I'd also like to search his *studio* and any *personal* rooms he may have had.
He's obviously not done any *work* in there for *quite* a while. Could *you* tell?
Yes, guv. The paint tubes were covered in a layer of *dust* and there were *cobwebs* on his easel. The oil paint on his palette was all *dried up*.
Yes. Depending upon *thickness*, it can take over six months to dry properly.
Now, the *kitchen*.

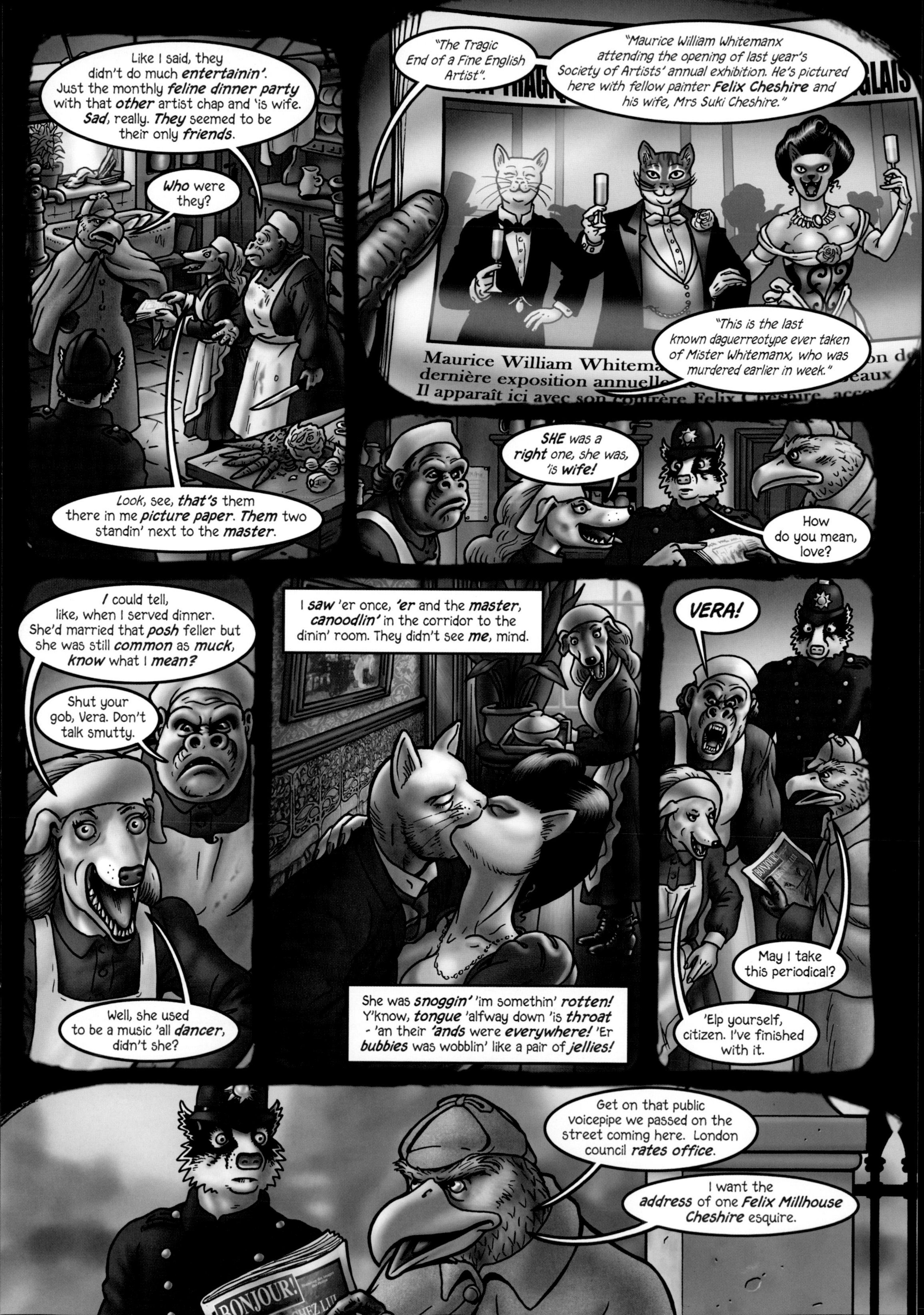
Like I said, they didn't do much *entertainin'*. Just the monthly *feline dinner party* with that *other* artist chap and 'is wife. *Sad*, really. *They* seemed to be their only *friends*.
Who were they?
Look, see, *that's* them there in me *picture paper*. *Them* two standin' next to the *master*.
"The Tragic End of a Fine English Artist".
"Maurice William Whitemanx attending the opening of last year's Society of Artists' annual exhibition. He's pictured here with fellow painter *Felix Cheshire* and his wife, Mrs Suki Cheshire."
"This is the last known daguerreotype ever taken of Mister Whitemanx, who was murdered earlier in week."
SHE was a *right* one, she was, 'is *wife!*
How do you mean, love?
I could tell, like, when I served dinner. She'd married that *posh* feller but she was still *common* as *muck*, *know* what I *mean?*
Shut your gob, Vera. Don't talk smutty.
Well, she used to be a music 'all *dancer*, didn't she?
I *saw* 'er once, *'er* and the *master*, *canoodlin'* in the corridor to the dinin' room. They didn't see *me*, mind.
She was *snoggin'* 'im somethin' *rotten!* Y'know, *tongue* 'alfway down 'is *throat* - 'an their *'ands* were *everywhere!* 'Er *bubbies* was wobblin' like a pair of *jellies!*
VERA!
May I take this periodical?
'Elp yourself, citizen. I've finished with it.
Get on that public voicepipe we passed on the street coming here. London council *rates office*.
I want the *address* of one *Felix Millhouse Cheshire* esquire.
BONJOUR!

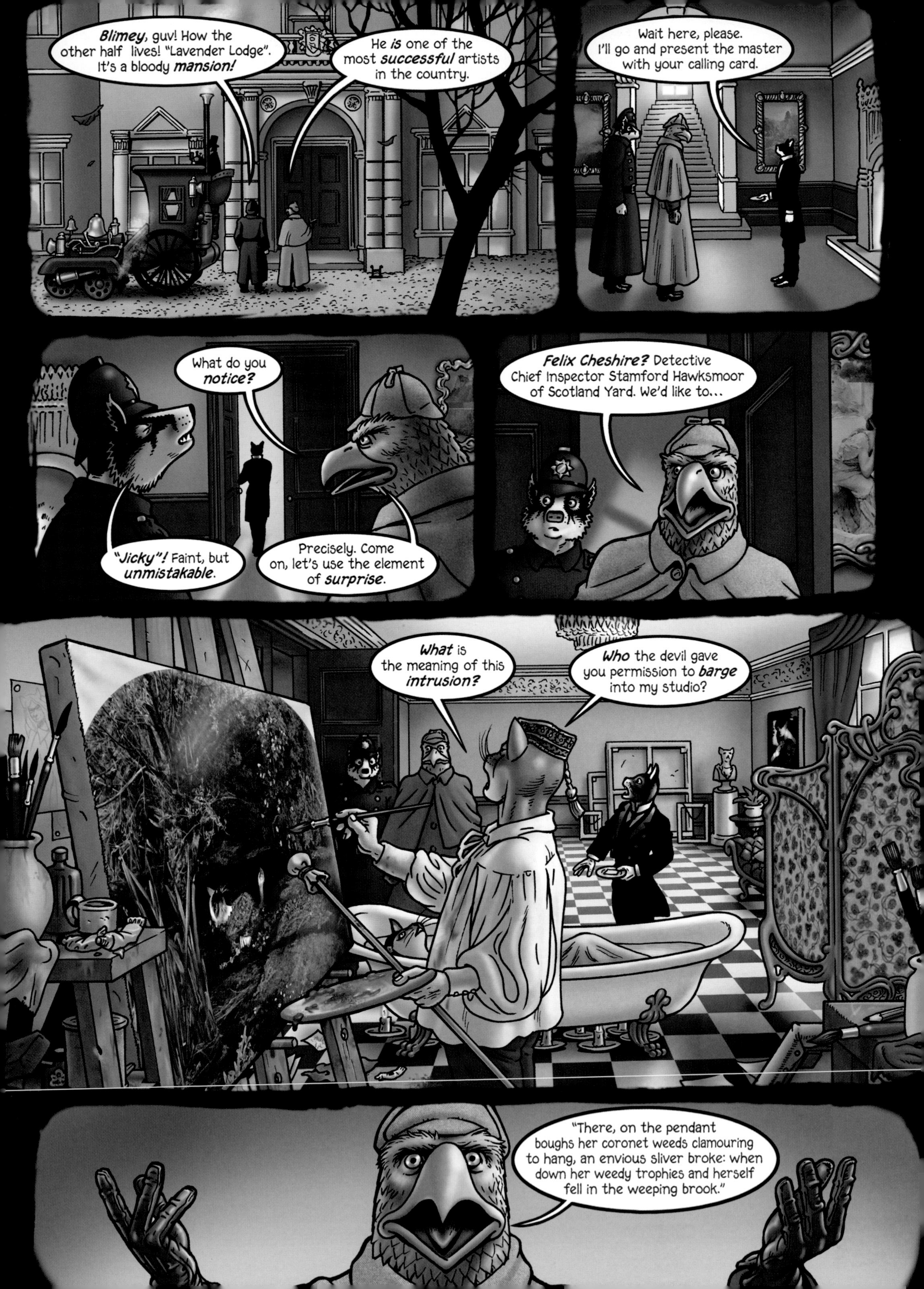
Blimey, guv! How the other half lives! "Lavender Lodge". It's a bloody mansion!
He is one of the most successful artists in the country.
Wait here, please. I'll go and present the master with your calling card.
What do you notice?
"Jicky"! Faint, but unmistakable.
Precisely. Come on, let's use the element of surprise.
Felix Cheshire? Detective Chief Inspector Stamford Hawksmoor of Scotland Yard. We'd like to...
What is the meaning of this intrusion?
Who the devil gave you permission to barge into my studio?
"There, on the pendant boughs her coronet weeds clamouring to hang, an envious sliver broke: when down her weedy trophies and herself fell in the weeping brook."

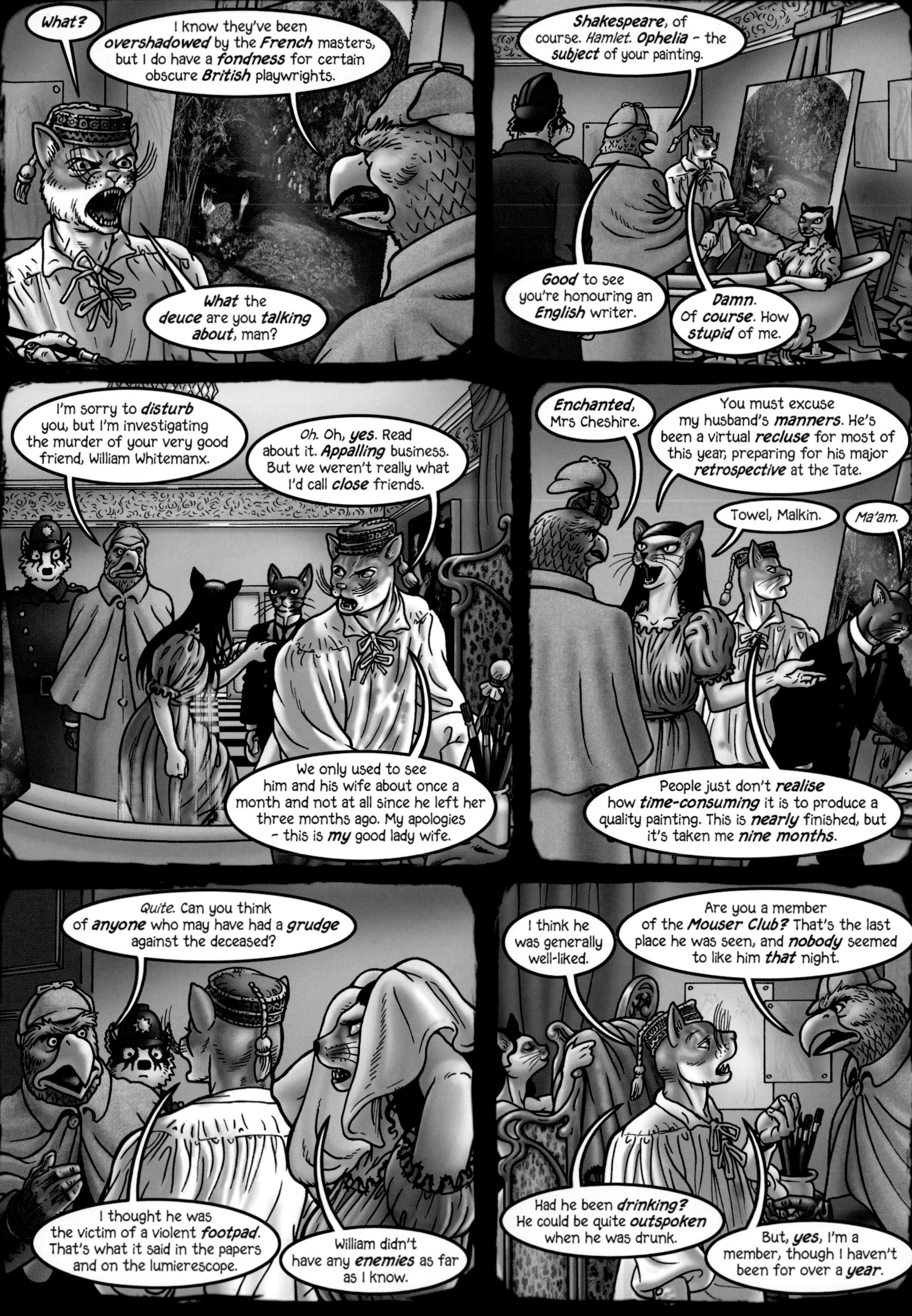

What?
I know they've been overshadowed by the French masters, but I do have a fondness for certain obscure British playwrights.
What the deuce are you talking about, man?
Shakespeare, of course. Hamlet. Ophelia – the subject of your painting.
Good to see you're honouring an English writer.
Damn. Of course. How stupid of me.
I'm sorry to disturb you, but I'm investigating the murder of your very good friend, William Whitemanx.
Oh. Oh, yes. Read about it. Appalling business. But we weren't really what I'd call close friends.
We only used to see him and his wife about once a month and not at all since he left her three months ago. My apologies – this is my good lady wife.
Enchanted, Mrs Cheshire.
You must excuse my husband's manners. He's been a virtual recluse for most of this year, preparing for his major retrospective at the Tate.
Towel, Malkin.
Ma'am.
People just don't realise how time-consuming it is to produce a quality painting. This is nearly finished, but it's taken me nine months.
Quite. Can you think of anyone who may have had a grudge against the deceased?
I thought he was the victim of a violent footpad. That's what it said in the papers and on the lumierescope.
William didn't have any enemies as far as I know.
I think he was generally well-liked.
Are you a member of the Mouser Club? That's the last place he was seen, and nobody seemed to like him that night.
Had he been drinking? He could be quite outspoken when he was drunk.
But, yes, I'm a member, though I haven't been for over a year.

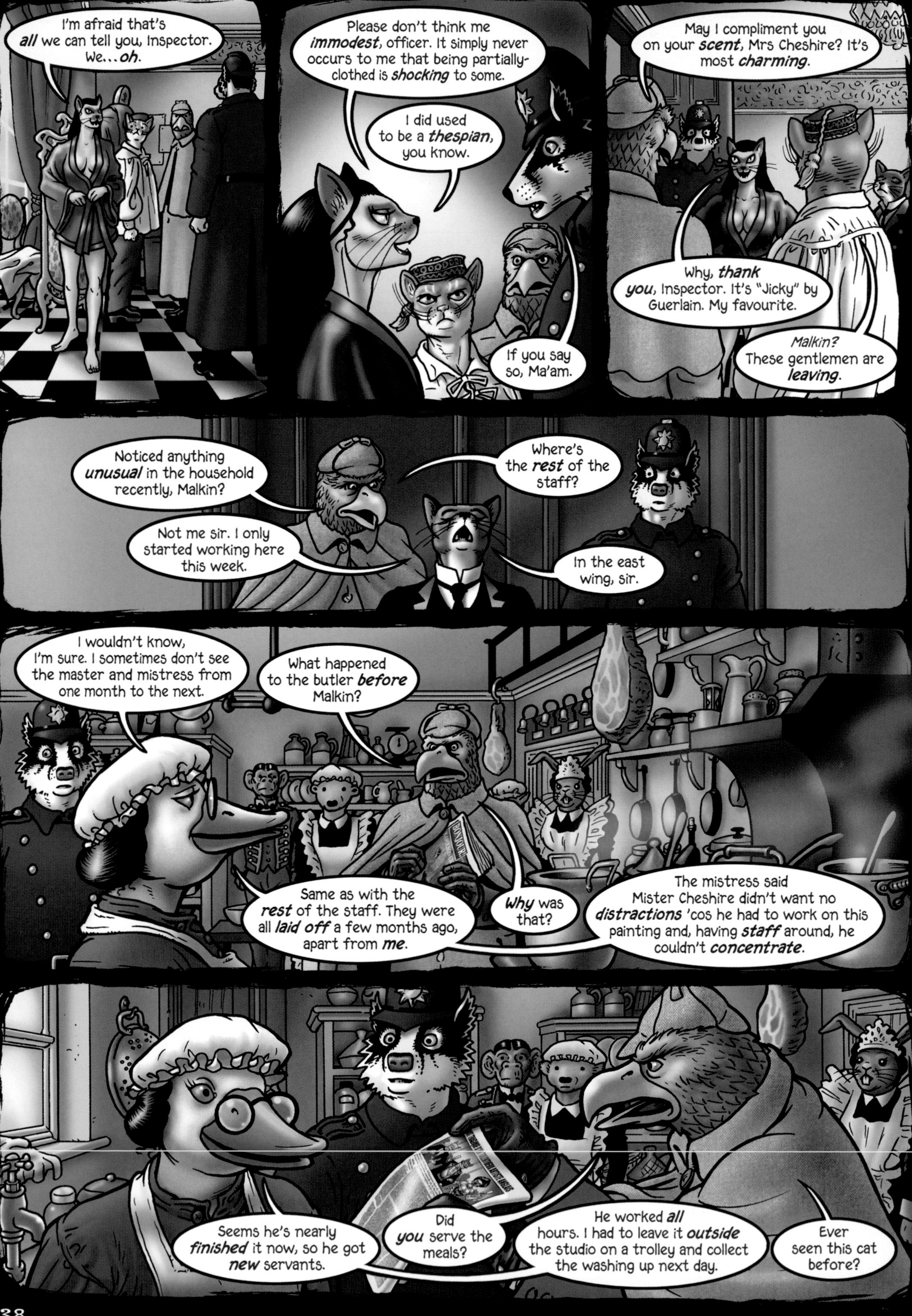

I'm afraid that's all we can tell you, Inspector. We... oh.
Please don't think me immodest, officer. It simply never occurs to me that being partially-clothed is shocking to some.
I did used to be a thespian, you know.
If you say so, Ma'am.
May I compliment you on your scent, Mrs Cheshire? It's most charming.
Why, thank you, Inspector. It's "Jicky" by Guerlain. My favourite.
Malkin? These gentlemen are leaving.
Noticed anything unusual in the household recently, Malkin?
Not me sir. I only started working here this week.
Where's the rest of the staff?
In the east wing, sir.
I wouldn't know, I'm sure. I sometimes don't see the master and mistress from one month to the next.
What happened to the butler before Malkin?
Same as with the rest of the staff. They were all laid off a few months ago, apart from me.
Why was that?
The mistress said Mister Cheshire didn't want no distractions 'cos he had to work on this painting and, having staff around, he couldn't concentrate.
Seems he's nearly finished it now, so he got new servants.
Did you serve the meals?
He worked all hours. I had to leave it outside the studio on a trolley and collect the washing up next day.
Ever seen this cat before?

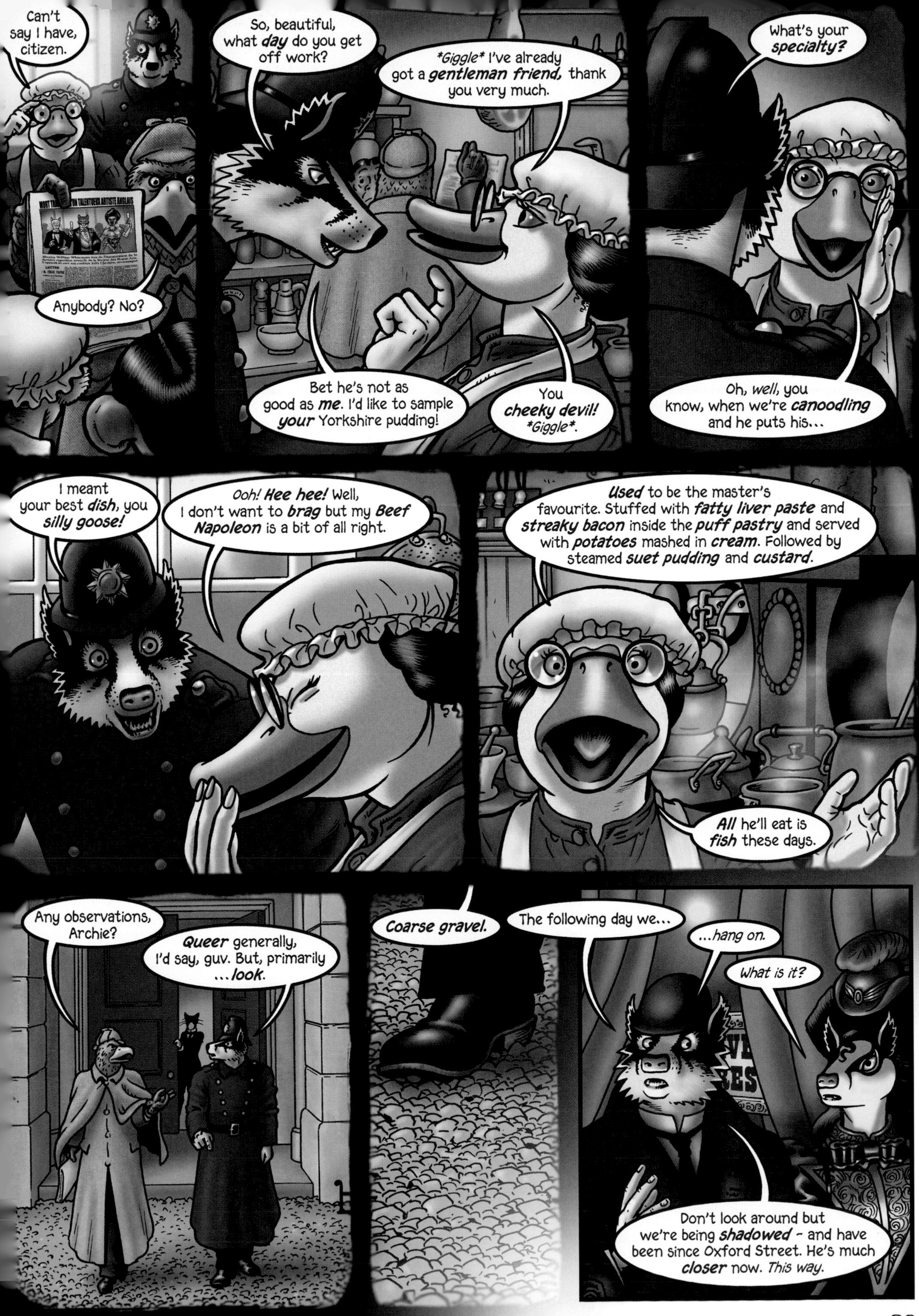
Can't say I have, citizen.
Anybody? No?
So, beautiful, what day do you get off work?
Giggle I've already got a gentleman friend, thank you very much.
Bet he's not as good as me. I'd like to sample your Yorkshire pudding!
You cheeky devil! *Giggle*.
What's your specialty?
Oh, well, you know, when we're canoodling and he puts his...
I meant your best dish, you silly goose!
Ooh! Hee hee! Well, I don't want to brag but my Beef Napoleon is a bit of all right.
Used to be the master's favourite. Stuffed with fatty liver paste and streaky bacon inside the puff pastry and served with potatoes mashed in cream. Followed by steamed suet pudding and custard.
All he'll eat is fish these days.
Any observations, Archie?
Queer generally, I'd say, guv. But, primarily ...look.
Coarse gravel.
The following day we...
...hang on.
What is it?
Don't look around but we're being shadowed - and have been since Oxford Street. He's much closer now. This way.

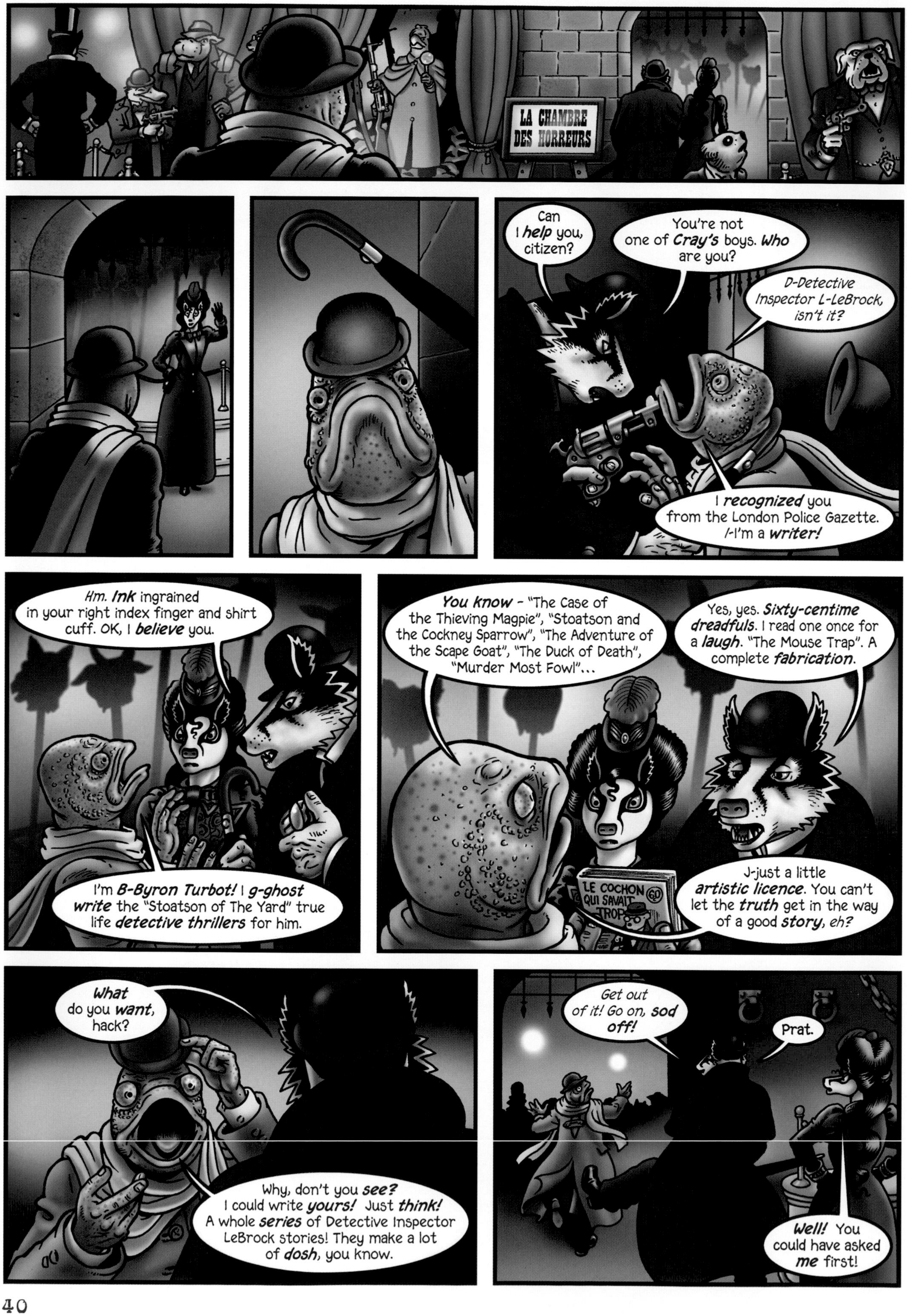
LA CHAMBRE DES HORREURS
Can I help you, citizen?
You're not one of Cray's boys. Who are you?
D-Detective Inspector L-LeBrock, isn't it?
I recognized you from the London Police Gazette. I-I'm a writer!
Hm. Ink ingrained in your right index finger and shirt cuff. OK, I believe you.
I'm B-Byron Turbot! I g-ghost write the "Stoatson of The Yard" true life detective thrillers for him.
You know - "The Case of the Thieving Magpie", "Stoatson and the Cockney Sparrow", "The Adventure of the Scape Goat", "The Duck of Death", "Murder Most Fowl"...
Yes, yes. Sixty-centime dreadfuls. I read one once for a laugh. "The Mouse Trap". A complete fabrication.
LE COCHON QUI SAVAIT TROP
J-just a little artistic licence. You can't let the truth get in the way of a good story, eh?
What do you want, hack?
Why, don't you see? I could write yours! Just think! A whole series of Detective Inspector LeBrock stories! They make a lot of dosh, you know.
Get out of it! Go on, sod off!
Prat.
Well! You could have asked me first!

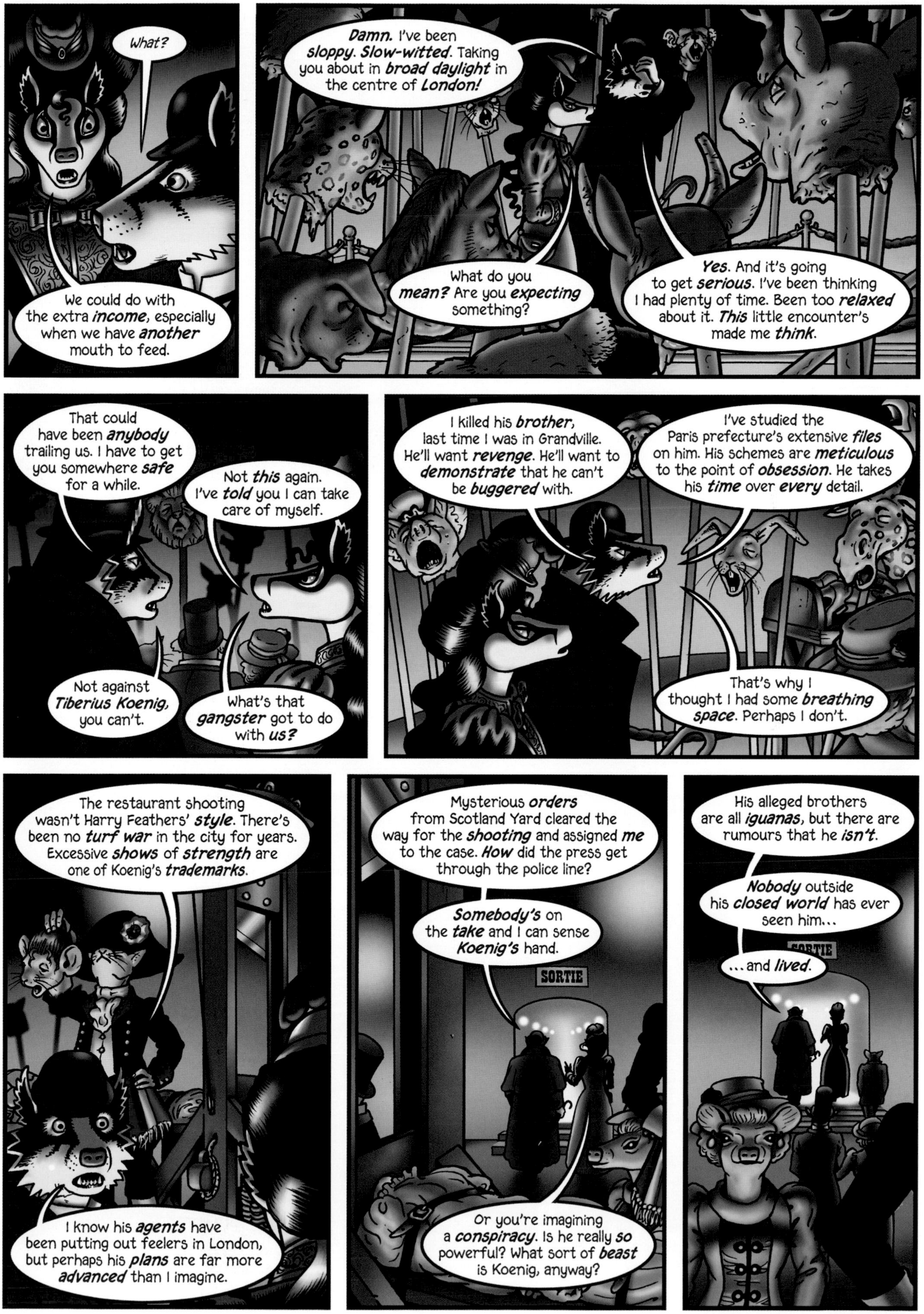
What?
We could do with the extra income, especially when we have another mouth to feed.
Damn. I've been sloppy. Slow-witted. Taking you about in broad daylight in the centre of London!
What do you mean? Are you expecting something?
Yes. And it's going to get serious. I've been thinking I had plenty of time. Been too relaxed about it. This little encounter's made me think.
That could have been anybody trailing us. I have to get you somewhere safe for a while.
Not this again. I've told you I can take care of myself.
Not against Tiberius Koenig, you can't.
What's that gangster got to do with us?
I killed his brother, last time I was in Grandville. He'll want revenge. He'll want to demonstrate that he can't be buggered with.
I've studied the Paris prefecture's extensive files on him. His schemes are meticulous to the point of obsession. He takes his time over every detail.
That's why I thought I had some breathing space. Perhaps I don't.
The restaurant shooting wasn't Harry Feathers' style. There's been no turf war in the city for years. Excessive shows of strength are one of Koenig's trademarks.
I know his agents have been putting out feelers in London, but perhaps his plans are far more advanced than I imagine.
Mysterious orders from Scotland Yard cleared the way for the shooting and assigned me to the case. How did the press get through the police line?
Somebody's on the take and I can sense Koenig's hand.
SORTIE
Or you're imagining a conspiracy. Is he really so powerful? What sort of beast is Koenig, anyway?
His alleged brothers are all iguanas, but there are rumours that he isn't.
Nobody outside his closed world has ever seen him...
SORTIE
...and lived.

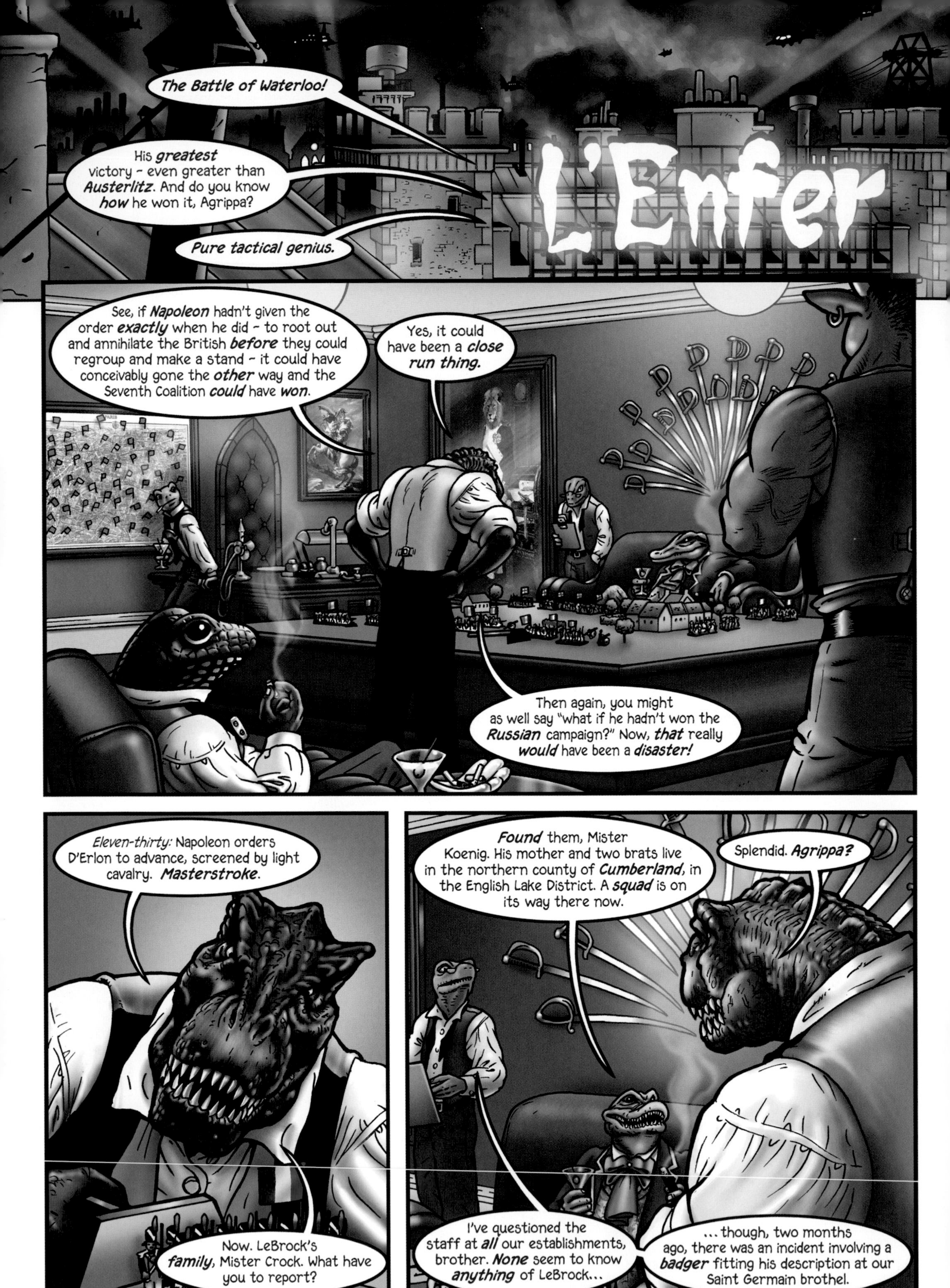

The Battle of Waterloo!
His greatest victory - even greater than Austerlitz. And do you know how he won it, Agrippa?
Pure tactical genius.
L'Enfer
See, if Napoleon hadn't given the order exactly when he did - to root out and annihilate the British before they could regroup and make a stand - it could have conceivably gone the other way and the Seventh Coalition could have won.
Yes, it could have been a close run thing.
Then again, you might as well say "what if he hadn't won the Russian campaign?" Now, that really would have been a disaster!
Eleven-thirty: Napoleon orders D'Erlon to advance, screened by light cavalry. Masterstroke.
Now. LeBrock's family, Mister Crock. What have you to report?
Found them, Mister Koenig. His mother and two brats live in the northern county of Cumberland, in the English Lake District. A squad is on its way there now.
Splendid. Agrippa?
I've questioned the staff at all our establishments, brother. None seem to know anything of LeBrock...
...though, two months ago, there was an incident involving a badger fitting his description at our Saint Germain brothel.

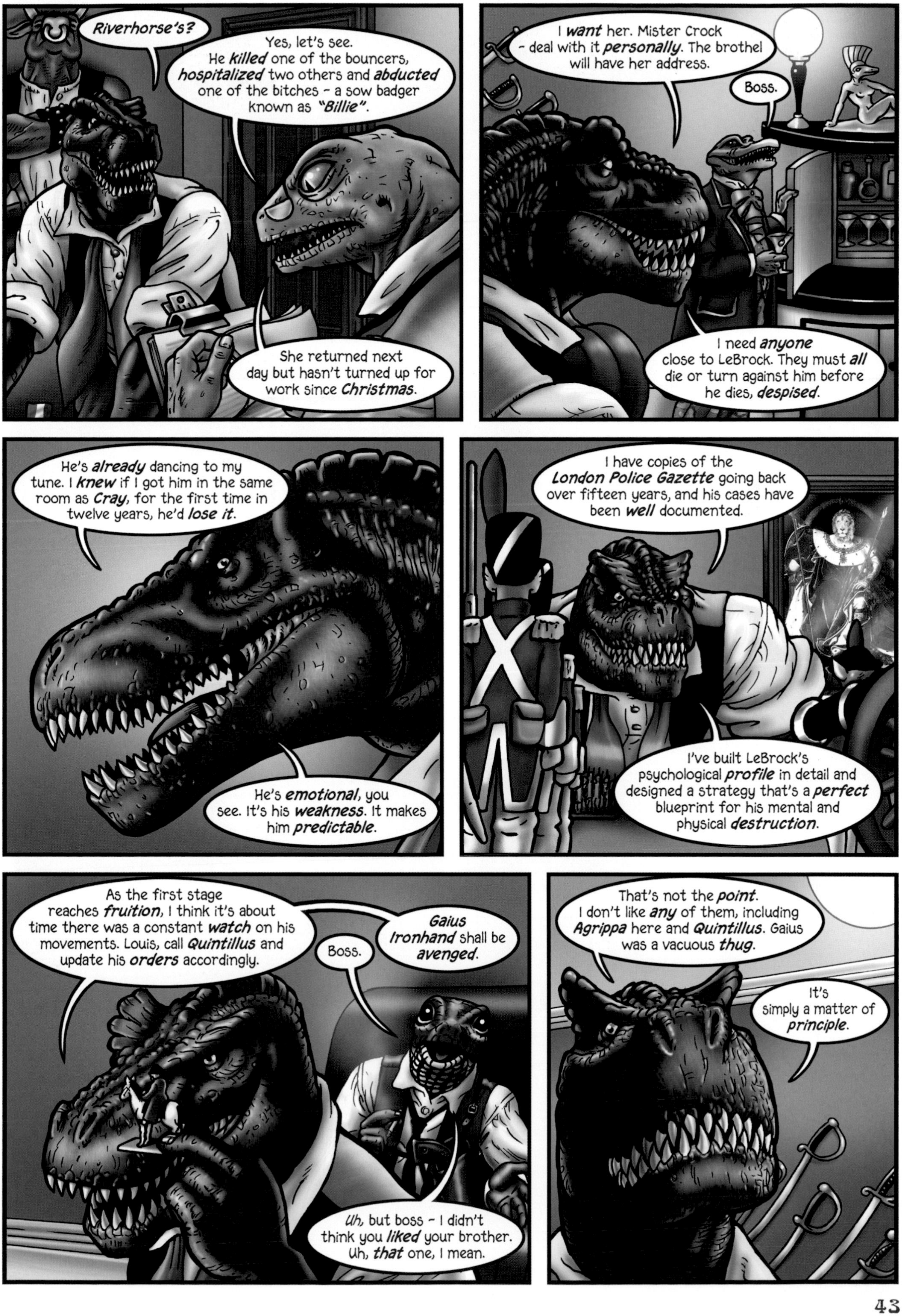
Riverhorse's?
Yes, let's see. He killed one of the bouncers, hospitalized two others and abducted one of the bitches - a sow badger known as "Billie".
She returned next day but hasn't turned up for work since Christmas.
I want her. Mister Crock - deal with it personally. The brothel will have her address.
Boss.
I need anyone close to LeBrock. They must all die or turn against him before he dies, despised.
He's already dancing to my tune. I knew if I got him in the same room as Cray, for the first time in twelve years, he'd lose it.
He's emotional, you see. It's his weakness. It makes him predictable.
I have copies of the London Police Gazette going back over fifteen years, and his cases have been well documented.
I've built LeBrock's psychological profile in detail and designed a strategy that's a perfect blueprint for his mental and physical destruction.
As the first stage reaches fruition, I think it's about time there was a constant watch on his movements. Louis, call Quintillus and update his orders accordingly.
Boss.
Gaius Ironhand shall be avenged.
Uh, but boss - I didn't think you liked your brother. Uh, that one, I mean.
That's not the point. I don't like any of them, including Agrippa here and Quintillus. Gaius was a vacuous thug.
It's simply a matter of principle.

Jesus! It's *pitch-dark* in here. The street lighting in London is *pathetic*. What a *backward* city! Why is *everything* better in *France?*

Yes, not like *Paris*, the *city of light*. Speaking of *light*, anyone *got* one?

Yeah, just a minute.

Here you go.

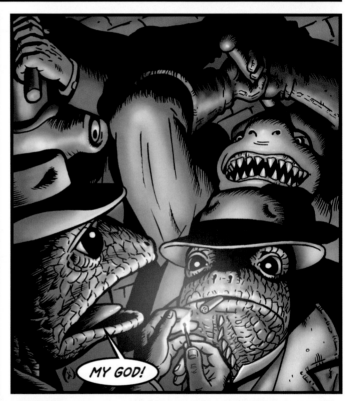

MY GOD!

44

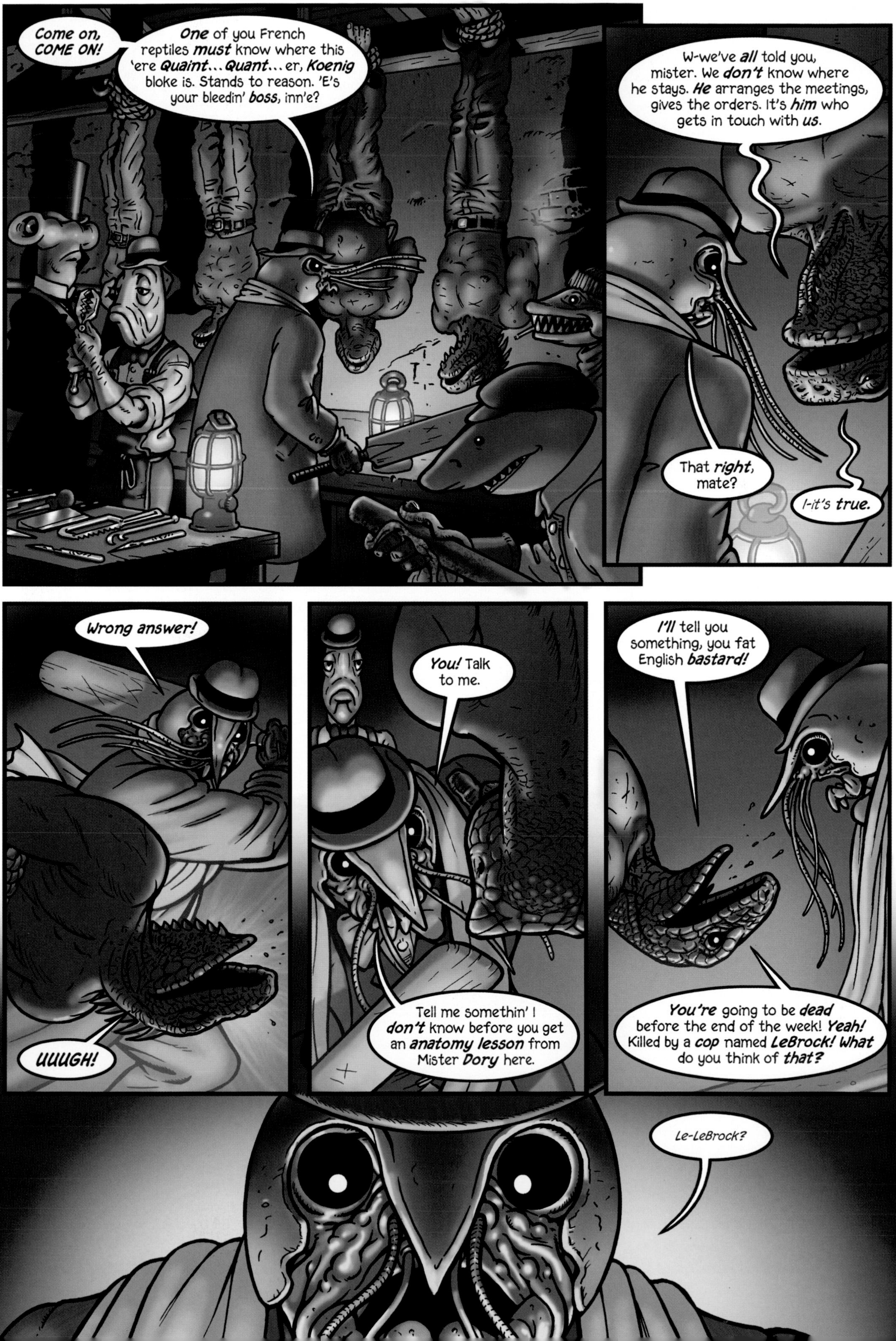

Come on, COME ON!
One of you French reptiles must know where this 'ere Quaint... Quant... er, Koenig bloke is. Stands to reason. 'E's your bleedin' boss, inn'e?
W-we've all told you, mister. We don't know where he stays. He arranges the meetings, gives the orders. It's him who gets in touch with us.
That right, mate?
I-it's true.
Wrong answer!
UUUGH!
You! Talk to me.
Tell me somethin' I don't know before you get an anatomy lesson from Mister Dory here.
I'll tell you something, you fat English bastard!
You're going to be dead before the end of the week! Yeah! Killed by a cop named LeBrock! What do you think of that?
Le-LeBrock?

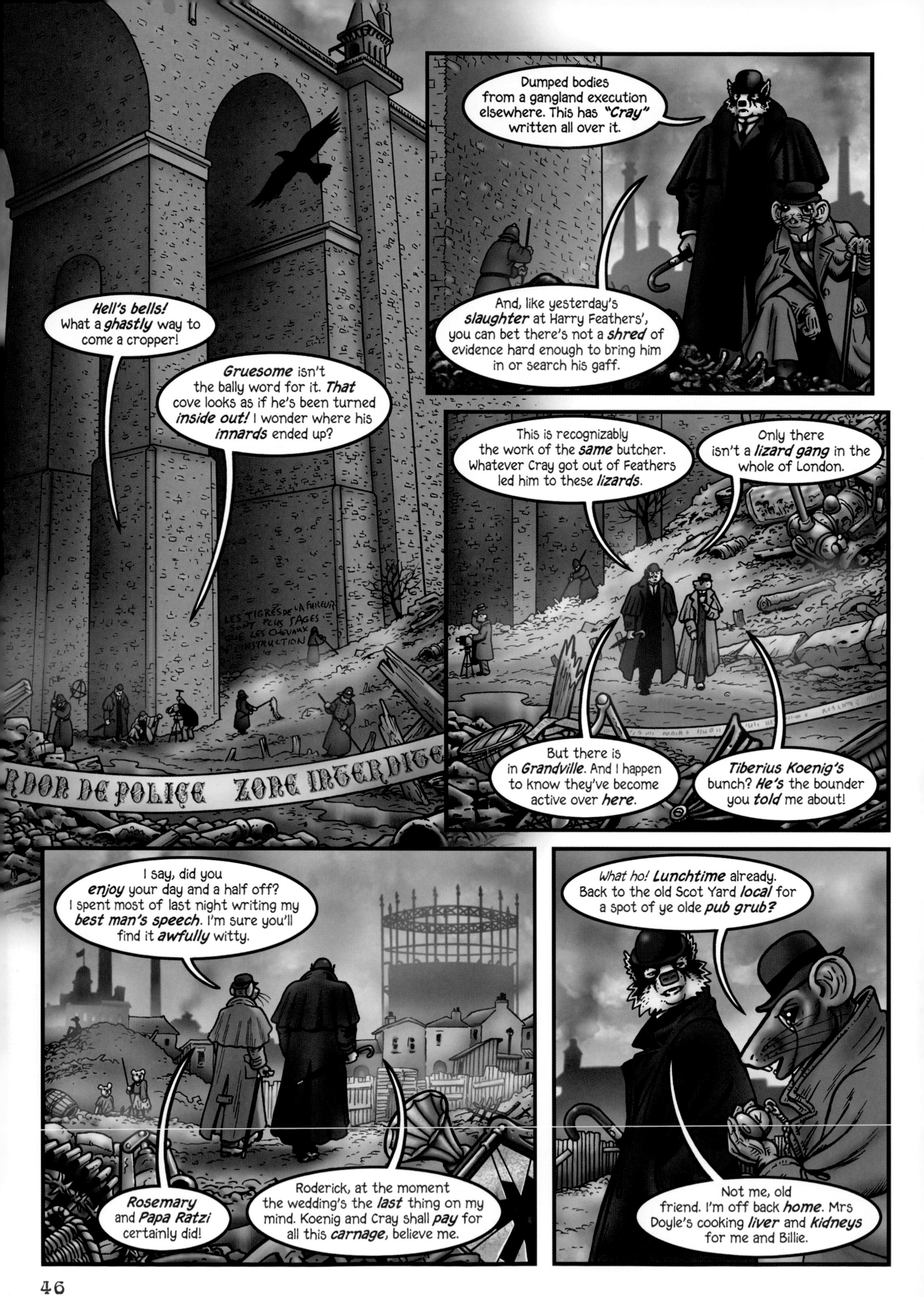
Hell's bells! What a ghastly way to come a cropper!
Gruesome isn't the bally word for it. That cove looks as if he's been turned inside out! I wonder where his innards ended up?
LES TIGRES DE LA FUREUR SONT PLUS SAGES QUE LES CHEVAUX
RDON DE POLICE ZONE INTERDIT
Dumped bodies from a gangland execution elsewhere. This has "Cray" written all over it.
And, like yesterday's slaughter at Harry Feathers', you can bet there's not a shred of evidence hard enough to bring him in or search his gaff.
This is recognizably the work of the same butcher. Whatever Cray got out of Feathers led him to these lizards.
Only there isn't a lizard gang in the whole of London.
But there is in Grandville. And I happen to know they've become active over here.
Tiberius Koenig's bunch? He's the bounder you told me about!
I say, did you enjoy your day and a half off? I spent most of last night writing my best man's speech. I'm sure you'll find it awfully witty.
Rosemary and Papa Ratzi certainly did!
Roderick, at the moment the wedding's the last thing on my mind. Koenig and Cray shall pay for all this carnage, believe me.
What ho! Lunchtime already. Back to the old Scot Yard local for a spot of ye olde pub grub?
Not me, old friend. I'm off back home. Mrs Doyle's cooking liver and kidneys for me and Billie.

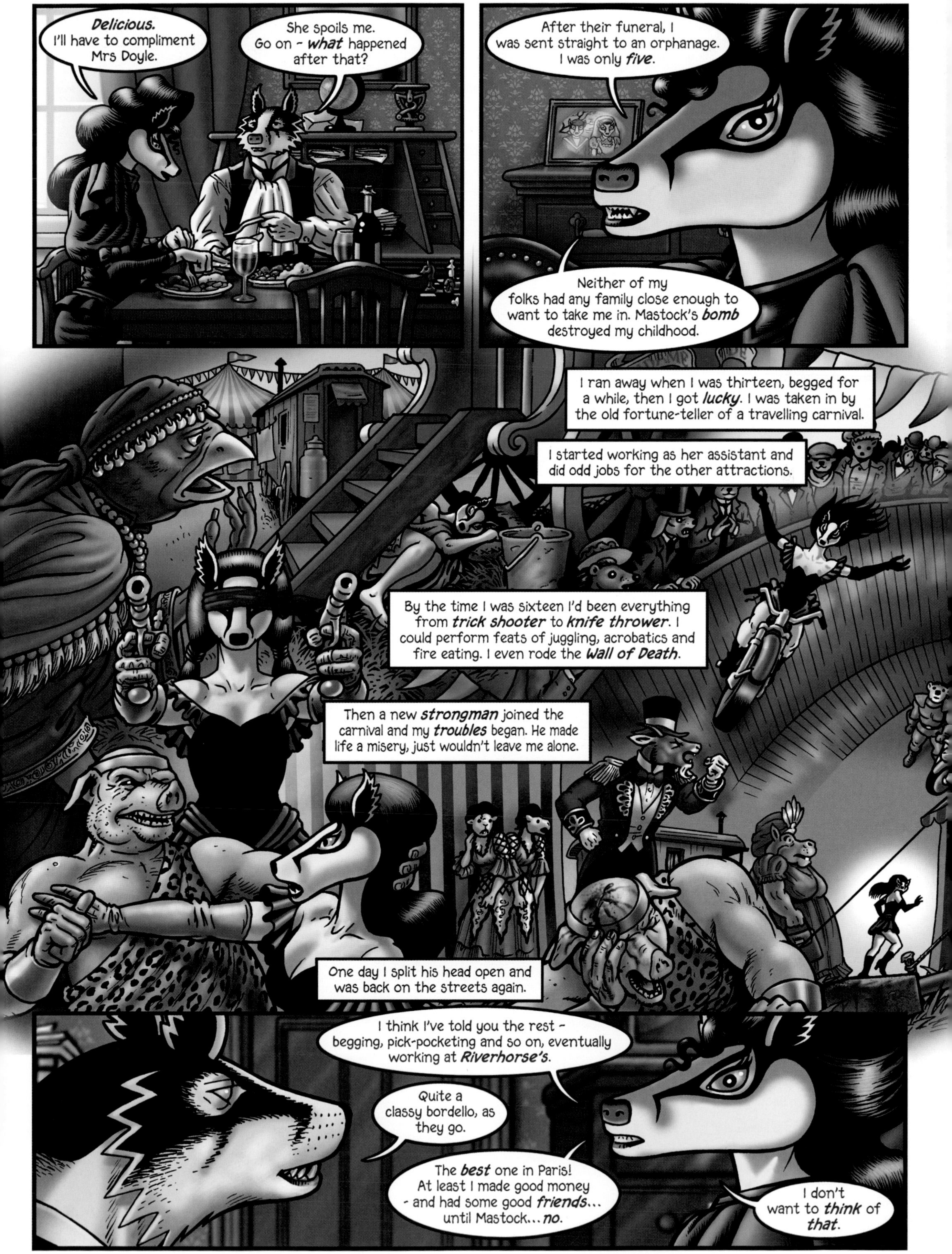

Delicious. I'll have to compliment Mrs Doyle.
She spoils me. Go on - what happened after that?
After their funeral, I was sent straight to an orphanage. I was only five.
Neither of my folks had any family close enough to want to take me in. Mastock's bomb destroyed my childhood.
I ran away when I was thirteen, begged for a while, then I got lucky. I was taken in by the old fortune-teller of a travelling carnival.
I started working as her assistant and did odd jobs for the other attractions.
By the time I was sixteen I'd been everything from trick shooter to knife thrower. I could perform feats of juggling, acrobatics and fire eating. I even rode the Wall of Death.
Then a new strongman joined the carnival and my troubles began. He made life a misery, just wouldn't leave me alone.
One day I split his head open and was back on the streets again.
I think I've told you the rest - begging, pick-pocketing and so on, eventually working at Riverhorse's.
Quite a classy bordello, as they go.
The best one in Paris! At least I made good money - and had some good friends... until Mastock... no.
I don't want to think of that.

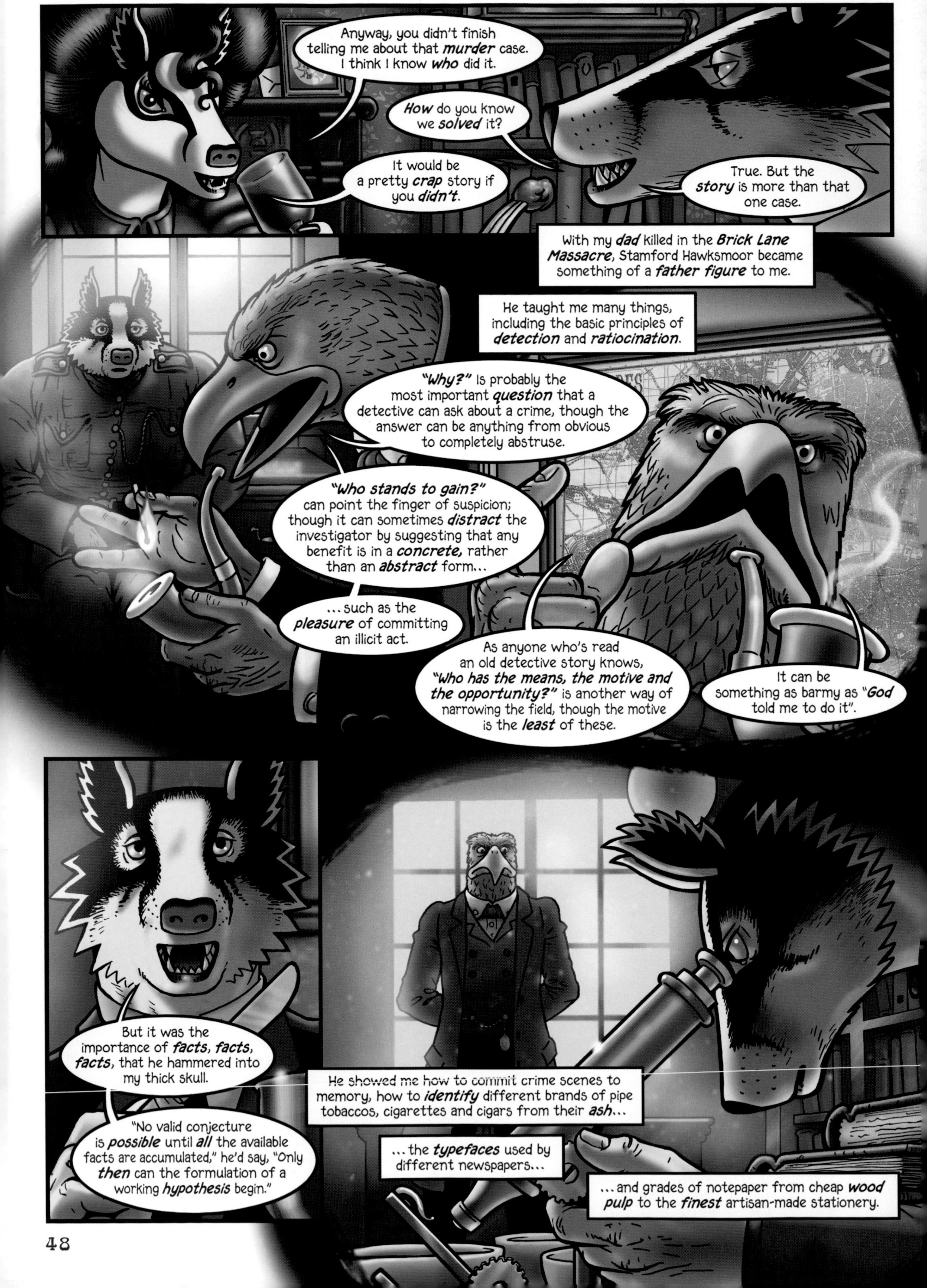
Anyway, you didn't finish telling me about that *murder* case. I think I know *who* did it.
How do you know we *solved* it?
It would be a pretty *crap* story if you *didn't*.
True. But the *story* is more than that one case.
With my *dad* killed in the *Brick Lane Massacre*, Stamford Hawksmoor became something of a *father figure* to me.
He taught me many things, including the basic principles of *detection* and *ratiocination*.
"Why?" is probably the most important *question* that a detective can ask about a crime, though the answer can be anything from obvious to completely abstruse.
"Who stands to gain?" can point the finger of suspicion; though it can sometimes *distract* the investigator by suggesting that any benefit is in a *concrete,* rather than an *abstract* form...
...such as the *pleasure* of committing an illicit act.
As anyone who's read an old detective story knows, *"Who has the means, the motive and the opportunity?"* is another way of narrowing the field, though the motive is the *least* of these.
It can be something as barmy as "*God* told me to do it".
But it was the importance of *facts, facts, facts,* that he hammered into my thick skull.
He showed me how to commit crime scenes to memory, how to *identify* different brands of pipe tobaccos, cigarettes and cigars from their *ash*...
"No valid conjecture is *possible* until *all* the available facts are accumulated," he'd say, "Only *then* can the formulation of a working *hypothesis* begin."
...the *typefaces* used by different newspapers...
...and grades of notepaper from cheap *wood pulp* to the *finest* artisan-made stationery.

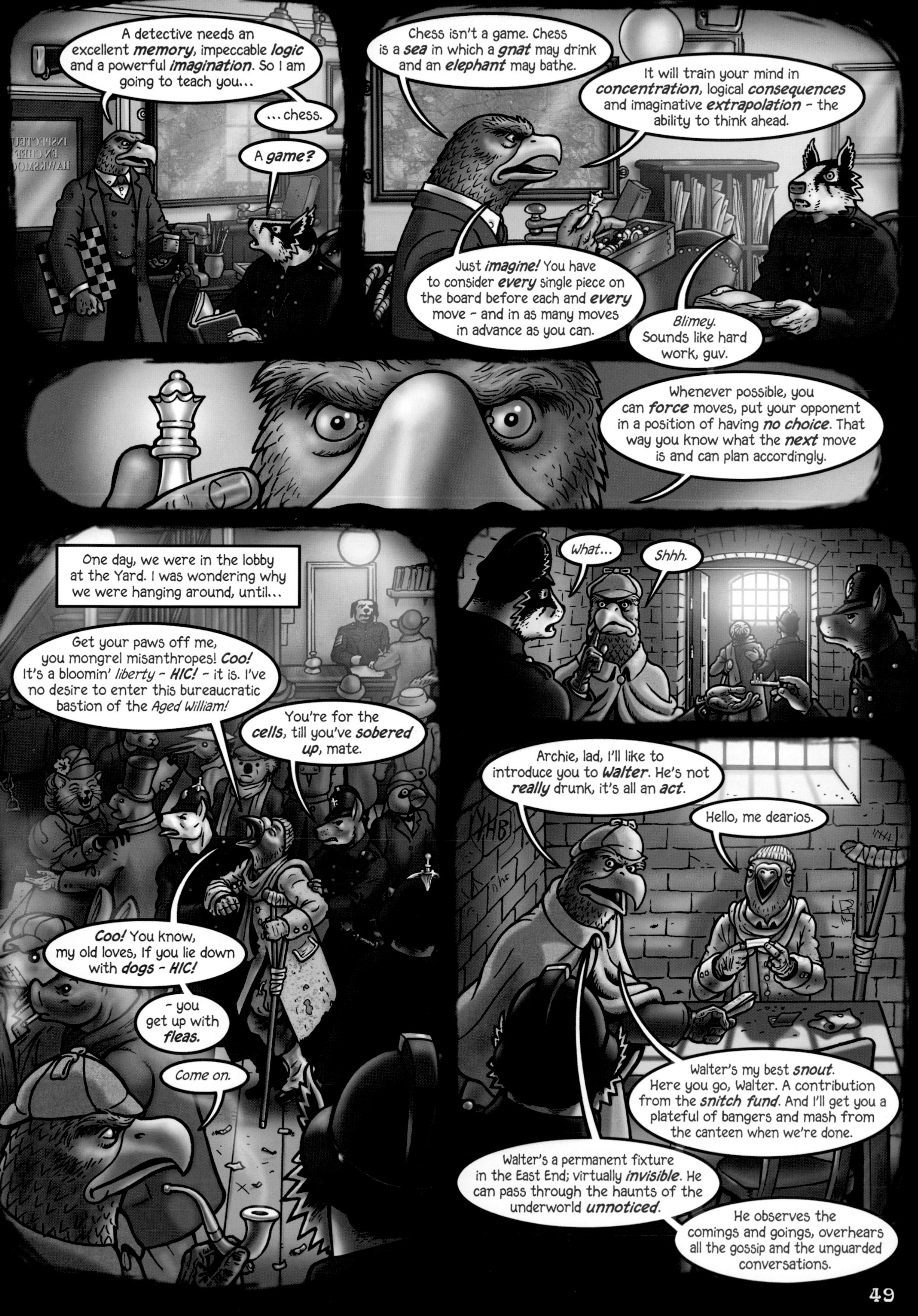
A detective needs an excellent *memory*, impeccable *logic* and a powerful *imagination*. So I am going to teach you...
...chess.
A *game?*
Chess isn't a game. Chess is a *sea* in which a *gnat* may drink and an *elephant* may bathe.
It will train your mind in *concentration*, logical *consequences* and imaginative *extrapolation* – the ability to think ahead.
Just *imagine!* You have to consider *every* single piece on the board before each and *every* move – and in as many moves in advance as you can.
Blimey. Sounds like hard work, guv.
Whenever possible, you can *force* moves, put your opponent in a position of having *no choice*. That way you know what the *next* move is and can plan accordingly.
One day, we were in the lobby at the Yard. I was wondering why we were hanging around, until...
Get your paws off me, you mongrel misanthropes! *Coo!* It's a bloomin' *liberty* – *HIC!* – it is. I've no desire to enter this bureaucratic bastion of the *Aged William!*
You're for the *cells*, till you've *sobered up*, mate.
Coo! You know, my old loves, If you lie down with *dogs* – *HIC!*
– you get up with *fleas.*
Come on.
What...
Shhh.
Archie, lad, I'll like to introduce you to *Walter*. He's not *really* drunk, it's all an *act*.
Hello, me dearios.
Walter's my best *snout*. Here you go, Walter. A contribution from the *snitch fund*. And I'll get you a plateful of bangers and mash from the canteen when we're done.
Walter's a permanent fixture in the East End; virtually *invisible*. He can pass through the haunts of the underworld *unnoticed*.
He observes the comings and goings, overhears all the gossip and the unguarded conversations.

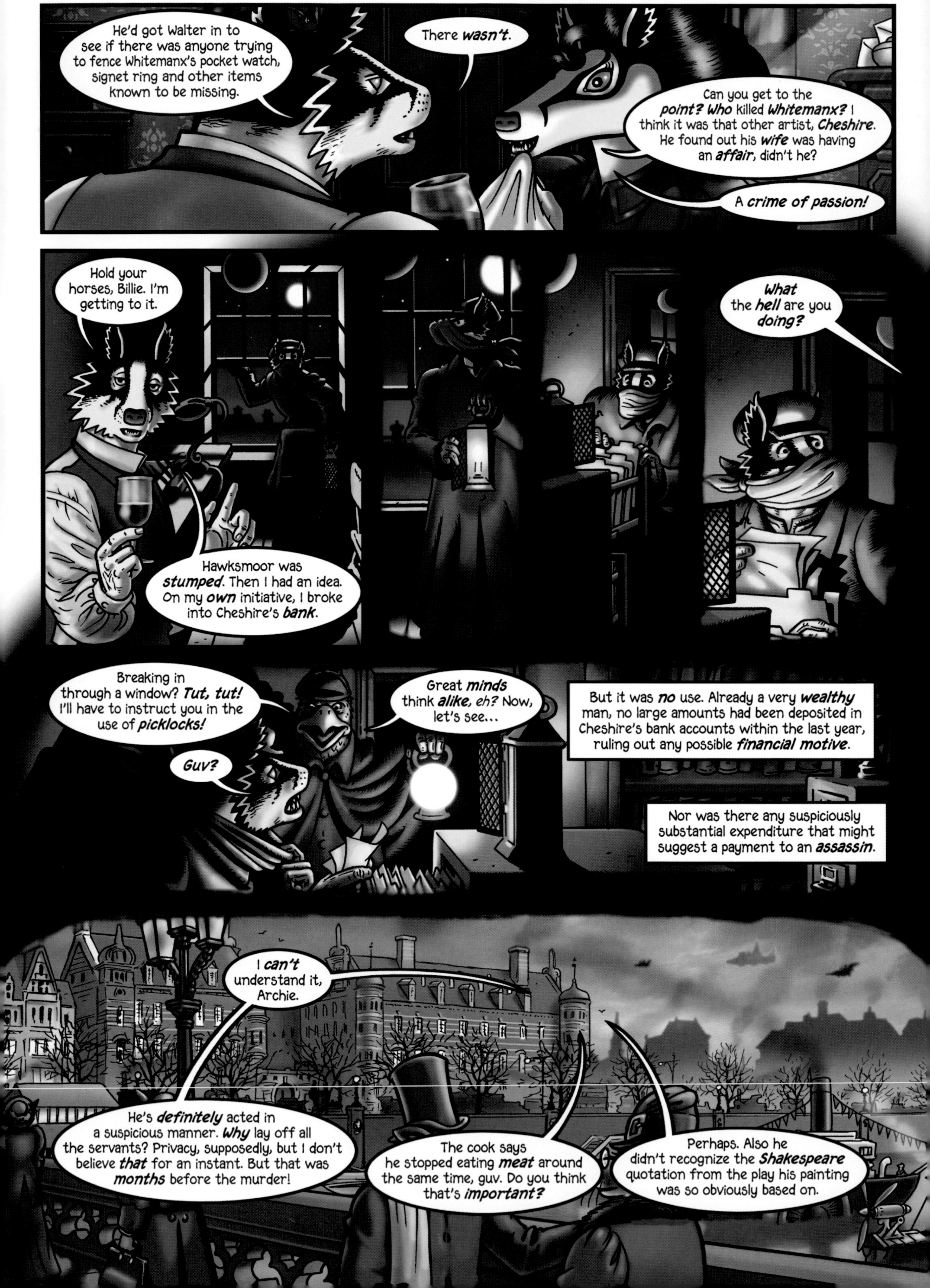
He'd got Walter in to see if there was anyone trying to fence Whitemanx's pocket watch, signet ring and other items known to be missing.
There *wasn't*.
Can you get to the *point? Who* killed *Whitemanx?* I think it was that other artist, *Cheshire*. He found out his *wife* was having an *affair*, didn't he?
A *crime of passion!*
Hold your horses, Billie. I'm getting to it.
Hawksmoor was *stumped*. Then I had an idea. On my *own* initiative, I broke into Cheshire's *bank*.
What the *hell* are you *doing?*
Breaking in through a window? *Tut, tut!* I'll have to instruct you in the use of *picklocks!*
Guv?
Great *minds* think *alike, eh?* Now, let's see...
But it was *no* use. Already a very *wealthy* man, no large amounts had been deposited in Cheshire's bank accounts within the last year, ruling out any possible *financial motive*.
Nor was there any suspiciously substantial expenditure that might suggest a payment to an *assassin*.
I *can't* understand it, Archie.
He's *definitely* acted in a suspicious manner. *Why* lay off all the servants? Privacy, supposedly, but I don't believe *that* for an instant. But that was *months* before the murder!
The cook says he stopped eating *meat* around the same time, guv. Do you think that's *important?*
Perhaps. Also he didn't recognize the *Shakespeare* quotation from the play his painting was so obviously based on.

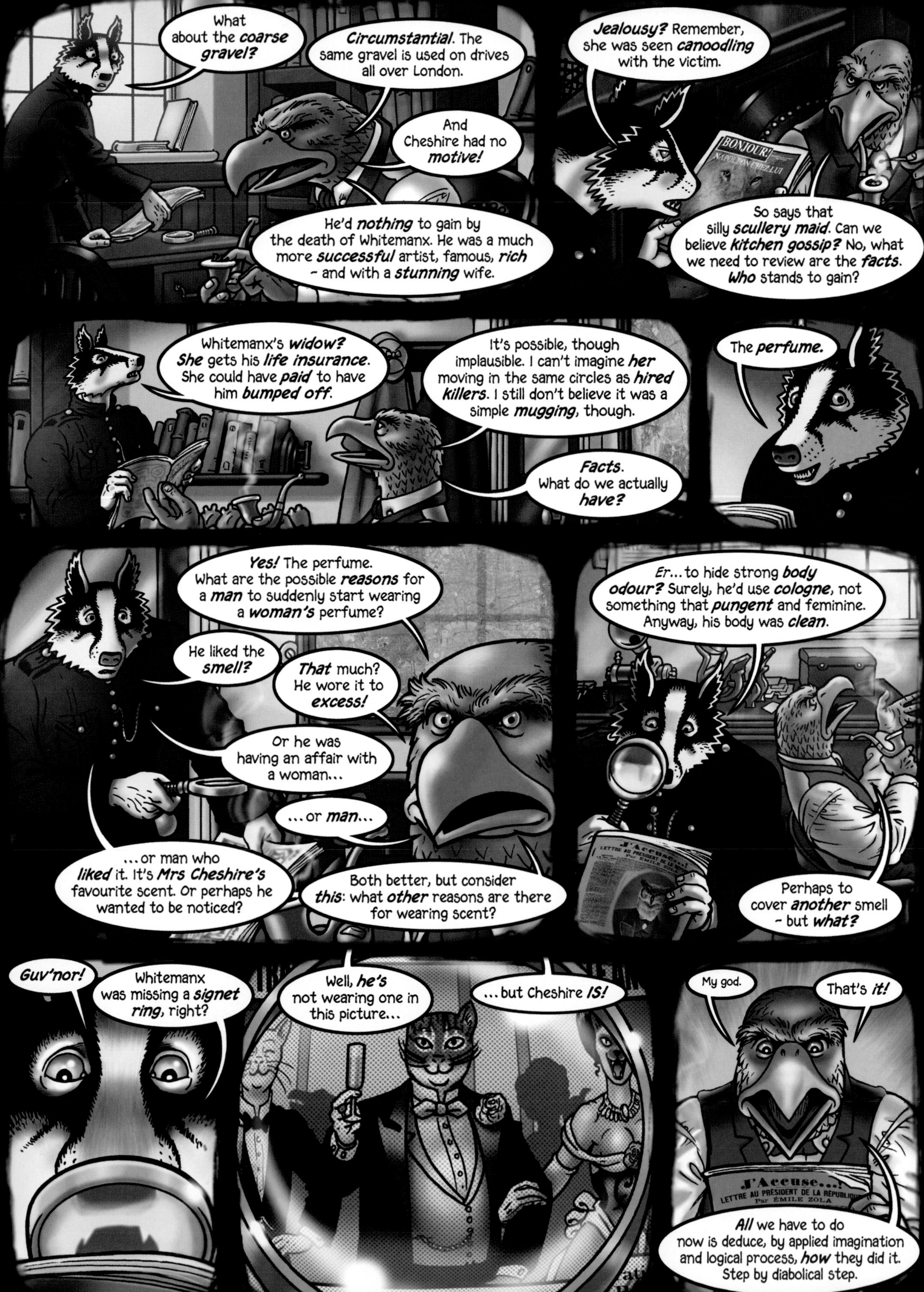
What about the *coarse gravel?*
Circumstantial. The same gravel is used on drives all over London.
And Cheshire had no *motive!*
He'd *nothing* to gain by the death of Whitemanx. He was a much more *successful* artist, famous, *rich* – and with a *stunning* wife.
Jealousy? Remember, she was seen *canoodling* with the victim.
BONJOUR!
NAPOLÉON CHEZ LUI
So says that silly *scullery maid*. Can we believe *kitchen gossip?* No, what we need to review are the *facts*. *Who* stands to gain?
Whitemanx's *widow? She* gets his *life insurance*. She could have *paid* to have him *bumped off*.
It's possible, though implausible. I can't imagine *her* moving in the same circles as *hired killers*. I still don't believe it was a simple *mugging*, though.
Facts. What do we actually *have?*
The *perfume*.
Yes! The perfume. What are the possible *reasons* for a *man* to suddenly start wearing a *woman's* perfume?
He liked the *smell?*
That much? He wore it to *excess!*
Or he was having an affair with a woman...
...or *man*...
...or man who *liked* it. It's *Mrs Cheshire's* favourite scent. Or perhaps he wanted to be noticed?
Both better, but consider *this*: what *other* reasons are there for wearing scent?
Er... to hide strong *body odour?* Surely, he'd use *cologne*, not something that *pungent* and feminine. Anyway, his body was *clean*.
Perhaps to cover *another* smell – but *what?*
Guv'nor!
Whitemanx was missing a *signet ring*, right?
Well, *he's* not wearing one in this picture...
...but Cheshire *IS!*
My god.
That's *it!*
J'Accuse...!
LETTRE AU PRÉSIDENT DE LA RÉPUBLIQUE
Par ÉMILE ZOLA
All we have to do now is deduce, by applied imagination and logical process, *how* they did it. Step by diabolical step.

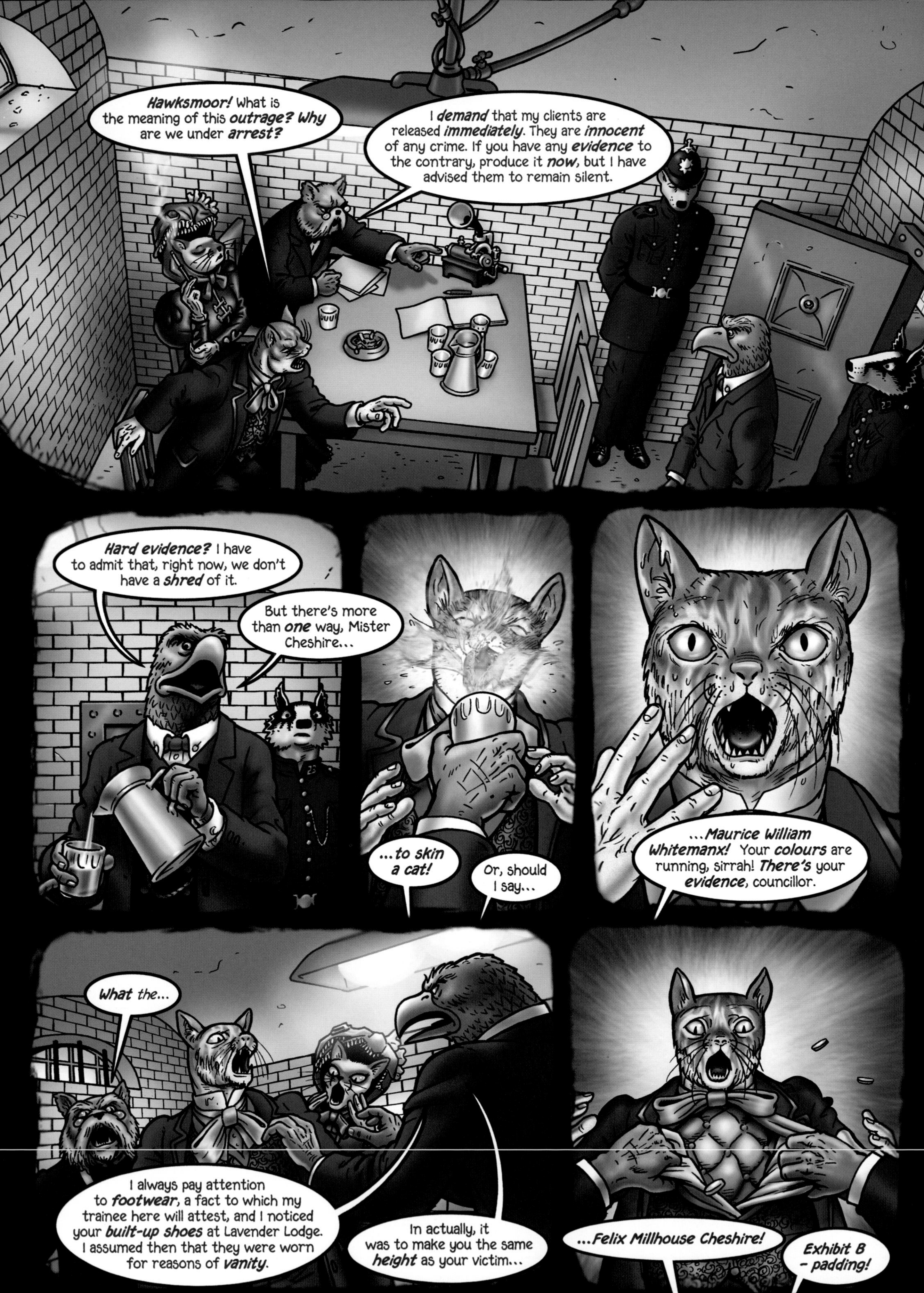

Hawksmoor! What is the meaning of this outrage? Why are we under arrest?
I demand that my clients are released immediately. They are innocent of any crime. If you have any evidence to the contrary, produce it now, but I have advised them to remain silent.
Hard evidence? I have to admit that, right now, we don't have a shred of it.
But there's more than one way, Mister Cheshire...
...to skin a cat!
Or, should I say...
...Maurice William Whitemanx! Your colours are running, sirrah! There's your evidence, councillor.
What the...
I always pay attention to footwear, a fact to which my trainee here will attest, and I noticed your built-up shoes at Lavender Lodge. I assumed then that they were worn for reasons of vanity.
In actually, it was to make you the same height as your victim...
...Felix Millhouse Cheshire!
Exhibit B – padding!

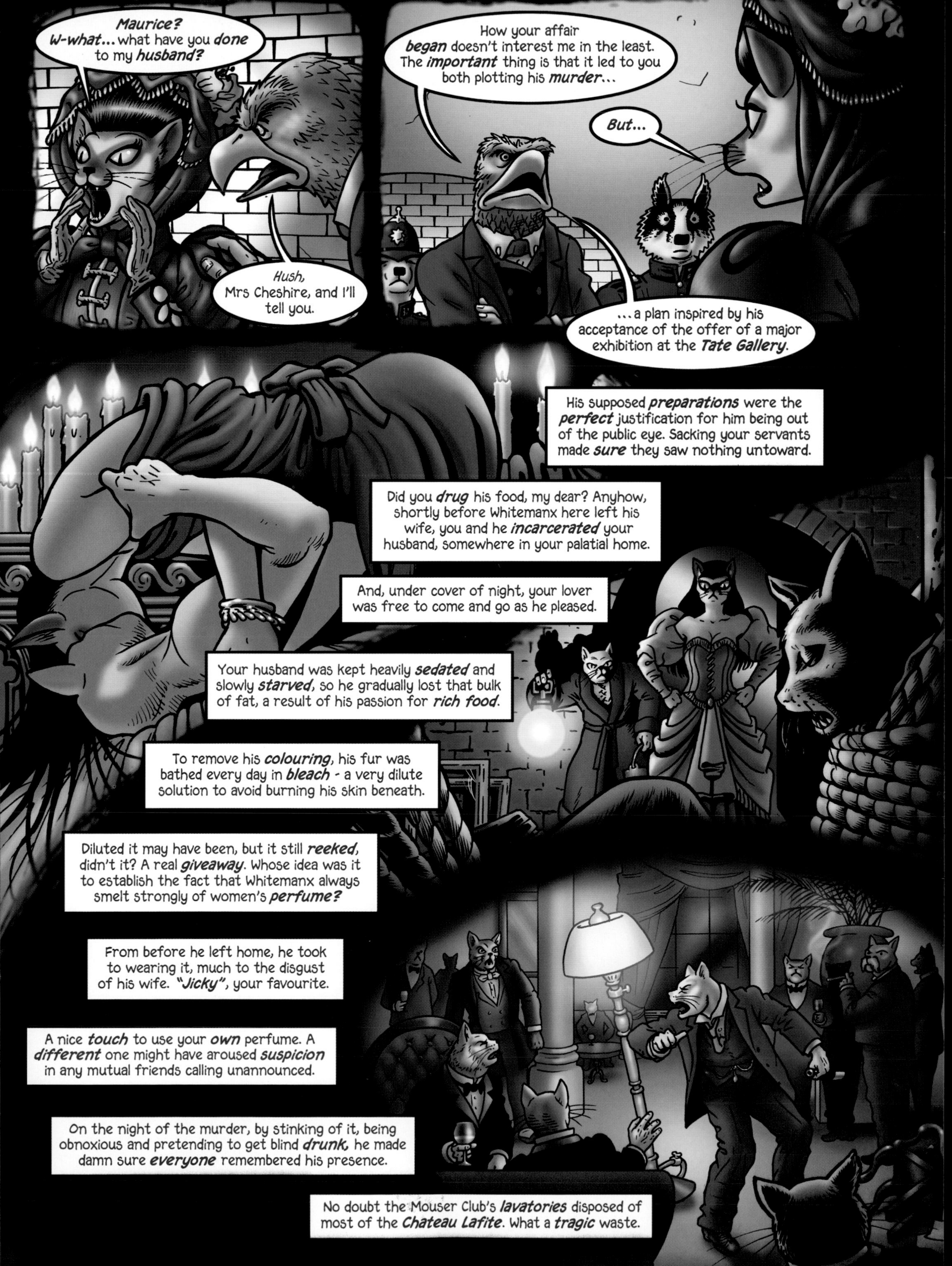

Maurice? W-what... what have you done to my husband?
Hush, Mrs Cheshire, and I'll tell you.
How your affair began doesn't interest me in the least. The important thing is that it led to you both plotting his murder...
But...
...a plan inspired by his acceptance of the offer of a major exhibition at the Tate Gallery.
His supposed preparations were the perfect justification for him being out of the public eye. Sacking your servants made sure they saw nothing untoward.
Did you drug his food, my dear? Anyhow, shortly before Whitemanx here left his wife, you and he incarcerated your husband, somewhere in your palatial home.
And, under cover of night, your lover was free to come and go as he pleased.
Your husband was kept heavily sedated and slowly starved, so he gradually lost that bulk of fat, a result of his passion for rich food.
To remove his colouring, his fur was bathed every day in bleach - a very dilute solution to avoid burning his skin beneath.
Diluted it may have been, but it still reeked, didn't it? A real giveaway. Whose idea was it to establish the fact that Whitemanx always smelt strongly of women's perfume?
From before he left home, he took to wearing it, much to the disgust of his wife. "Jicky", your favourite.
A nice touch to use your own perfume. A different one might have aroused suspicion in any mutual friends calling unannounced.
On the night of the murder, by stinking of it, being obnoxious and pretending to get blind drunk, he made damn sure everyone remembered his presence.
No doubt the Mouser Club's lavatories disposed of most of the Chateau Lafite. What a tragic waste.

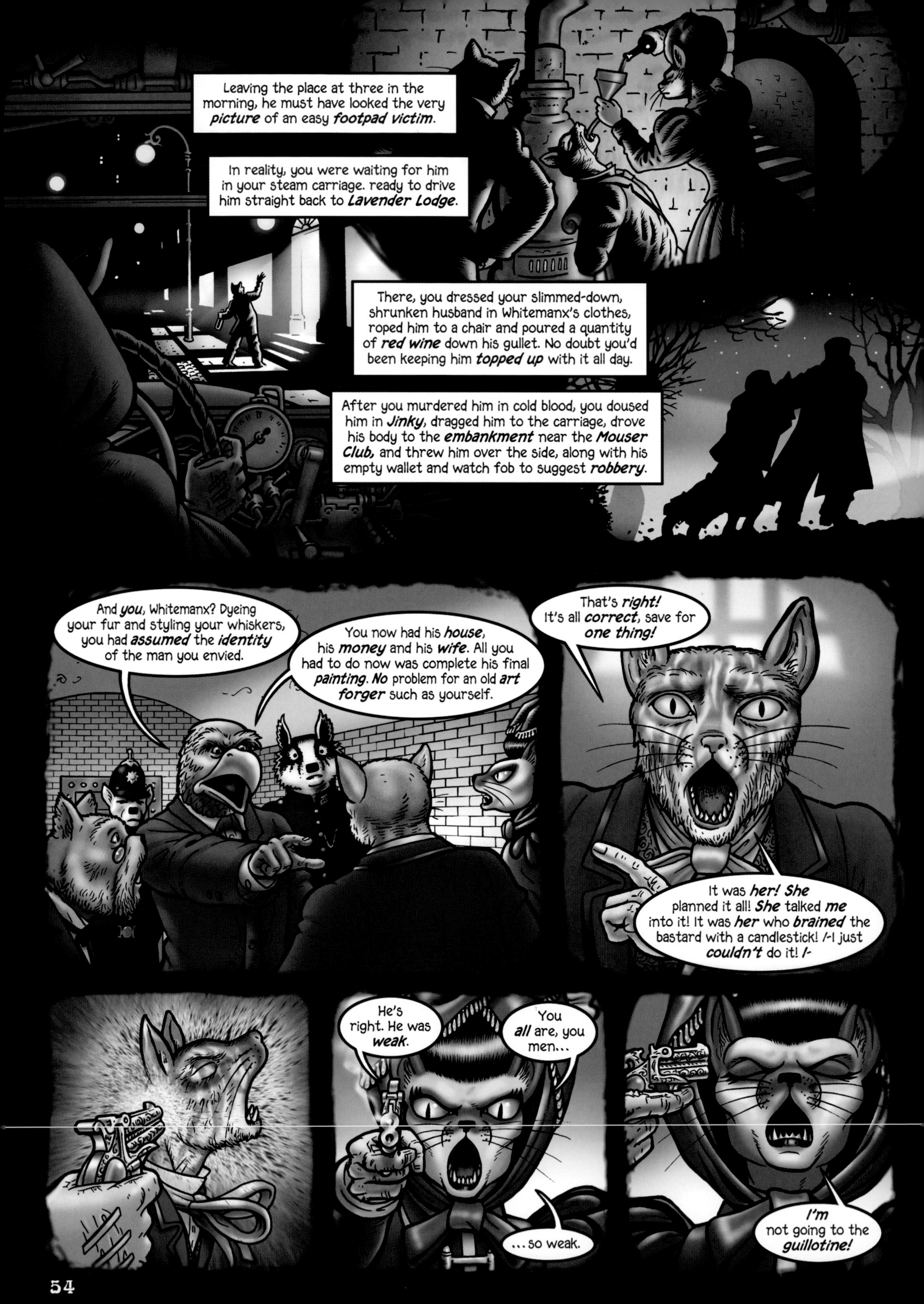
Leaving the place at three in the morning, he must have looked the very picture of an easy footpad victim.
In reality, you were waiting for him in your steam carriage. ready to drive him straight back to Lavender Lodge.
There, you dressed your slimmed-down, shrunken husband in Whitemanx's clothes, roped him to a chair and poured a quantity of red wine down his gullet. No doubt you'd been keeping him topped up with it all day.
After you murdered him in cold blood, you doused him in Jinky, dragged him to the carriage, drove his body to the embankment near the Mouser Club, and threw him over the side, along with his empty wallet and watch fob to suggest robbery.
And you, Whitemanx? Dyeing your fur and styling your whiskers, you had assumed the identity of the man you envied.
You now had his house, his money and his wife. All you had to do now was complete his final painting. No problem for an old art forger such as yourself.
That's right! It's all correct, save for one thing!
It was her! She planned it all! She talked me into it! It was her who brained the bastard with a candlestick! I-I just couldn't do it! I-
He's right. He was weak.
You all are, you men...
...so weak.
I'm not going to the guillotine!

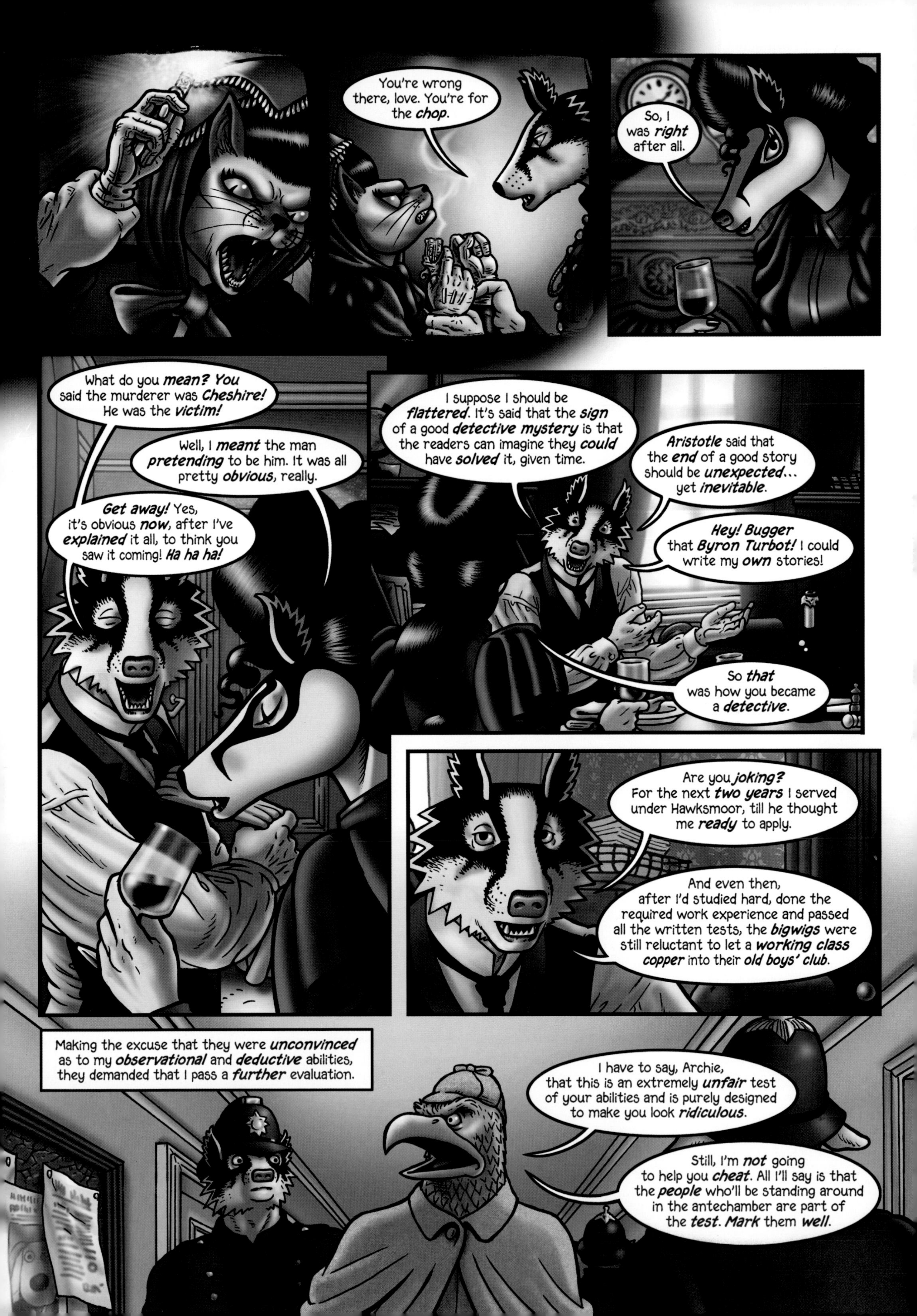

You're wrong there, love. You're for the chop.
So, I was right after all.
What do you mean? You said the murderer was Cheshire! He was the victim!
Well, I meant the man pretending to be him. It was all pretty obvious, really.
Get away! Yes, it's obvious now, after I've explained it all, to think you saw it coming! Ha ha ha!
I suppose I should be flattered. It's said that the sign of a good detective mystery is that the readers can imagine they could have solved it, given time.
Aristotle said that the end of a good story should be unexpected... yet inevitable.
Hey! Bugger that Byron Turbot! I could write my own stories!
So that was how you became a detective.
Are you joking? For the next two years I served under Hawksmoor, till he thought me ready to apply.
And even then, after I'd studied hard, done the required work experience and passed all the written tests, the bigwigs were still reluctant to let a working class copper into their old boys' club.
Making the excuse that they were unconvinced as to my observational and deductive abilities, they demanded that I pass a further evaluation.
I have to say, Archie, that this is an extremely unfair test of your abilities and is purely designed to make you look ridiculous.
Still, I'm not going to help you cheat. All I'll say is that the people who'll be standing around in the antechamber are part of the test. Mark them well.

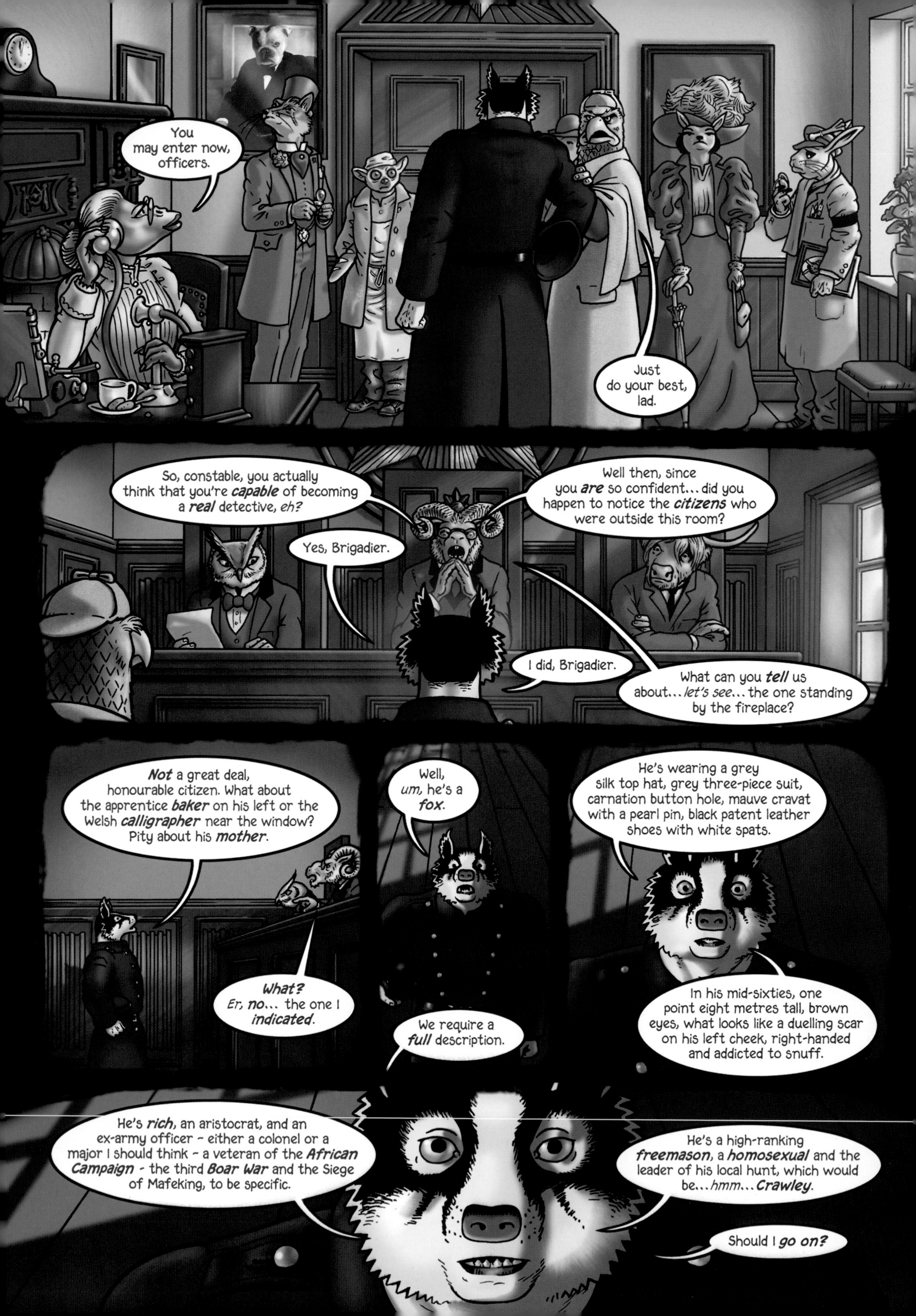
You may enter now, officers.
Just do your best, lad.
So, constable, you actually think that you're *capable* of becoming a *real* detective, *eh?*
Yes, Brigadier.
Well then, since you *are* so confident... did you happen to notice the *citizens* who were outside this room?
I did, Brigadier.
What can you *tell* us about... *let's see*... the one standing by the fireplace?
Well, *um*, he's a *fox*.
We require a *full* description.
He's wearing a grey silk top hat, grey three-piece suit, carnation button hole, mauve cravat with a pearl pin, black patent leather shoes with white spats.
In his mid-sixties, one point eight metres tall, brown eyes, what looks like a duelling scar on his left cheek, right-handed and addicted to snuff.
He's *rich*, an aristocrat, and an ex-army officer - either a colonel or a major I should think - a veteran of the *African Campaign* - the third *Boar War* and the Siege of Mafeking, to be specific.
He's a high-ranking *freemason*, a *homosexual* and the leader of his local hunt, which would be... *hmm*... *Crawley*.
Should I *go on?*
Not a great deal, honourable citizen. What about the apprentice *baker* on his left or the Welsh *calligrapher* near the window? Pity about his *mother*.
What? *Er, no*... the one I *indicated*.

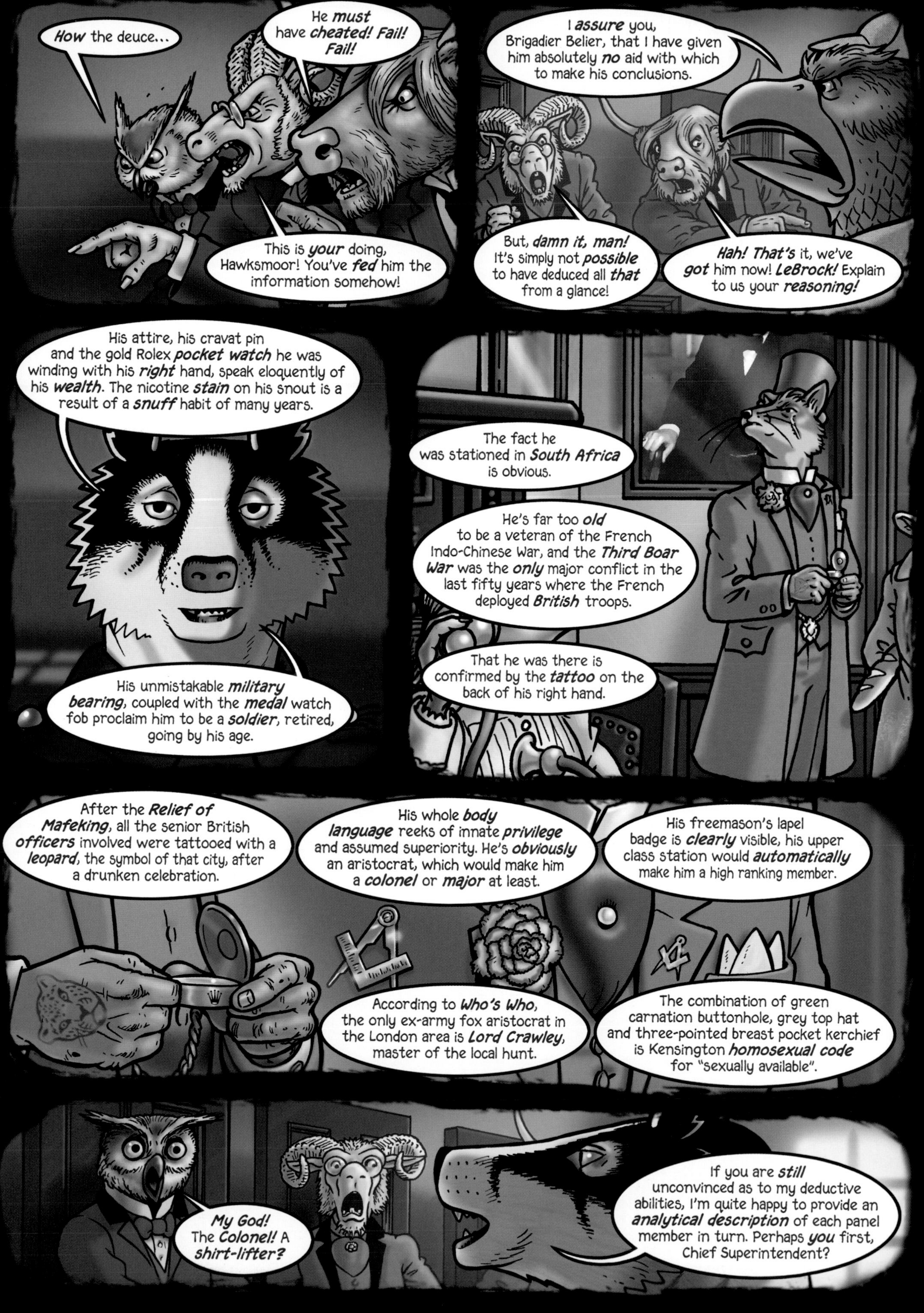
How the deuce...
He must have cheated! Fail! Fail!
This is your doing, Hawksmoor! You've fed him the information somehow!
I assure you, Brigadier Belier, that I have given him absolutely no aid with which to make his conclusions.
But, damn it, man! It's simply not possible to have deduced all that from a glance!
Hah! That's it, we've got him now! LeBrock! Explain to us your reasoning!
His attire, his cravat pin and the gold Rolex pocket watch he was winding with his right hand, speak eloquently of his wealth. The nicotine stain on his snout is a result of a snuff habit of many years.
His unmistakable military bearing, coupled with the medal watch fob proclaim him to be a soldier, retired, going by his age.
The fact he was stationed in South Africa is obvious.
He's far too old to be a veteran of the French Indo-Chinese War, and the Third Boar War was the only major conflict in the last fifty years where the French deployed British troops.
That he was there is confirmed by the tattoo on the back of his right hand.
After the Relief of Mafeking, all the senior British officers involved were tattooed with a leopard, the symbol of that city, after a drunken celebration.
His whole body language reeks of innate privilege and assumed superiority. He's obviously an aristocrat, which would make him a colonel or major at least.
His freemason's lapel badge is clearly visible, his upper class station would automatically make him a high ranking member.
According to Who's Who, the only ex-army fox aristocrat in the London area is Lord Crawley, master of the local hunt.
The combination of green carnation buttonhole, grey top hat and three-pointed breast pocket kerchief is Kensington homosexual code for "sexually available".
My God! The Colonel! A shirt-lifter?
If you are still unconvinced as to my deductive abilities, I'm quite happy to provide an analytical description of each panel member in turn. Perhaps you first, Chief Superintendent?

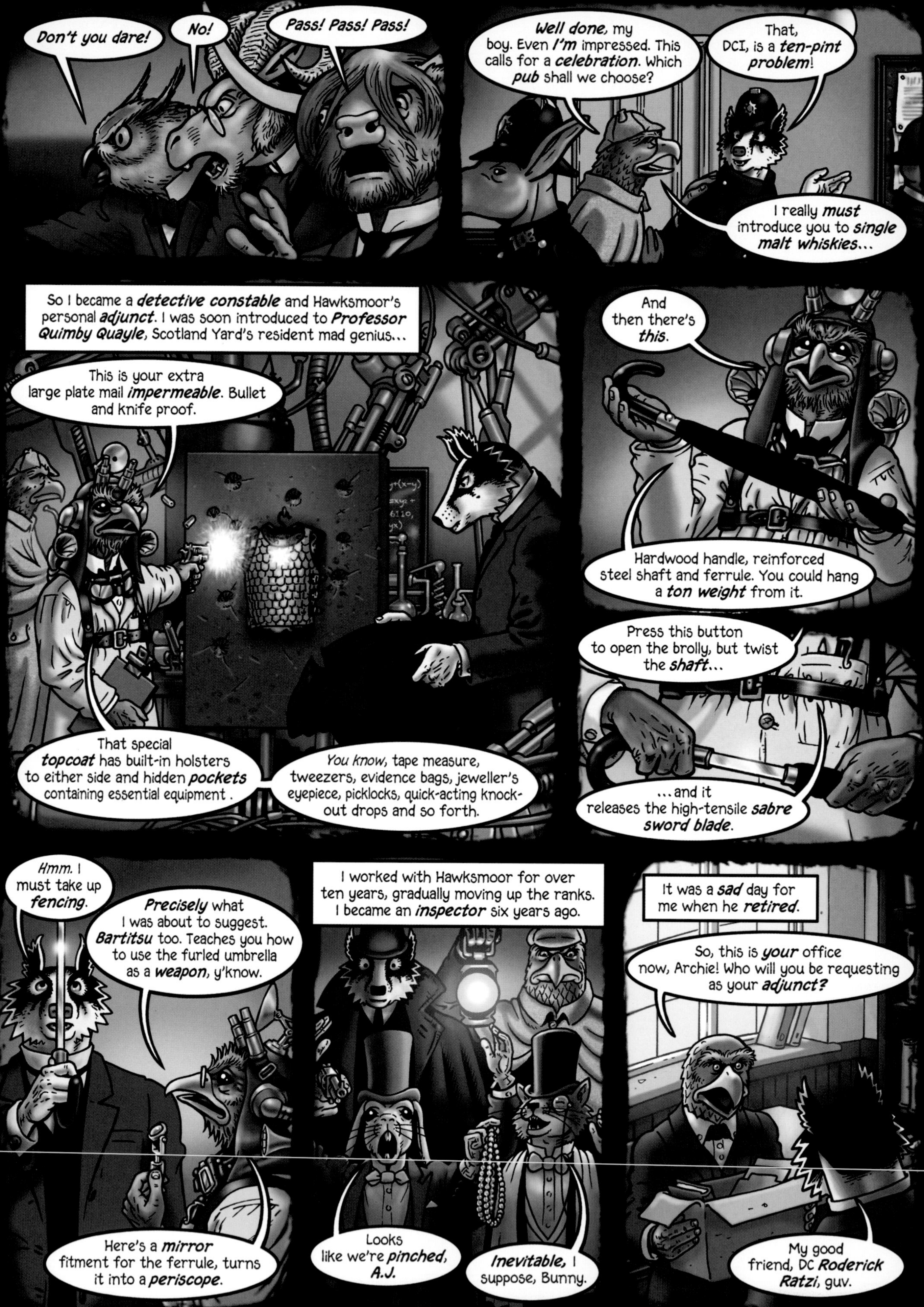
Don't you dare!
No!
Pass! Pass! Pass!
Well done, my boy. Even I'm impressed. This calls for a celebration. Which pub shall we choose?
That, DCI, is a ten-pint problem!
I really must introduce you to single malt whiskies...
So I became a detective constable and Hawksmoor's personal adjunct. I was soon introduced to Professor Quimby Quayle, Scotland Yard's resident mad genius...
This is your extra large plate mail impermeable. Bullet and knife proof.
That special topcoat has built-in holsters to either side and hidden pockets containing essential equipment .
You know, tape measure, tweezers, evidence bags, jeweller's eyepiece, picklocks, quick-acting knock-out drops and so forth.
And then there's this.
Hardwood handle, reinforced steel shaft and ferrule. You could hang a ton weight from it.
Press this button to open the brolly, but twist the shaft...
...and it releases the high-tensile sabre sword blade.
Hmm. I must take up fencing.
Precisely what I was about to suggest. Bartitsu too. Teaches you how to use the furled umbrella as a weapon, y'know.
Here's a mirror fitment for the ferrule, turns it into a periscope.
I worked with Hawksmoor for over ten years, gradually moving up the ranks. I became an inspector six years ago.
Looks like we're pinched, A.J.
Inevitable, I suppose, Bunny.
It was a sad day for me when he retired.
So, this is your office now, Archie! Who will you be requesting as your adjunct?
My good friend, DC Roderick Ratzi, guv.

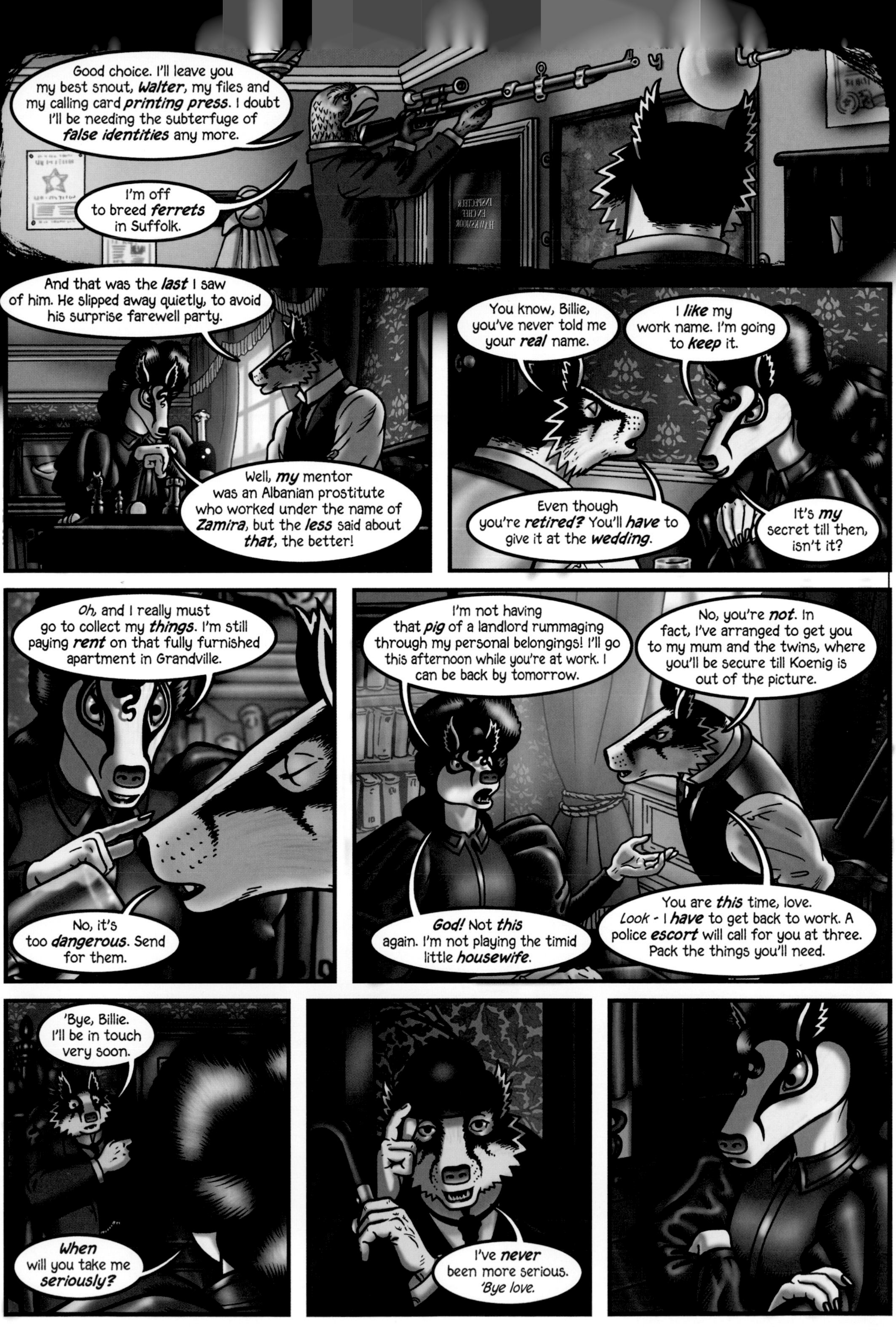

Good choice. I'll leave you my best snout, *Walter*, my files and my calling card *printing press*. I doubt I'll be needing the subterfuge of *false identities* any more.
I'm off to breed *ferrets* in Suffolk.
INSPECTEUR EN CHEF HAWKSHOOR
And that was the *last* I saw of him. He slipped away quietly, to avoid his surprise farewell party.
Well, *my* mentor was an Albanian prostitute who worked under the name of *Zamira*, but the *less* said about *that*, the better!
You know, Billie, you've never told me your *real* name.
I *like* my work name. I'm going to *keep* it.
Even though you're *retired?* You'll *have* to give it at the *wedding*.
It's *my* secret till then, isn't it?
Oh, and I really must go to collect my *things*. I'm still paying *rent* on that fully furnished apartment in Grandville.
No, it's too *dangerous*. Send for them.
I'm not having that *pig* of a landlord rummaging through my personal belongings! I'll go this afternoon while you're at work. I can be back by tomorrow.
No, you're *not*. In fact, I've arranged to get you to my mum and the twins, where you'll be secure till Koenig is out of the picture.
God! Not *this* again. I'm not playing the timid little *housewife*.
You are *this* time, love. *Look* - I *have* to get back to work. A police *escort* will call for you at three. Pack the things you'll need.
'Bye, Billie. I'll be in touch very soon.
When will you take me *seriously?*
I've *never* been more serious. *'Bye love.*

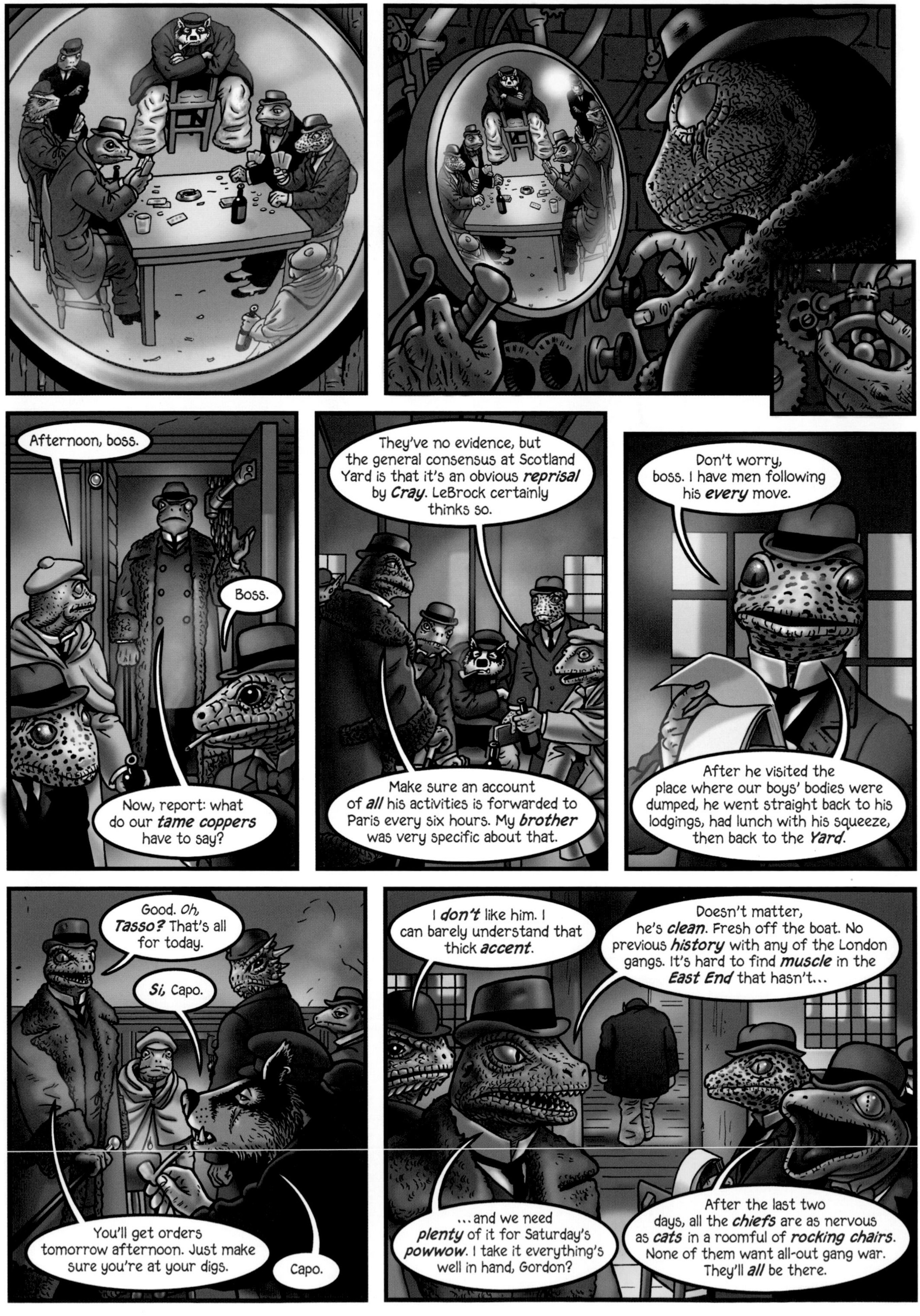
Afternoon, boss.
Boss.
Now, report: what do our *tame coppers* have to say?
They've no evidence, but the general consensus at Scotland Yard is that it's an obvious *reprisal* by *Cray*. LeBrock certainly thinks so.
Make sure an account of *all* his activities is forwarded to Paris every six hours. My *brother* was very specific about that.
Don't worry, boss. I have men following his *every* move.
After he visited the place where our boys' bodies were dumped, he went straight back to his lodgings, had lunch with his squeeze, then back to the *Yard*.
Good. *Oh, Tasso?* That's all for today.
Si, Capo.
You'll get orders tomorrow afternoon. Just make sure you're at your digs.
Capo.
I *don't* like him. I can barely understand that thick *accent*.
Doesn't matter, he's *clean*. Fresh off the boat. No previous *history* with any of the London gangs. It's hard to find *muscle* in the *East End* that hasn't...
...and we need *plenty* of it for Saturday's *powwow*. I take it everything's well in hand, Gordon?
After the last two days, all the *chiefs* are as nervous as *cats* in a roomful of *rocking chairs*. None of them want all-out gang war. They'll *all* be there.

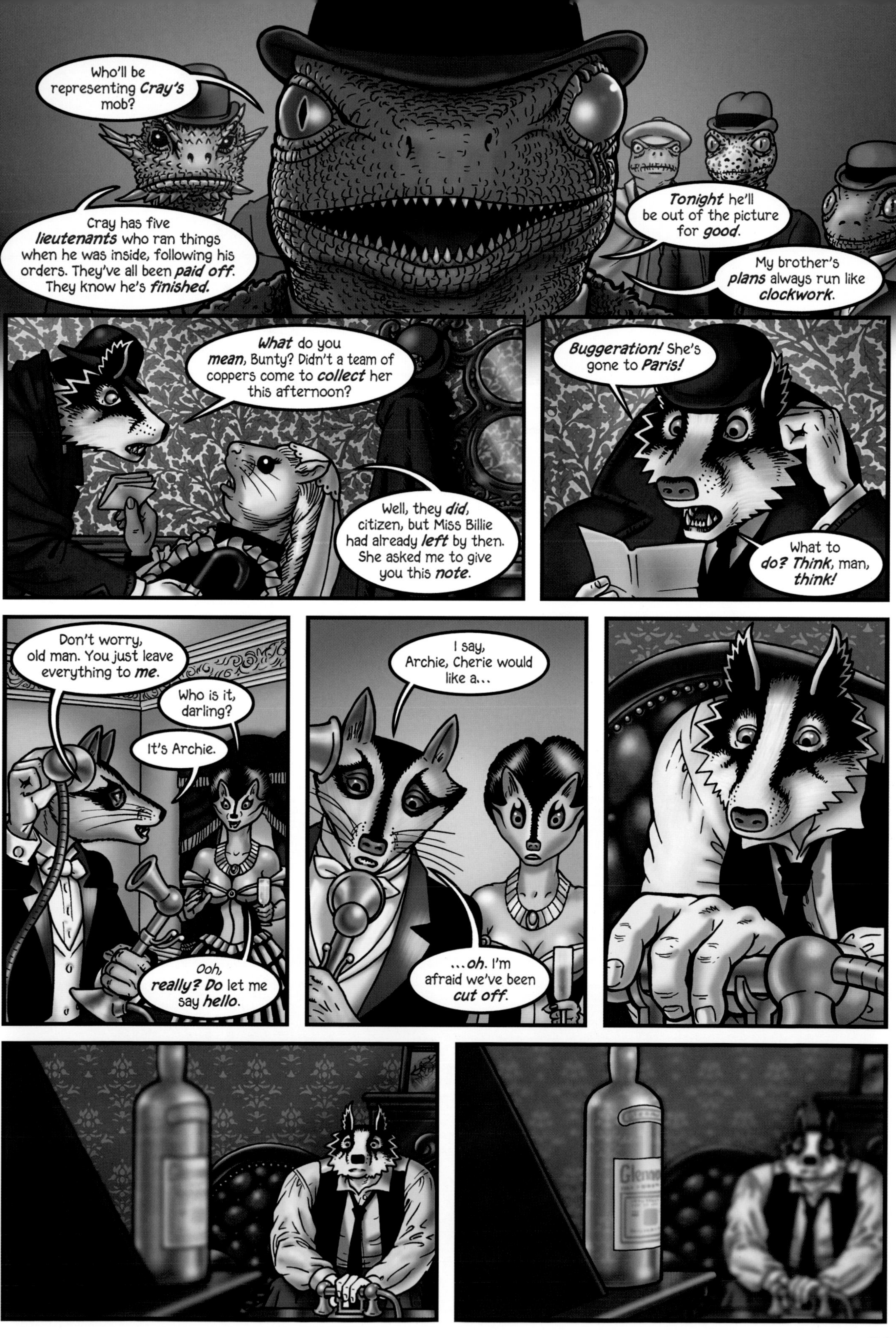

Who'll be representing Cray's mob?
Cray has five lieutenants who ran things when he was inside, following his orders. They've all been paid off. They know he's finished.
Tonight he'll be out of the picture for good.
My brother's plans always run like clockwork.
What do you mean, Bunty? Didn't a team of coppers come to collect her this afternoon?
Well, they did, citizen, but Miss Billie had already left by then. She asked me to give you this note.
Buggeration! She's gone to Paris!
What to do? Think, man, think!
Don't worry, old man. You just leave everything to me.
Who is it, darling?
It's Archie.
Ooh, really? Do let me say hello.
I say, Archie, Cherie would like a...
...oh. I'm afraid we've been cut off.

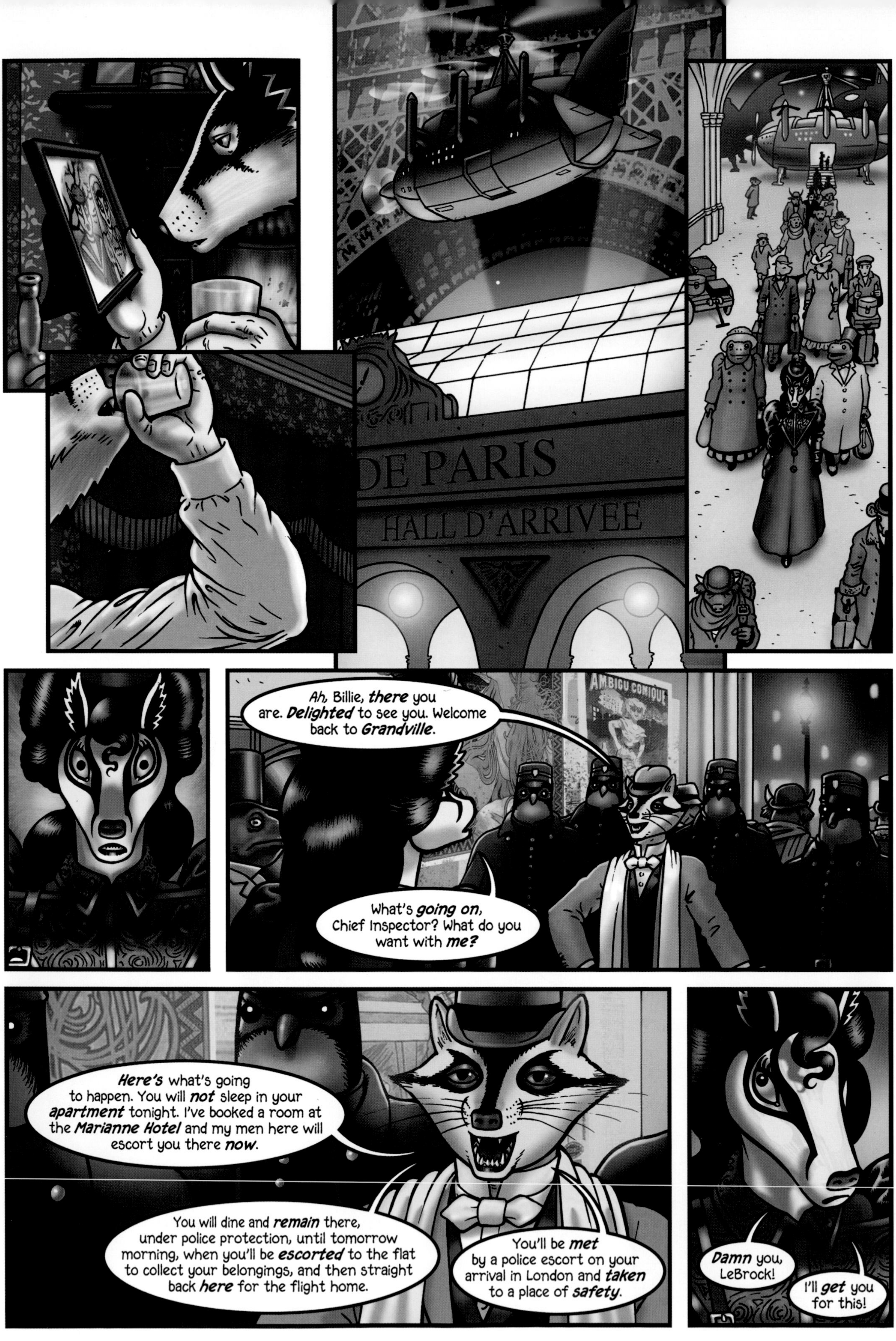
DE PARIS
HALL D'ARRIVEE
AMBIGU COMIQUE
Ah, Billie, ***there*** you are. ***Delighted*** to see you. Welcome back to ***Grandville***.
What's ***going on***, Chief Inspector? What do you want with ***me?***
Here's what's going to happen. You will ***not*** sleep in your ***apartment*** tonight. I've booked a room at the ***Marianne Hotel*** and my men here will escort you there ***now***.
You will dine and ***remain*** there, under police protection, until tomorrow morning, when you'll be ***escorted*** to the flat to collect your belongings, and then straight back ***here*** for the flight home.
You'll be ***met*** by a police escort on your arrival in London and ***taken*** to a place of ***safety***.
Damn you, LeBrock!
I'll ***get*** you for this!

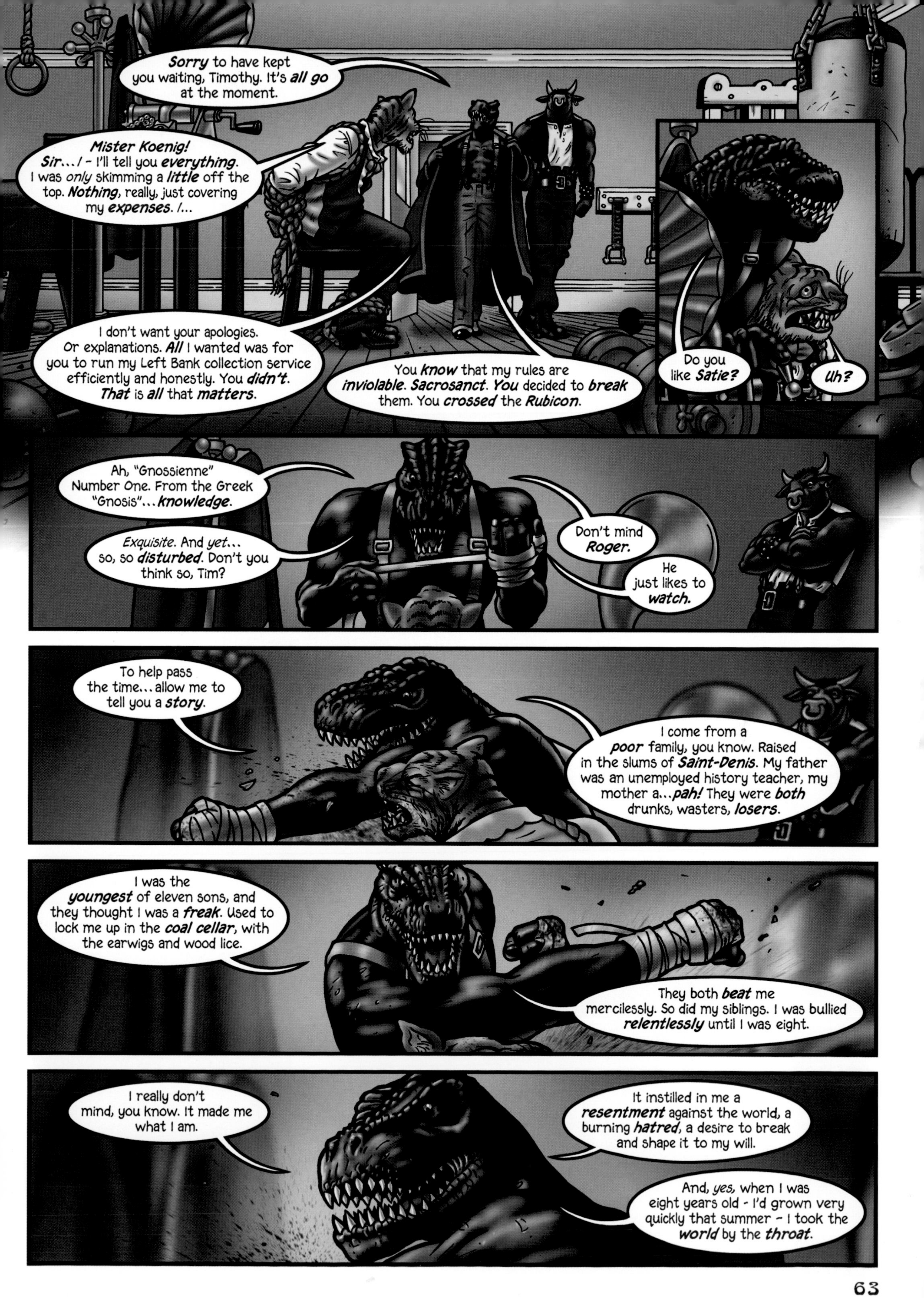
Sorry to have kept you waiting, Timothy. It's *all go* at the moment.
Mister Koenig! Sir... / - I'll tell you *everything*. I was *only* skimming a *little* off the top. *Nothing*, really, just covering my *expenses*. /...
I don't want your apologies. Or explanations. *All* I wanted was for you to run my Left Bank collection service efficiently and honestly. You *didn't*. *That* is *all* that *matters*.
You *know* that my rules are *inviolable*. *Sacrosanct*. *You* decided to *break* them. You *crossed* the *Rubicon*.
Do you like *Satie?*
Uh?
Ah, "Gnossienne" Number One. From the Greek "Gnosis"... *knowledge*.
Exquisite. And *yet*... so, so *disturbed*. Don't you think so, Tim?
Don't mind *Roger*.
He just likes to *watch*.
To help pass the time... allow me to tell you a *story*.
I come from a *poor* family, you know. Raised in the slums of *Saint-Denis*. My father was an unemployed history teacher, my mother a... *pah!* They were *both* drunks, wasters, *losers*.
I was the *youngest* of eleven sons, and they thought I was a *freak*. Used to lock me up in the *coal cellar*, with the earwigs and wood lice.
They both *beat* me mercilessly. So did my siblings. I was bullied *relentlessly* until I was eight.
I really don't mind, you know. It made me what I am.
It instilled in me a *resentment* against the world, a burning *hatred*, a desire to break and shape it to my will.
And, *yes*, when I was eight years old - I'd grown very quickly that summer - I took the *world* by the *throat*.

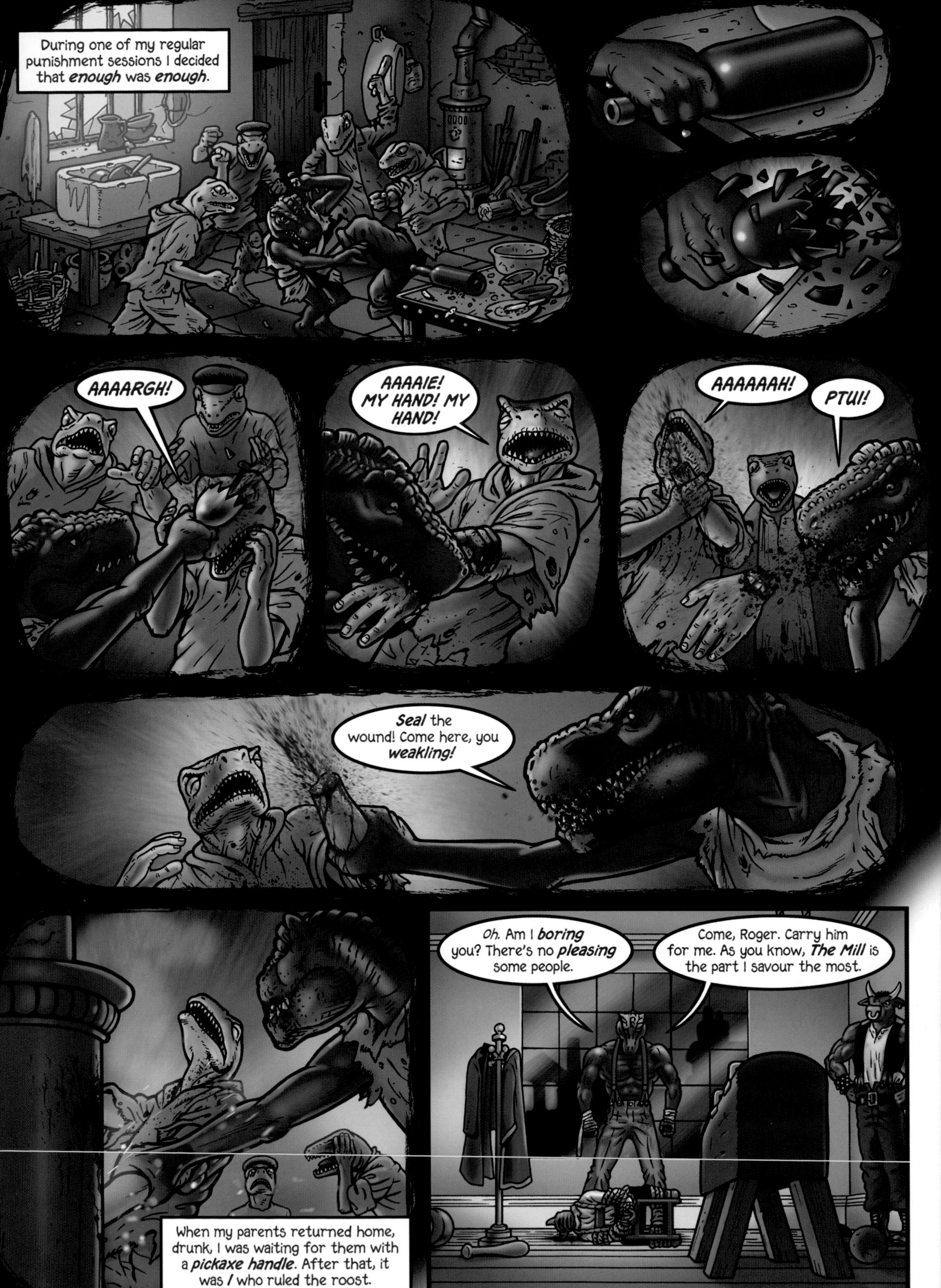
During one of my regular punishment sessions I decided that *enough* was *enough*.
AAAARGH!
AAAAIE! MY HAND! MY HAND!
AAAAAAH!
PTUI!
Seal the wound! Come here, you *weakling!*
When my parents returned home, drunk, I was waiting for them with a *pickaxe handle*. After that, it was *I* who ruled the roost.
Oh. Am I *boring* you? There's no *pleasing* some people.
Come, Roger. Carry him for me. As you know, *The Mill* is the part I savour the most.

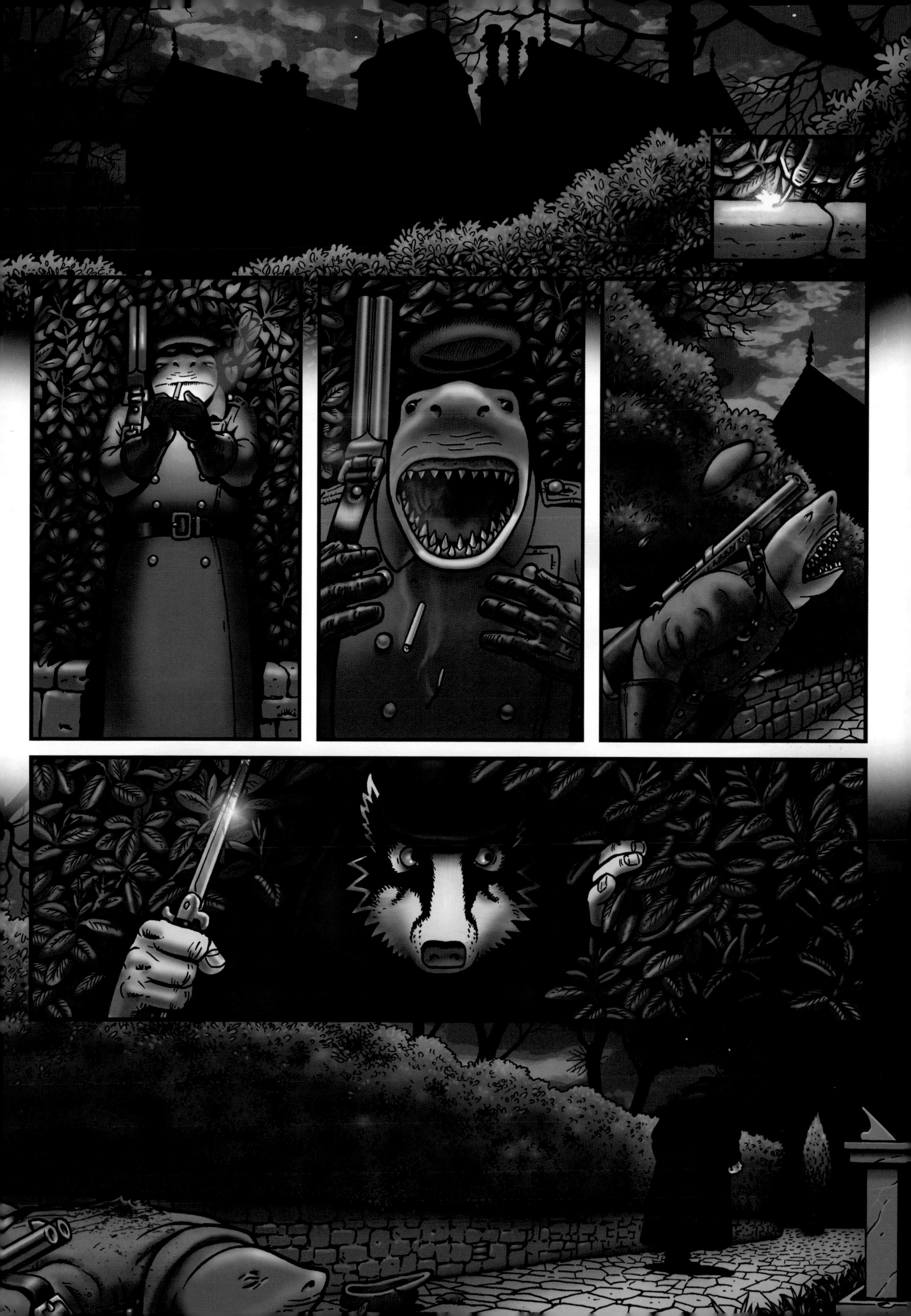

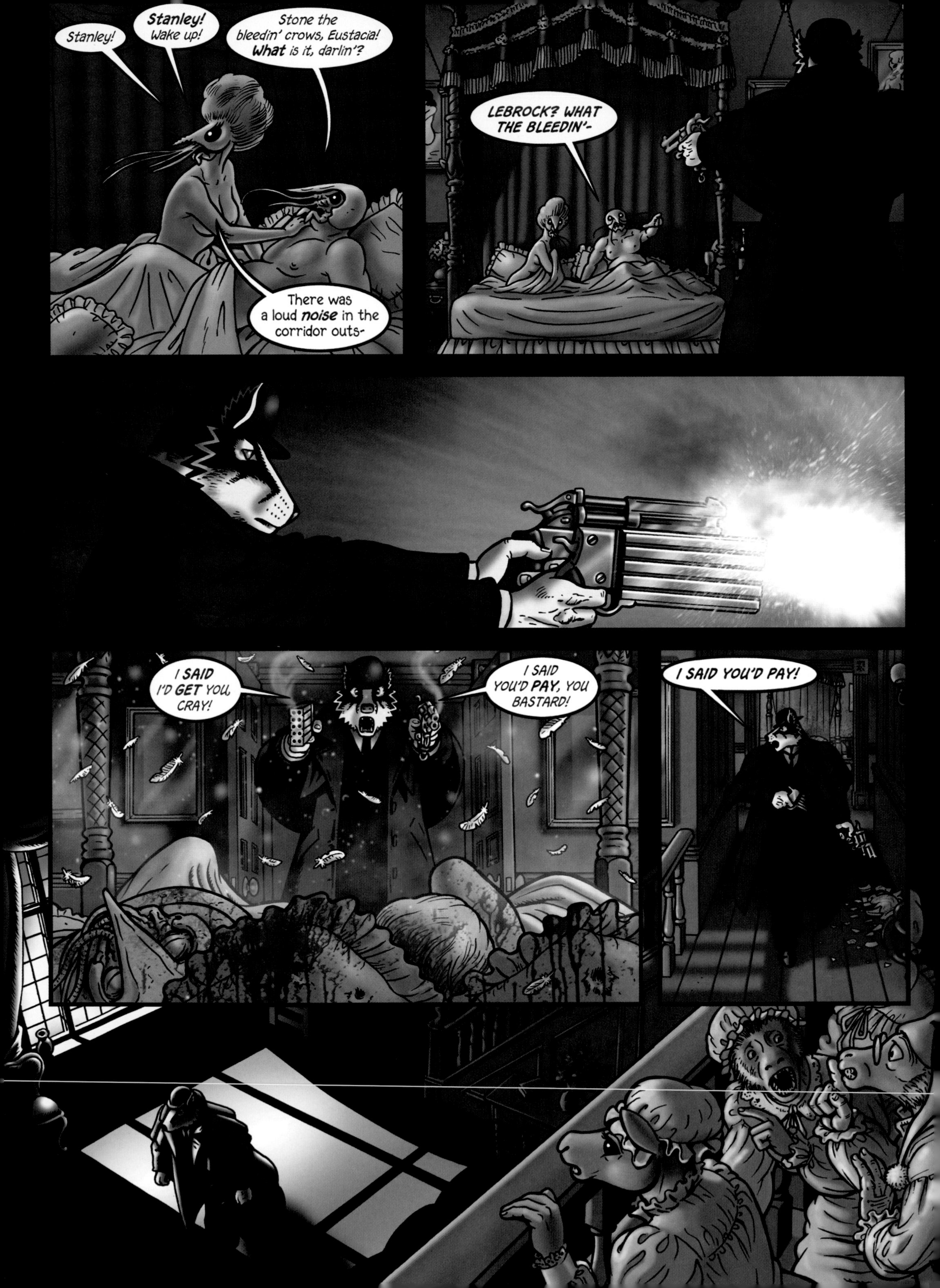
Stanley!
Stanley! Wake up!
Stone the bleedin' crows, Eustacia! What is it, darlin'?
There was a loud noise in the corridor outs-
LEBROCK? WHAT THE BLEEDIN'-
I SAID I'D GET YOU, CRAY!
I SAID YOU'D PAY, YOU BASTARD!
I SAID YOU'D PAY!

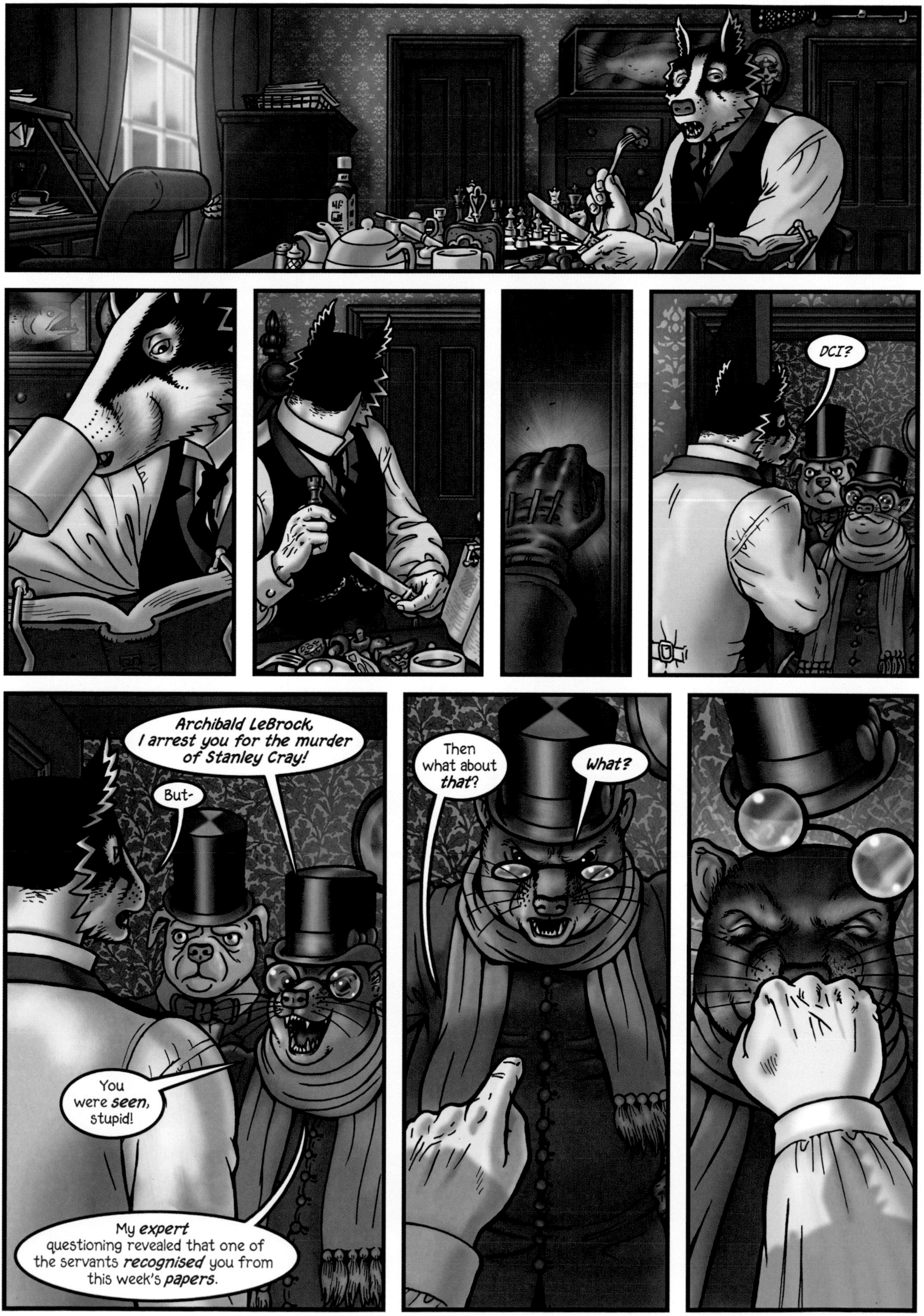
DCI?
Archibald LeBrock, I arrest you for the murder of Stanley Cray!
But-
You were seen, stupid!
My expert questioning revealed that one of the servants recognised you from this week's papers.
Then what about that?
What?

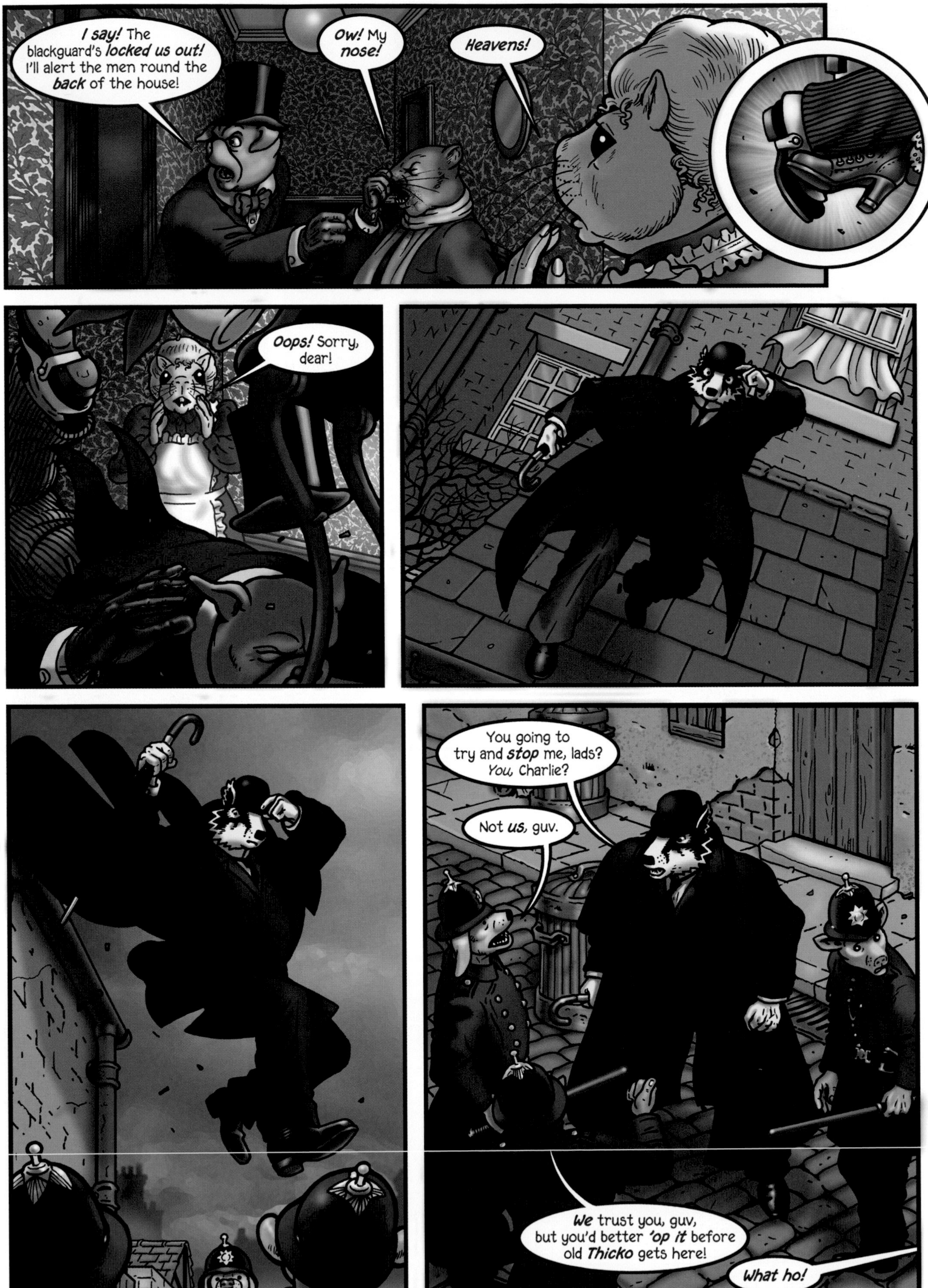
I say! The blackguard's locked us out! I'll alert the men round the back of the house!
Ow! My nose!
Heavens!
Oops! Sorry, dear!
You going to try and stop me, lads? You, Charlie?
Not us, guv.
We trust you, guv, but you'd better 'op it before old Thicko gets here!
What ho!

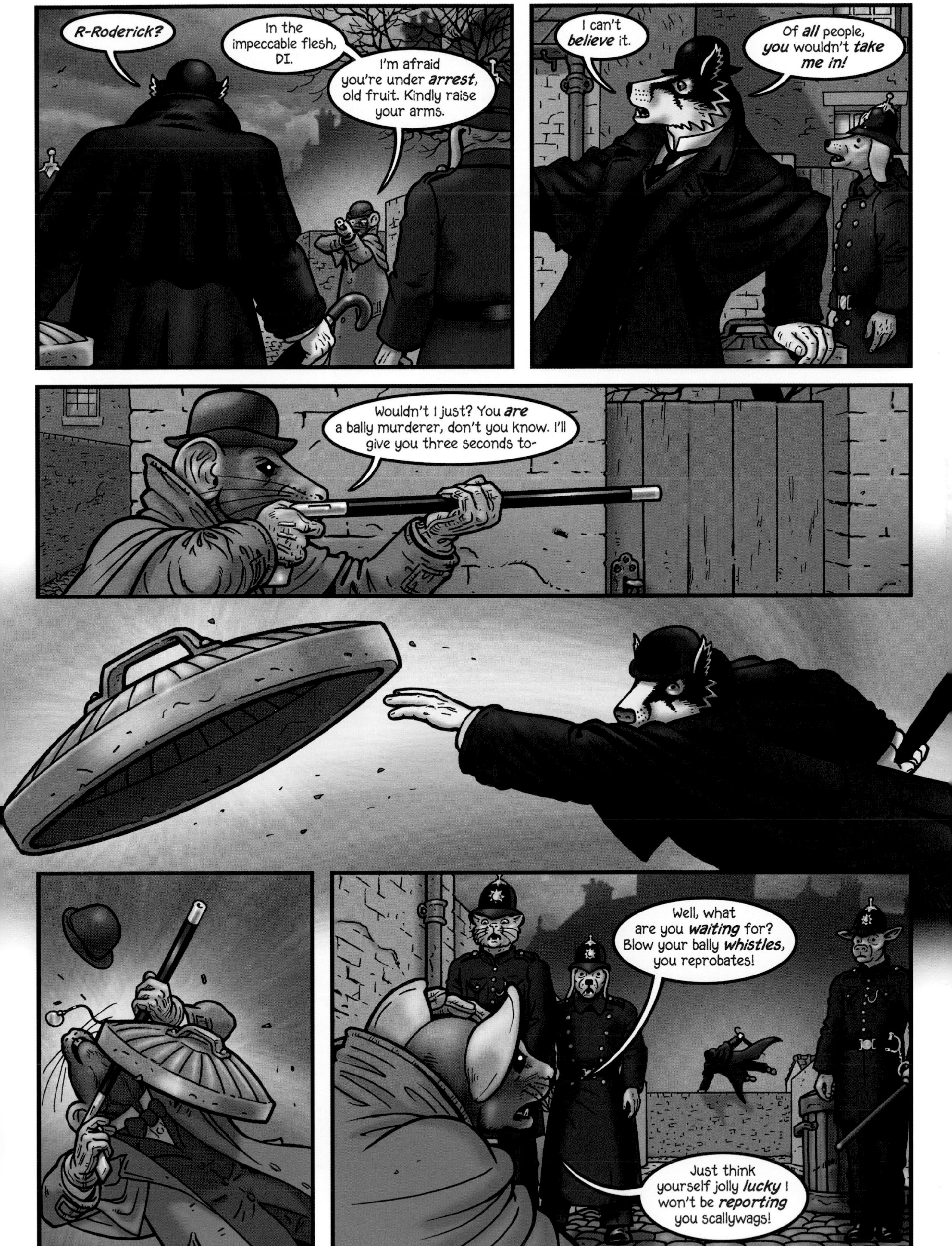
R-Roderick?
In the impeccable flesh, DI.
I'm afraid you're under *arrest*, old fruit. Kindly raise your arms.
I can't *believe* it.
Of *all* people, *you* wouldn't *take me in!*
Wouldn't I just? You *are* a bally murderer, don't you know. I'll give you three seconds to-
Well, what are you *waiting* for? Blow your bally *whistles*, you reprobates!
Just think yourself jolly *lucky* I won't be *reporting* you scallywags!

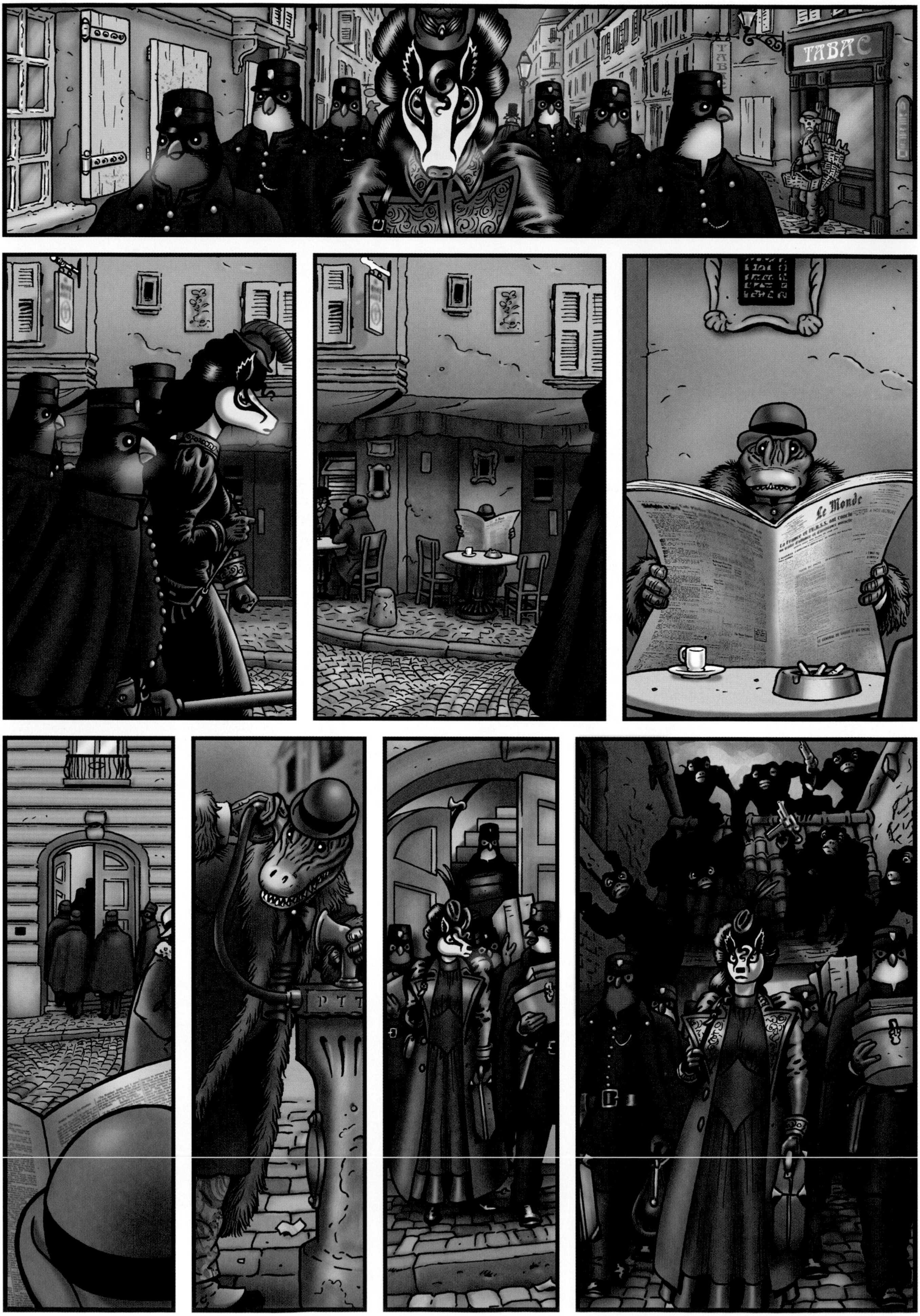
TABAC
Le Monde
PTT

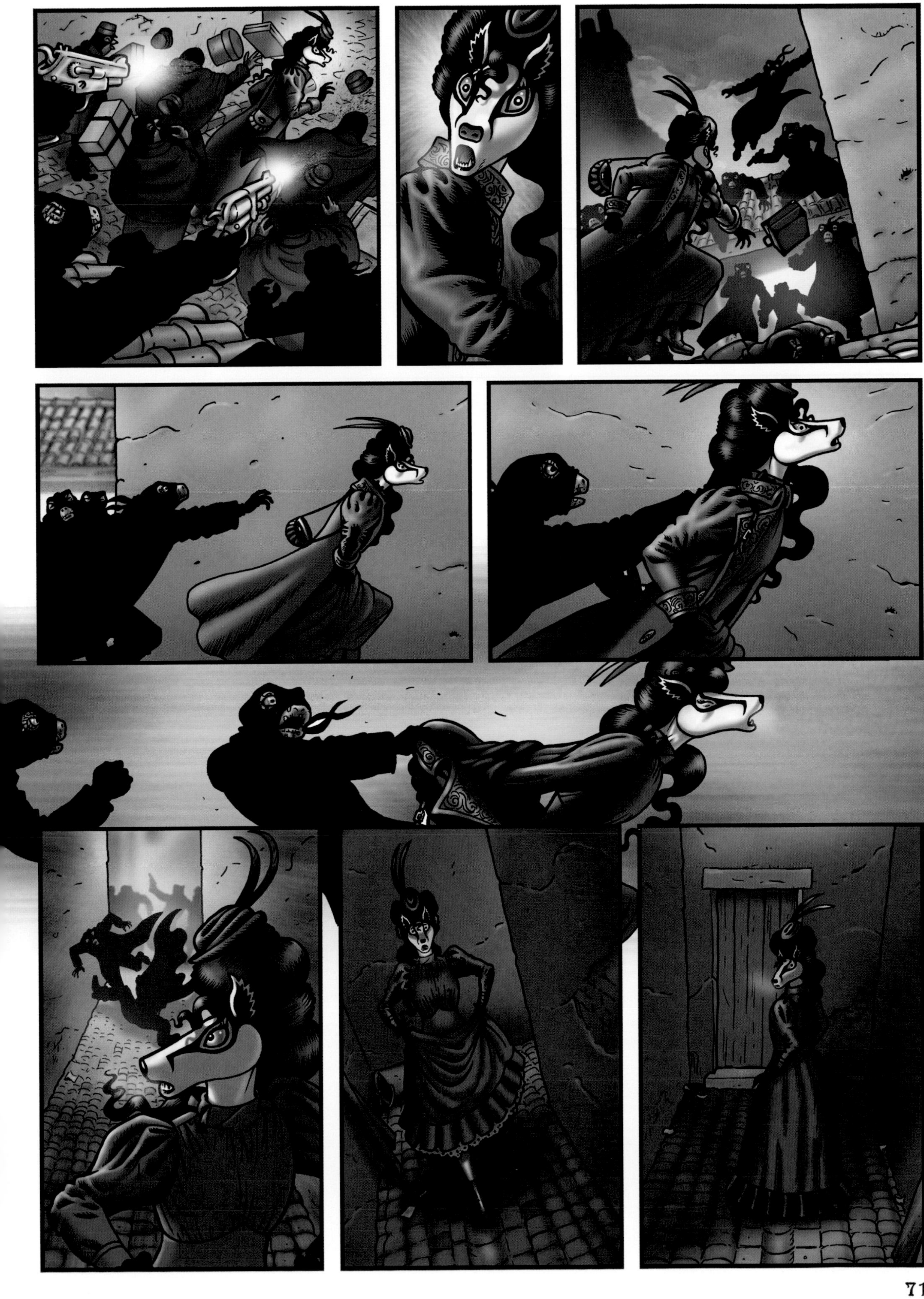

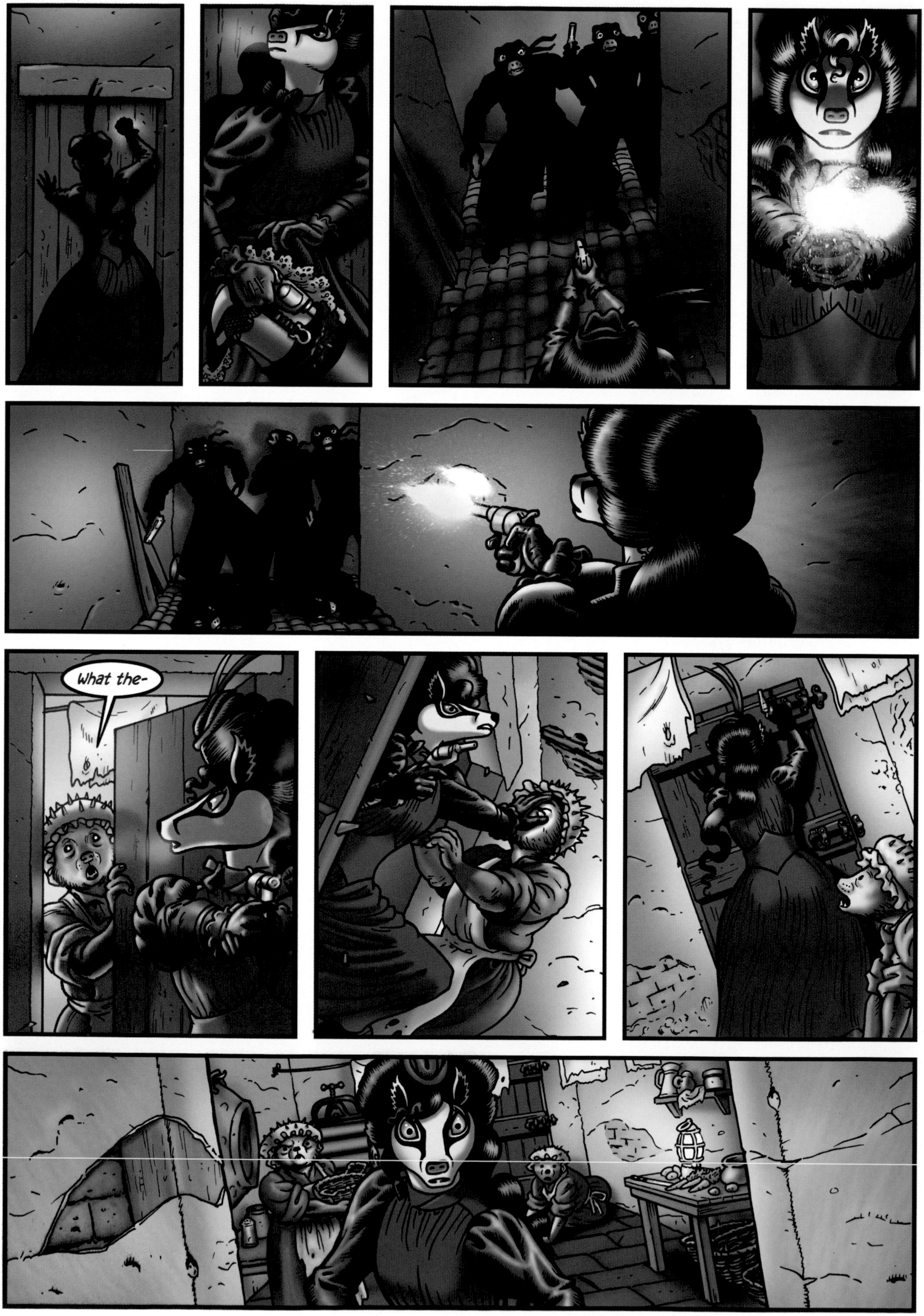
What the-

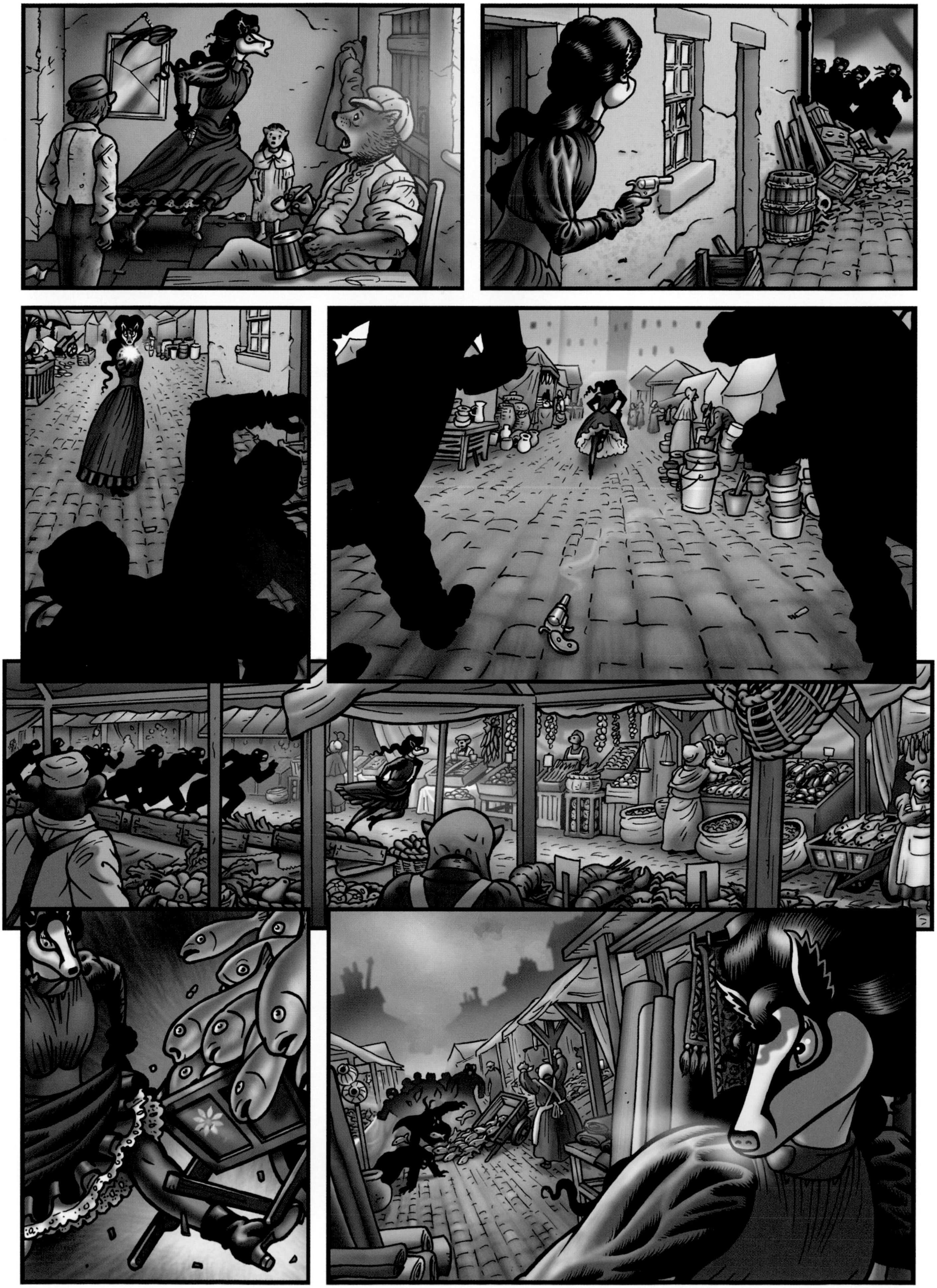

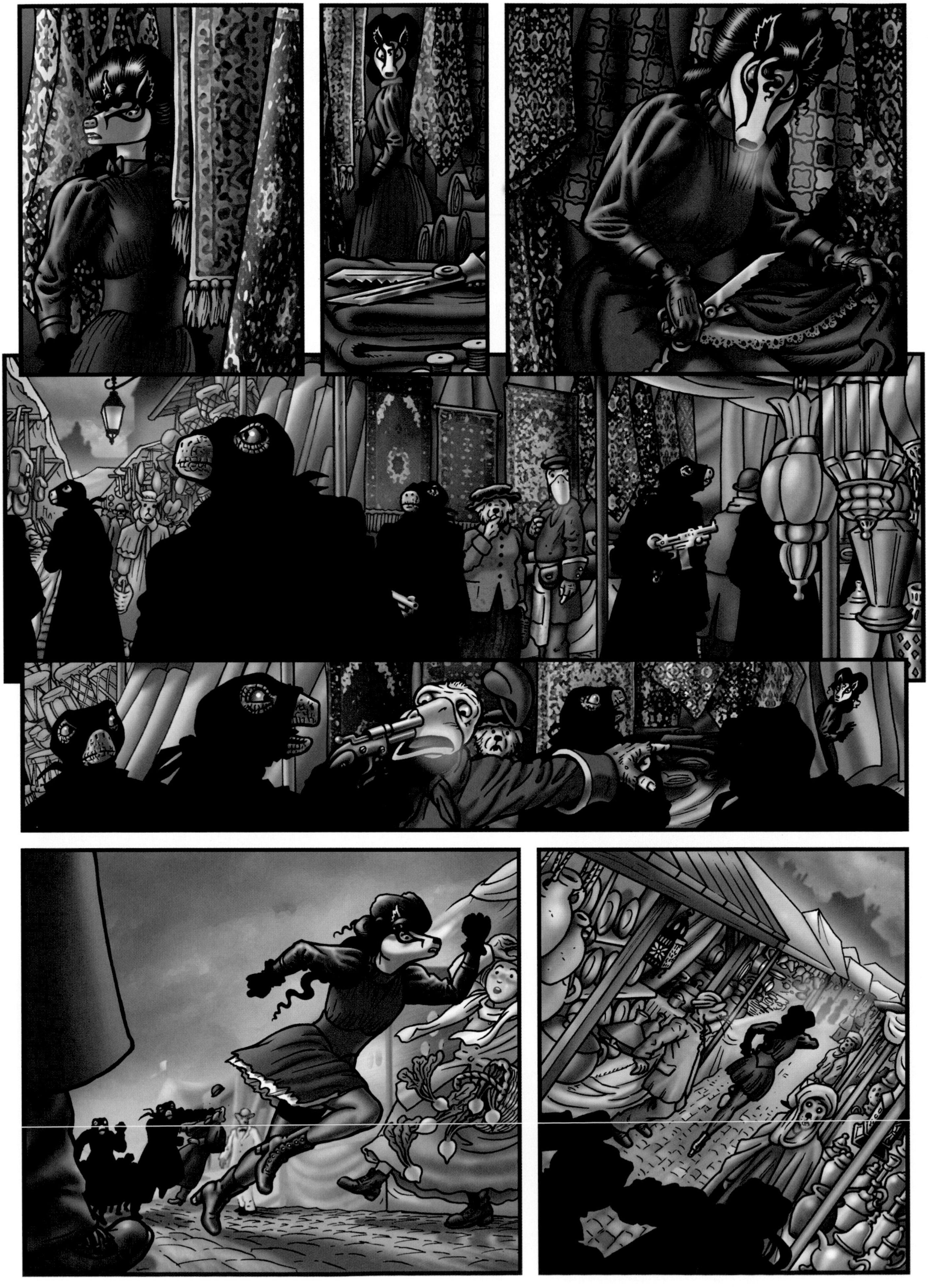

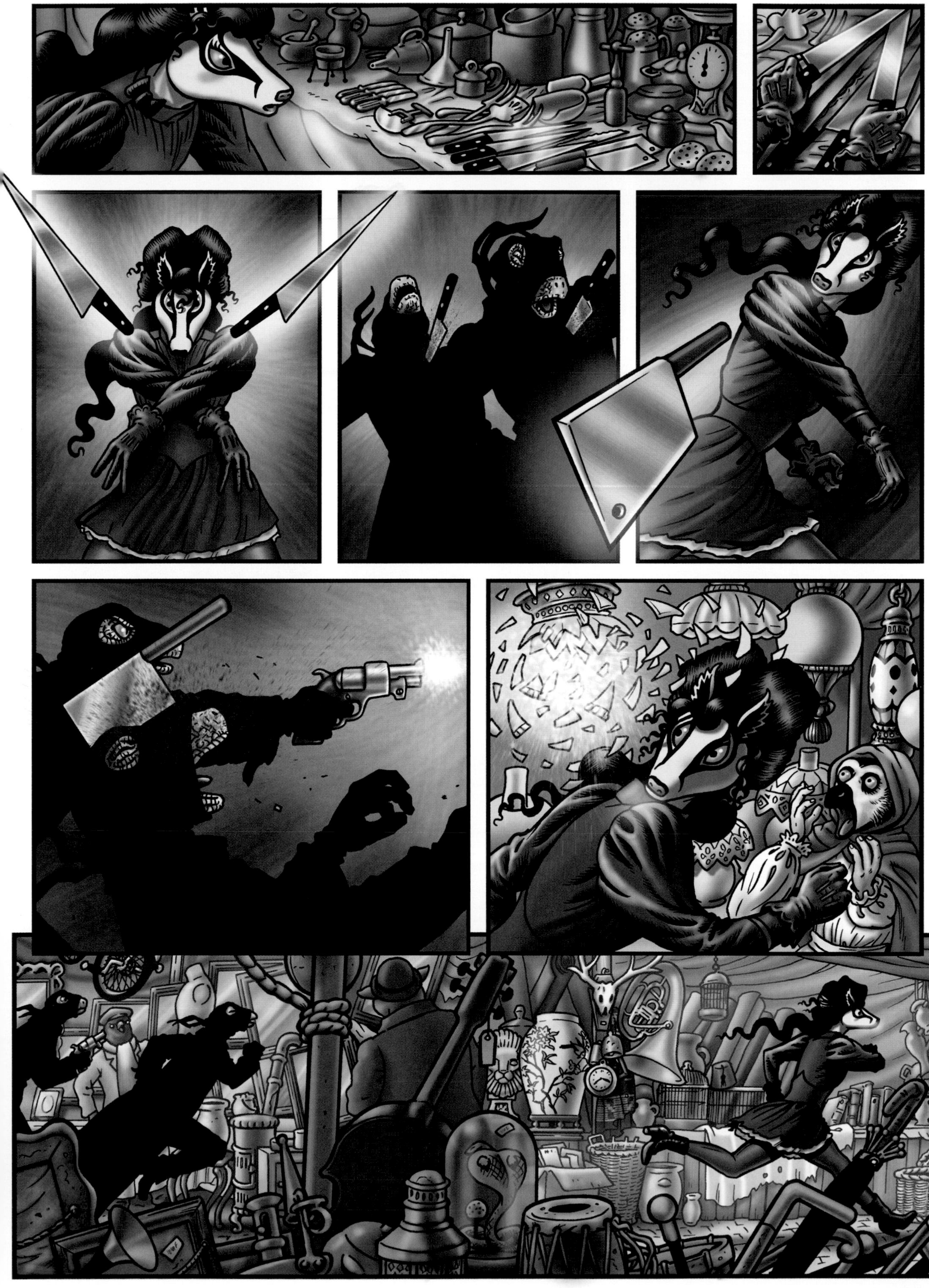

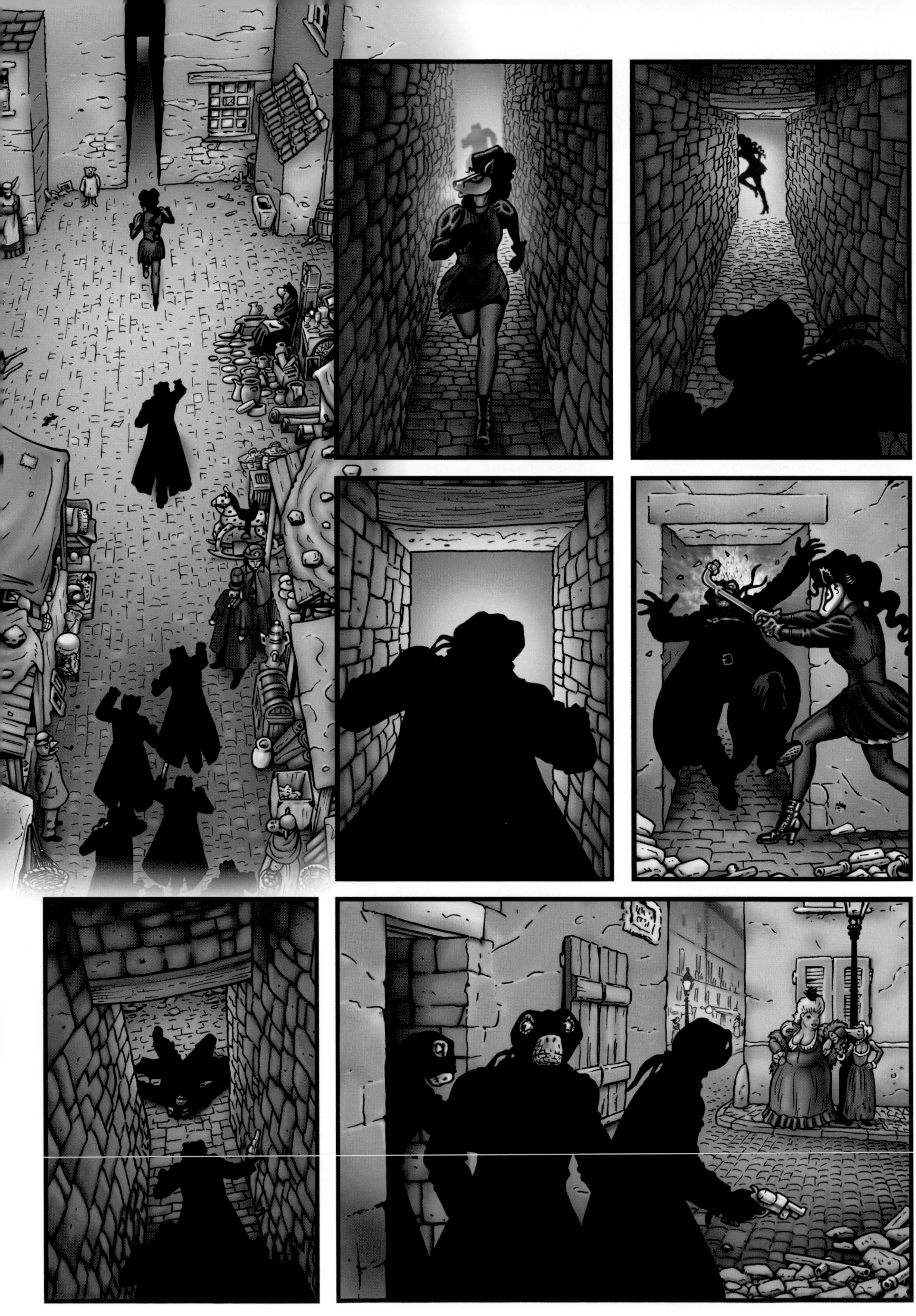

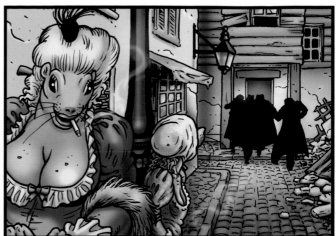

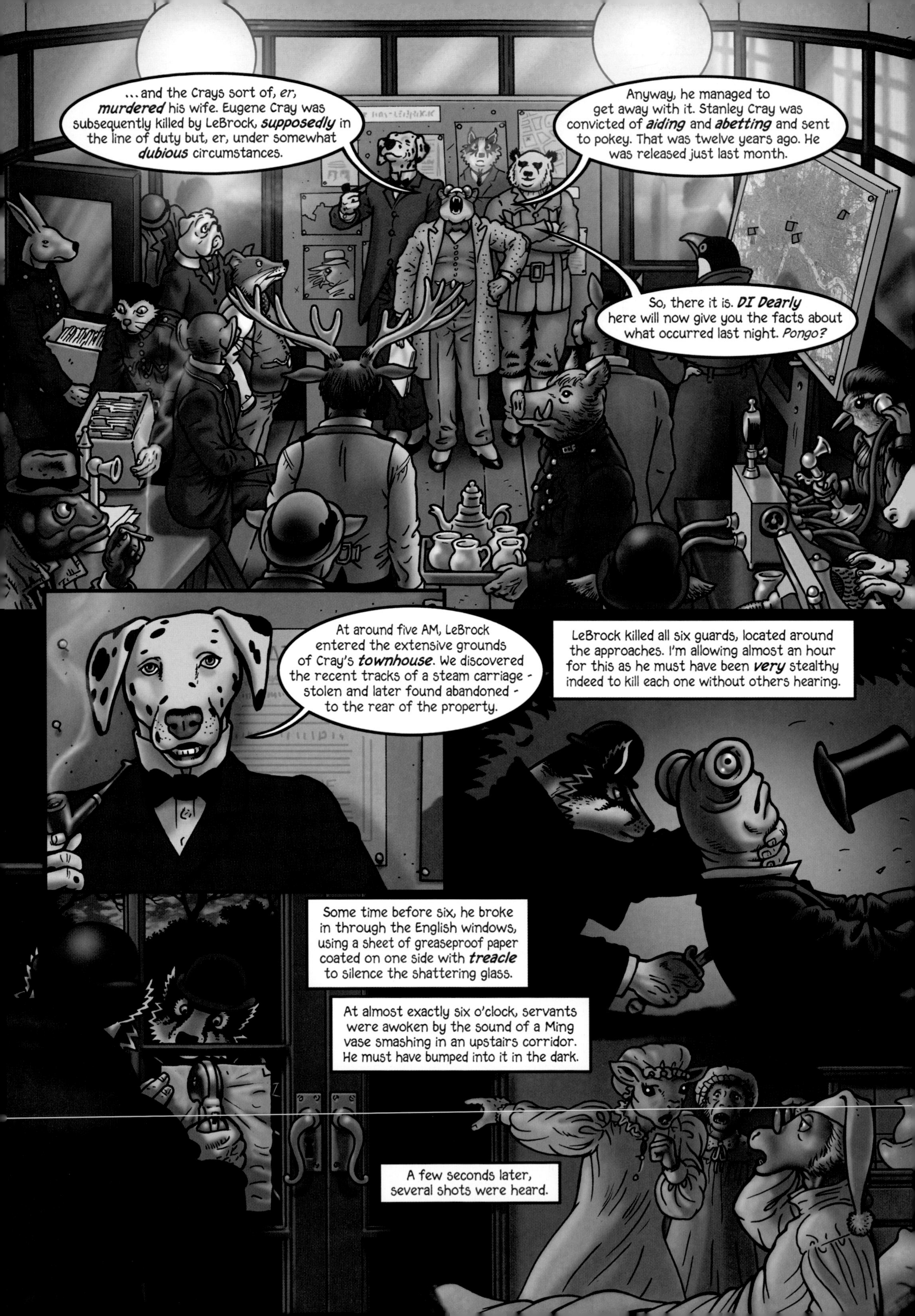
...and the Crays sort of, *er*, ***murdered*** his wife. Eugene Cray was subsequently killed by LeBrock, ***supposedly*** in the line of duty but, er, under somewhat ***dubious*** circumstances.
Anyway, he managed to get away with it. Stanley Cray was convicted of ***aiding*** and ***abetting*** and sent to pokey. That was twelve years ago. He was released just last month.
So, there it is. ***DI Dearly*** here will now give you the facts about what occurred last night. *Pongo?*
At around five AM, LeBrock entered the extensive grounds of Cray's ***townhouse***. We discovered the recent tracks of a steam carriage - stolen and later found abandoned - to the rear of the property.
LeBrock killed all six guards, located around the approaches. I'm allowing almost an hour for this as he must have been ***very*** stealthy indeed to kill each one without others hearing.
Some time before six, he broke in through the English windows, using a sheet of greaseproof paper coated on one side with ***treacle*** to silence the shattering glass.
At almost exactly six o'clock, servants were awoken by the sound of a Ming vase smashing in an upstairs corridor. He must have bumped into it in the dark.
A few seconds later, several shots were heard.

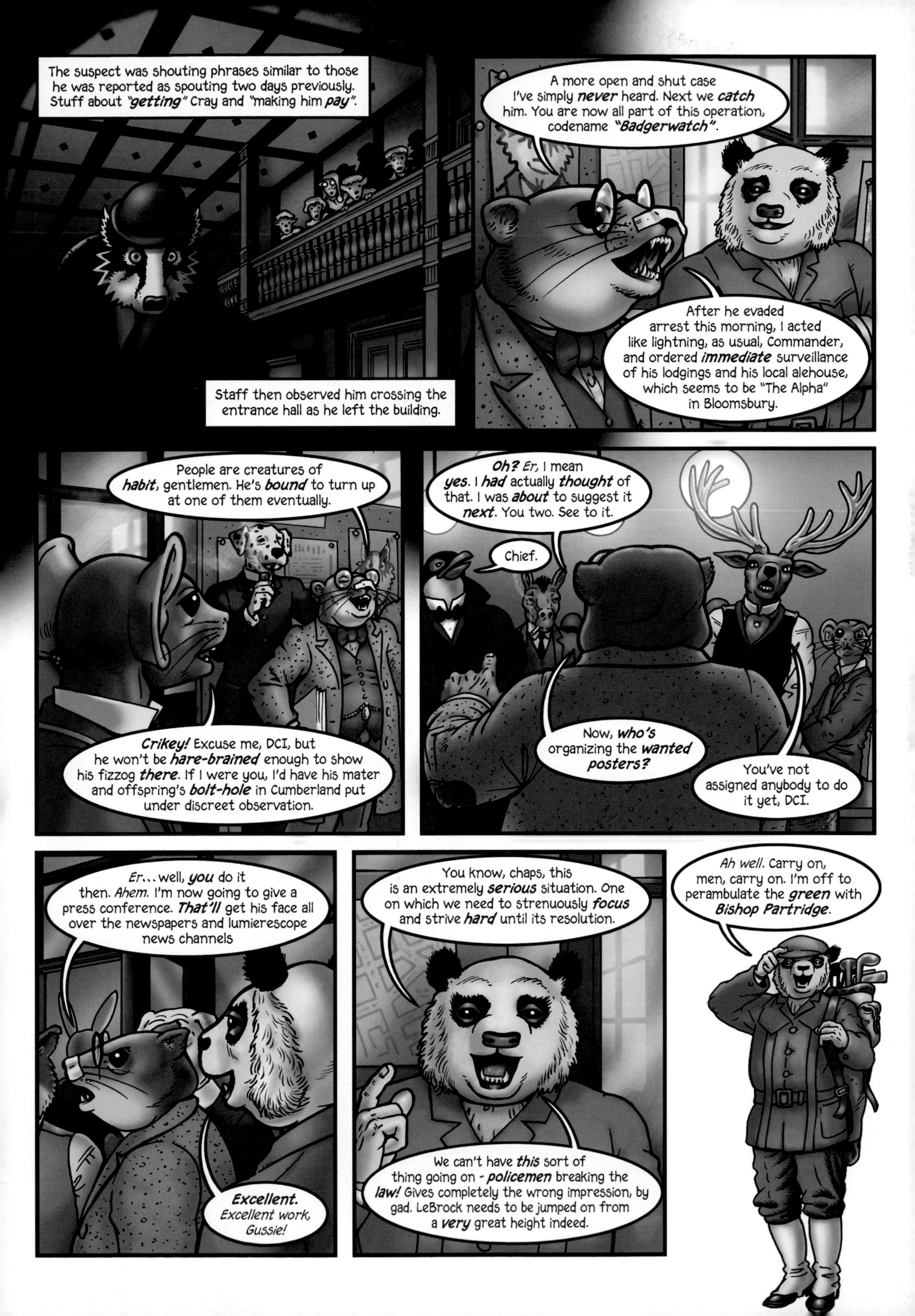
The suspect was shouting phrases similar to those he was reported as spouting two days previously. Stuff about "getting" Cray and "making him pay".
Staff then observed him crossing the entrance hall as he left the building.
A more open and shut case I've simply never heard. Next we catch him. You are now all part of this operation, codename "Badgerwatch".
After he evaded arrest this morning, I acted like lightning, as usual, Commander, and ordered immediate surveillance of his lodgings and his local alehouse, which seems to be "The Alpha" in Bloomsbury.
People are creatures of habit, gentlemen. He's bound to turn up at one of them eventually.
Crikey! Excuse me, DCI, but he won't be hare-brained enough to show his fizzog there. If I were you, I'd have his mater and offspring's bolt-hole in Cumberland put under discreet observation.
Oh? Er, I mean yes. I had actually thought of that. I was about to suggest it next. You two. See to it.
Chief.
Now, who's organizing the wanted posters?
You've not assigned anybody to do it yet, DCI.
Er... well, you do it then. Ahem. I'm now going to give a press conference. That'll get his face all over the newspapers and lumierescope news channels
Excellent. Excellent work, Gussie!
You know, chaps, this is an extremely serious situation. One on which we need to strenuously focus and strive hard until its resolution.
We can't have this sort of thing going on - policemen breaking the law! Gives completely the wrong impression, by gad. LeBrock needs to be jumped on from a very great height indeed.
Ah well. Carry on, men, carry on. I'm off to perambulate the green with Bishop Partridge.

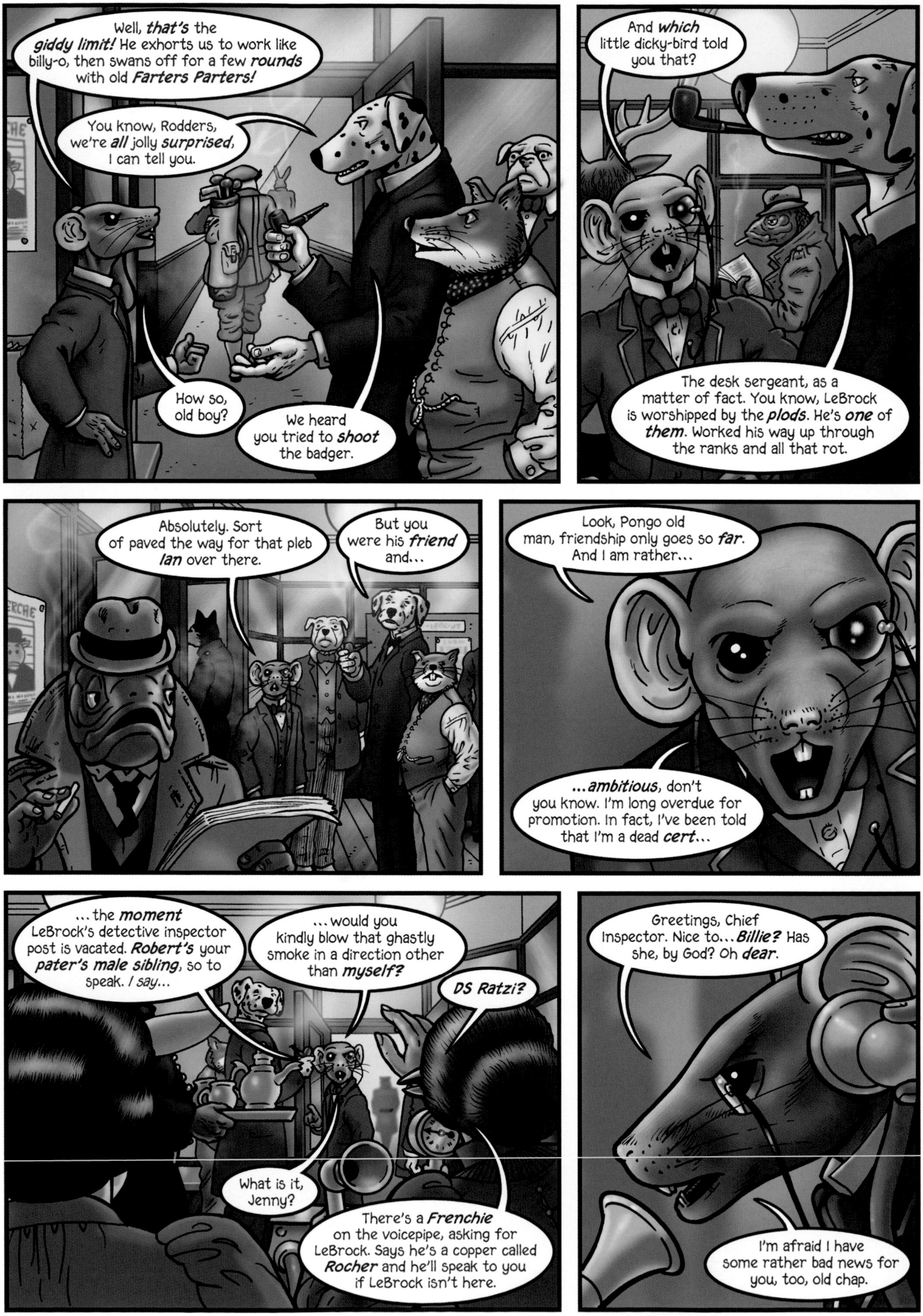
Well, that's the giddy limit! He exhorts us to work like billy-o, then swans off for a few rounds with old Farters Parters!
You know, Rodders, we're all jolly surprised, I can tell you.
How so, old boy?
We heard you tried to shoot the badger.
And which little dicky-bird told you that?
The desk sergeant, as a matter of fact. You know, LeBrock is worshipped by the plods. He's one of them. Worked his way up through the ranks and all that rot.
Absolutely. Sort of paved the way for that pleb Ian over there.
But you were his friend and...
Look, Pongo old man, friendship only goes so far. And I am rather...
...ambitious, don't you know. I'm long overdue for promotion. In fact, I've been told that I'm a dead cert...
...the moment LeBrock's detective inspector post is vacated. Robert's your pater's male sibling, so to speak. I say...
...would you kindly blow that ghastly smoke in a direction other than myself?
DS Ratzi?
What is it, Jenny?
There's a Frenchie on the voicepipe, asking for LeBrock. Says he's a copper called Rocher and he'll speak to you if LeBrock isn't here.
Greetings, Chief Inspector. Nice to... Billie? Has she, by God? Oh dear.
I'm afraid I have some rather bad news for you, too, old chap.

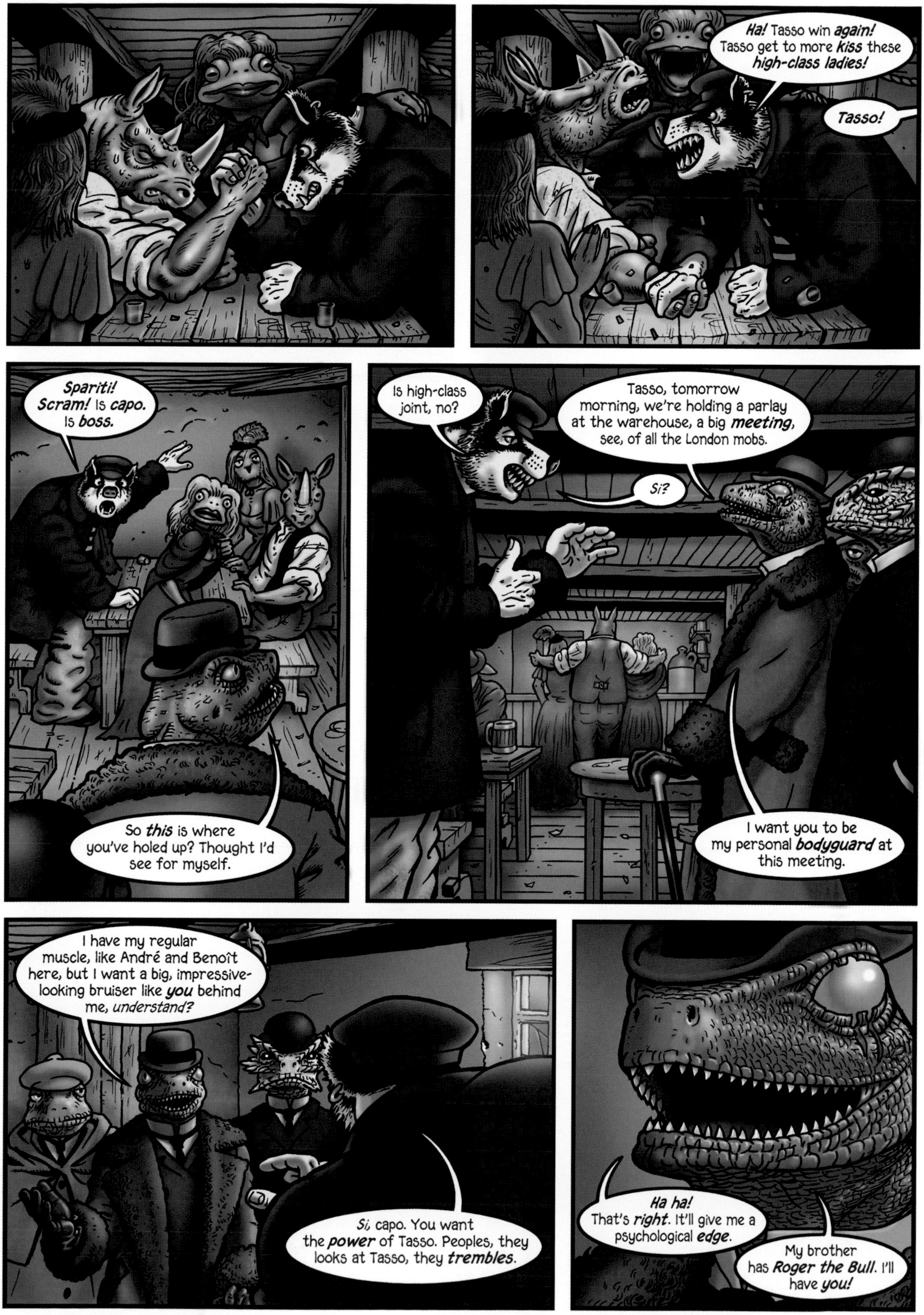
Ha! Tasso win again! Tasso get to more kiss these high-class ladies!
Tasso!
Sparìti! Scram! Is capo. Is boss.
So this is where you've holed up? Thought I'd see for myself.
Is high-class joint, no?
Tasso, tomorrow morning, we're holding a parlay at the warehouse, a big meeting, see, of all the London mobs.
Sì?
I want you to be my personal bodyguard at this meeting.
I have my regular muscle, like André and Benoît here, but I want a big, impressive-looking bruiser like you behind me, understand?
Sì, capo. You want the power of Tasso. Peoples, they looks at Tasso, they trembles.
Ha ha! That's right. It'll give me a psychological edge.
My brother has Roger the Bull. I'll have you!

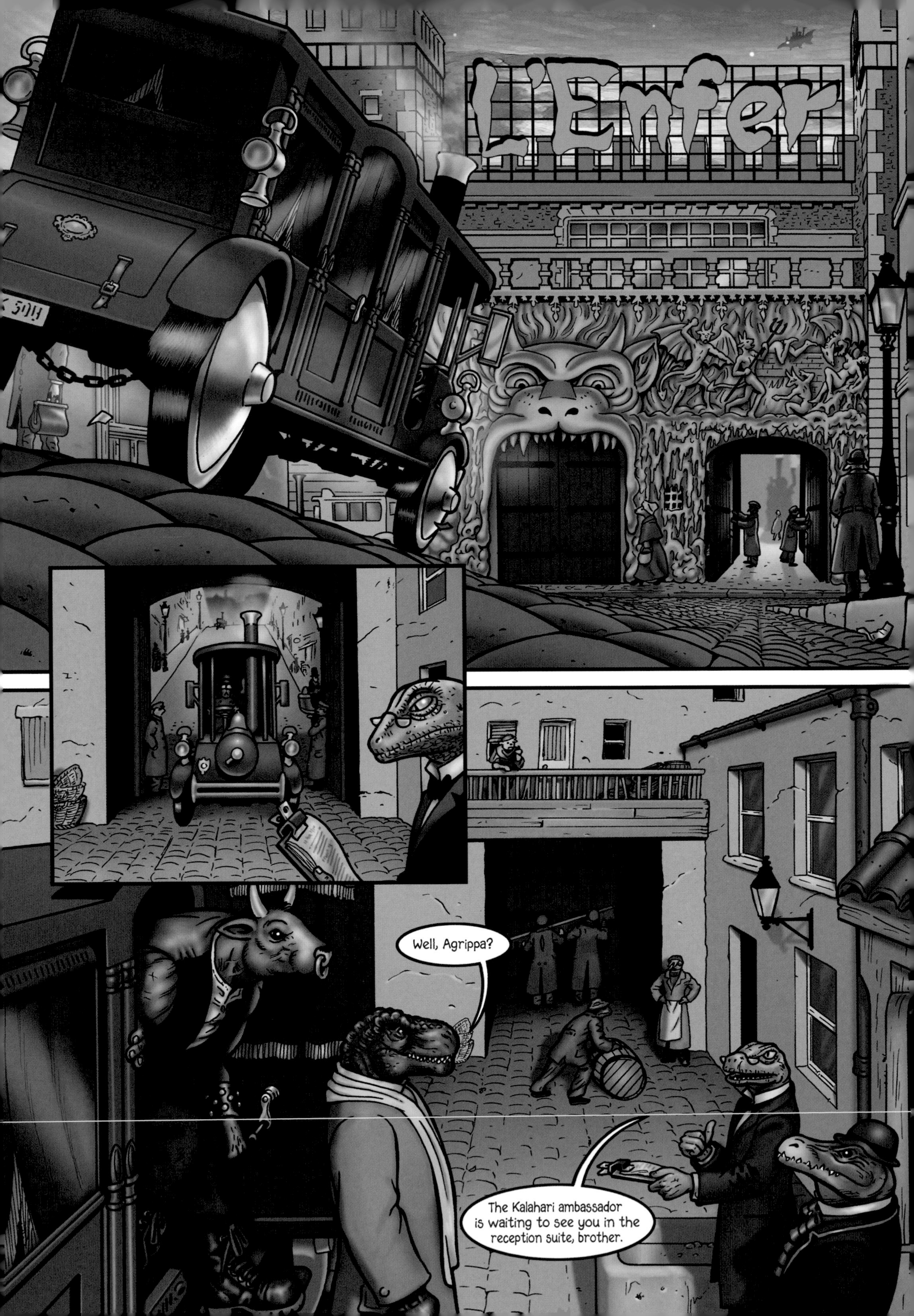
L'Enfer
Well, Agrippa?
The Kalahari ambassador is waiting to see you in the reception suite, brother.

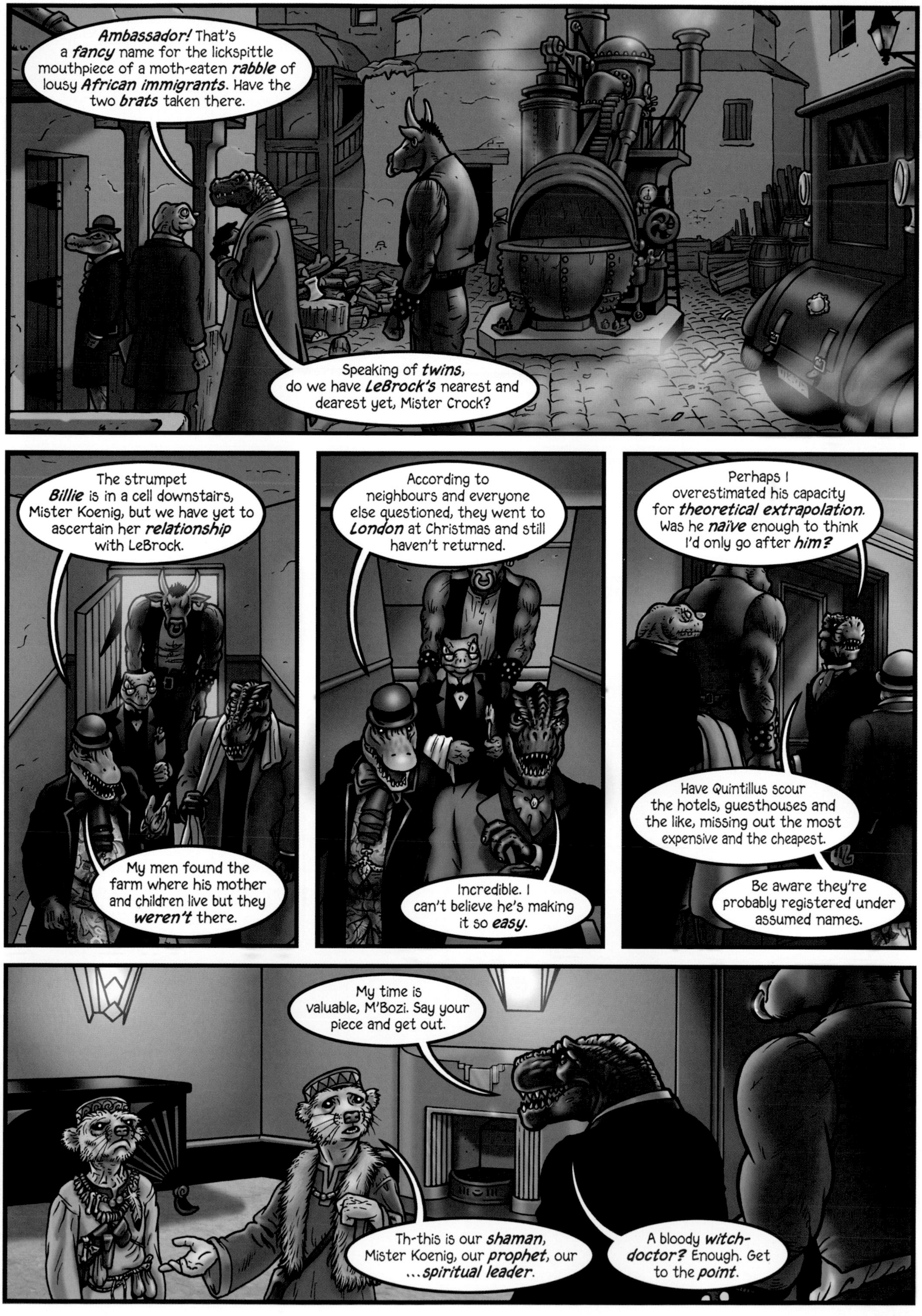
Ambassador! That's a fancy name for the lickspittle mouthpiece of a moth-eaten rabble of lousy African immigrants. Have the two brats taken there.
Speaking of twins, do we have LeBrock's nearest and dearest yet, Mister Crock?
The strumpet Billie is in a cell downstairs, Mister Koenig, but we have yet to ascertain her relationship with LeBrock.
My men found the farm where his mother and children live but they weren't there.
According to neighbours and everyone else questioned, they went to London at Christmas and still haven't returned.
Incredible. I can't believe he's making it so easy.
Perhaps I overestimated his capacity for theoretical extrapolation. Was he naïve enough to think I'd only go after him?
Have Quintillus scour the hotels, guesthouses and the like, missing out the most expensive and the cheapest.
Be aware they're probably registered under assumed names.
My time is valuable, M'Bozi. Say your piece and get out.
Th-this is our shaman, Mister Koenig, our prophet, our ...spiritual leader.
A bloody witch-doctor? Enough. Get to the point.

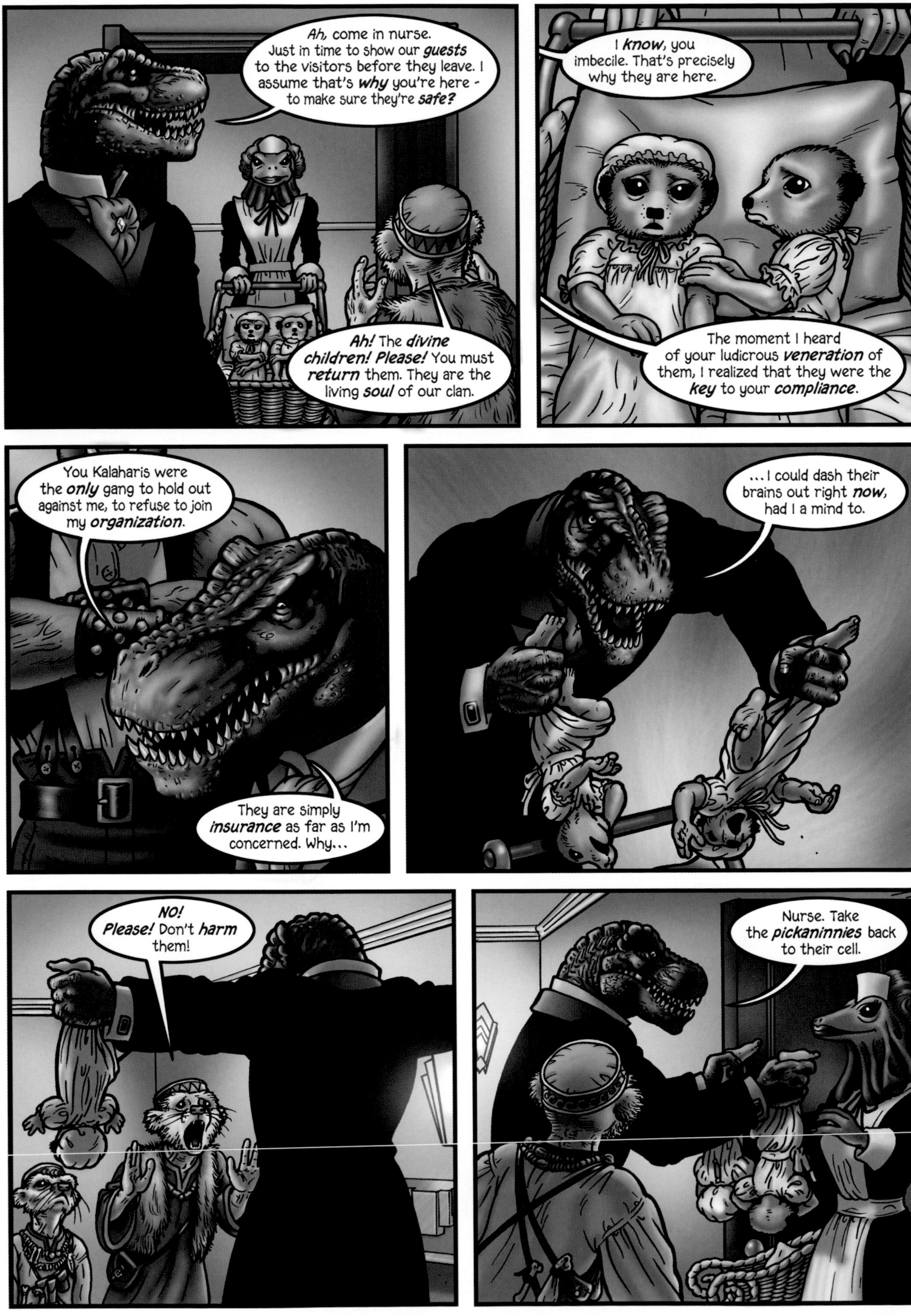
Ah, come in nurse. Just in time to show our guests to the visitors before they leave. I assume that's why you're here - to make sure they're safe?
Ah! The divine children! Please! You must return them. They are the living soul of our clan.
I know, you imbecile. That's precisely why they are here.
The moment I heard of your ludicrous veneration of them, I realized that they were the key to your compliance.
You Kalaharis were the only gang to hold out against me, to refuse to join my organization.
They are simply insurance as far as I'm concerned. Why...
...I could dash their brains out right now, had I a mind to.
NO! Please! Don't harm them!
Nurse. Take the pickaninnies back to their cell.

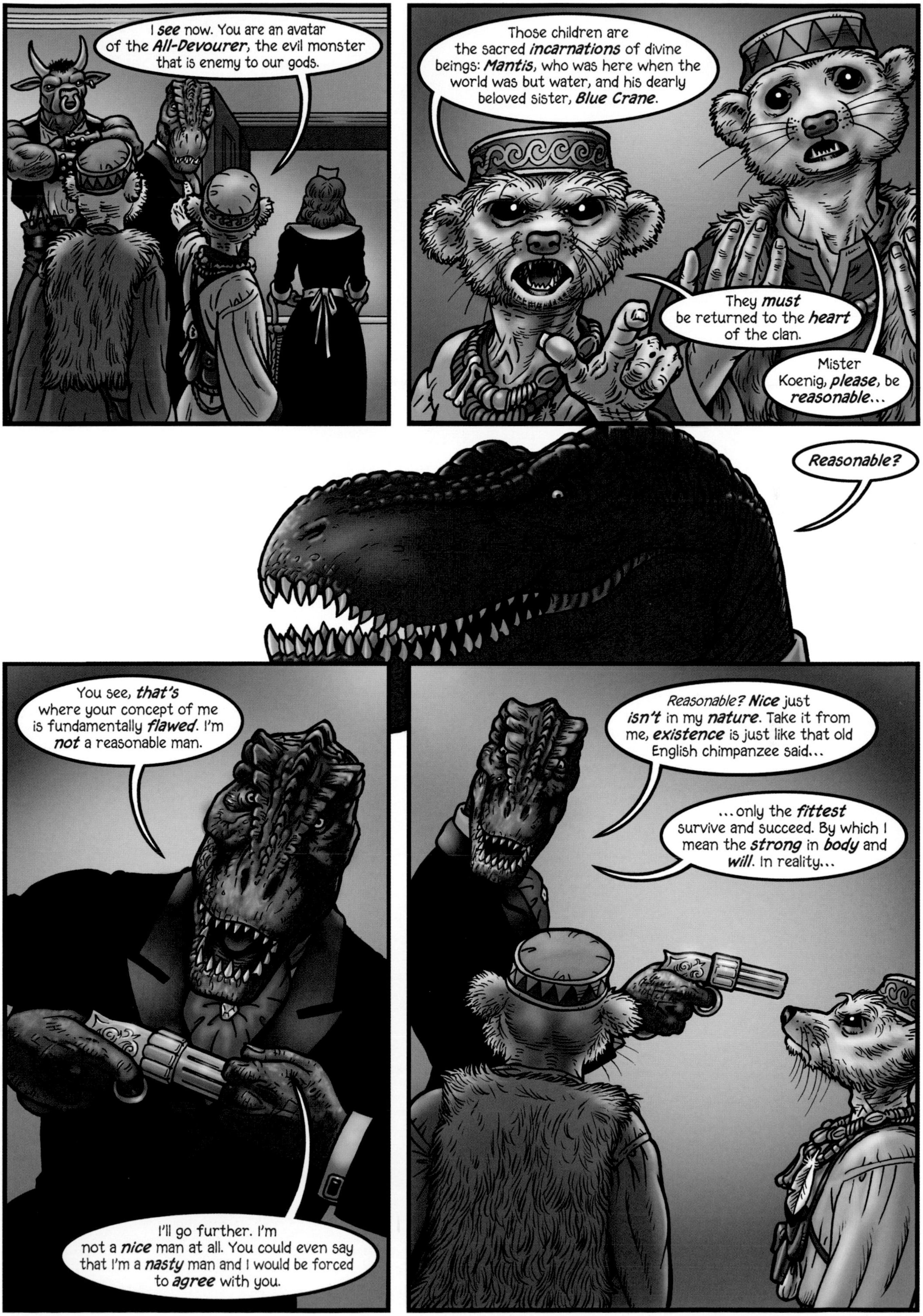
I *see* now. You are an avatar of the *All-Devourer*, the evil monster that is enemy to our gods.
Those children are the sacred *incarnations* of divine beings: *Mantis*, who was here when the world was but water, and his dearly beloved sister, *Blue Crane*.
They *must* be returned to the *heart* of the clan.
Mister Koenig, *please*, be *reasonable*...
Reasonable?
You see, *that's* where your concept of me is fundamentally *flawed*. I'm *not* a reasonable man.
I'll go further. I'm not a *nice* man at all. You could even say that I'm a *nasty* man and I would be forced to *agree* with you.
Reasonable? Nice just *isn't* in my *nature*. Take it from me, *existence* is just like that old English chimpanzee said...
...only the *fittest* survive and succeed. By which I mean the *strong* in *body* and *will*. In reality...

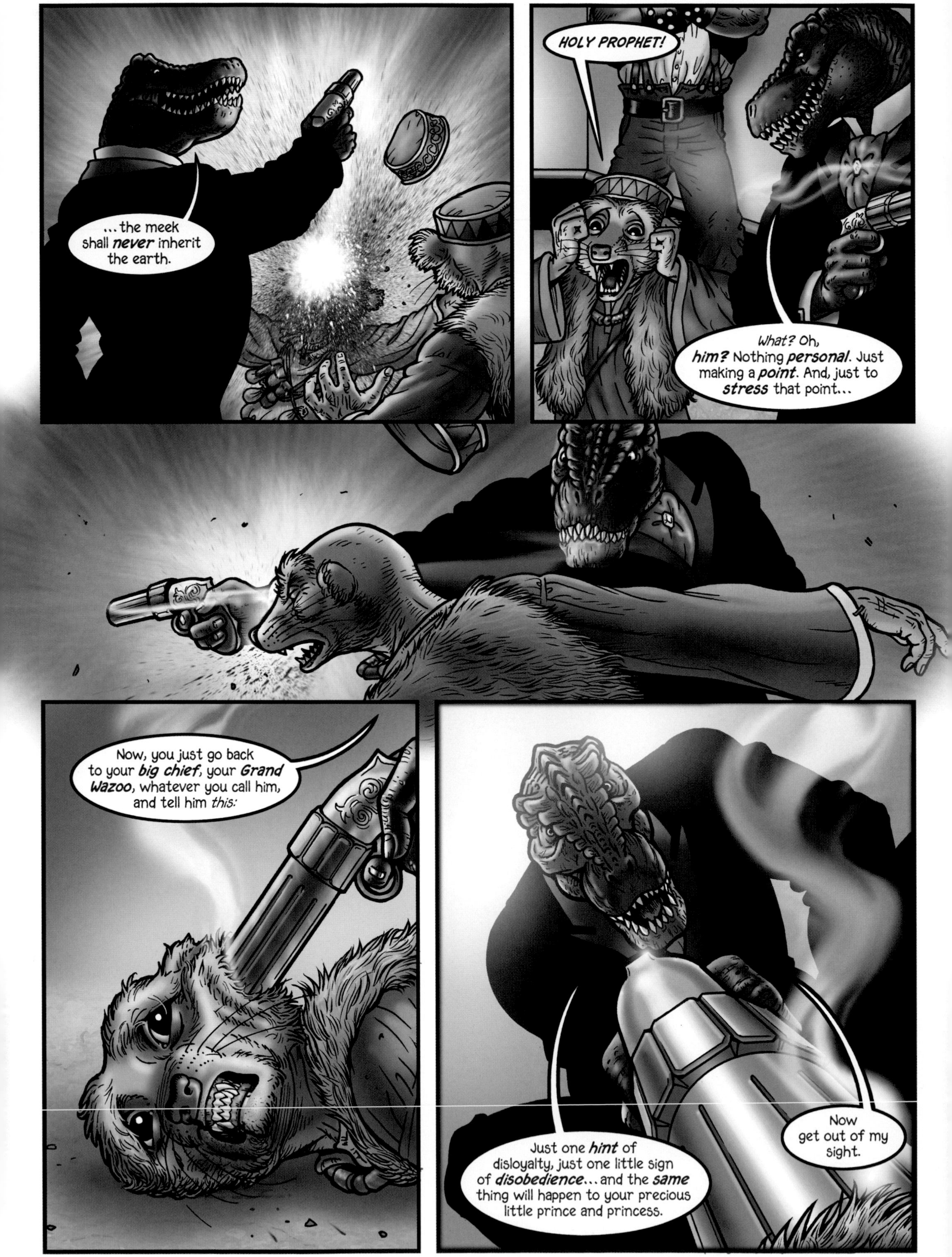
...the meek shall **never** inherit the earth.
HOLY PROPHET!
What? Oh, **him?** Nothing **personal**. Just making a **point**. And, just to **stress** that point...
Now, you just go back to your **big chief**, your **Grand Wazoo**, whatever you call him, and tell him *this:*
Just one **hint** of disloyalty, just one little sign of **disobedience**... and the **same** thing will happen to your precious little prince and princess.
Now get out of my sight.

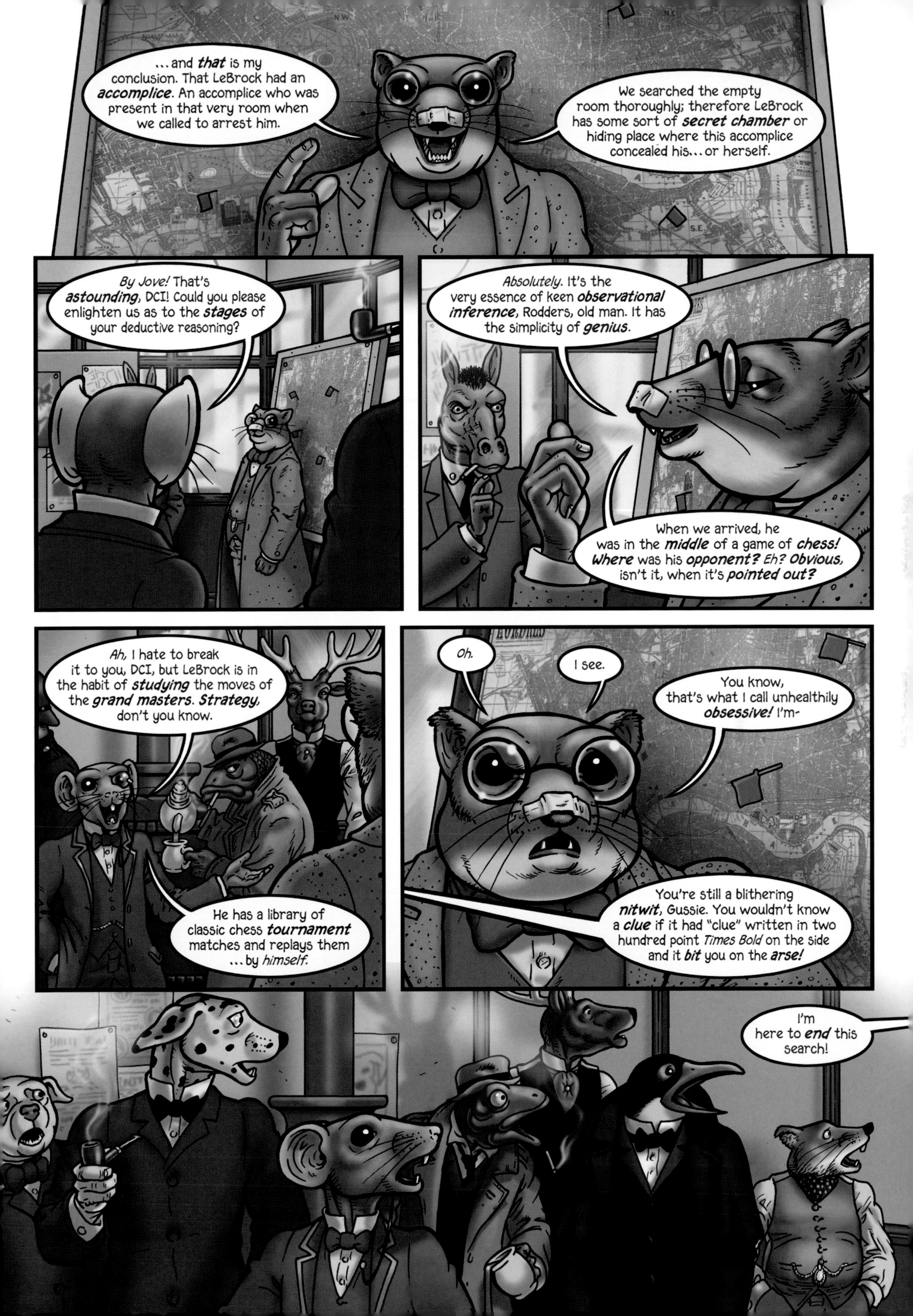

...and *that* is my conclusion. That LeBrock had an *accomplice*. An accomplice who was present in that very room when we called to arrest him.
We searched the empty room thoroughly; therefore LeBrock has some sort of *secret chamber* or hiding place where this accomplice concealed his... or herself.
By Jove! That's *astounding*, DCI! Could you please enlighten us as to the *stages* of your deductive reasoning?
Absolutely. It's the very essence of keen *observational inference*, Rodders, old man. It has the simplicity of *genius*.
When we arrived, he was in the *middle* of a game of *chess! Where* was his *opponent? Eh? Obvious*, isn't it, when it's *pointed out?*
Ah, I hate to break it to you, DCI, but LeBrock is in the habit of *studying* the moves of the *grand masters*. *Strategy*, don't you know.
He has a library of classic chess *tournament* matches and replays them ...by *himself*.
Oh.
I see.
You know, that's what I call unhealthily *obsessive!* I'm-
You're still a blithering *nitwit*, Gussie. You wouldn't know a *clue* if it had "clue" written in two hundred point *Times Bold* on the side and it *bit* you on the *arse!*
I'm here to *end* this search!

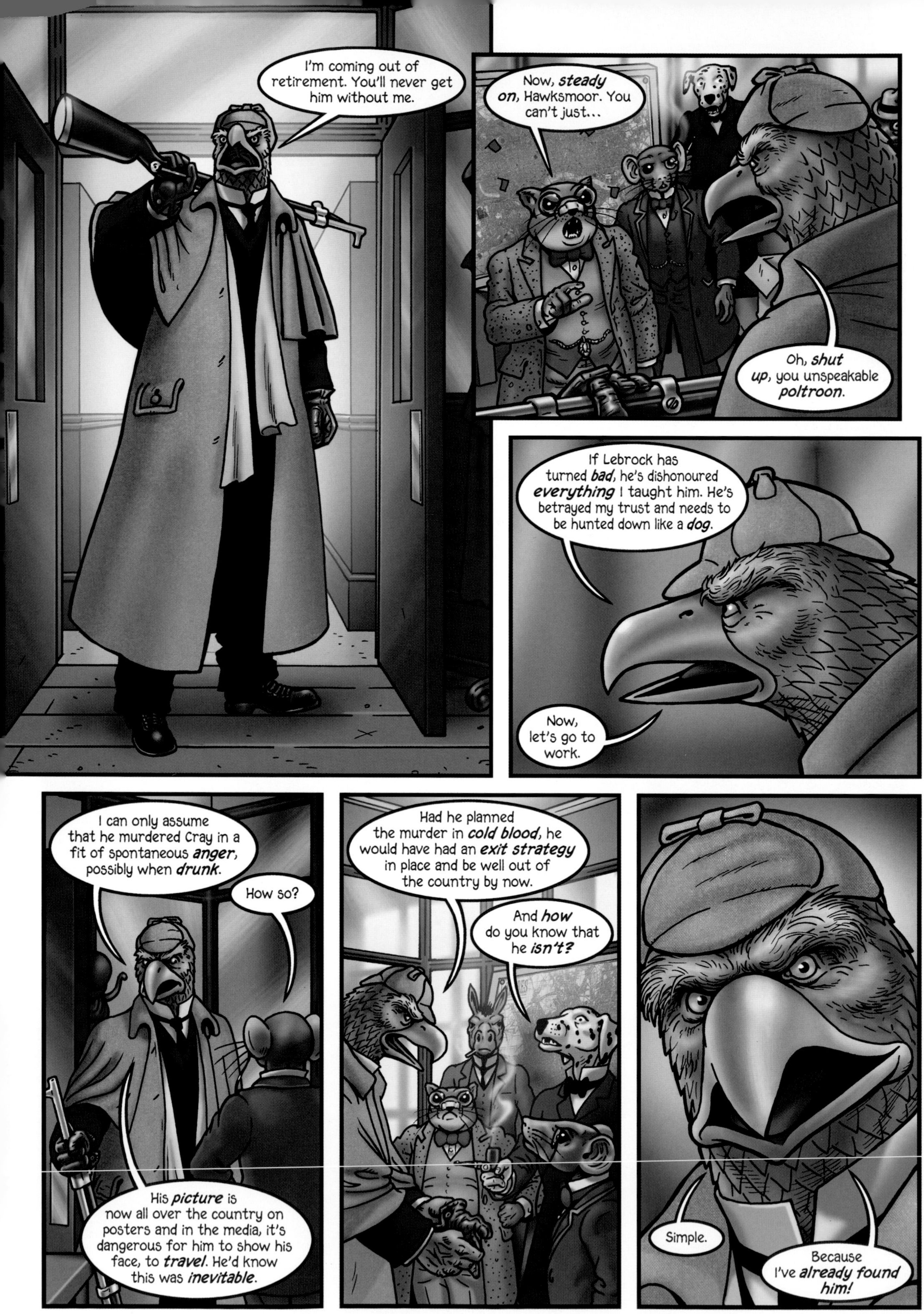
I'm coming out of retirement. You'll never get him without me.
Now, steady on, Hawksmoor. You can't just...
Oh, shut up, you unspeakable poltroon.
If Lebrock has turned bad, he's dishonoured everything I taught him. He's betrayed my trust and needs to be hunted down like a dog.
Now, let's go to work.
I can only assume that he murdered Cray in a fit of spontaneous anger, possibly when drunk.
How so?
His picture is now all over the country on posters and in the media, it's dangerous for him to show his face, to travel. He'd know this was inevitable.
Had he planned the murder in cold blood, he would have had an exit strategy in place and be well out of the country by now.
And how do you know that he isn't?
Simple.
Because I've already found him!

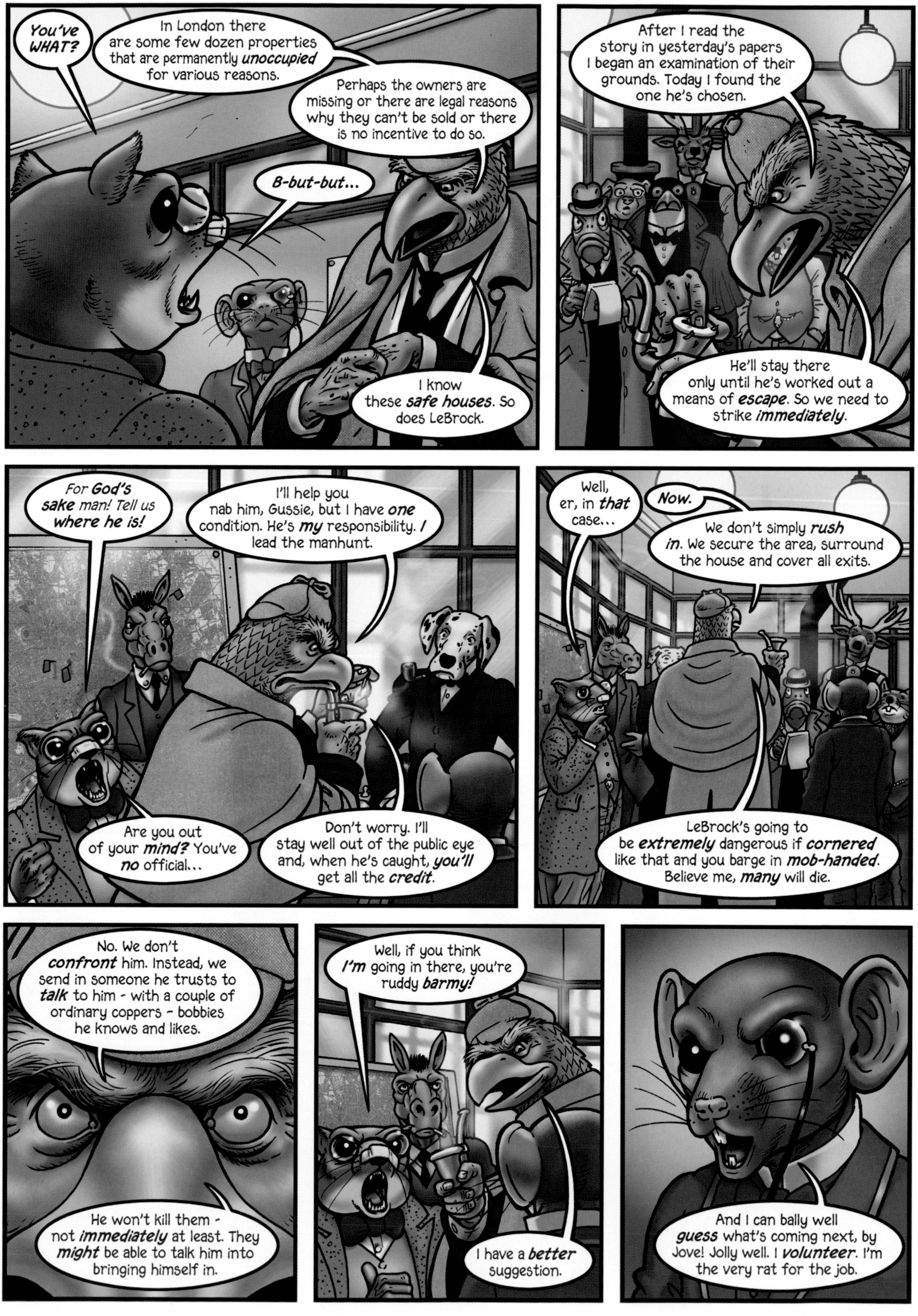
You've WHAT?
In London there are some few dozen properties that are permanently unoccupied for various reasons.
Perhaps the owners are missing or there are legal reasons why they can't be sold or there is no incentive to do so.
B-but-but...
I know these safe houses. So does LeBrock.
After I read the story in yesterday's papers I began an examination of their grounds. Today I found the one he's chosen.
He'll stay there only until he's worked out a means of escape. So we need to strike immediately.
For God's sake man! Tell us where he is!
I'll help you nab him, Gussie, but I have one condition. He's my responsibility. I lead the manhunt.
Are you out of your mind? You've no official...
Don't worry. I'll stay well out of the public eye and, when he's caught, you'll get all the credit.
Well, er, in that case...
Now.
We don't simply rush in. We secure the area, surround the house and cover all exits.
LeBrock's going to be extremely dangerous if cornered like that and you barge in mob-handed. Believe me, many will die.
No. We don't confront him. Instead, we send in someone he trusts to talk to him - with a couple of ordinary coppers - bobbies he knows and likes.
He won't kill them - not immediately at least. They might be able to talk him into bringing himself in.
Well, if you think I'm going in there, you're ruddy barmy!
I have a better suggestion.
And I can bally well guess what's coming next, by Jove! Jolly well. I volunteer. I'm the very rat for the job.

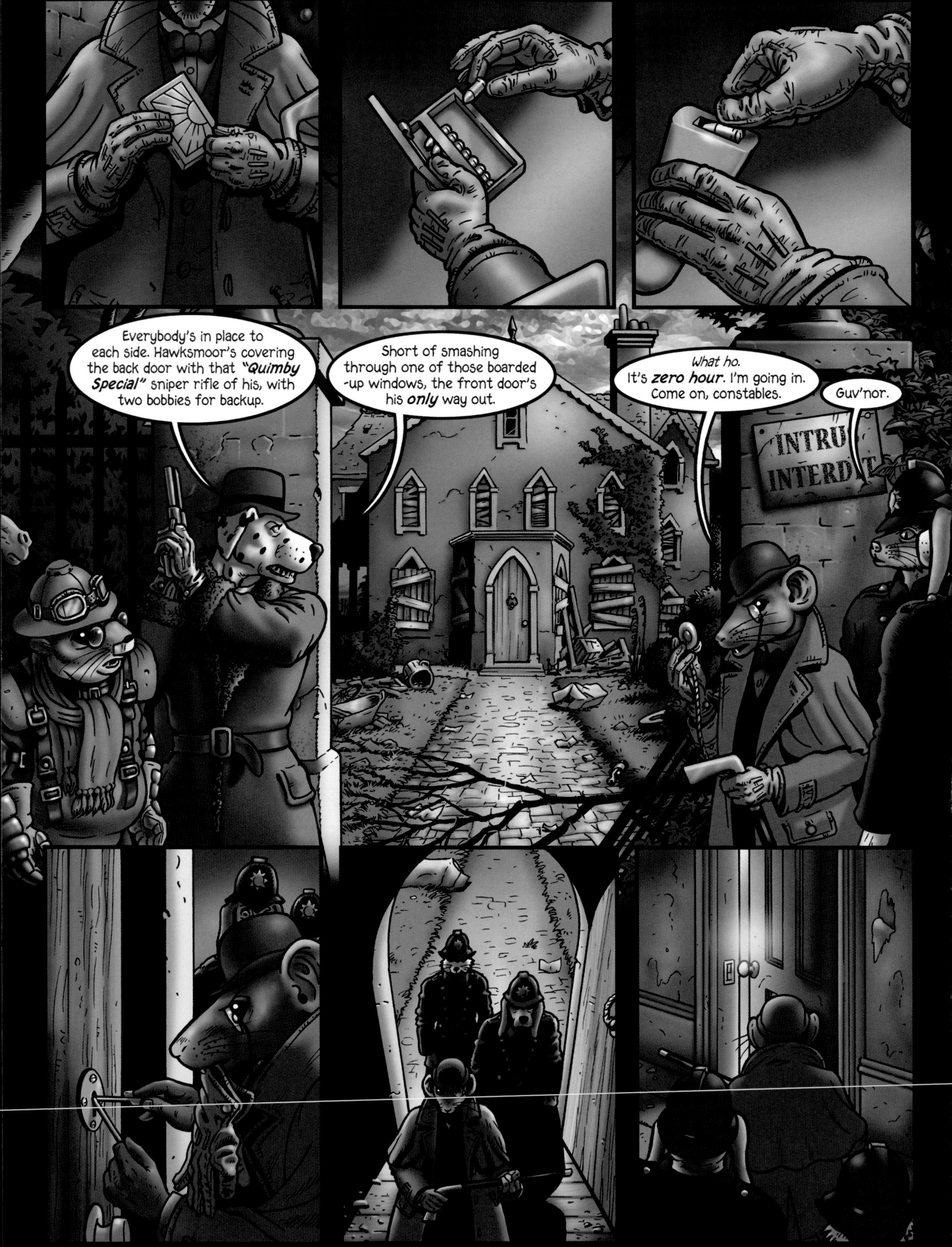
Everybody's in place to each side. Hawksmoor's covering the back door with that "Quimby Special" sniper rifle of his, with two bobbies for backup.
Short of smashing through one of those boarded -up windows, the front door's his only way out.
What ho. It's zero hour. I'm going in. Come on, constables.
Guv'nor.
INTRU
INTERDIT

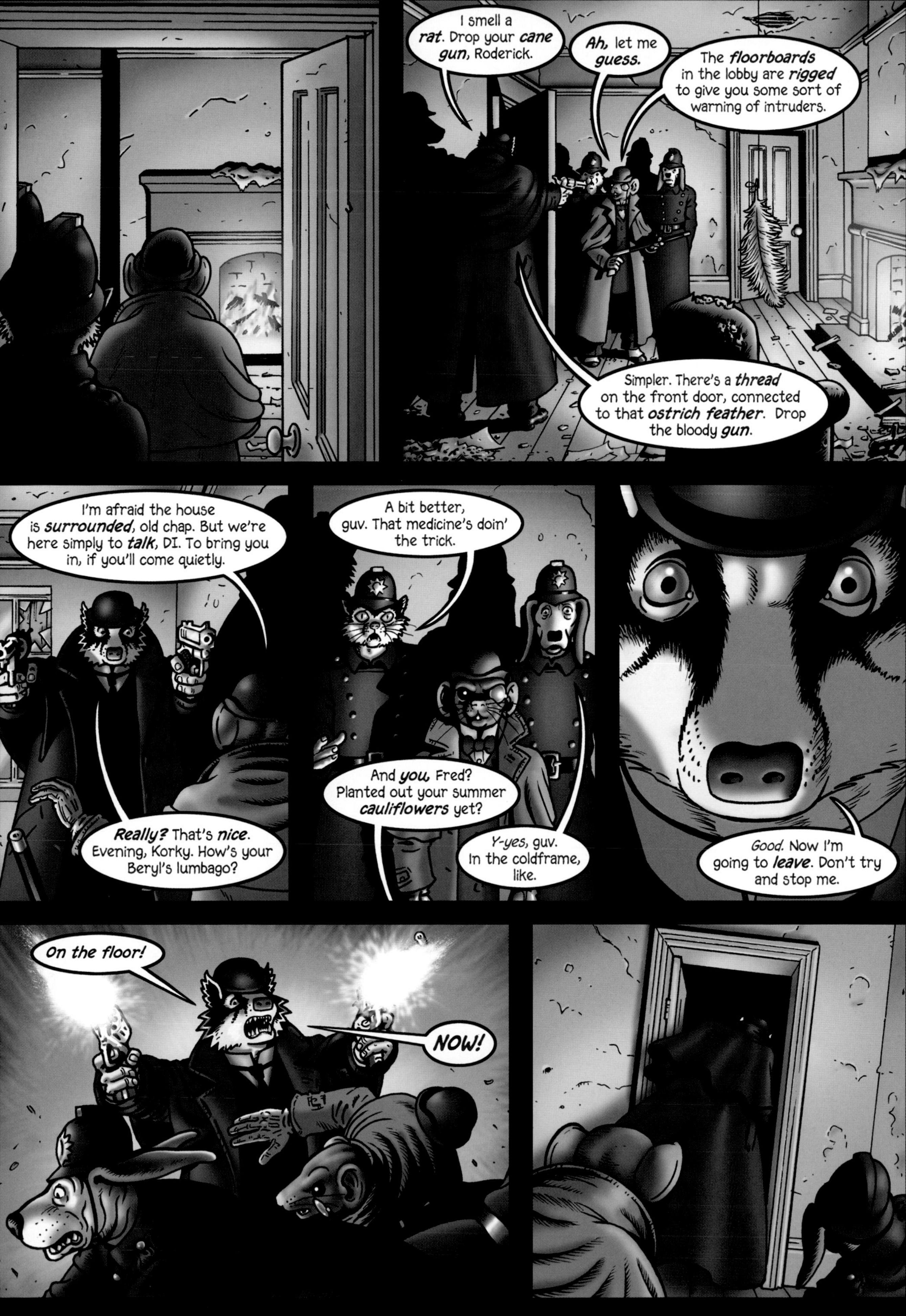
I smell a rat. Drop your cane gun, Roderick.
Ah, let me guess.
The floorboards in the lobby are rigged to give you some sort of warning of intruders.
Simpler. There's a thread on the front door, connected to that ostrich feather. Drop the bloody gun.
I'm afraid the house is surrounded, old chap. But we're here simply to talk, DI. To bring you in, if you'll come quietly.
Really? That's nice. Evening, Korky. How's your Beryl's lumbago?
A bit better, guv. That medicine's doin' the trick.
And you, Fred? Planted out your summer cauliflowers yet?
Y-yes, guv. In the coldframe, like.
Good. Now I'm going to leave. Don't try and stop me.
On the floor!
NOW!

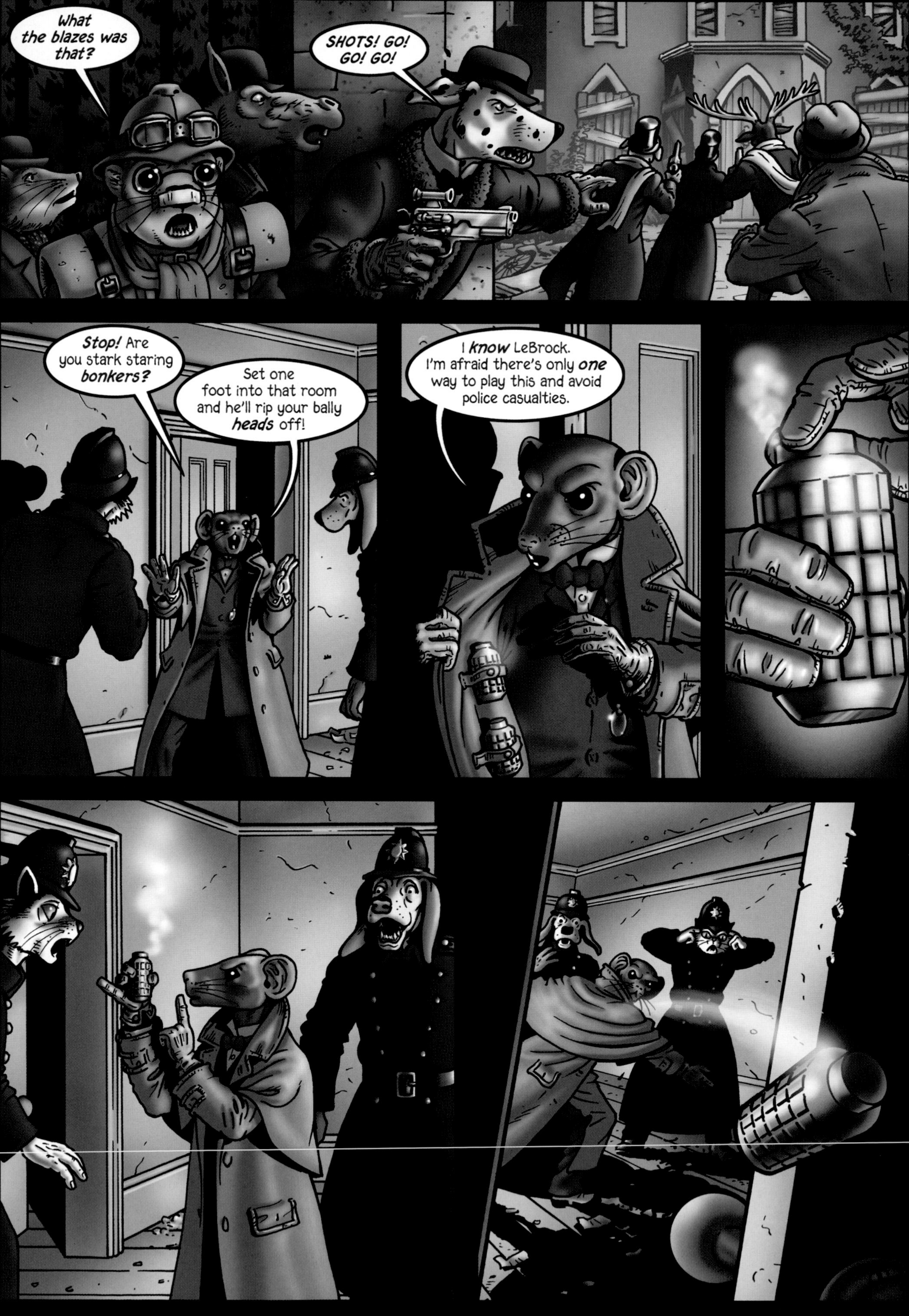
What the blazes was that?
SHOTS! GO! GO! GO!
Stop! Are you stark staring bonkers?
Set one foot into that room and he'll rip your bally heads off!
I know LeBrock. I'm afraid there's only one way to play this and avoid police casualties.

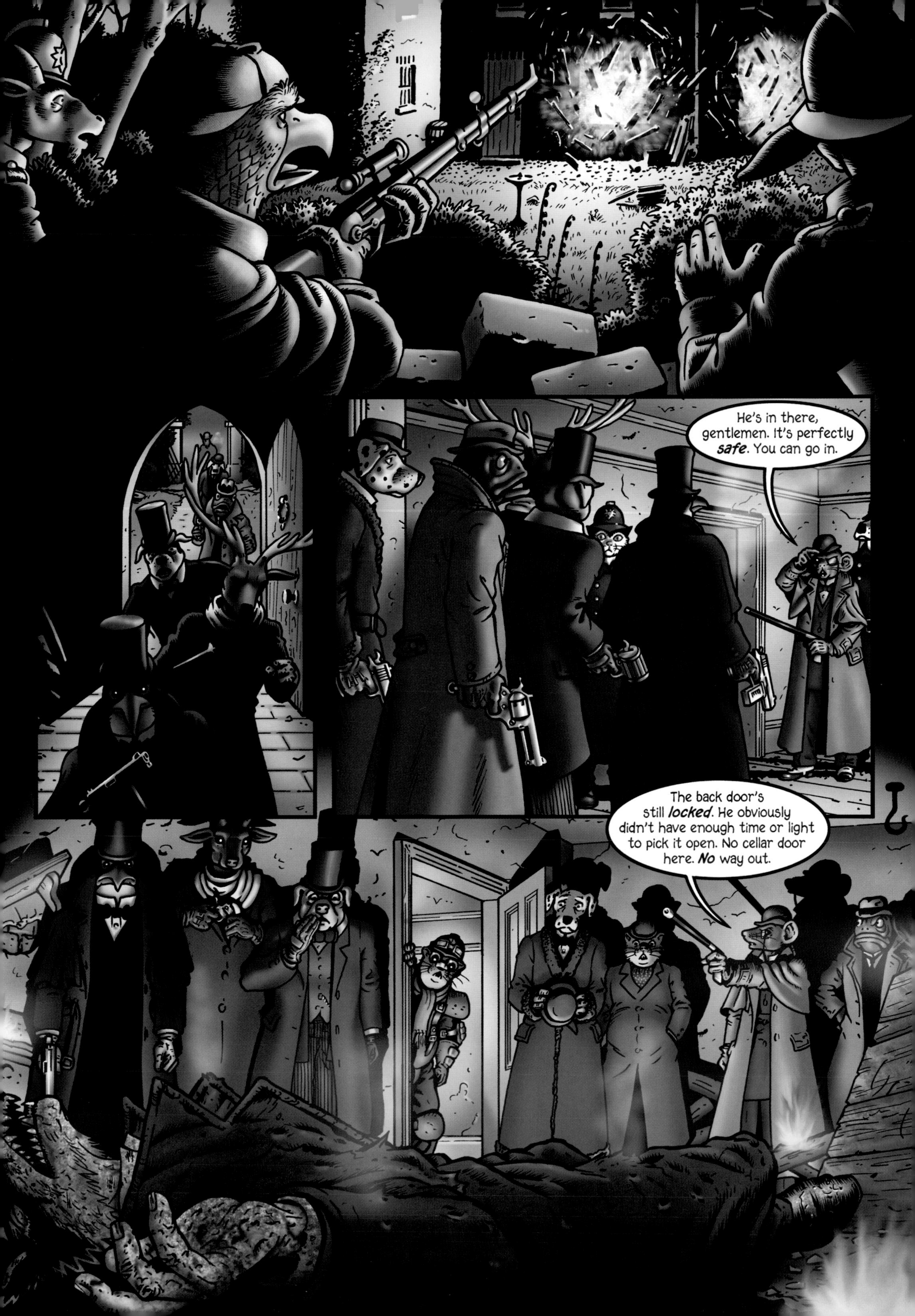
He's in there, gentlemen. It's perfectly *safe*. You can go in.
The back door's still *locked*. He obviously didn't have enough time or light to pick it open. No cellar door here. *No* way out.

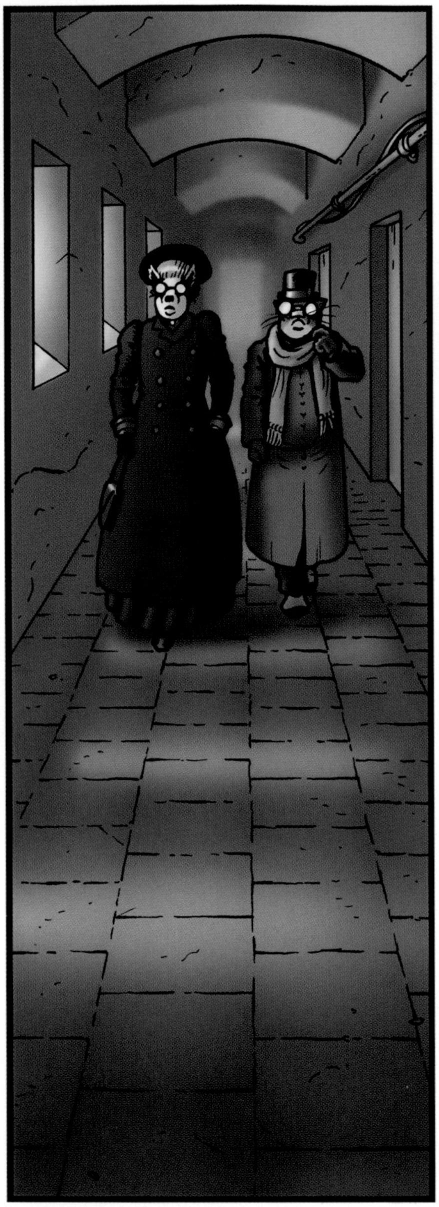

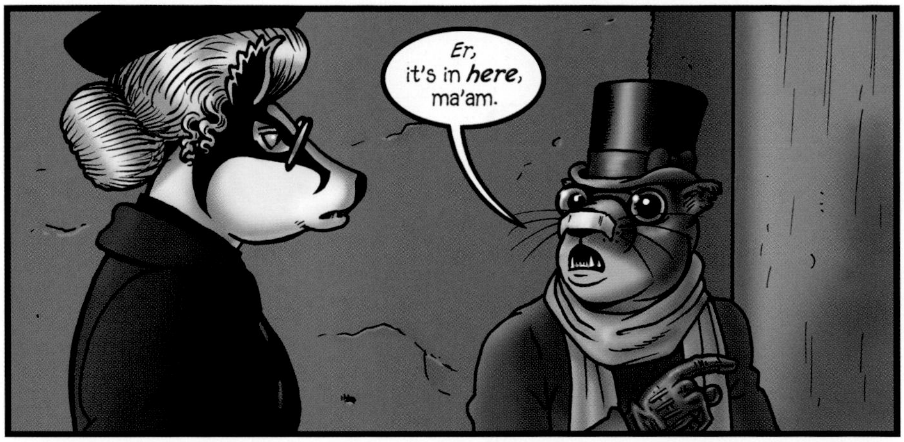
Er, it's in here, ma'am.

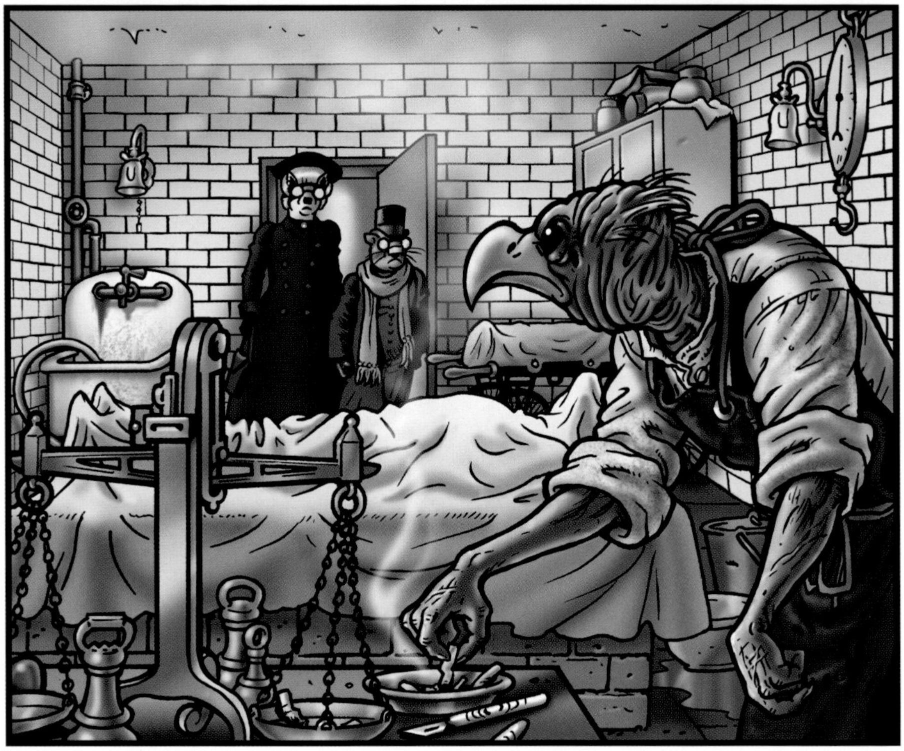

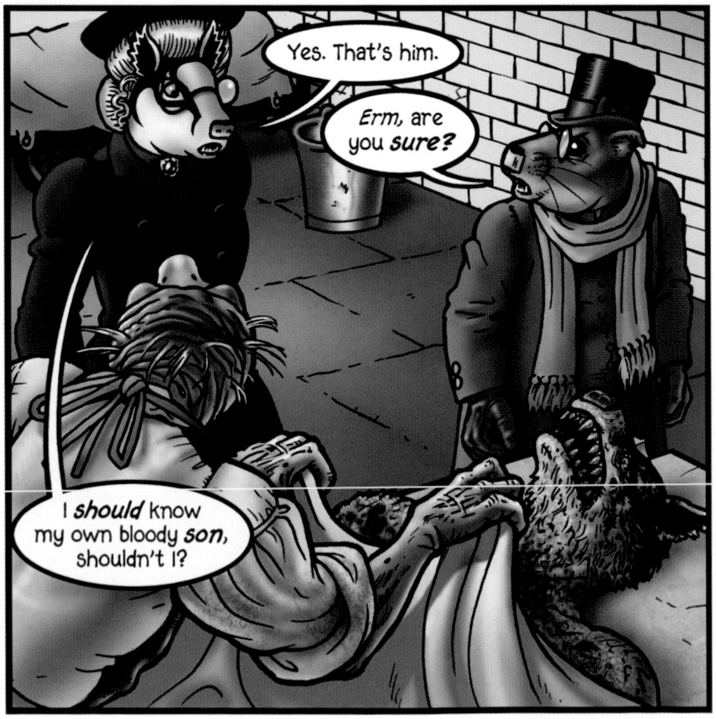
Yes. That's him.
Erm, are you sure?
I should know my own bloody son, shouldn't I?

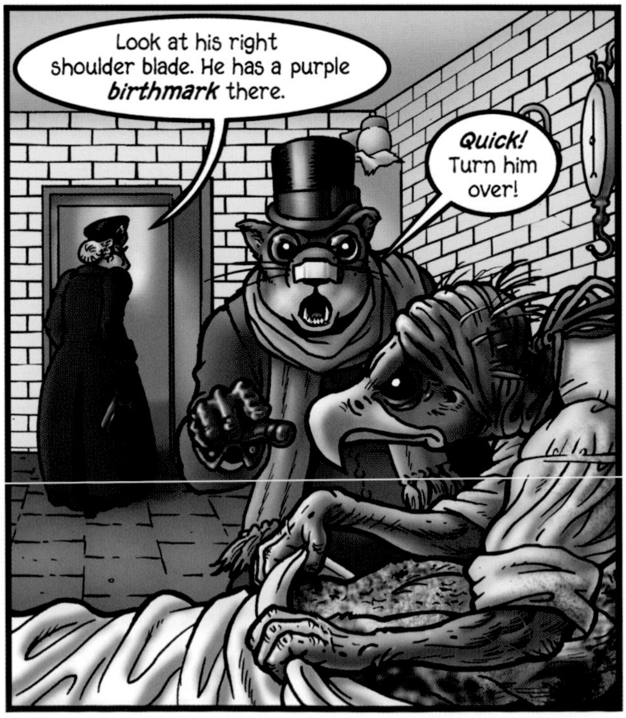
Look at his right shoulder blade. He has a purple birthmark there.
Quick! Turn him over!

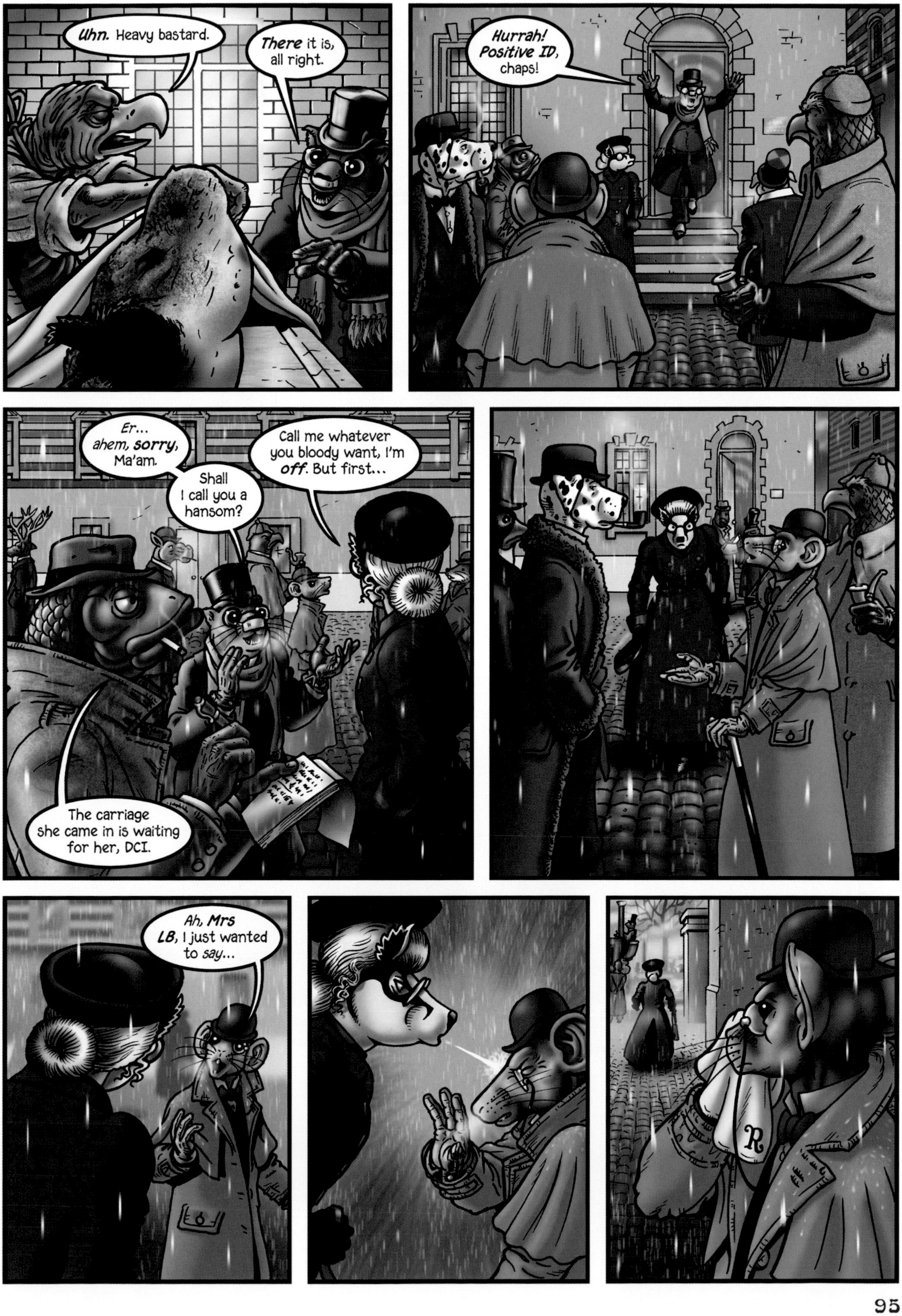

Uhn. Heavy bastard.
There it is, all right.
Hurrah! Positive ID, chaps!
Er... ahem, ***sorry,*** Ma'am.
Shall I call you a hansom?
Call me whatever you bloody want, I'm ***off***. But first...
The carriage she came in is waiting for her, DCI.
Ah, ***Mrs LB***, I just wanted to *say*...

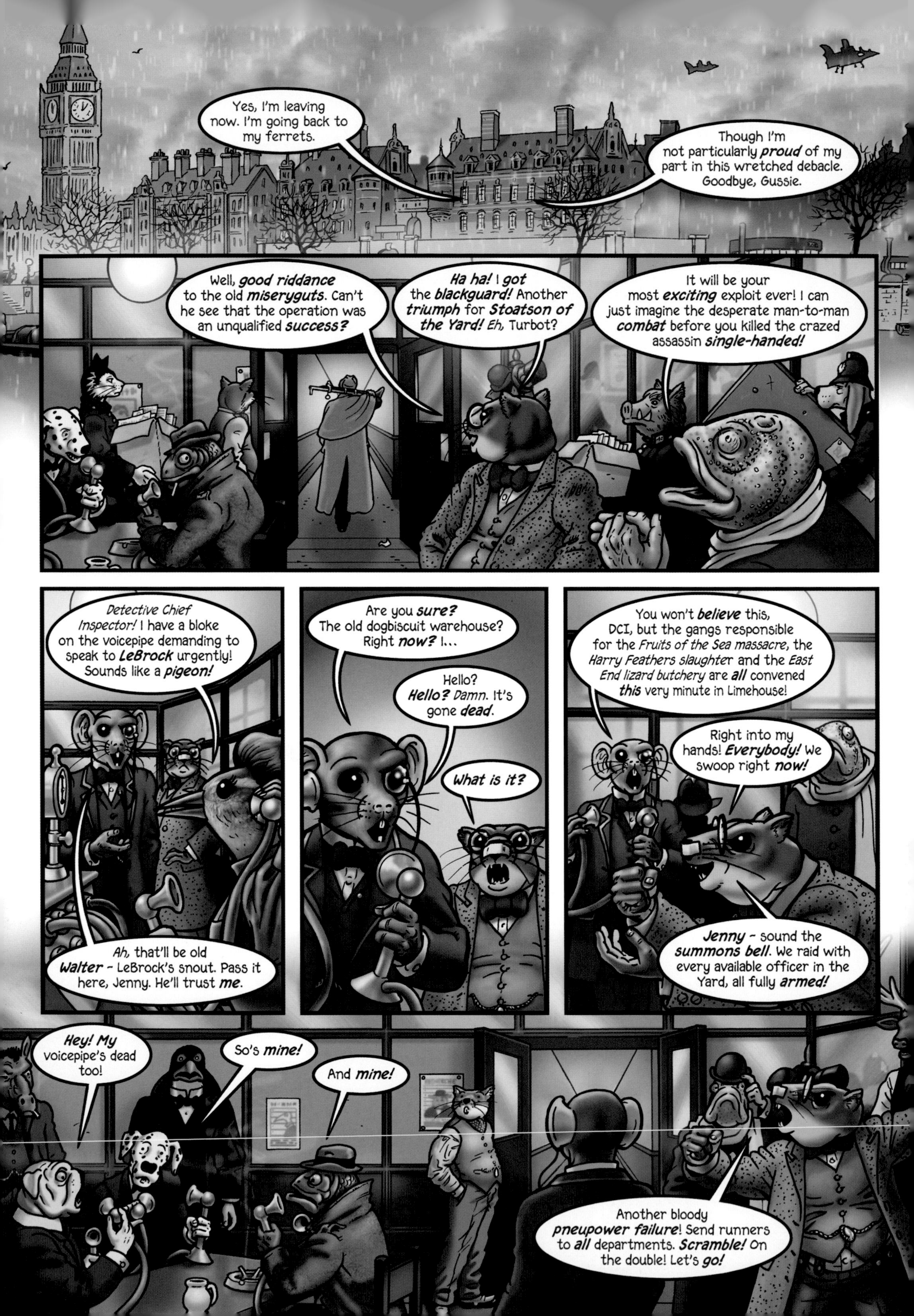

Yes, I'm leaving now. I'm going back to my ferrets.
Though I'm not particularly proud of my part in this wretched debacle. Goodbye, Gussie.
Well, good riddance to the old miseryguts. Can't he see that the operation was an unqualified success?
Ha ha! I got the blackguard! Another triumph for Stoatson of the Yard! Eh, Turbot?
It will be your most exciting exploit ever! I can just imagine the desperate man-to-man combat before you killed the crazed assassin single-handed!
Detective Chief Inspector! I have a bloke on the voicepipe demanding to speak to LeBrock urgently! Sounds like a pigeon!
Ah, that'll be old Walter – LeBrock's snout. Pass it here, Jenny. He'll trust me.
Are you sure? The old dogbiscuit warehouse? Right now? I...
Hello? Hello? Damn. It's gone dead.
What is it?
You won't believe this, DCI, but the gangs responsible for the Fruits of the Sea massacre, the Harry Feathers slaughter and the East End lizard butchery are all convened this very minute in Limehouse!
Right into my hands! Everybody! We swoop right now!
Jenny – sound the summons bell. We raid with every available officer in the Yard, all fully armed!
Hey! My voicepipe's dead too!
So's mine!
And mine!
Another bloody pneupower failure! Send runners to all departments. Scramble! On the double! Let's go!

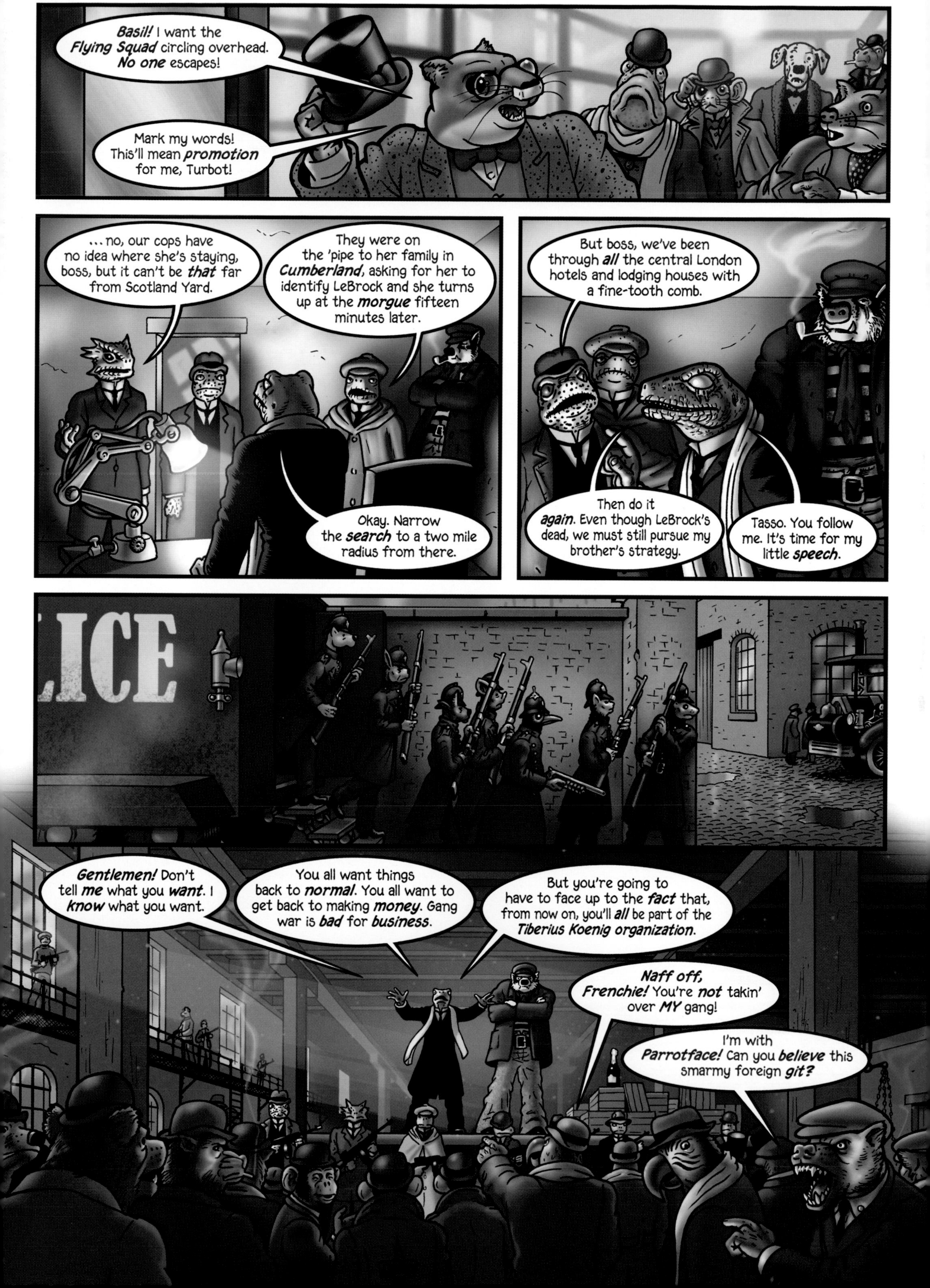
Basil! I want the Flying Squad circling overhead. No one escapes!
Mark my words! This'll mean promotion for me, Turbot!
... no, our cops have no idea where she's staying, boss, but it can't be that far from Scotland Yard.
They were on the 'pipe to her family in Cumberland, asking for her to identify LeBrock and she turns up at the morgue fifteen minutes later.
Okay. Narrow the search to a two mile radius from there.
But boss, we've been through all the central London hotels and lodging houses with a fine-tooth comb.
Then do it again. Even though LeBrock's dead, we must still pursue my brother's strategy.
Tasso. You follow me. It's time for my little speech.
LICE
Gentlemen! Don't tell me what you want. I know what you want.
You all want things back to normal. You all want to get back to making money. Gang war is bad for business.
But you're going to have to face up to the fact that, from now on, you'll all be part of the Tiberius Koenig organization.
Naff off, Frenchie! You're not takin' over MY gang!
I'm with Parrotface! Can you believe this smarmy foreign git?

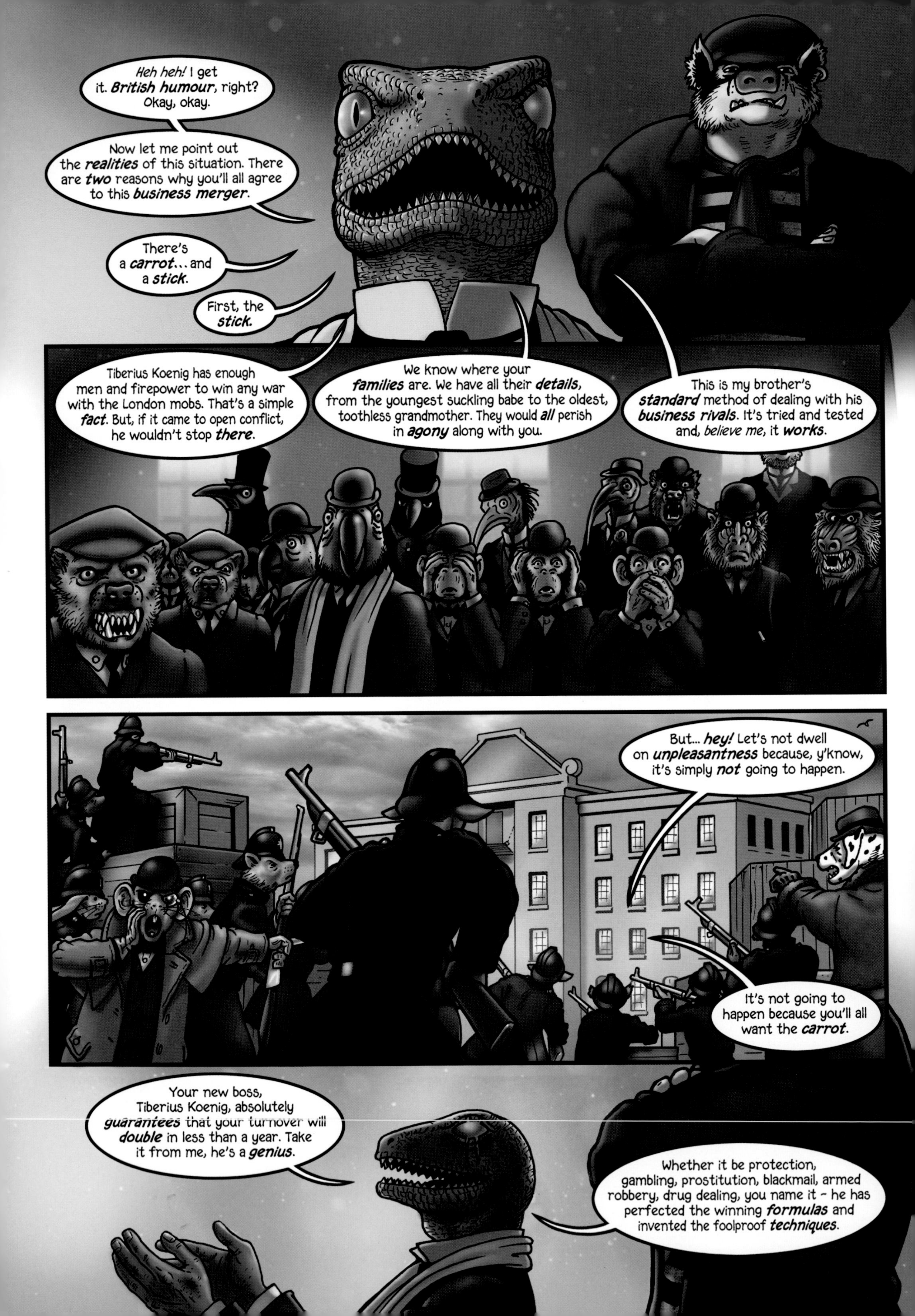
Heh heh! I get it. British humour, right? Okay, okay.
Now let me point out the realities of this situation. There are two reasons why you'll all agree to this business merger.
There's a carrot... and a stick.
First, the stick.
Tiberius Koenig has enough men and firepower to win any war with the London mobs. That's a simple fact. But, if it came to open conflict, he wouldn't stop there.
We know where your families are. We have all their details, from the youngest suckling babe to the oldest, toothless grandmother. They would all perish in agony along with you.
This is my brother's standard method of dealing with his business rivals. It's tried and tested and, believe me, it works.
But... hey! Let's not dwell on unpleasantness because, y'know, it's simply not going to happen.
It's not going to happen because you'll all want the carrot.
Your new boss, Tiberius Koenig, absolutely guarantees that your turnover will double in less than a year. Take it from me, he's a genius.
Whether it be protection, gambling, prostitution, blackmail, armed robbery, drug dealing, you name it - he has perfected the winning formulas and invented the foolproof techniques.

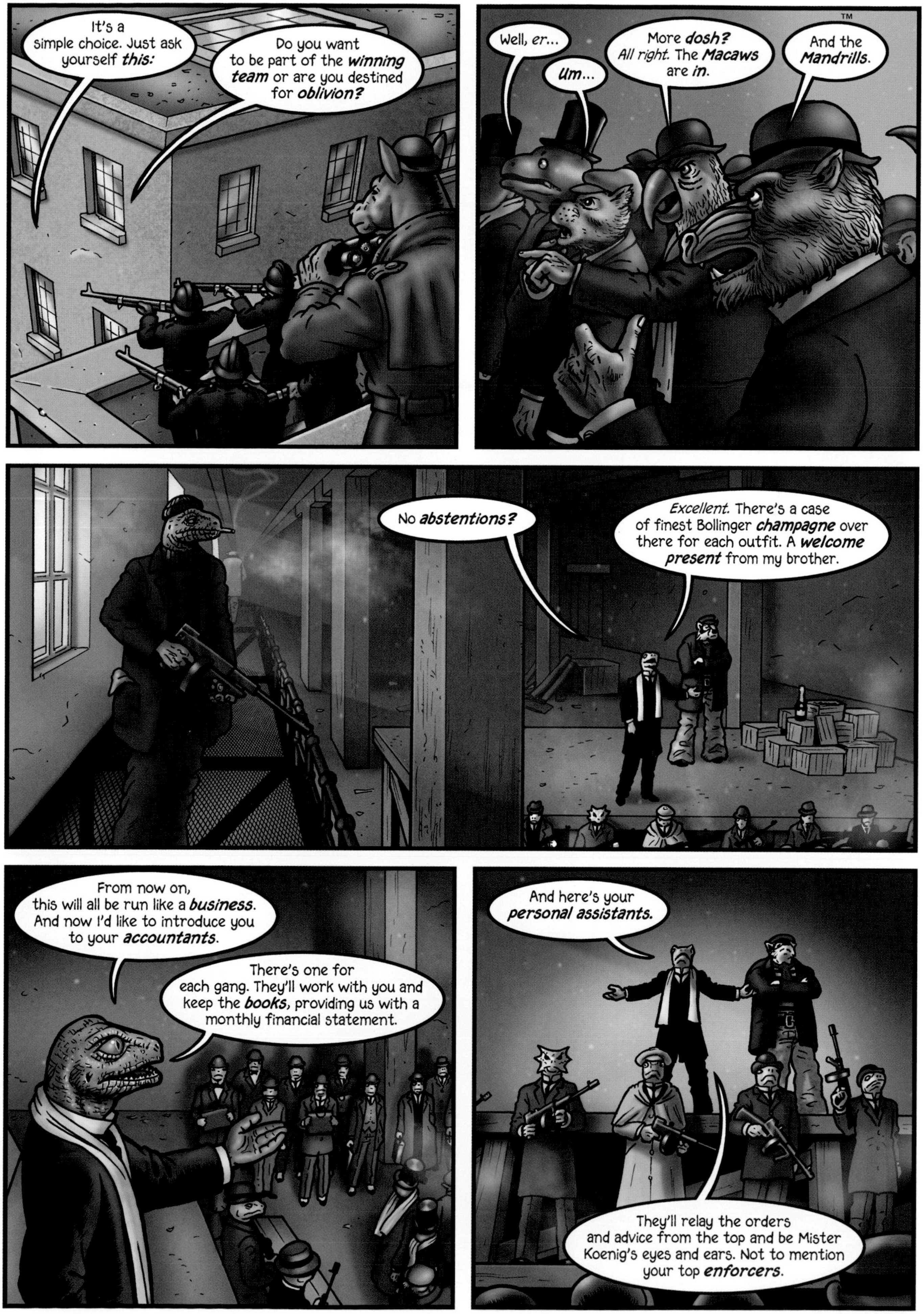

It's a simple choice. Just ask yourself this:
Do you want to be part of the winning team or are you destined for oblivion?
Well, er...
Um...
More dosh? All right. The Macaws are in.
And the Mandrills.
TM
No abstentions?
Excellent. There's a case of finest Bollinger champagne over there for each outfit. A welcome present from my brother.
From now on, this will all be run like a business. And now I'd like to introduce you to your accountants.
There's one for each gang. They'll work with you and keep the books, providing us with a monthly financial statement.
And here's your personal assistants.
They'll relay the orders and advice from the top and be Mister Koenig's eyes and ears. Not to mention your top enforcers.

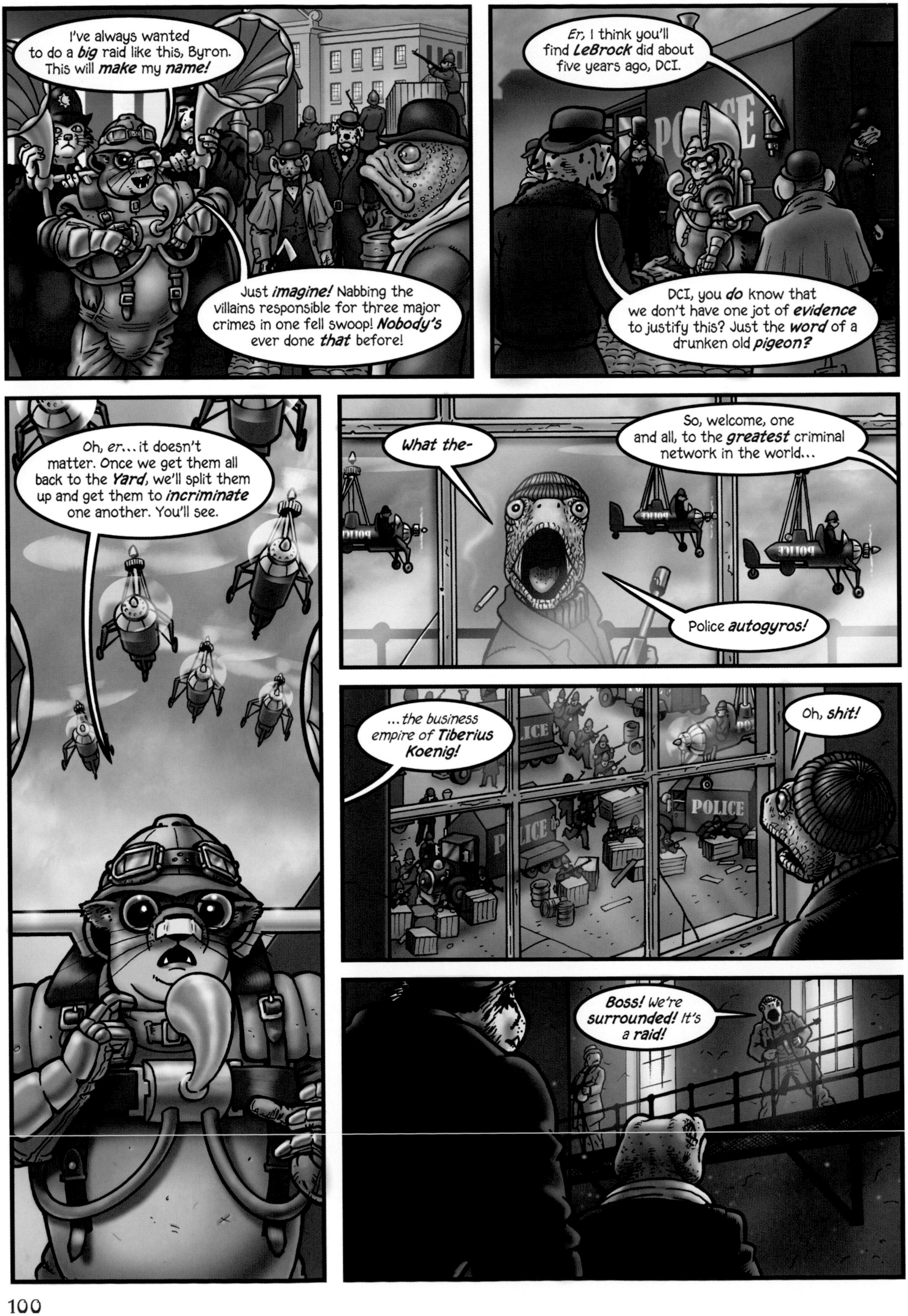
I've always wanted to do a *big* raid like this, Byron. This will *make* my *name!*
Just *imagine!* Nabbing the villains responsible for three major crimes in one fell swoop! *Nobody's* ever done *that* before!
Er, I think you'll find *LeBrock* did about five years ago, DCI.
DCI, you *do* know that we don't have one jot of *evidence* to justify this? Just the *word* of a drunken old *pigeon?*
Oh, *er*... it doesn't matter. Once we get them all back to the *Yard,* we'll split them up and get them to *incriminate* one another. You'll see.
POLICE
What the-
So, welcome, one and all, to the *greatest* criminal network in the world...
Police *autogyros!*
...the business empire of Tiberius Koenig!
POLICE
Oh, *shit!*
Boss! We're *surrounded!* It's a *raid!*

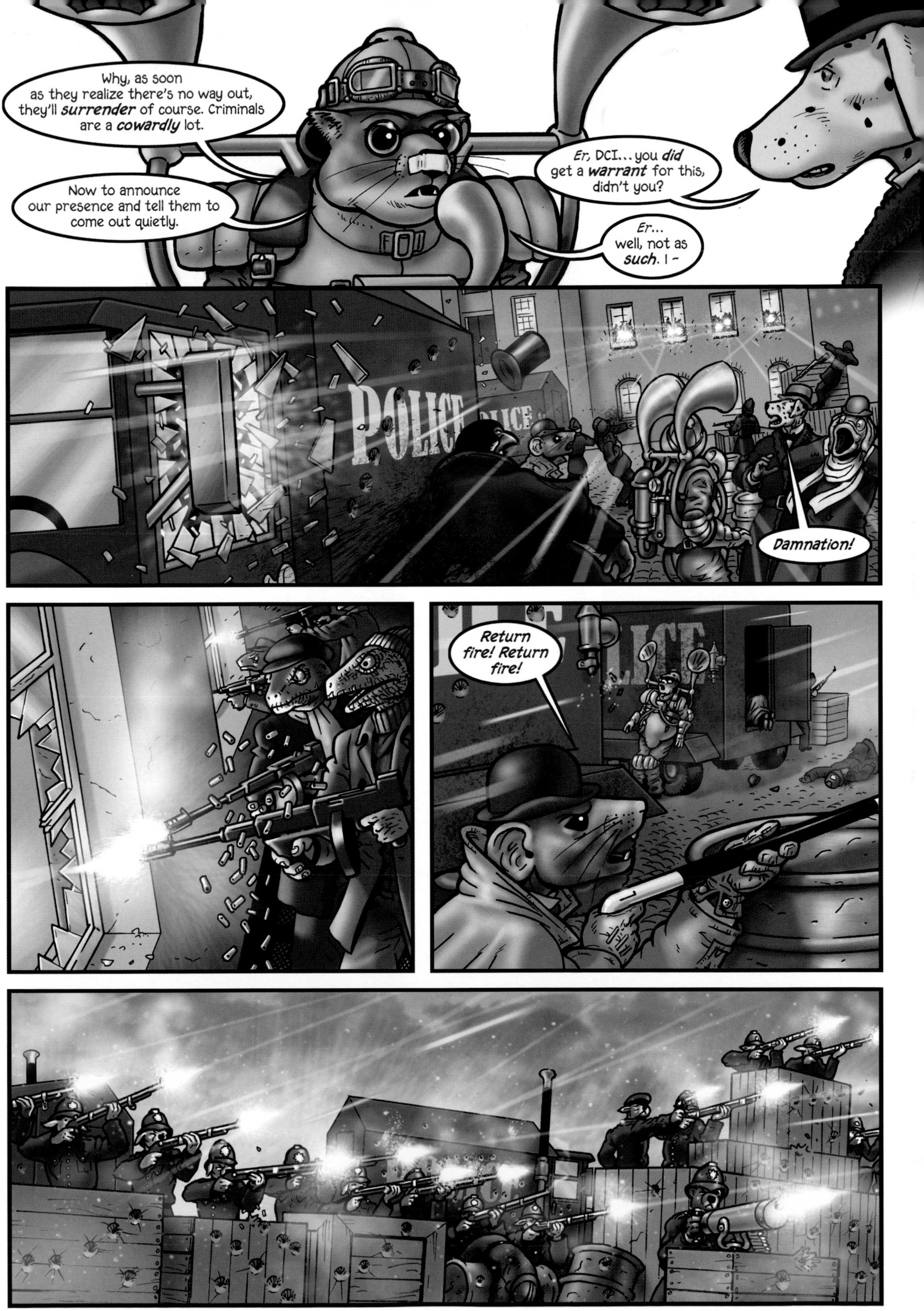
Why, as soon as they realize there's no way out, they'll *surrender* of course. Criminals are a *cowardly* lot.
Now to announce our presence and tell them to come out quietly.
Er, DCI... you *did* get a *warrant* for this, didn't you?
Er... well, not as *such*. I –
POLICE
Damnation!
Return fire! Return fire!

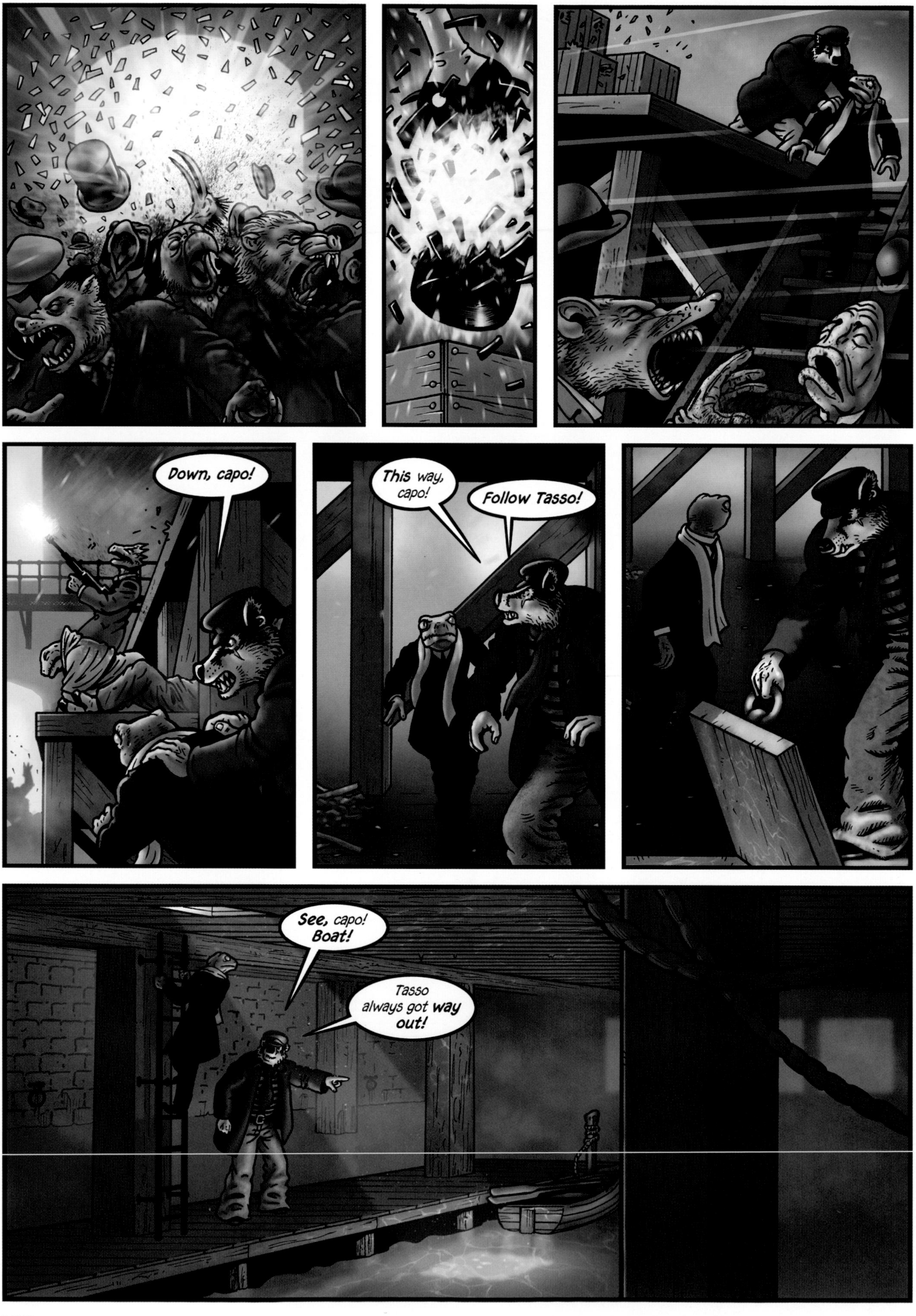

Down, capo!
This way, capo!
Follow Tasso!
See, capo! Boat!
Tasso always got way out!

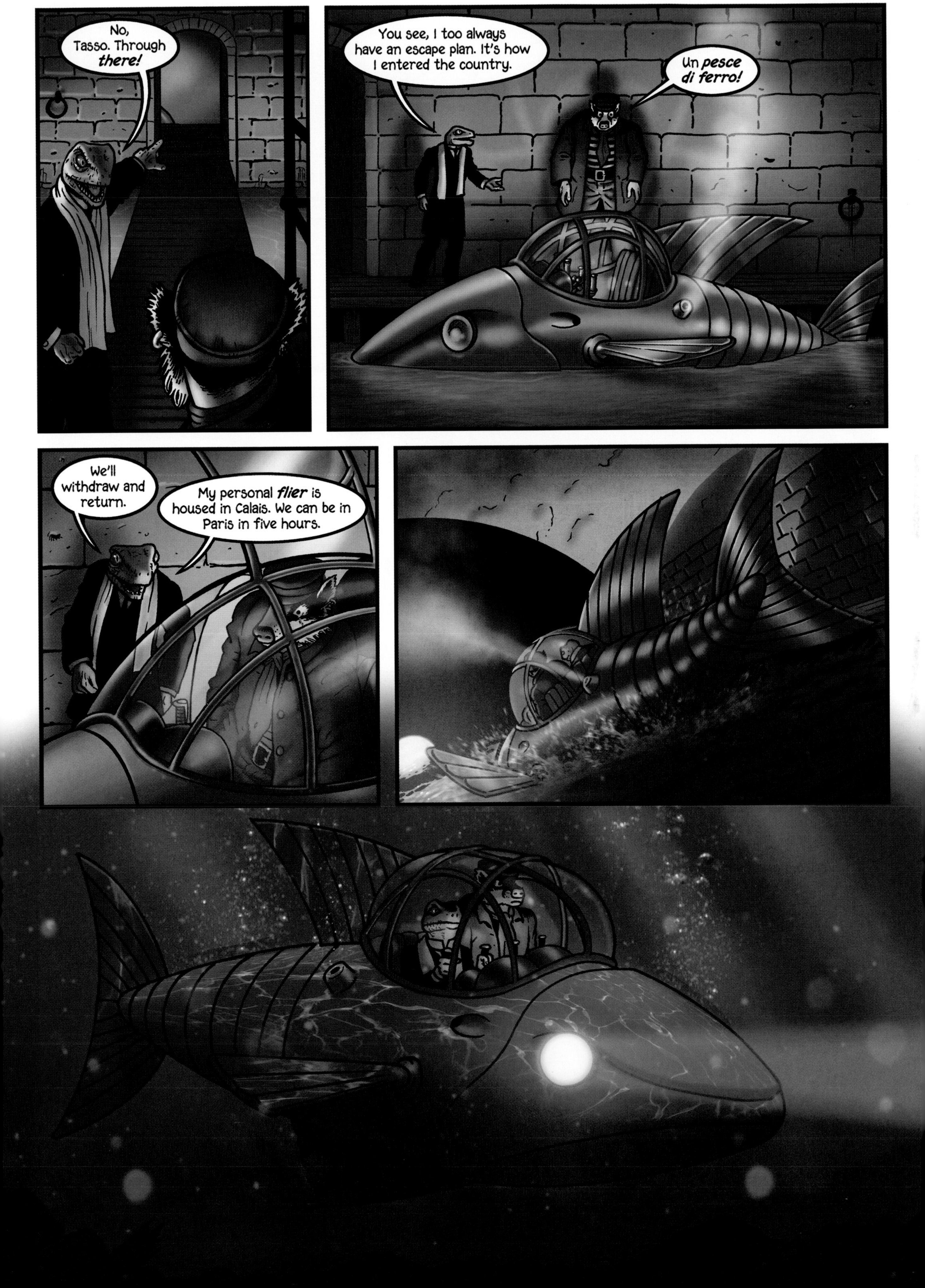

No, Tasso. Through *there!*
You see, I too always have an escape plan. It's how I entered the country.
Un *pesce di ferro!*
We'll withdraw and return.
My personal *flier* is housed in Calais. We can be in Paris in five hours.

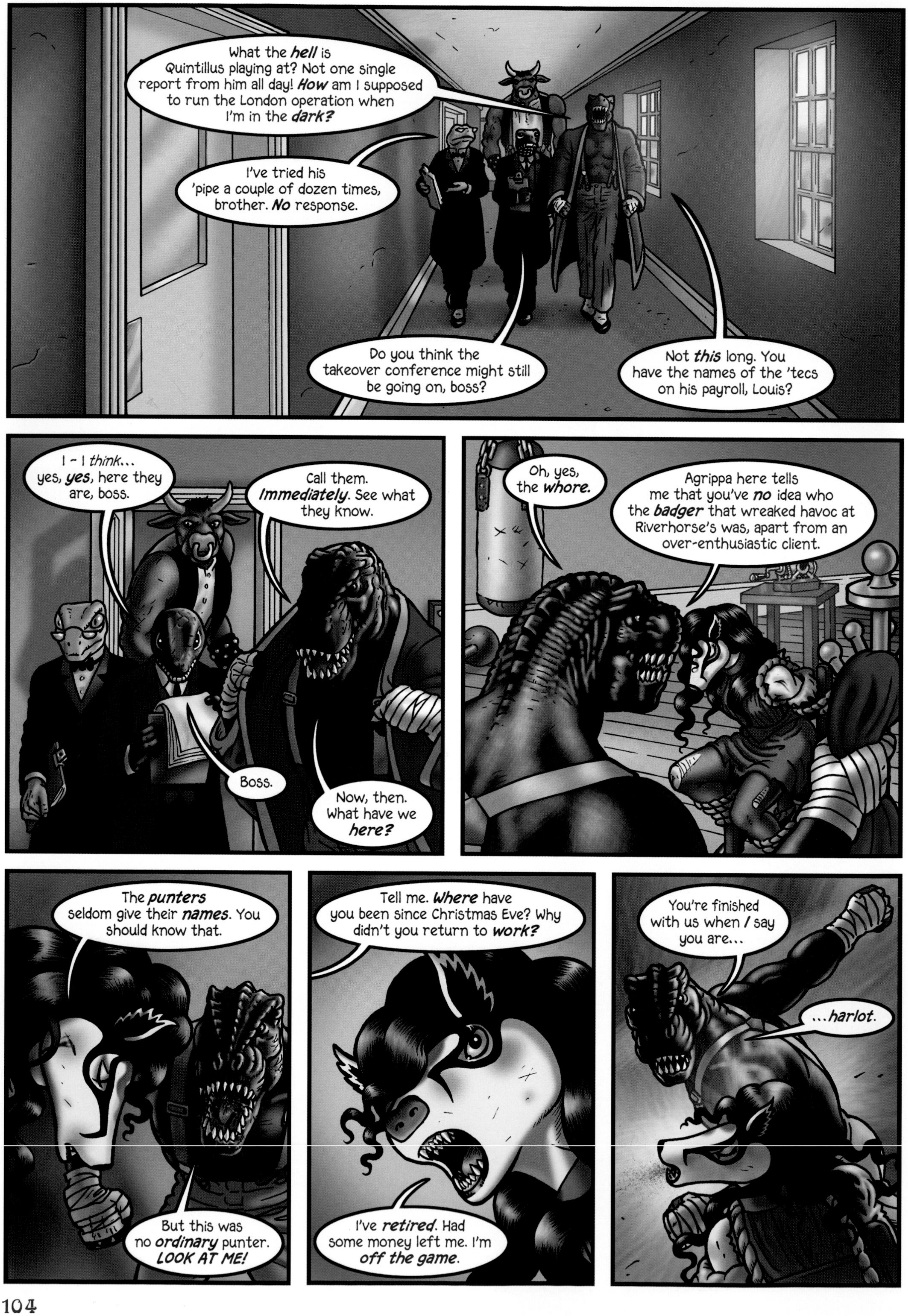

What the *hell* is Quintillus playing at? Not one single report from him all day! *How* am I supposed to run the London operation when I'm in the *dark?*
I've tried his 'pipe a couple of dozen times, brother. *No* response.
Do you think the takeover conference might still be going on, boss?
Not *this* long. You have the names of the 'tecs on his payroll, Louis?
I - I *think*... yes, *yes*, here they are, boss.
Call them. *Immediately*. See what they know.
Boss.
Now, then. What have we *here?*
Oh, yes, the *whore.*
Agrippa here tells me that you've *no* idea who the *badger* that wreaked havoc at Riverhorse's was, apart from an over-enthusiastic client.
The *punters* seldom give their *names*. You should know that.
But this was no *ordinary* punter. *LOOK AT ME!*
Tell me. *Where* have you been since Christmas Eve? Why didn't you return to *work?*
I've *retired*. Had some money left me. I'm *off the game*.
You're finished with us when *I* say you are...
...*harlot*.

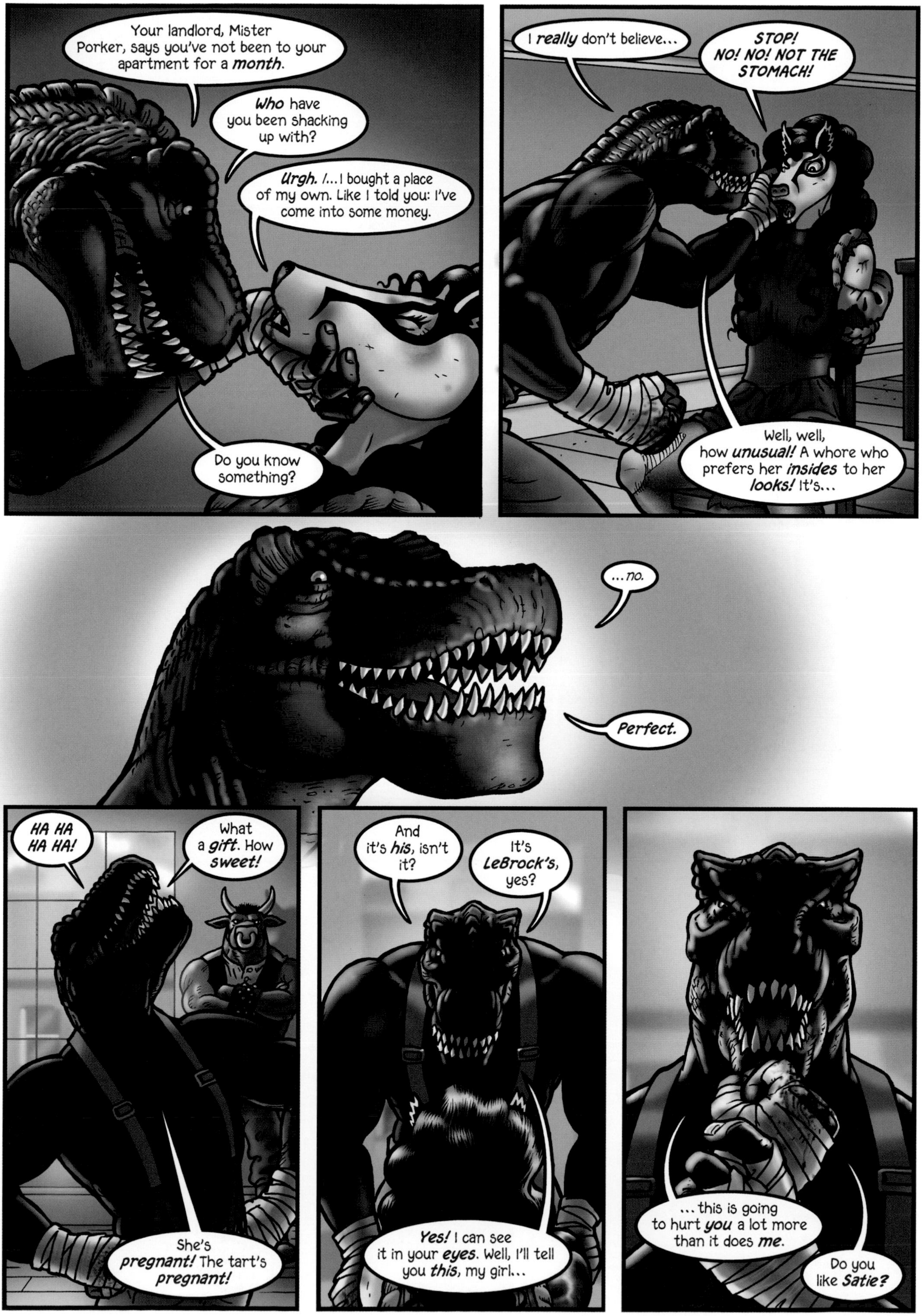
Your landlord, Mister Porker, says you've not been to your apartment for a *month*.
Who have you been shacking up with?
Urgh. I...I bought a place of my own. Like I told you: I've come into some money.
Do you know something?
I *really* don't believe...
STOP! NO! NO! NOT THE STOMACH!
Well, well, how *unusual!* A whore who prefers her *insides* to her *looks!* It's...
...no.
Perfect.
HA HA HA HA!
What a *gift*. How *sweet!*
She's *pregnant!* The tart's *pregnant!*
And it's *his*, isn't it?
It's *LeBrock's*, yes?
Yes! I can see it in your *eyes*. Well, I'll tell you *this*, my girl...
...this is going to hurt *you* a lot more than it does *me*.
Do you like *Satie?*

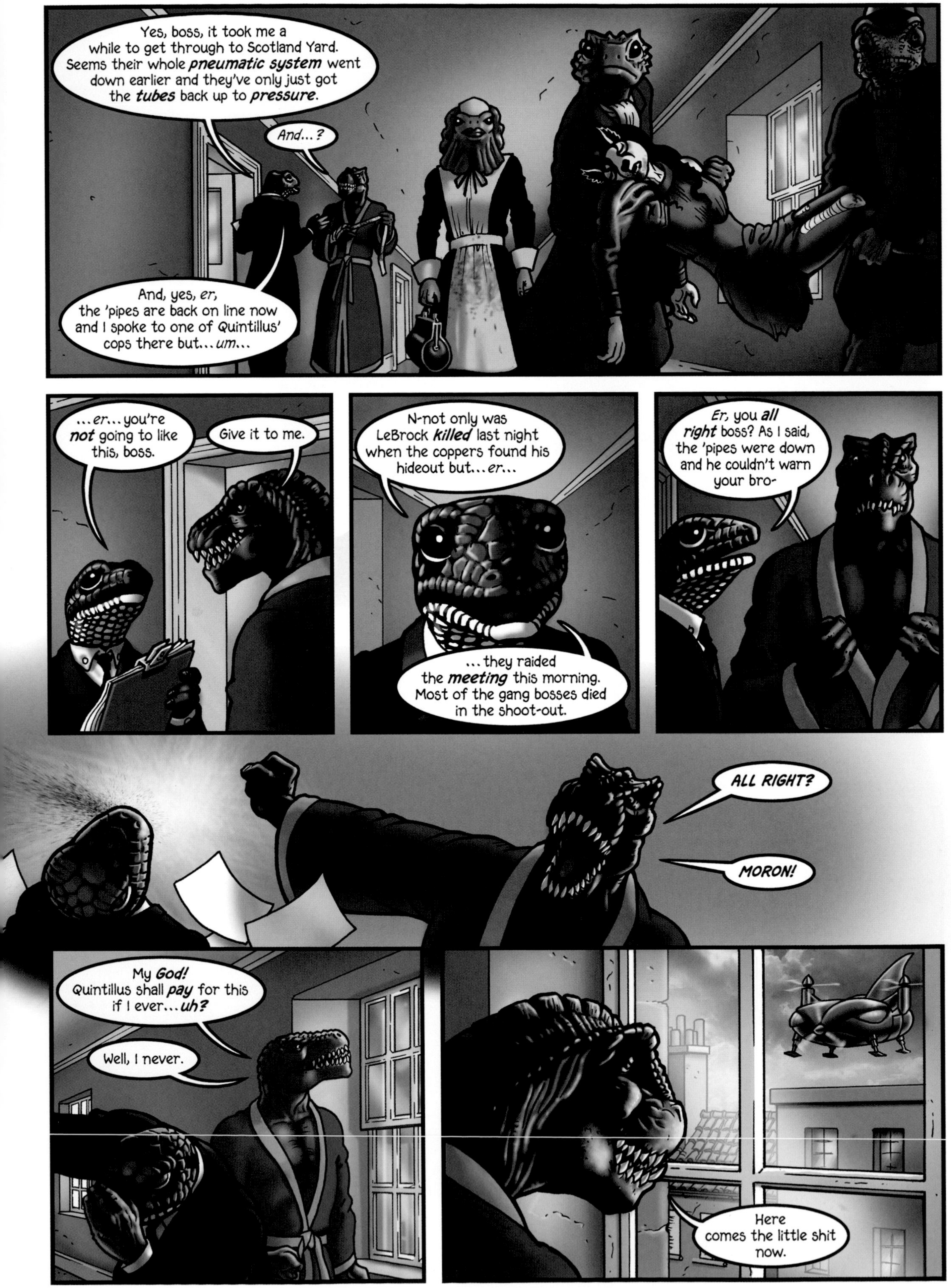

Yes, boss, it took me a while to get through to Scotland Yard. Seems their whole pneumatic system went down earlier and they've only just got the tubes back up to pressure.
And...?
And, yes, er, the 'pipes are back on line now and I spoke to one of Quintillus' cops there but...um...
...er...you're not going to like this, boss.
Give it to me.
N-not only was LeBrock killed last night when the coppers found his hideout but...er...
...they raided the meeting this morning. Most of the gang bosses died in the shoot-out.
Er, you all right boss? As I said, the 'pipes were down and he couldn't warn your bro-
ALL RIGHT?
MORON!
My God! Quintillus shall pay for this if I ever...uh?
Well, I never.
Here comes the little shit now.

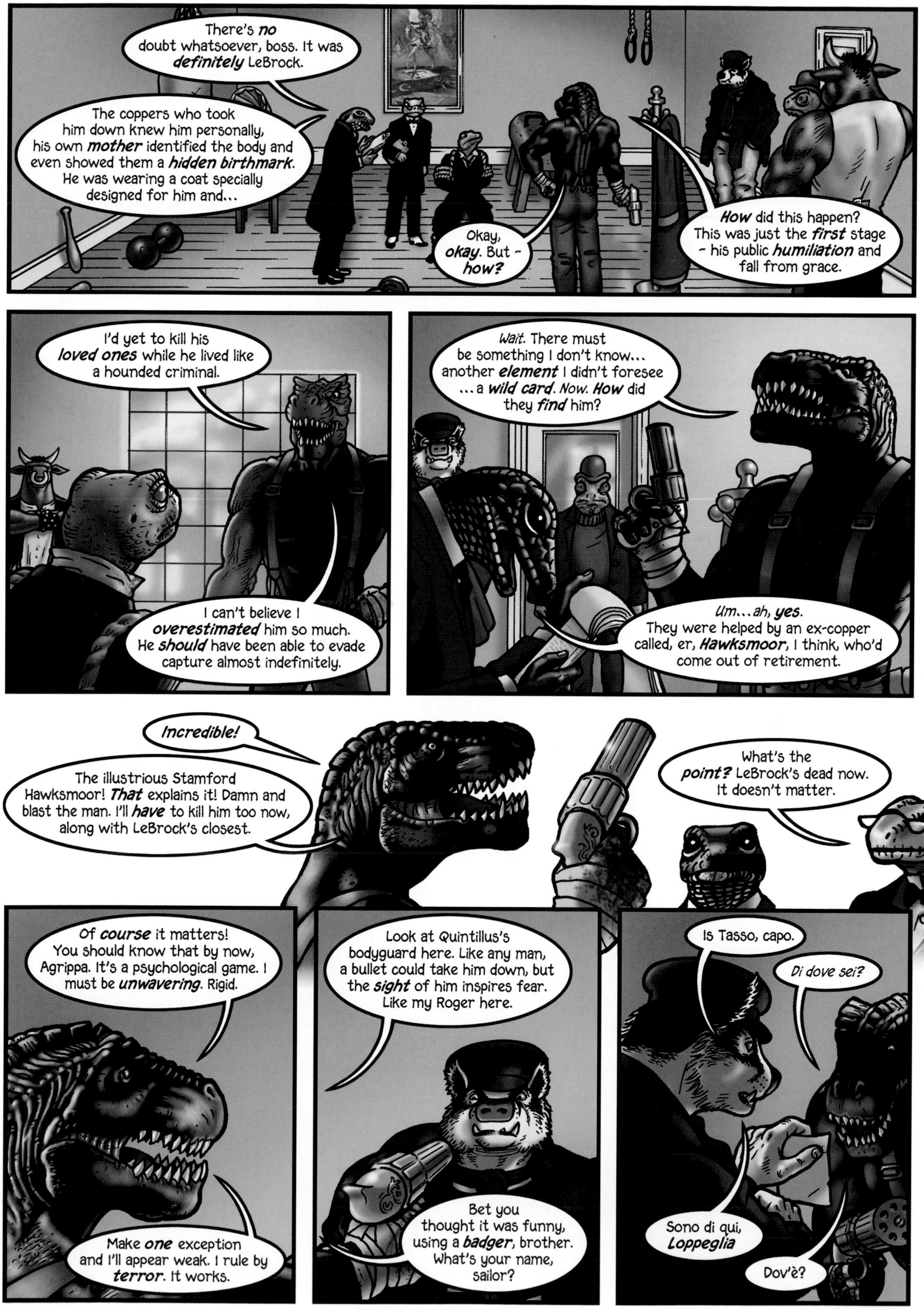
There's *no* doubt whatsoever, boss. It was *definitely* LeBrock.
The coppers who took him down knew him personally, his own *mother* identified the body and even showed them a *hidden birthmark*. He was wearing a coat specially designed for him and...
Okay, *okay*. But - *how?*
How did this happen? This was just the *first* stage - his public *humiliation* and fall from grace.
I'd yet to kill his *loved ones* while he lived like a hounded criminal.
I can't believe I *overestimated* him so much. He *should* have been able to evade capture almost indefinitely.
Wait. There must be something I don't know... another *element* I didn't foresee ... a *wild card*. *Now*. *How* did they *find* him?
Um...ah, yes. They were helped by an ex-copper called, er, *Hawksmoor*, I think, who'd come out of retirement.
Incredible!
The illustrious Stamford Hawksmoor! *That* explains it! Damn and blast the man. I'll *have* to kill him too now, along with LeBrock's closest.
What's the *point?* LeBrock's dead now. It doesn't matter.
Of *course* it matters! You should know that by now, Agrippa. It's a psychological game. I must be *unwavering*. Rigid.
Make *one* exception and I'll appear weak. I rule by *terror*. It works.
Look at Quintillus's bodyguard here. Like any man, a bullet could take him down, but the *sight* of him inspires fear. Like my Roger here.
Bet you thought it was funny, using a *badger*, brother. What's your name, sailor?
Is Tasso, capo.
Di dove sei?
Sono di qui, *Loppeglia*
Dov'è?

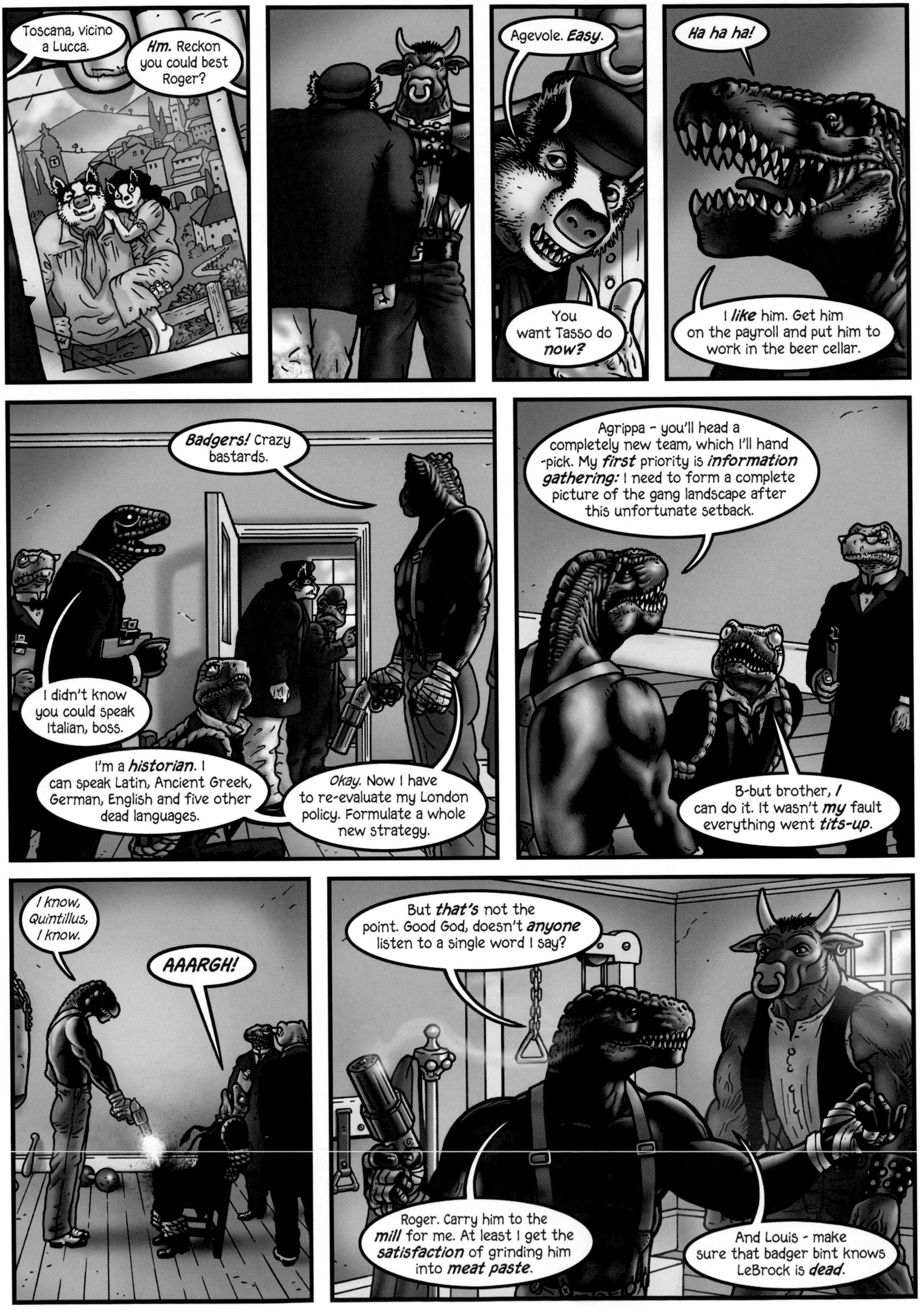
Toscana, vicino a Lucca.
Hm. Reckon you could best Roger?
Agevole. ***Easy.***
You want Tasso do ***now?***
Ha ha ha!
I ***like*** him. Get him on the payroll and put him to work in the beer cellar.
Badgers! Crazy bastards.
I didn't know you could speak Italian, boss.
I'm a ***historian***. I can speak Latin, Ancient Greek, German, English and five other dead languages.
Okay. Now I have to re-evaluate my London policy. Formulate a whole new strategy.
Agrippa - you'll head a completely new team, which I'll hand -pick. My ***first*** priority is ***information gathering:*** I need to form a complete picture of the gang landscape after this unfortunate setback.
B-but brother, ***I*** can do it. It wasn't ***my*** fault everything went ***tits-up***.
I know, Quintillus, I know.
AAARGH!
But ***that's*** not the point. Good God, doesn't ***anyone*** listen to a single word I say?
Roger. Carry him to the ***mill*** for me. At least I get the ***satisfaction*** of grinding him into ***meat paste***.
And Louis - make sure that badger bint knows LeBrock is ***dead***.

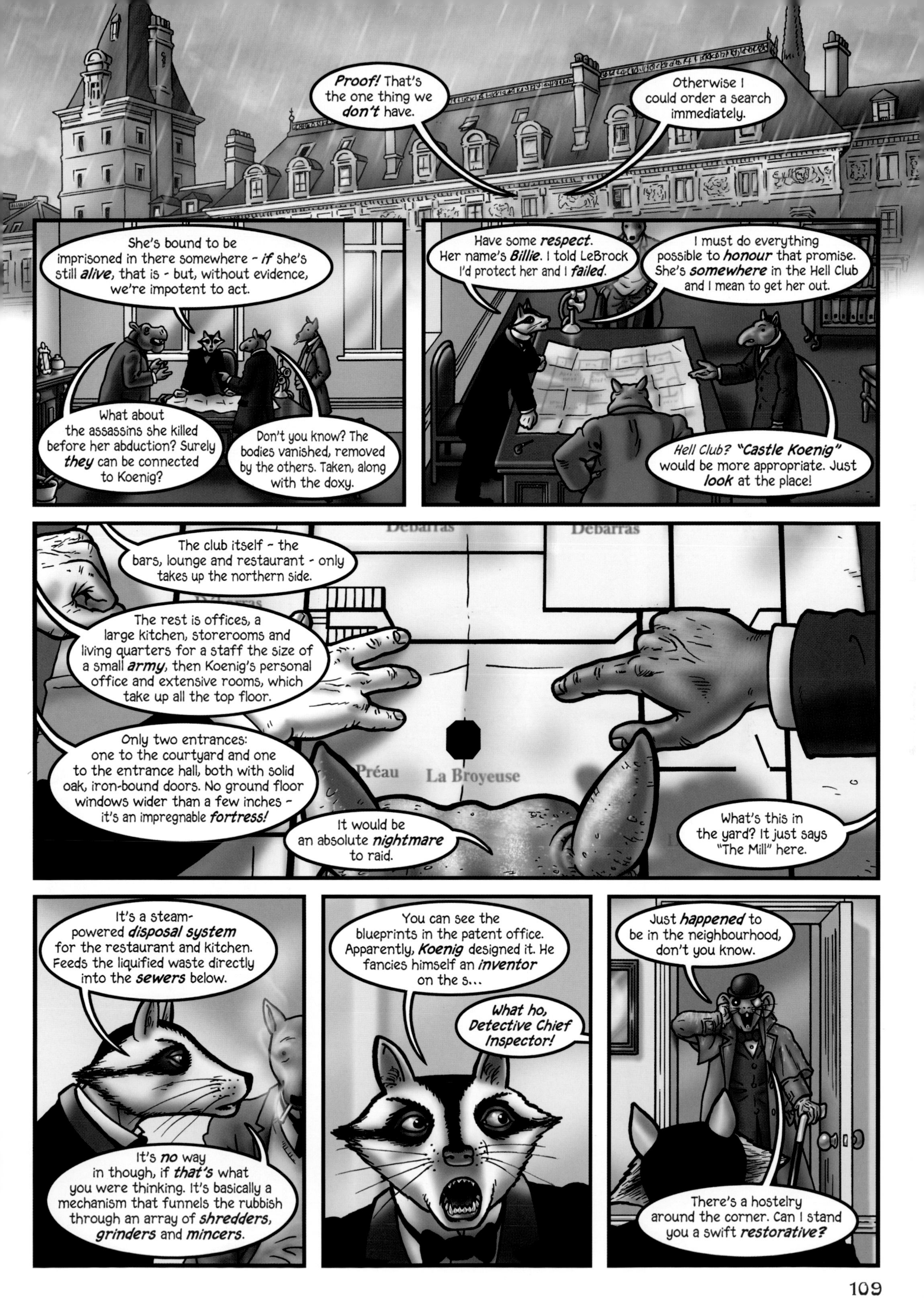
Proof! That's the one thing we don't have.
Otherwise I could order a search immediately.
She's bound to be imprisoned in there somewhere - if she's still alive, that is - but, without evidence, we're impotent to act.
What about the assassins she killed before her abduction? Surely they can be connected to Koenig?
Don't you know? The bodies vanished, removed by the others. Taken, along with the doxy.
Have some respect. Her name's Billie. I told LeBrock I'd protect her and I failed.
I must do everything possible to honour that promise. She's somewhere in the Hell Club and I mean to get her out.
Hell Club? "Castle Koenig" would be more appropriate. Just look at the place!
Debarras
Debarras
The club itself - the bars, lounge and restaurant - only takes up the northern side.
The rest is offices, a large kitchen, storerooms and living quarters for a staff the size of a small army, then Koenig's personal office and extensive rooms, which take up all the top floor.
Préau
La Broyeuse
Only two entrances: one to the courtyard and one to the entrance hall, both with solid oak, iron-bound doors. No ground floor windows wider than a few inches - it's an impregnable fortress!
It would be an absolute nightmare to raid.
What's this in the yard? It just says "The Mill" here.
It's a steam-powered disposal system for the restaurant and kitchen. Feeds the liquified waste directly into the sewers below.
It's no way in though, if that's what you were thinking. It's basically a mechanism that funnels the rubbish through an array of shredders, grinders and mincers.
You can see the blueprints in the patent office. Apparently, Koenig designed it. He fancies himself an inventor on the s...
What ho, Detective Chief Inspector!
Just happened to be in the neighbourhood, don't you know.
There's a hostelry around the corner. Can I stand you a swift restorative?

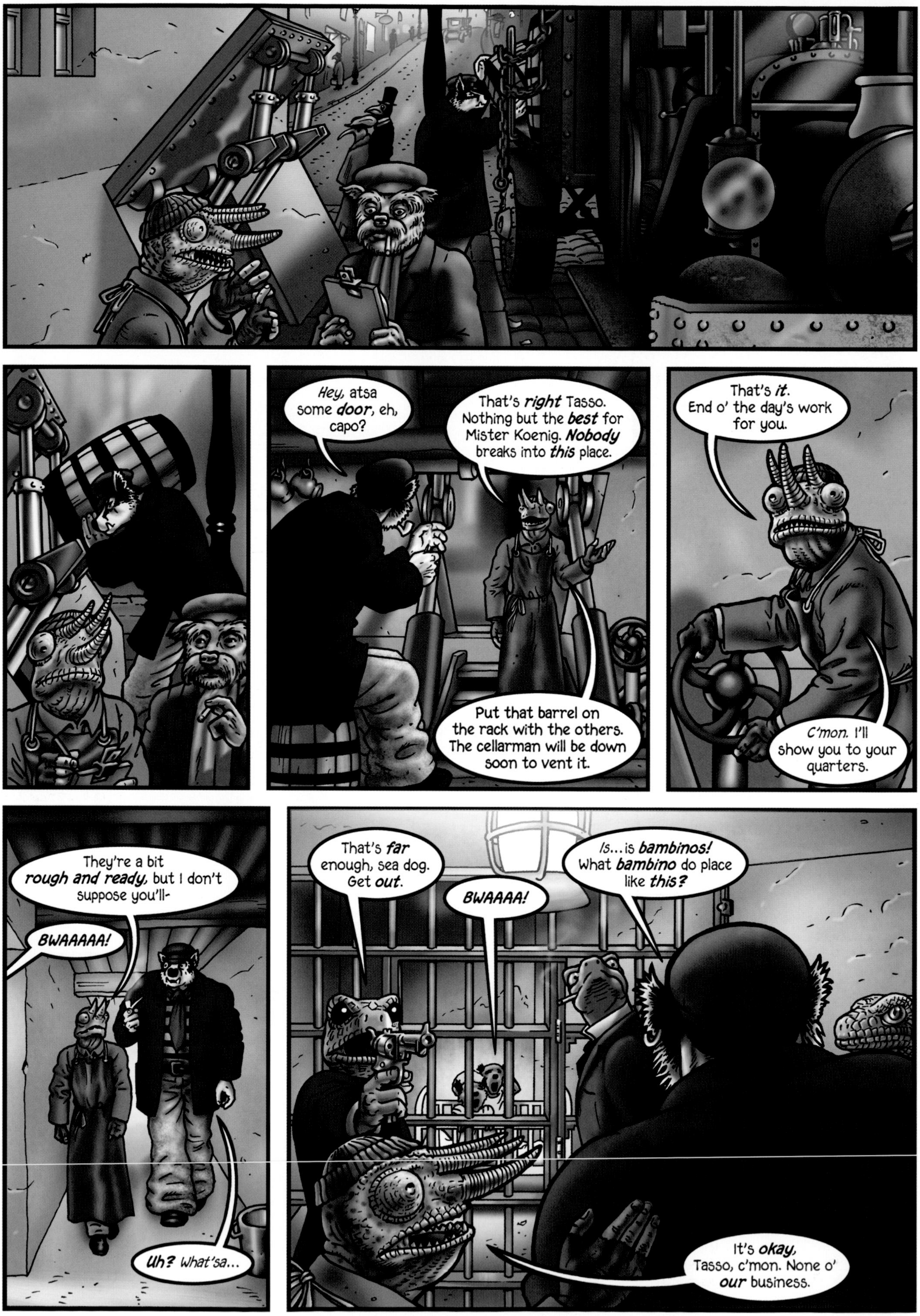
Hey, atsa some door, eh, capo?
That's right Tasso. Nothing but the best for Mister Koenig. Nobody breaks into this place.
Put that barrel on the rack with the others. The cellarman will be down soon to vent it.
That's it. End o' the day's work for you.
C'mon. I'll show you to your quarters.
They're a bit rough and ready, but I don't suppose you'll-
BWAAAAA!
Uh? What'sa...
That's far enough, sea dog. Get out.
BWAAAA!
Is... is bambinos! What bambino do place like this?
It's okay, Tasso, c'mon. None o' our business.

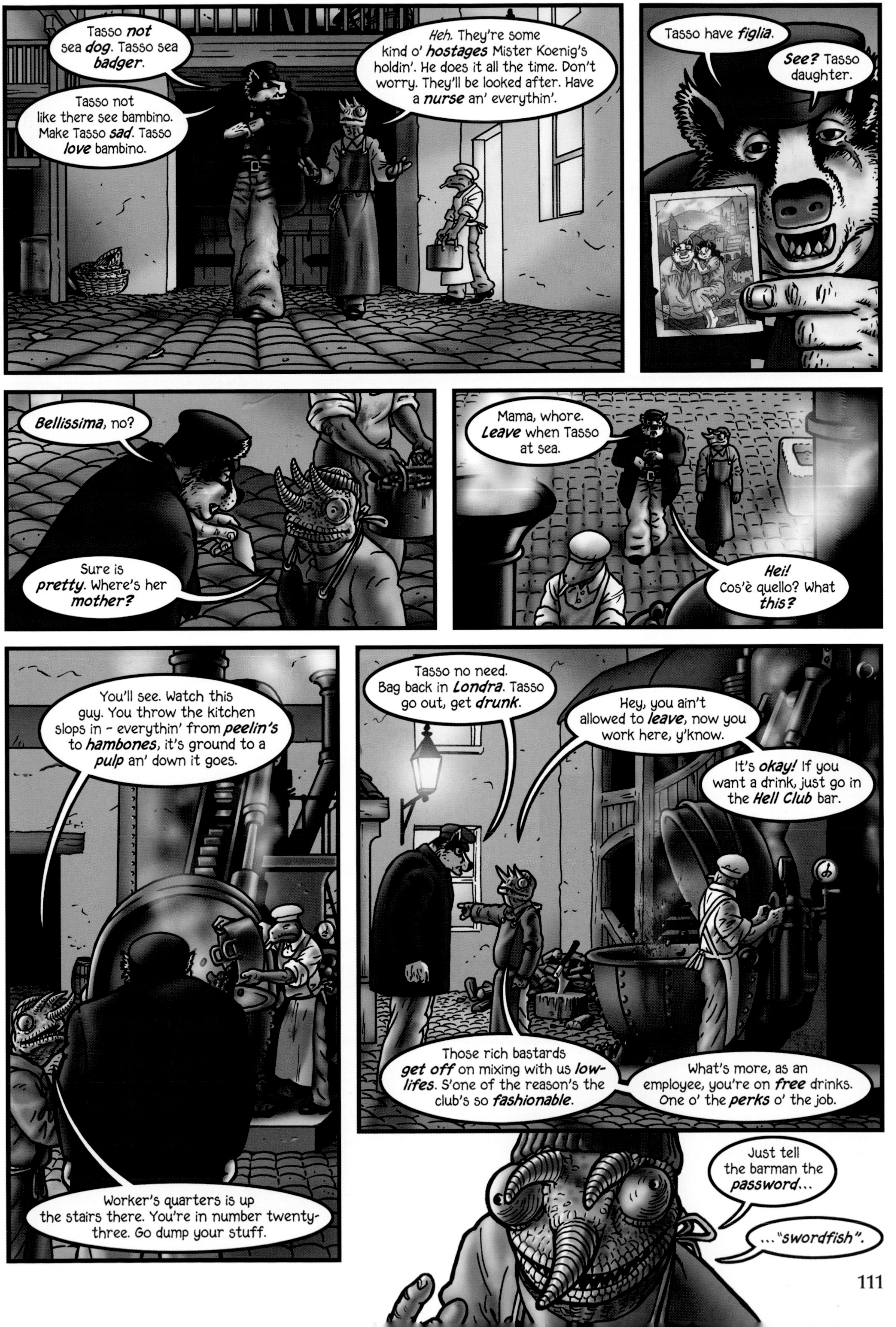
Tasso not sea dog. Tasso sea badger.
Tasso not like there see bambino. Make Tasso sad. Tasso love bambino.
Heh. They're some kind o' hostages Mister Koenig's holdin'. He does it all the time. Don't worry. They'll be looked after. Have a nurse an' everythin'.
Tasso have figlia.
See? Tasso daughter.
Bellissima, no?
Sure is pretty. Where's her mother?
Mama, whore. Leave when Tasso at sea.
Hei! Cos'è quello? What this?
You'll see. Watch this guy. You throw the kitchen slops in - everythin' from peelin's to hambones, it's ground to a pulp an' down it goes.
Worker's quarters is up the stairs there. You're in number twenty-three. Go dump your stuff.
Tasso no need. Bag back in Londra. Tasso go out, get drunk.
Hey, you ain't allowed to leave, now you work here, y'know.
It's okay! If you want a drink, just go in the Hell Club bar.
Those rich bastards get off on mixing with us low-lifes. S'one of the reason's the club's so fashionable.
What's more, as an employee, you're on free drinks. One o' the perks o' the job.
Just tell the barman the password...
..."swordfish".

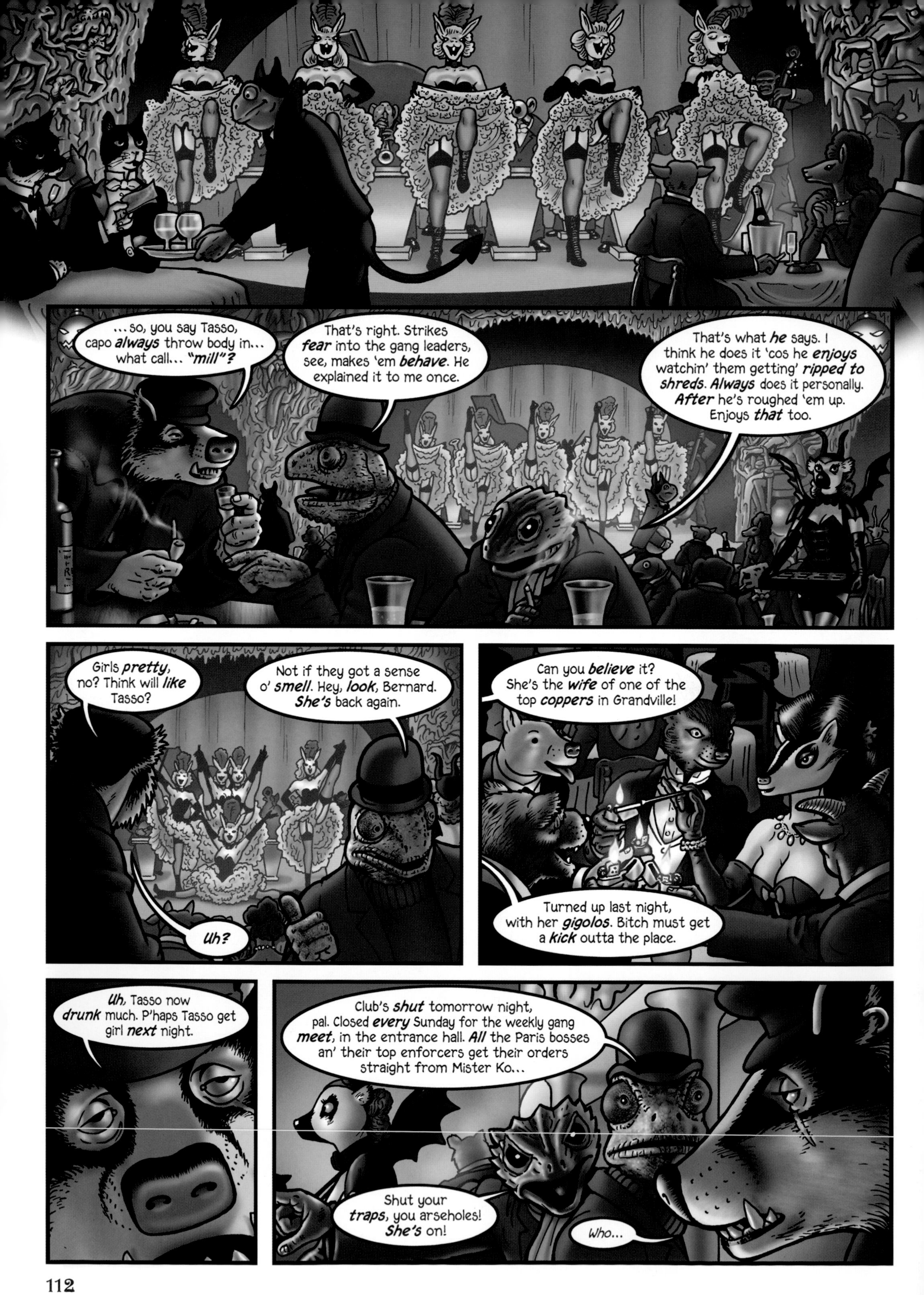
...so, you say Tasso, capo *always* throw body in... what call... *"mill"*?
That's right. Strikes *fear* into the gang leaders, see, makes 'em *behave*. He explained it to me once.
That's what *he* says. I think he does it 'cos he *enjoys* watchin' them getting' *ripped to shreds*. *Always* does it personally. *After* he's roughed 'em up. Enjoys *that* too.
Girls *pretty*, no? Think will *like* Tasso?
Not if they got a sense o' *smell*. Hey, *look*, Bernard. *She's* back again.
Uh?
Can you *believe* it? She's the *wife* of one of the top *coppers* in Grandville!
Turned up last night, with her *gigolos*. Bitch must get a *kick* outta the place.
Uh, Tasso now *drunk* much. P'haps Tasso get girl *next* night.
Club's *shut* tomorrow night, pal. Closed *every* Sunday for the weekly gang *meet*, in the entrance hall. *All* the Paris bosses an' their top enforcers get their orders straight from Mister Ko...
Shut your *traps*, you arseholes! *She's* on!
Who...

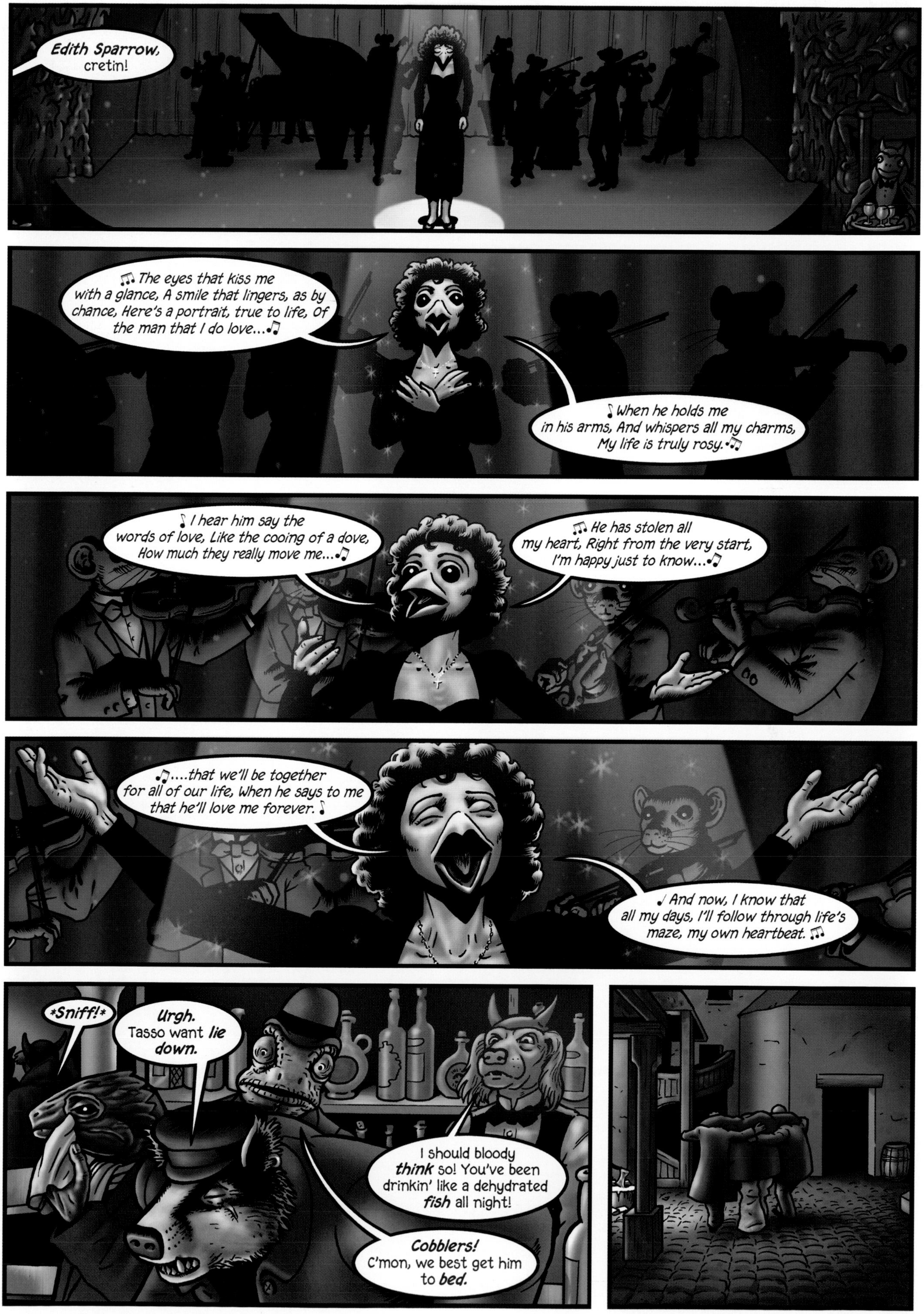
Edith Sparrow, cretin!
♫ The eyes that kiss me with a glance, A smile that lingers, as by chance, Here's a portrait, true to life, Of the man that I do love...♫
♪ When he holds me in his arms, And whispers all my charms, My life is truly rosy.•♫
♪ I hear him say the words of love, Like the cooing of a dove, How much they really move me...♫
♫ He has stolen all my heart, Right from the very start, I'm happy just to know...•♫
•♫....that we'll be together for all of our life, When he says to me that he'll love me forever. ♪
♩ And now, I know that all my days, I'll follow through life's maze, my own heartbeat. ♫
Sniff!
Urgh. Tasso want ***lie down.***
I should bloody ***think*** so! You've been drinkin' like a dehydrated ***fish*** all night!
Cobblers! C'mon, we best get him to ***bed.***

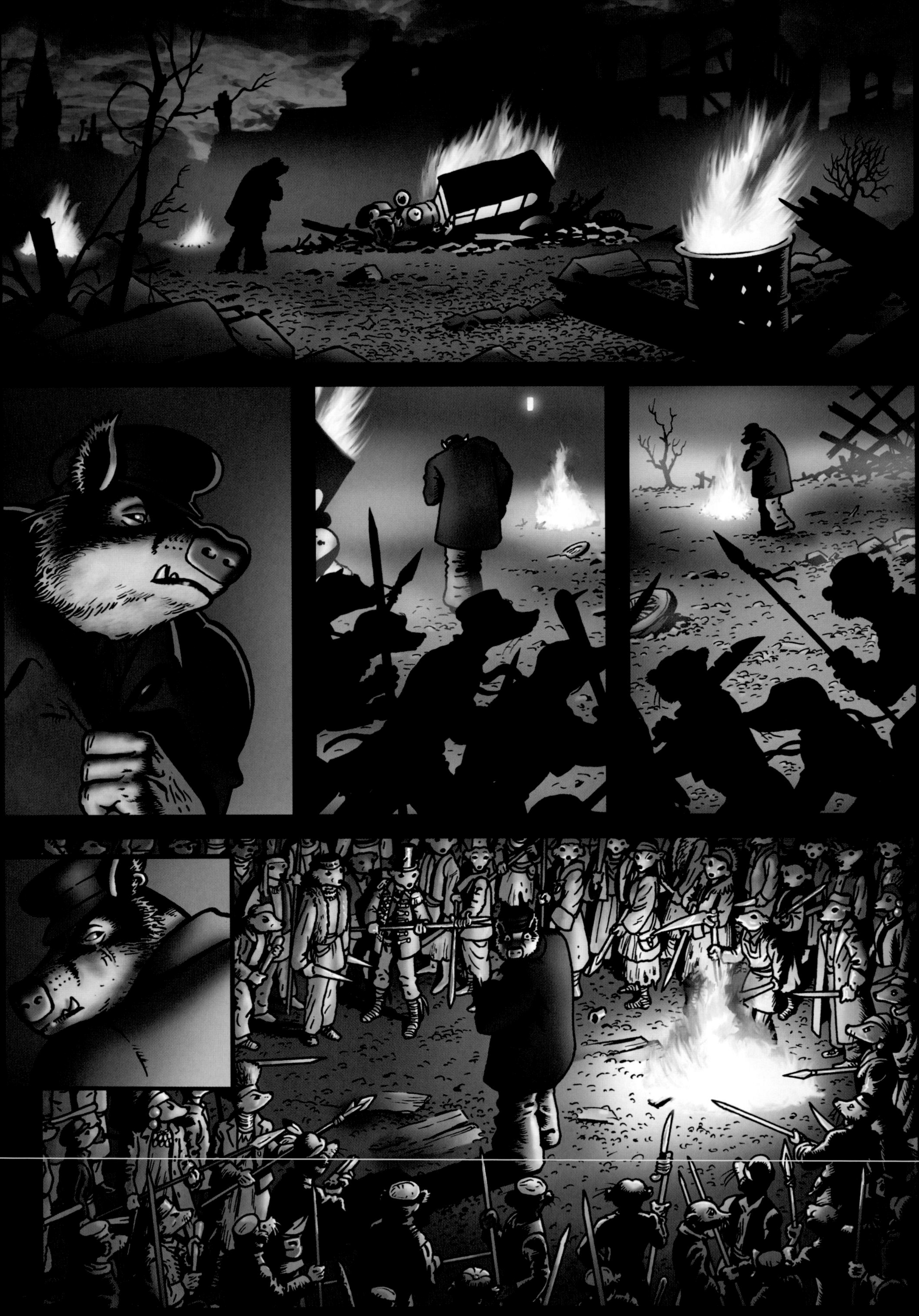

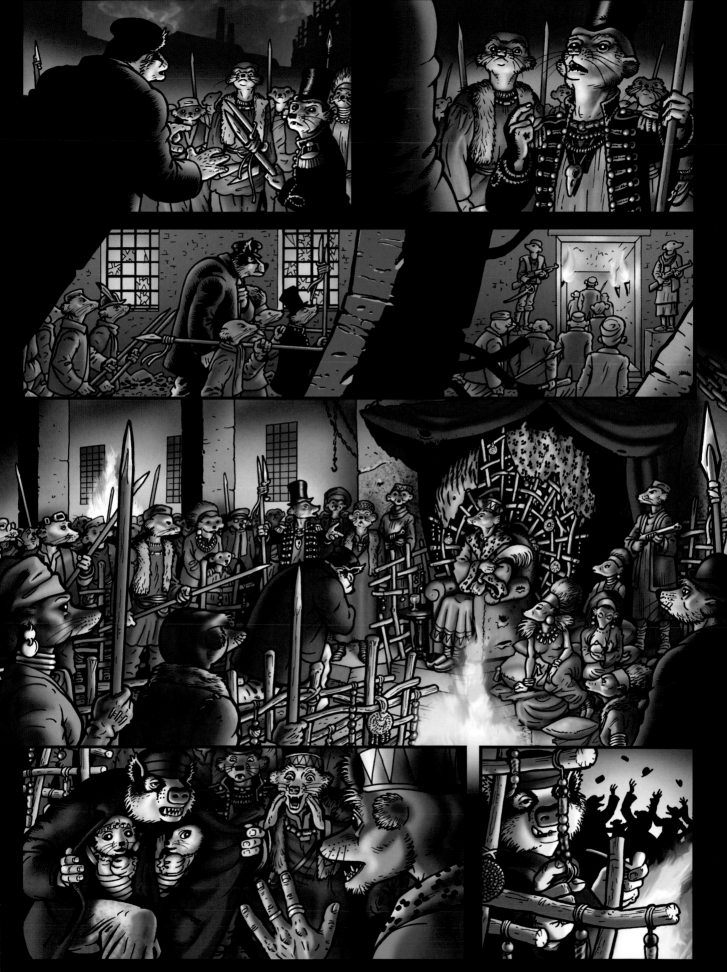

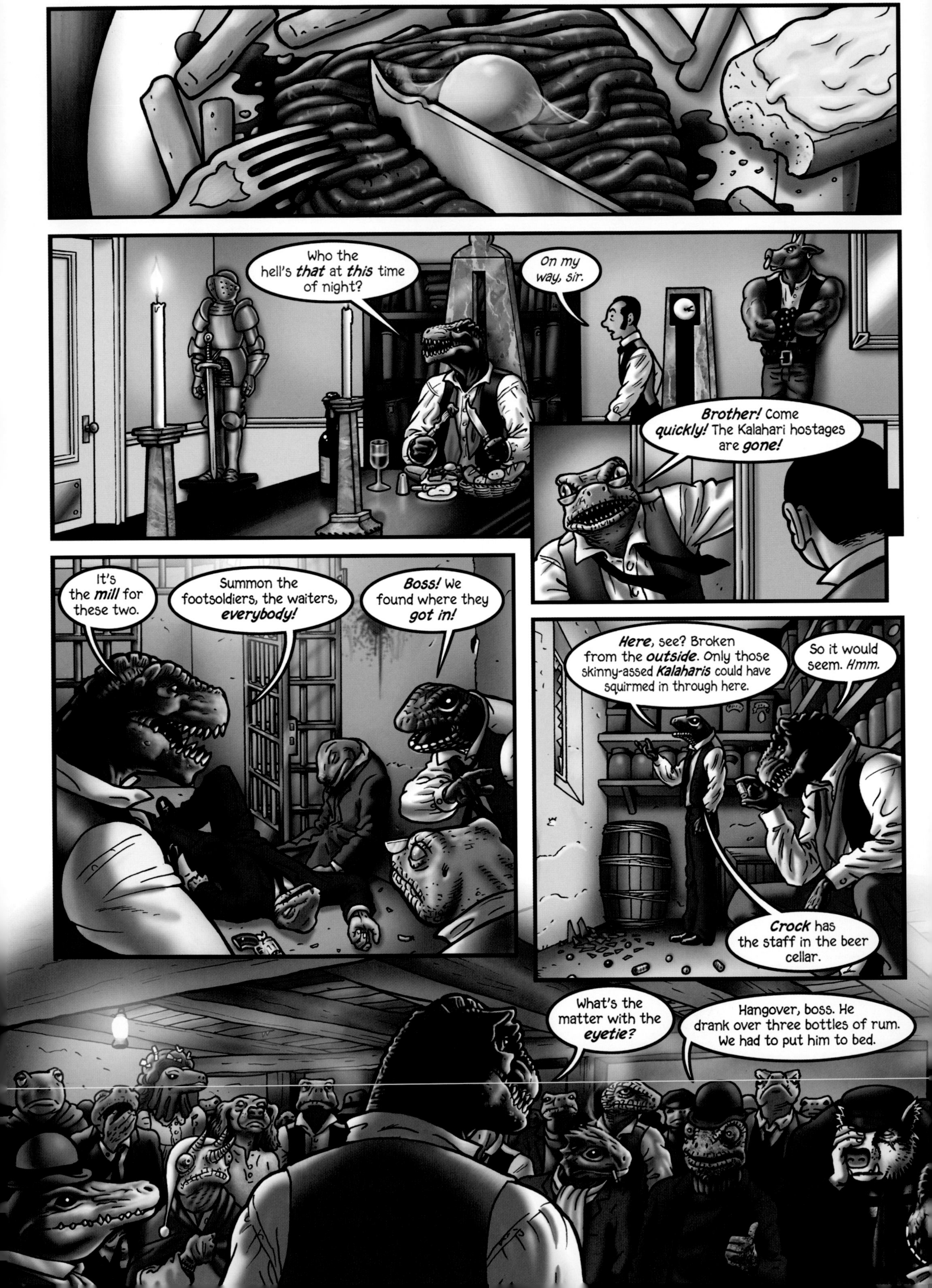
Who the hell's *that* at *this* time of night?
On my way, sir.
Brother! Come ***quickly!*** The Kalahari hostages are ***gone!***
It's the ***mill*** for these two.
Summon the footsoldiers, the waiters, ***everybody!***
Boss! We found where they ***got in!***
Here, see? Broken from the ***outside***. Only those skinny-assed ***Kalaharis*** could have squirmed in through here.
So it would seem. *Hmm.*
Crock has the staff in the beer cellar.
What's the matter with the ***eyetie?***
Hangover, boss. He drank over three bottles of rum. We had to put him to bed.

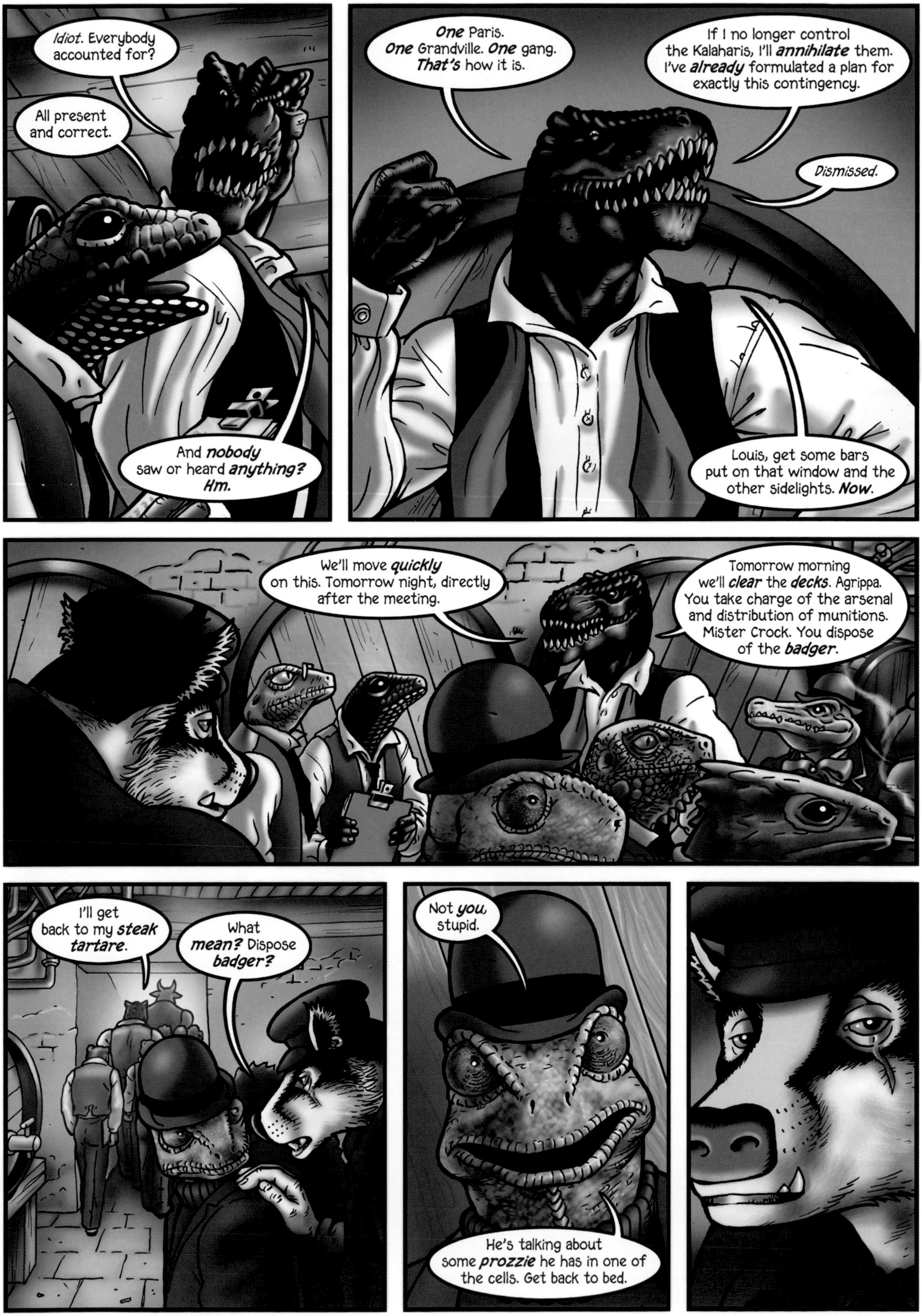
Idiot. Everybody accounted for?
All present and correct.
And nobody saw or heard anything? Hm.
One Paris. One Grandville. One gang. That's how it is.
If I no longer control the Kalaharis, I'll annihilate them. I've already formulated a plan for exactly this contingency.
Dismissed.
Louis, get some bars put on that window and the other sidelights. Now.
We'll move quickly on this. Tomorrow night, directly after the meeting.
Tomorrow morning we'll clear the decks. Agrippa. You take charge of the arsenal and distribution of munitions. Mister Crock. You dispose of the badger.
I'll get back to my steak tartare.
What mean? Dispose badger?
Not you, stupid.
He's talking about some prozzie he has in one of the cells. Get back to bed.

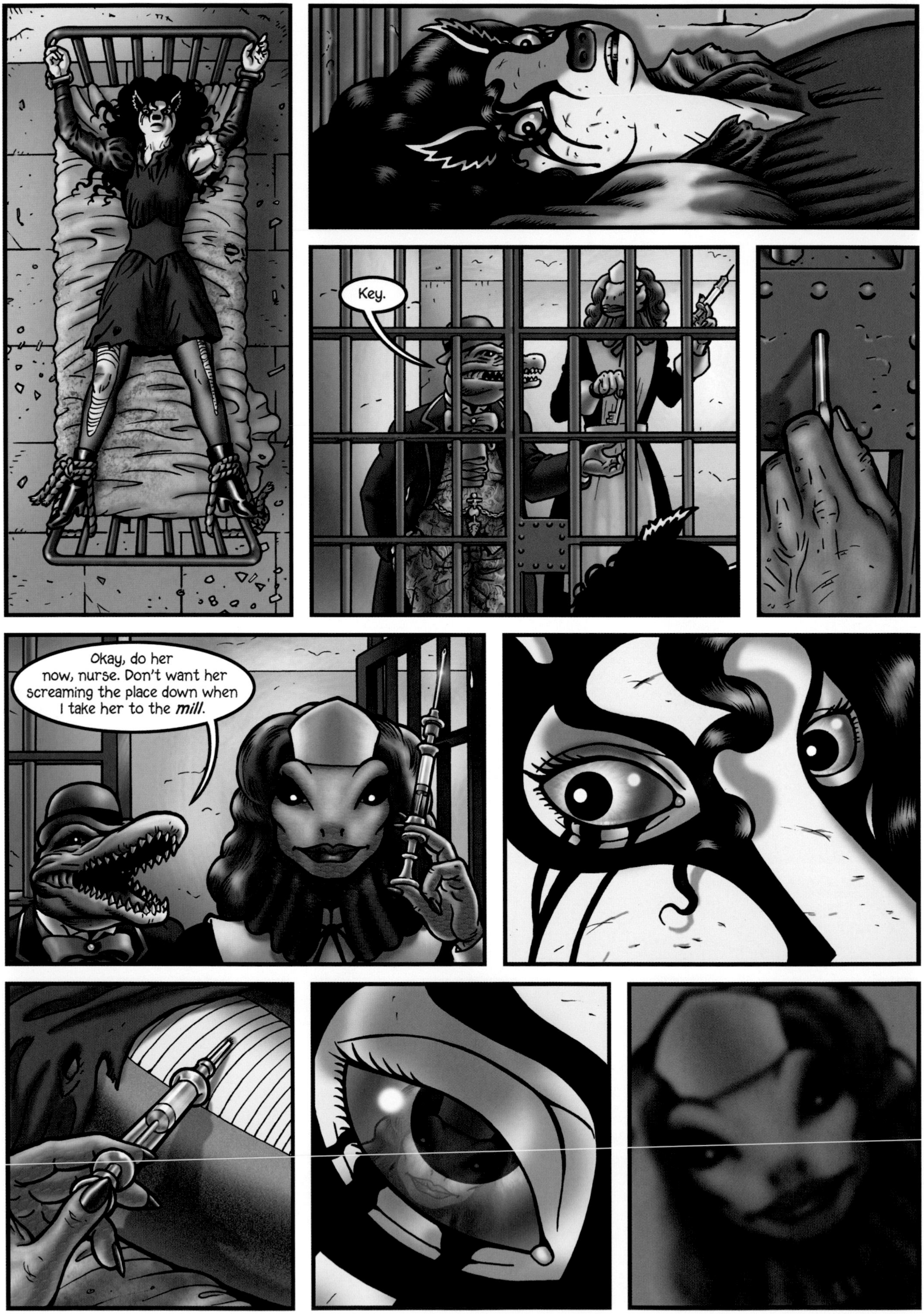
Key.
Okay, do her now, nurse. Don't want her screaming the place down when I take her to the *mill*.

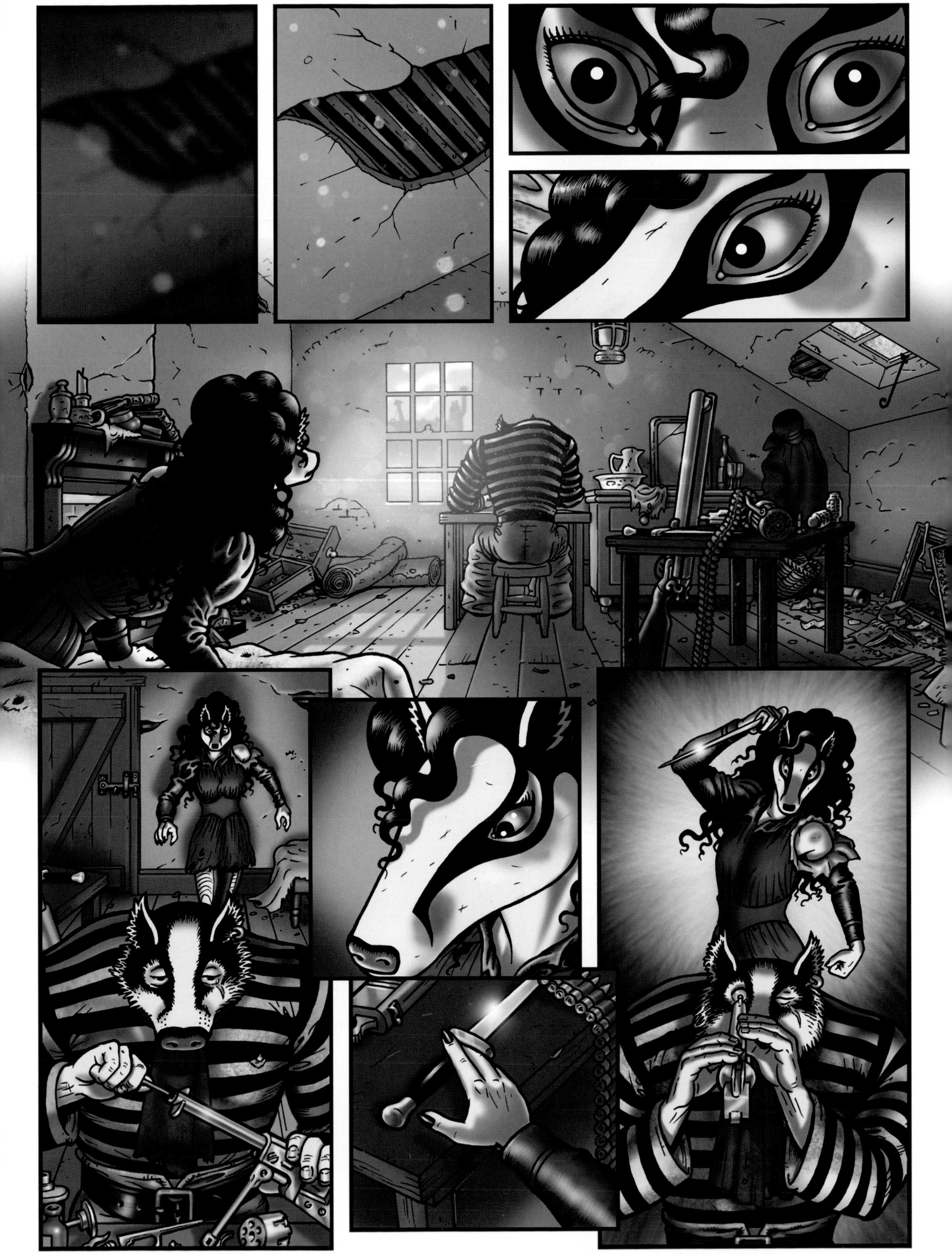

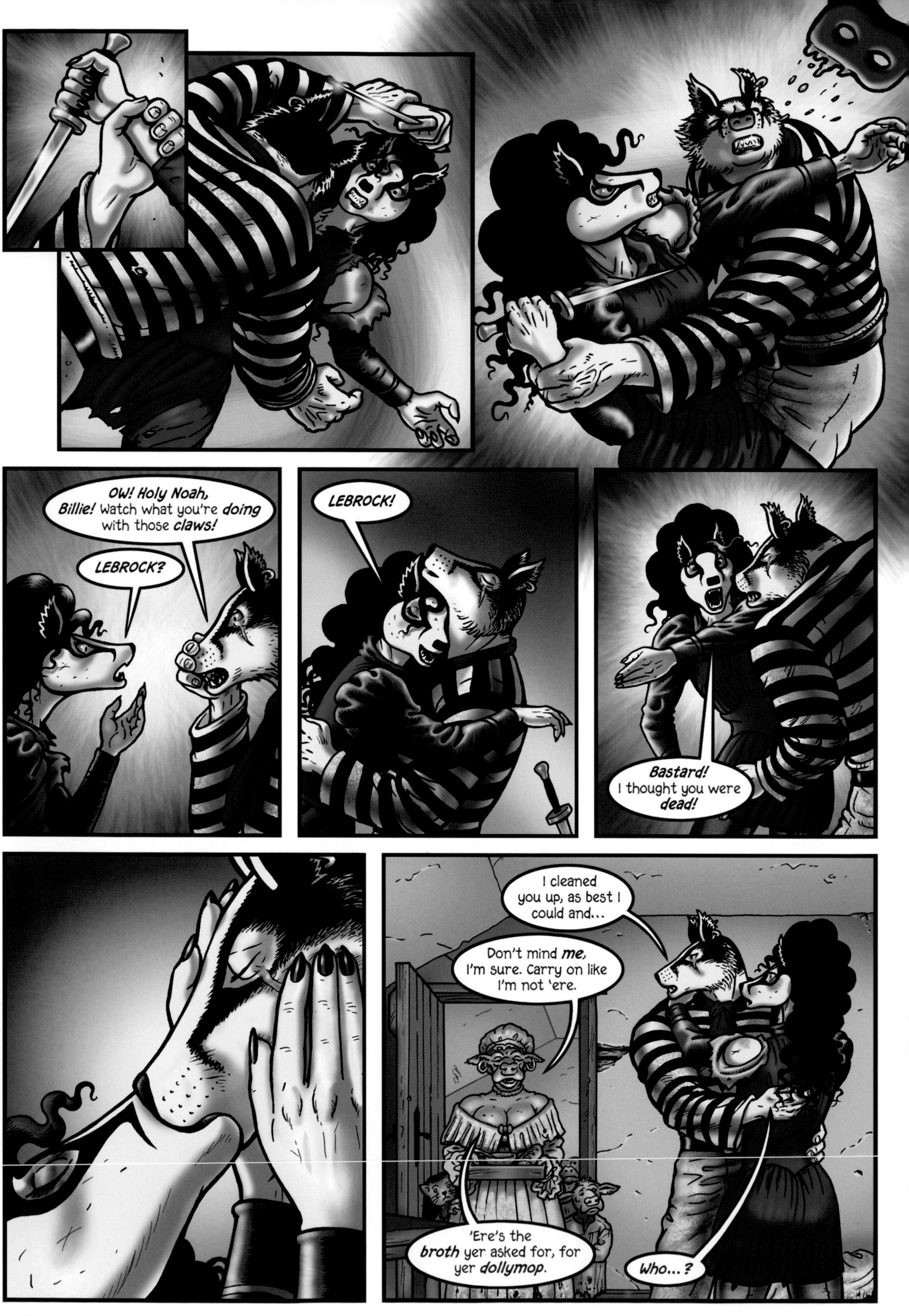
OW! Holy Noah, Billie! Watch what you're doing with those claws!
LEBROCK?
LEBROCK!
Bastard! I thought you were dead!
I cleaned you up, as best I could and...
Don't mind me, I'm sure. Carry on like I'm not 'ere.
'Ere's the broth yer asked for, for yer dollymop.
Who...?

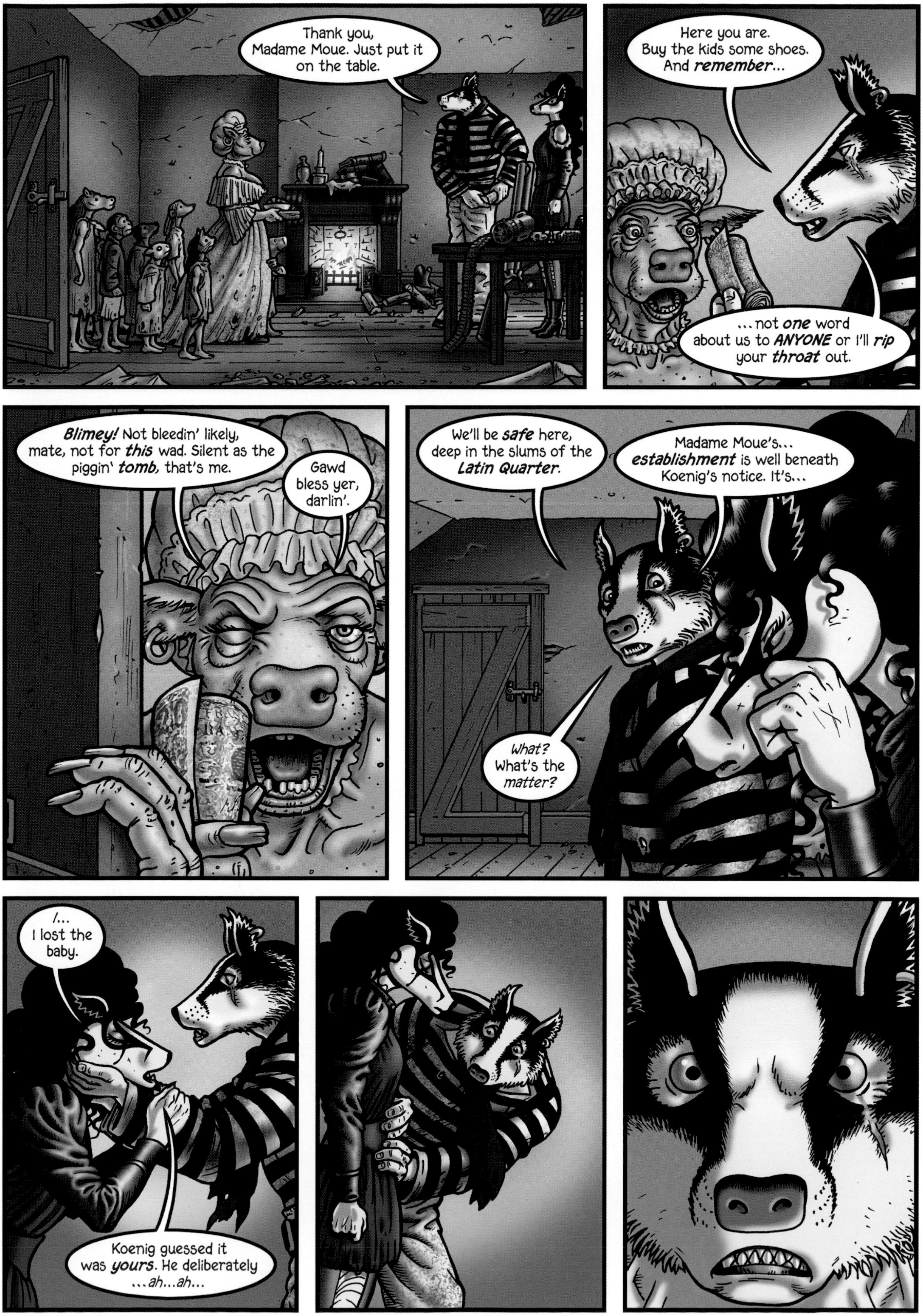
Thank you, Madame Moue. Just put it on the table.
Here you are. Buy the kids some shoes. And *remember*...
...not *one* word about us to *ANYONE* or I'll *rip* your *throat* out.
Blimey! Not bleedin' likely, mate, not for *this* wad. Silent as the piggin' *tomb,* that's me.
Gawd bless yer, darlin'.
We'll be *safe* here, deep in the slums of the *Latin Quarter*.
Madame Moue's... *establishment* is well beneath Koenig's notice. It's...
What? What's the matter?
I... I lost the baby.
Koenig guessed it was *yours*. He deliberately *...ah...ah...*

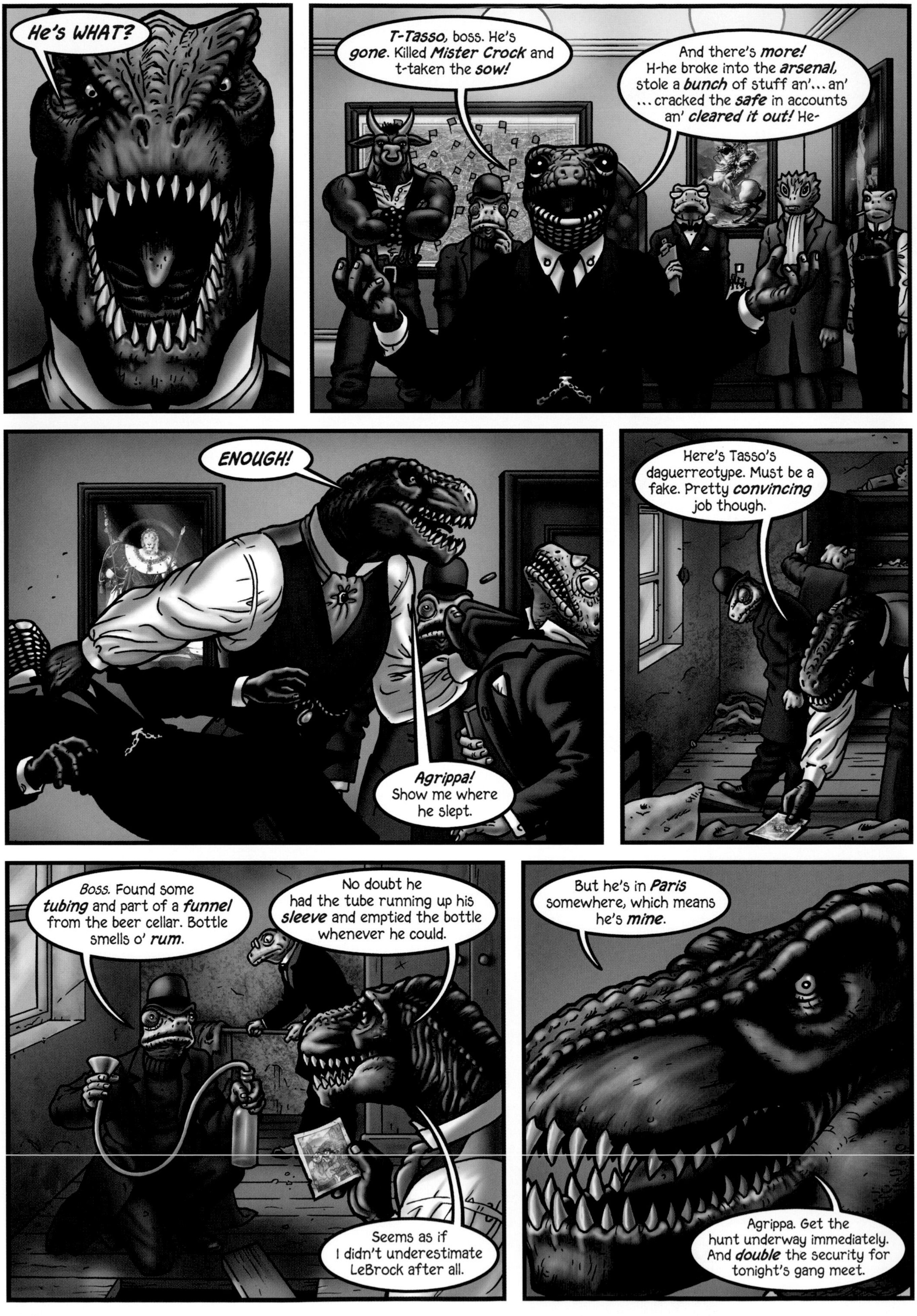
He's WHAT?
T-Tasso, boss. He's gone. Killed Mister Crock and t-taken the sow!
And there's more! H-he broke into the arsenal, stole a bunch of stuff an'... an' ... cracked the safe in accounts an' cleared it out! He-
ENOUGH!
Agrippa! Show me where he slept.
Here's Tasso's daguerreotype. Must be a fake. Pretty convincing job though.
Boss. Found some tubing and part of a funnel from the beer cellar. Bottle smells o' rum.
No doubt he had the tube running up his sleeve and emptied the bottle whenever he could.
Seems as if I didn't underestimate LeBrock after all.
But he's in Paris somewhere, which means he's mine.
Agrippa. Get the hunt underway immediately. And double the security for tonight's gang meet.

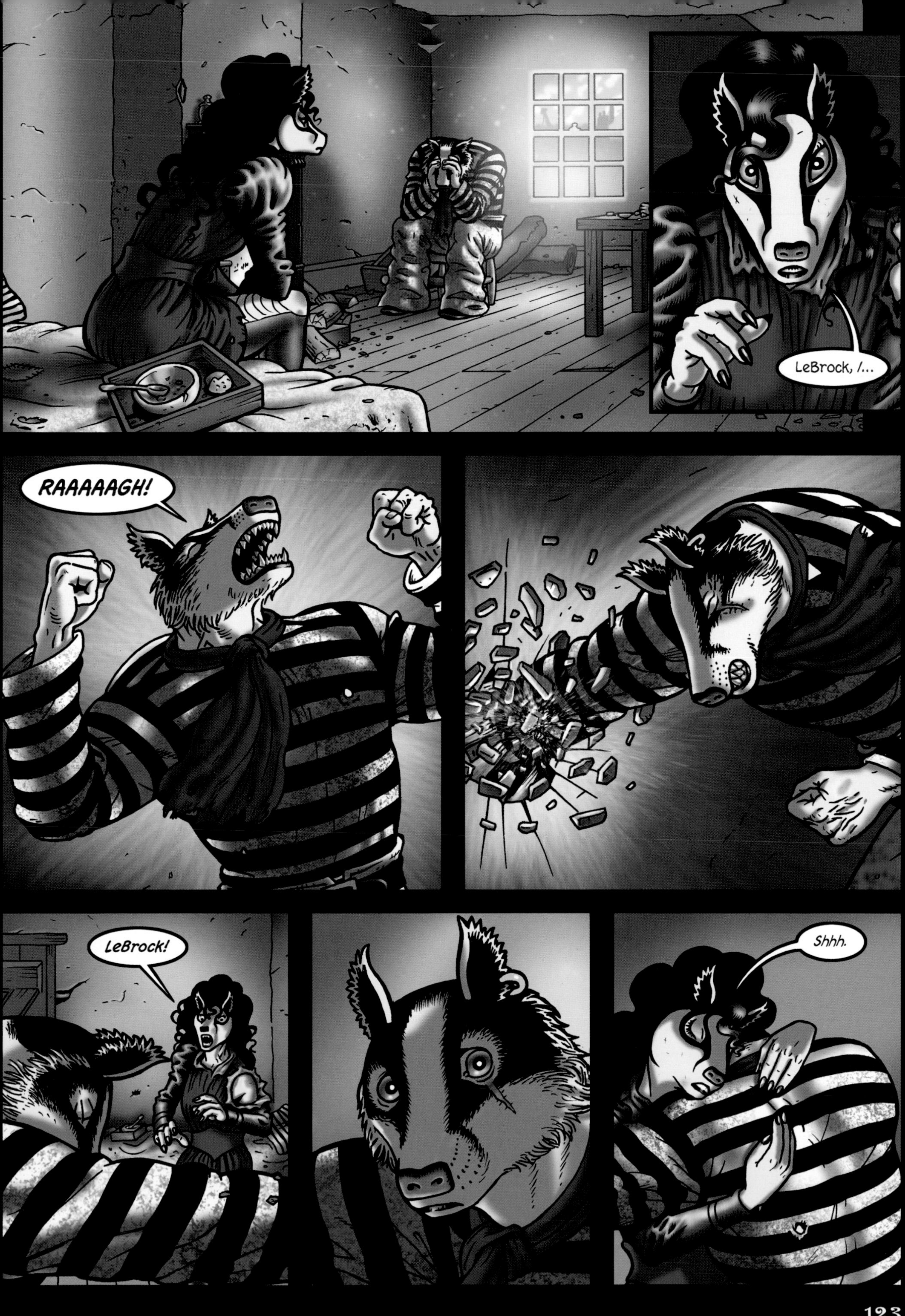
LeBrock, I...
RAAAAAGH!
LeBrock!
Shhh.

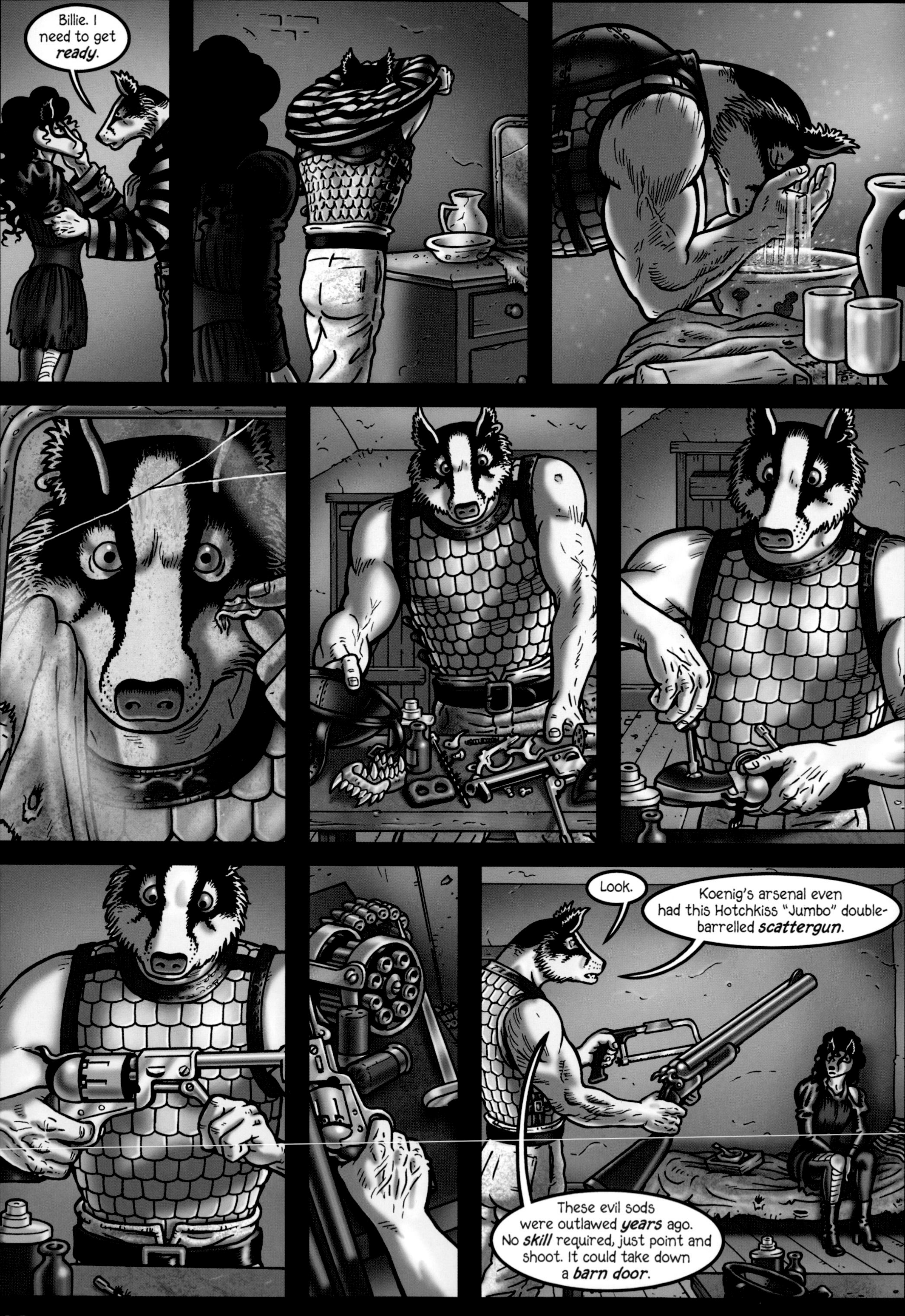

Billie. I need to get *ready*.
Look.
Koenig's arsenal even had this Hotchkiss "Jumbo" double-barrelled *scattergun*.
These evil sods were outlawed *years* ago. No *skill* required, just point and shoot. It could take down a *barn door*.

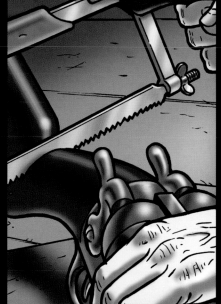

125

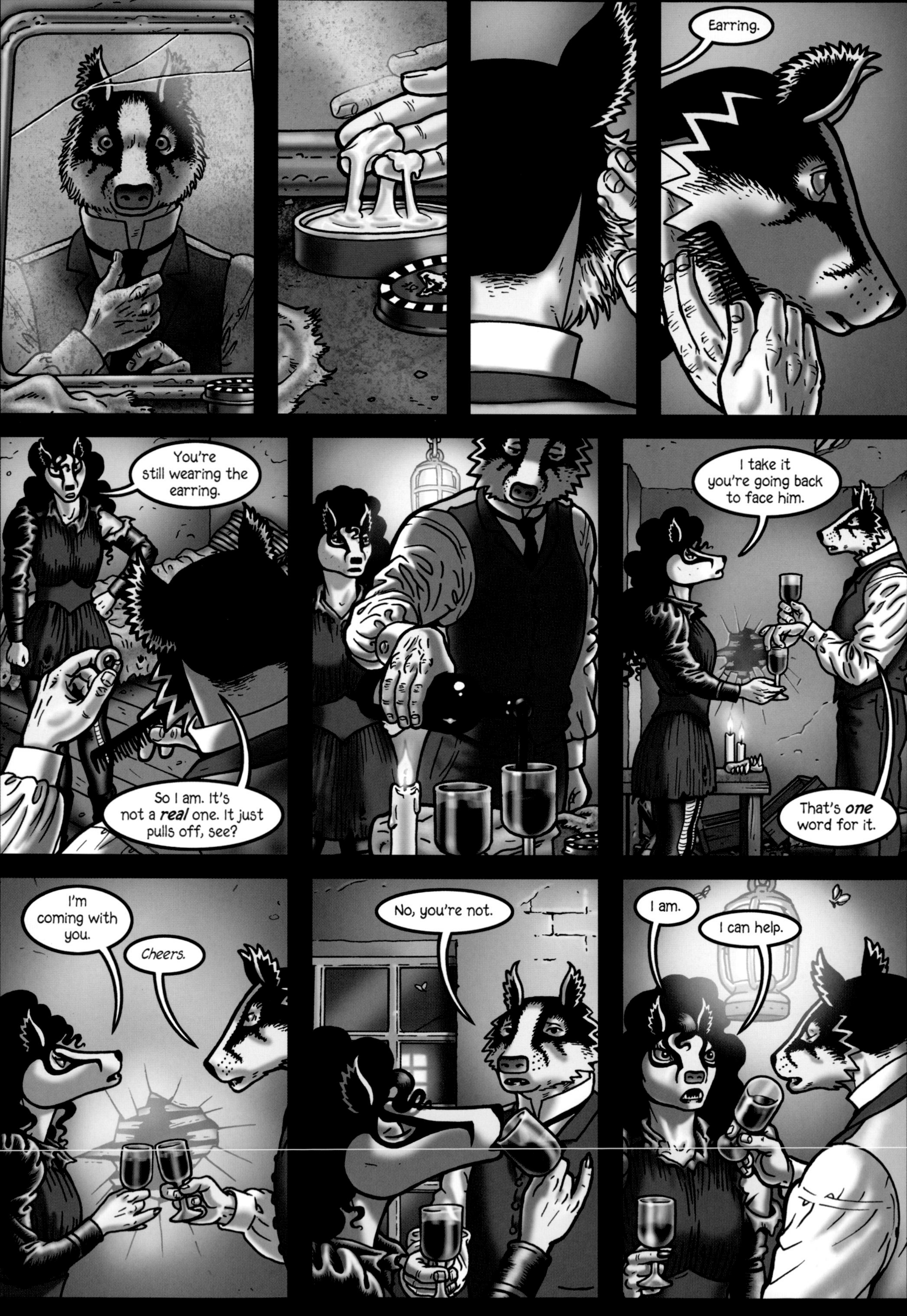
Earring.
You're still wearing the earring.
So I am. It's not a *real* one. It just pulls off, see?
I take it you're going back to face him.
That's *one* word for it.
I'm coming with you.
Cheers.
No, you're not.
I am.
I can help.

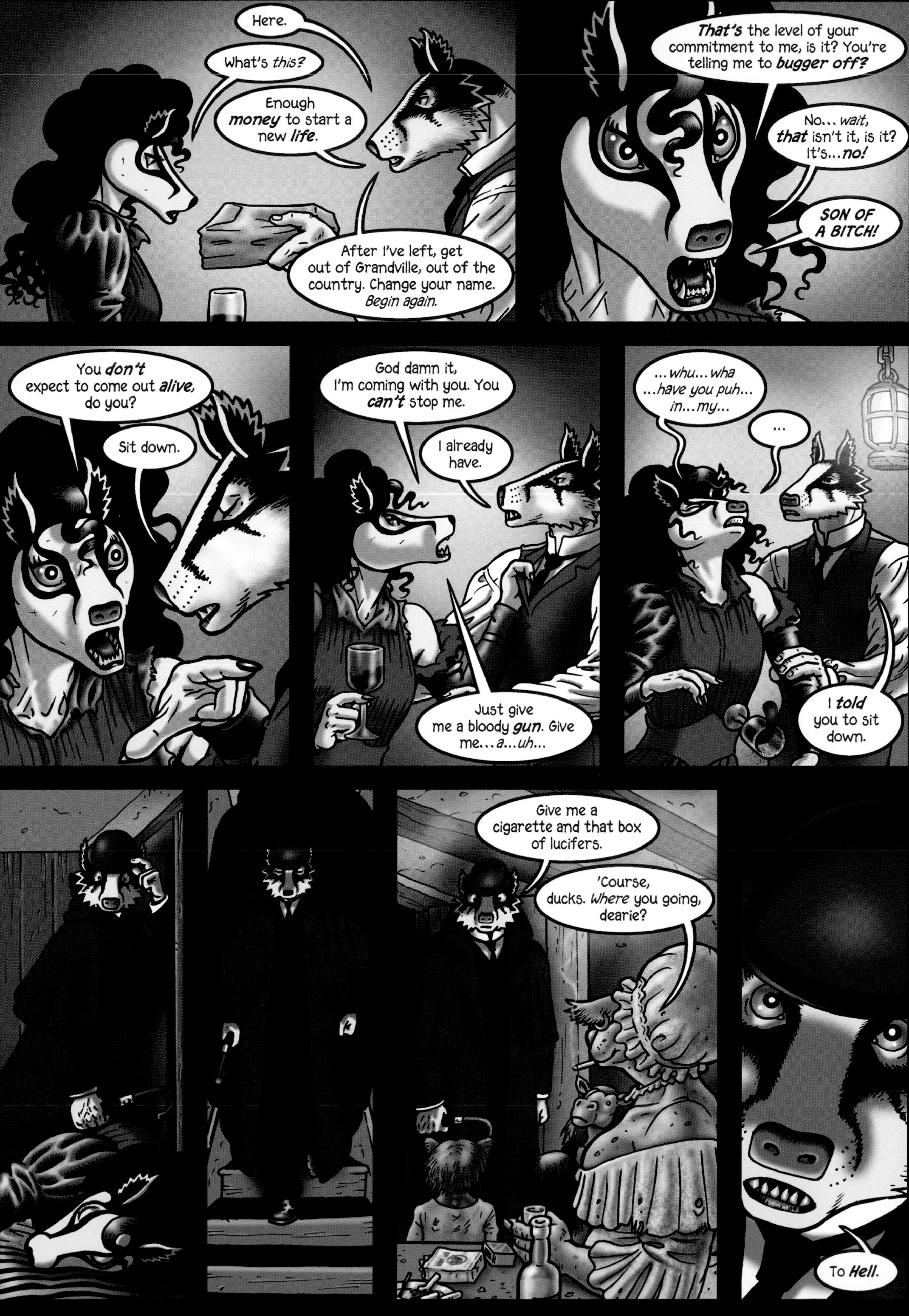

Here.
What's *this?*
Enough **money** to start a new **life**.
After I've left, get out of Grandville, out of the country. Change your name. *Begin again.*
That's the level of your commitment to me, is it? You're telling me to ***bugger off?***
No... *wait,* ***that*** isn't it, is it? It's... ***no!***
SON OF A BITCH!
You ***don't*** expect to come out ***alive,*** do you?
Sit down.
God damn it, I'm coming with you. You ***can't*** stop me.
I already have.
Just give me a bloody ***gun.*** Give me... *a... uh...*
...whu... wha ...have you puh... in... my...
...
I ***told*** you to sit down.
Give me a cigarette and that box of lucifers.
'Course, ducks. *Where* you going, dearie?
To ***Hell.***

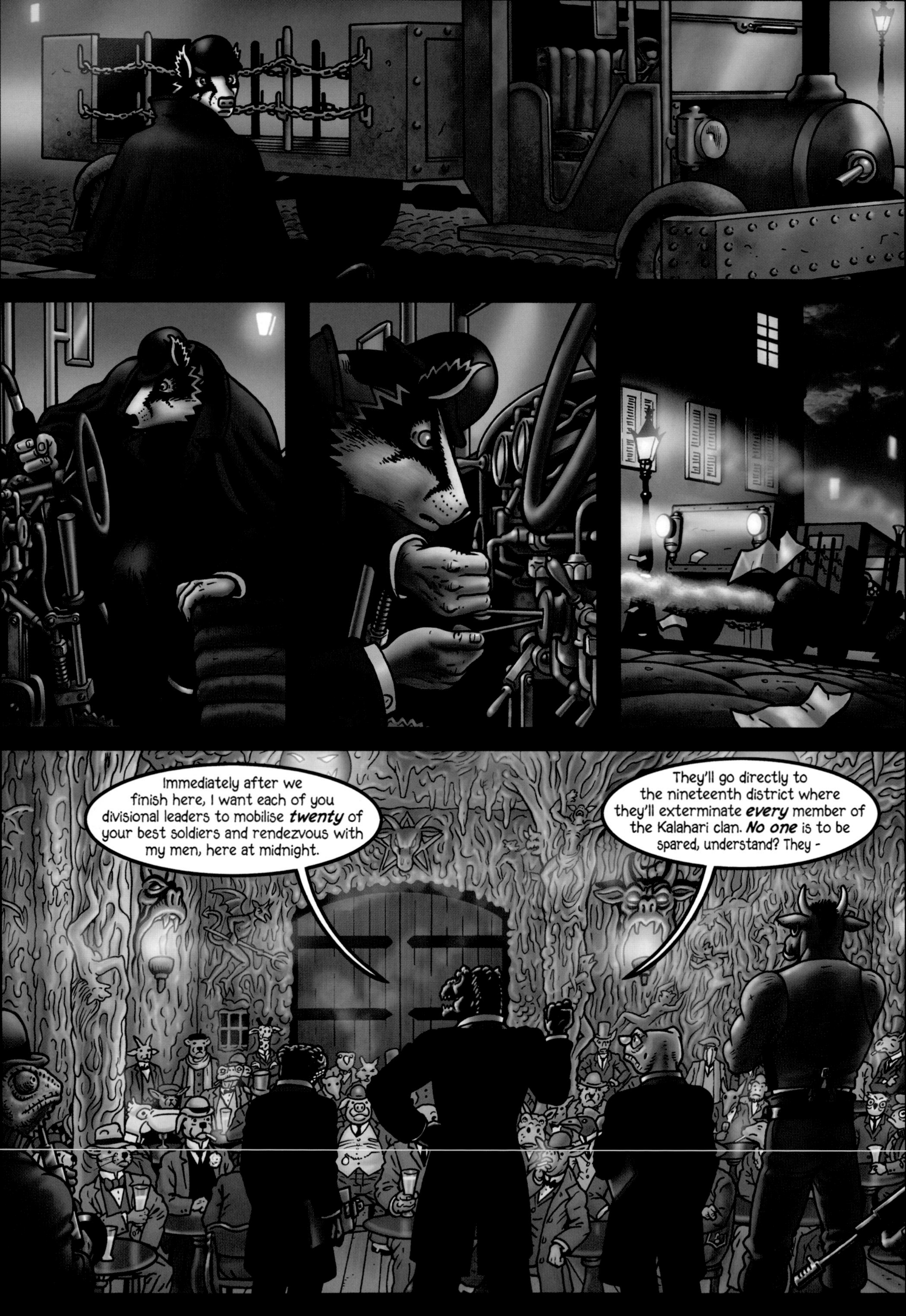
Immediately after we finish here, I want each of you divisional leaders to mobilise **twenty** of your best soldiers and rendezvous with my men, here at midnight.
They'll go directly to the nineteenth district where they'll exterminate **every** member of the Kalahari clan. **No one** is to be spared, understand? They -

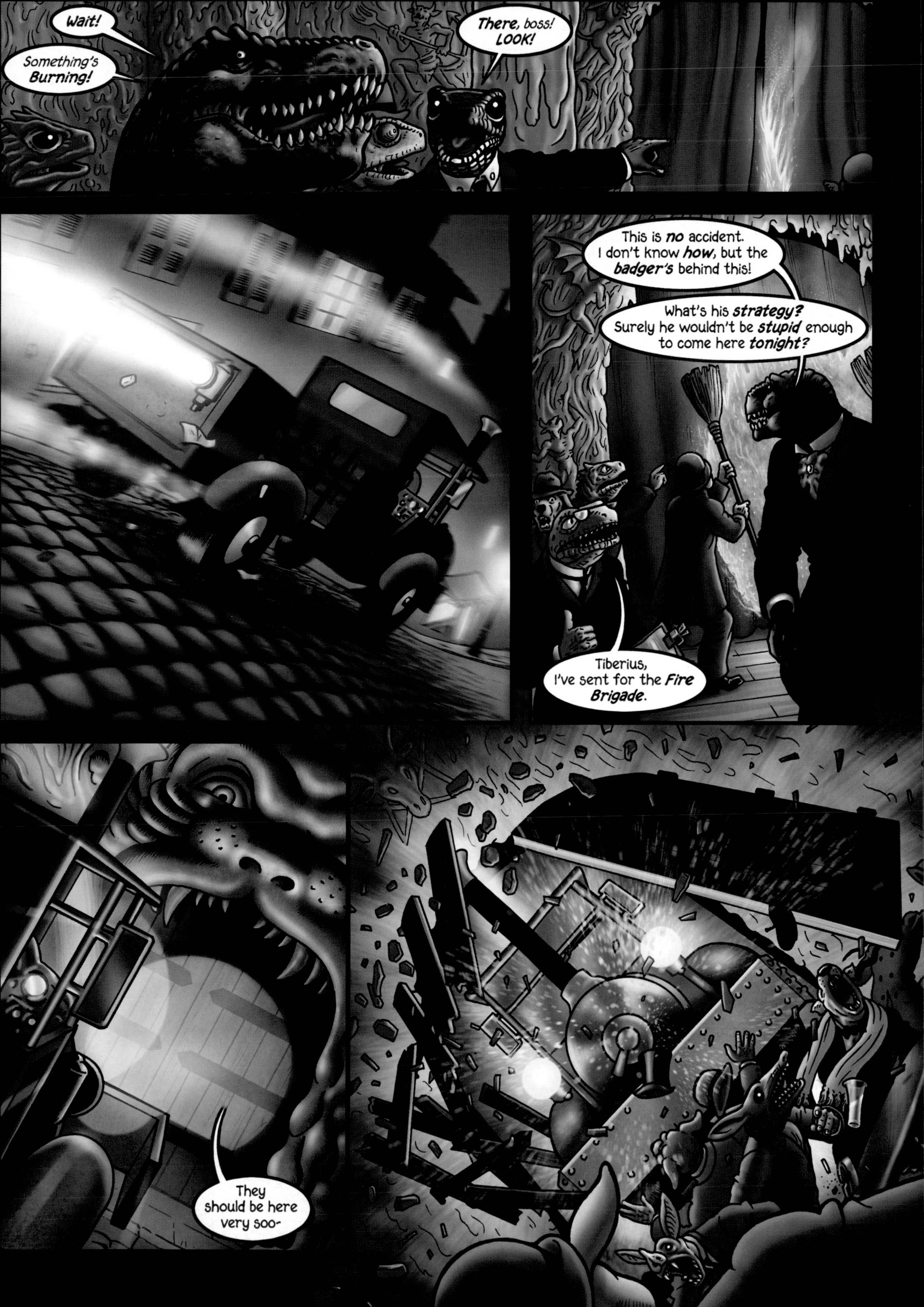
Wait!
Something's Burning!
There, boss! LOOK!
This is no accident. I don't know how, but the badger's behind this!
What's his strategy? Surely he wouldn't be stupid enough to come here tonight?
Tiberius, I've sent for the Fire Brigade.
They should be here very soo-

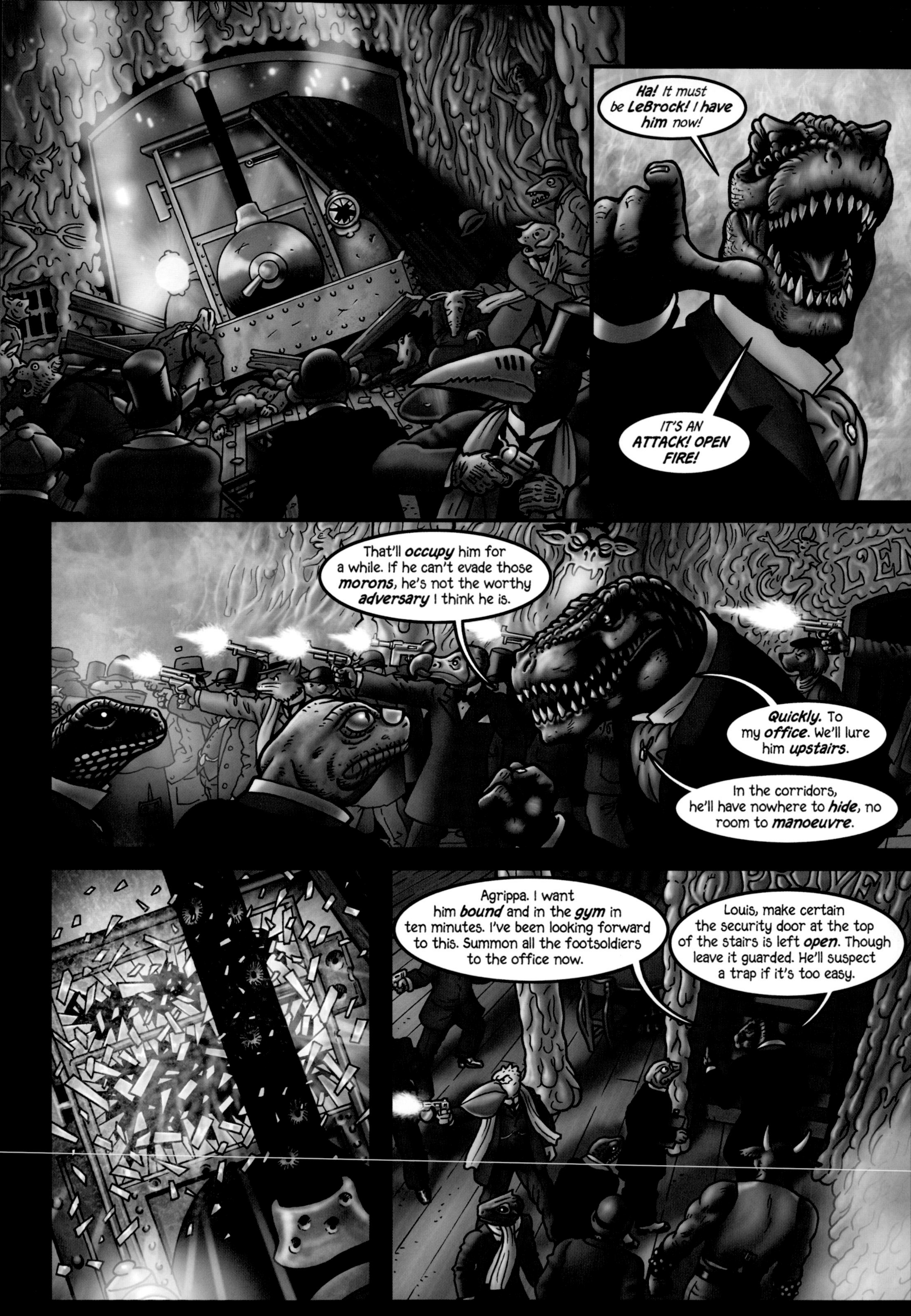
Ha! It must be LeBrock! I have him now!
IT'S AN ATTACK! OPEN FIRE!
That'll occupy him for a while. If he can't evade those morons, he's not the worthy adversary I think he is.
Quickly. To my office. We'll lure him upstairs.
In the corridors, he'll have nowhere to hide, no room to manoeuvre.
Agrippa. I want him bound and in the gym in ten minutes. I've been looking forward to this. Summon all the footsoldiers to the office now.
Louis, make certain the security door at the top of the stairs is left open. Though leave it guarded. He'll suspect a trap if it's too easy.

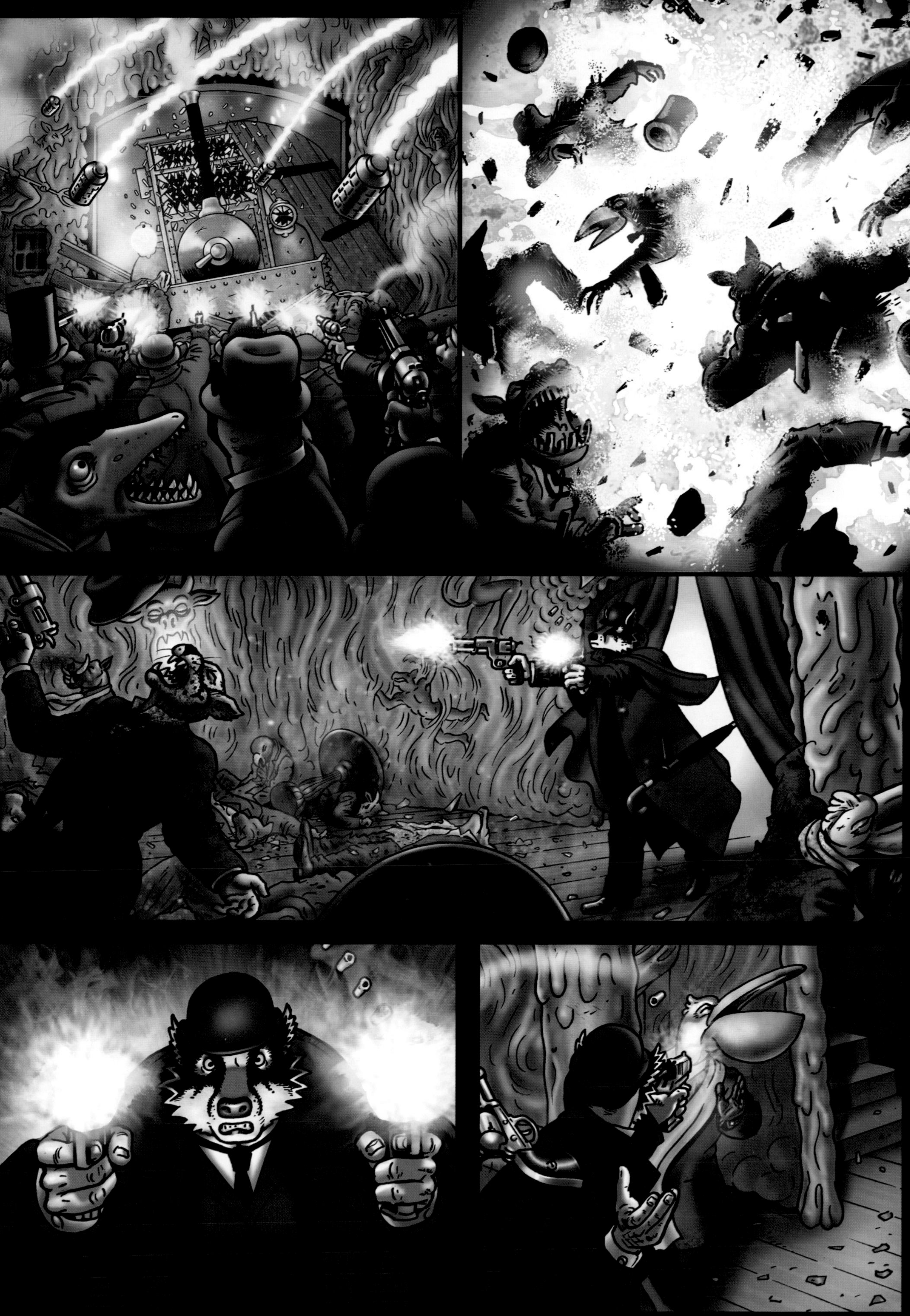

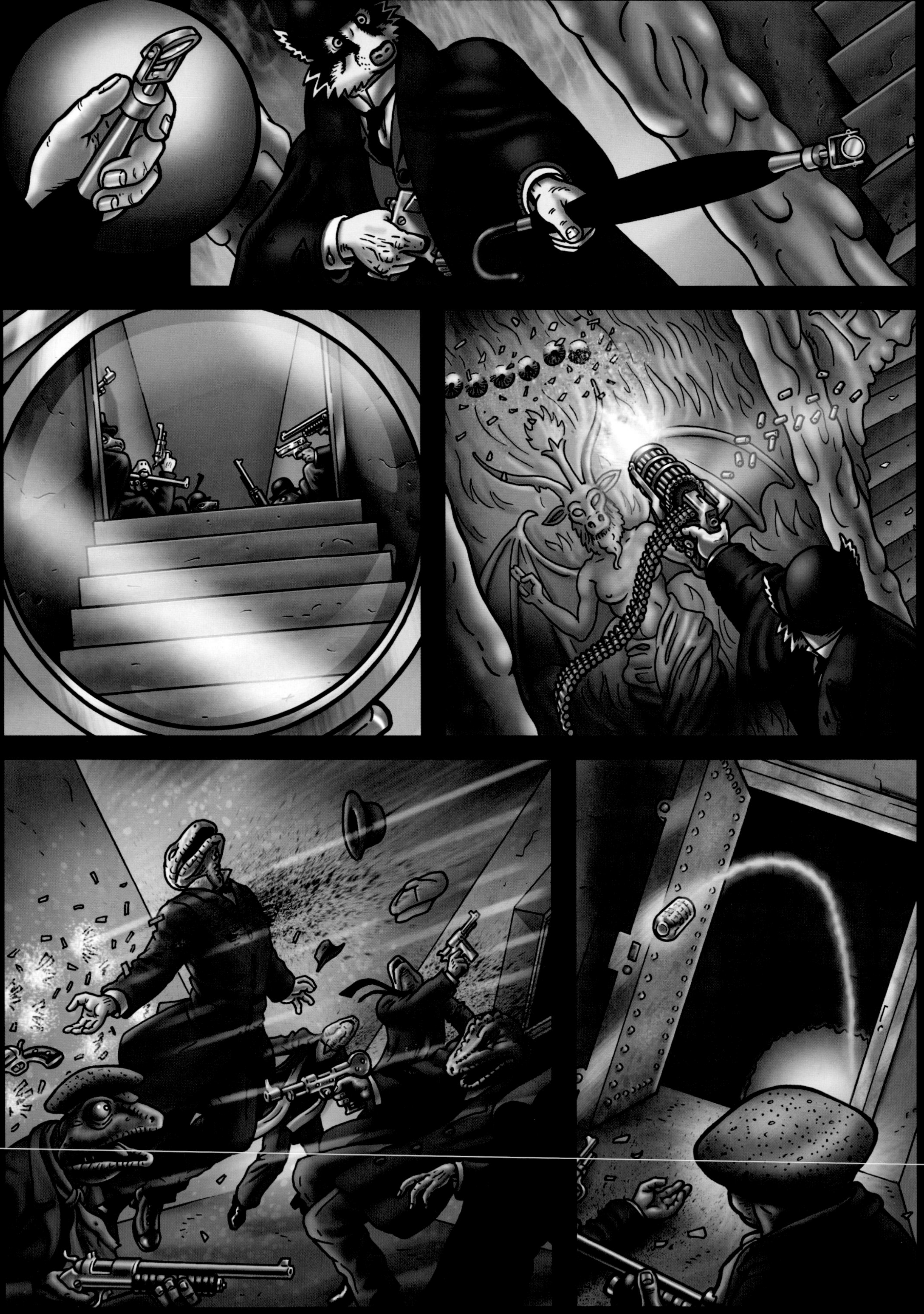

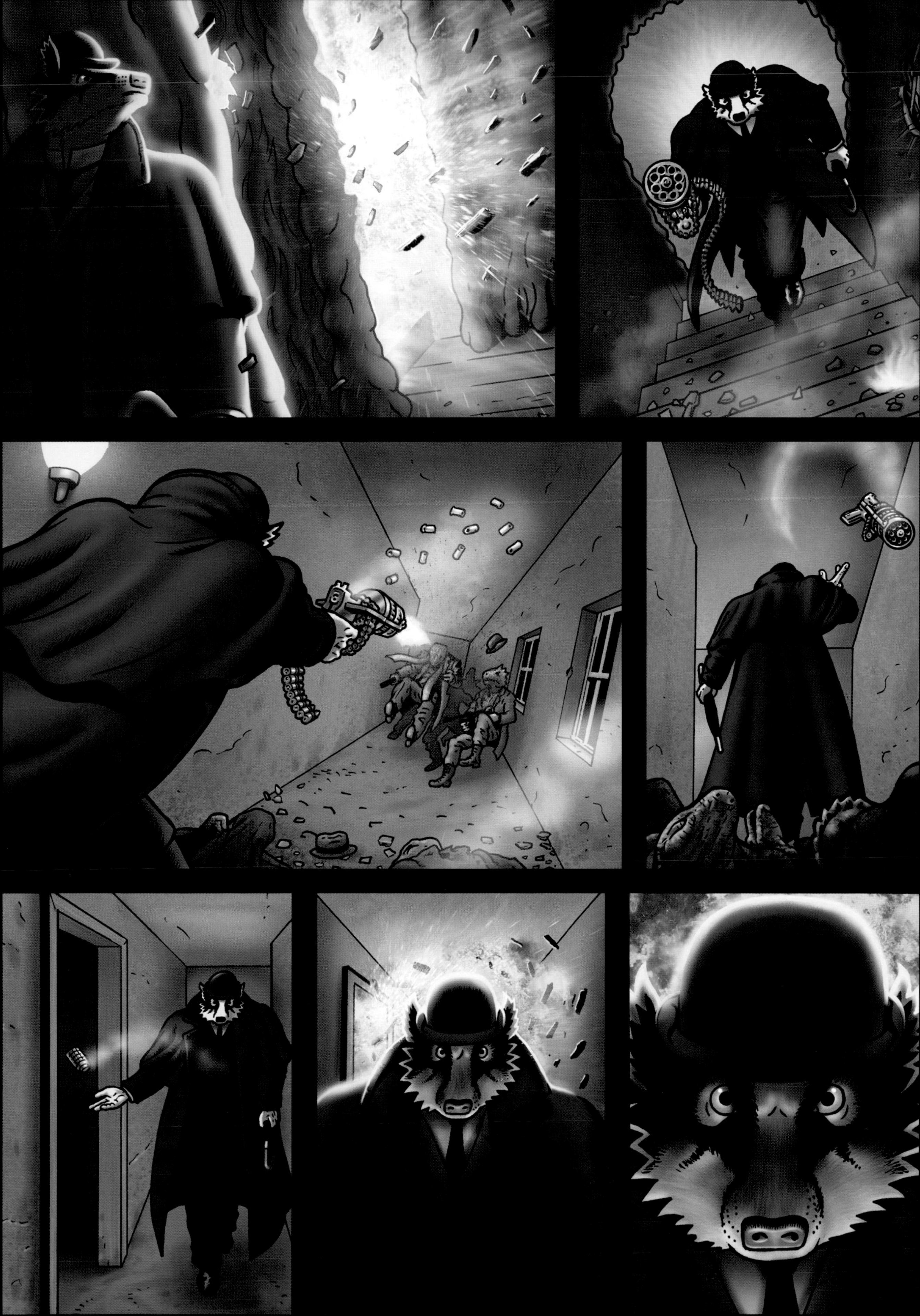

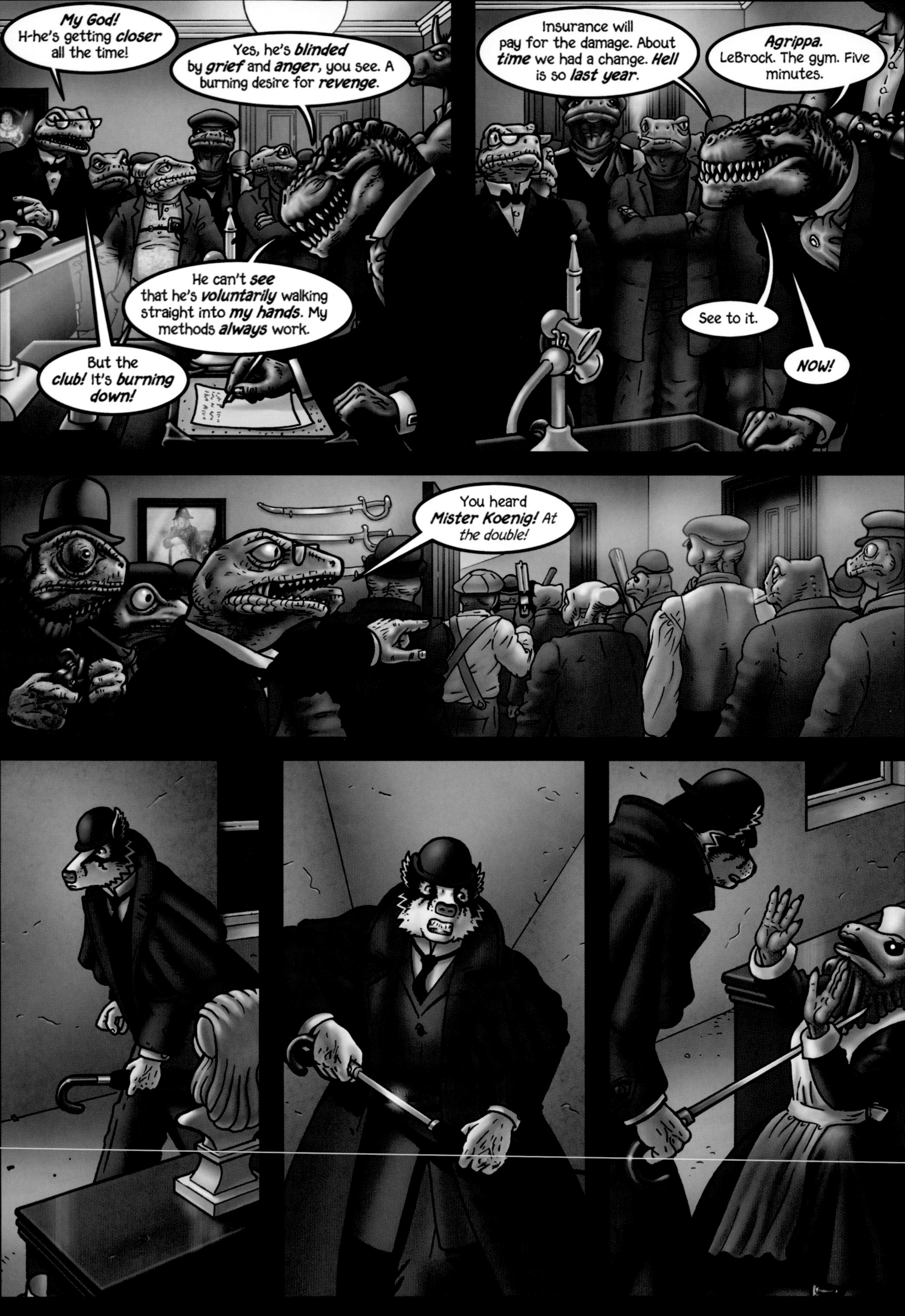

My God! H-he's getting closer all the time!
Yes, he's blinded by grief and anger, you see. A burning desire for revenge.
He can't see that he's voluntarily walking straight into my hands. My methods always work.
But the club! It's burning down!
Insurance will pay for the damage. About time we had a change. Hell is so last year.
Agrippa. LeBrock. The gym. Five minutes.
See to it.
NOW!
You heard Mister Koenig! At the double!

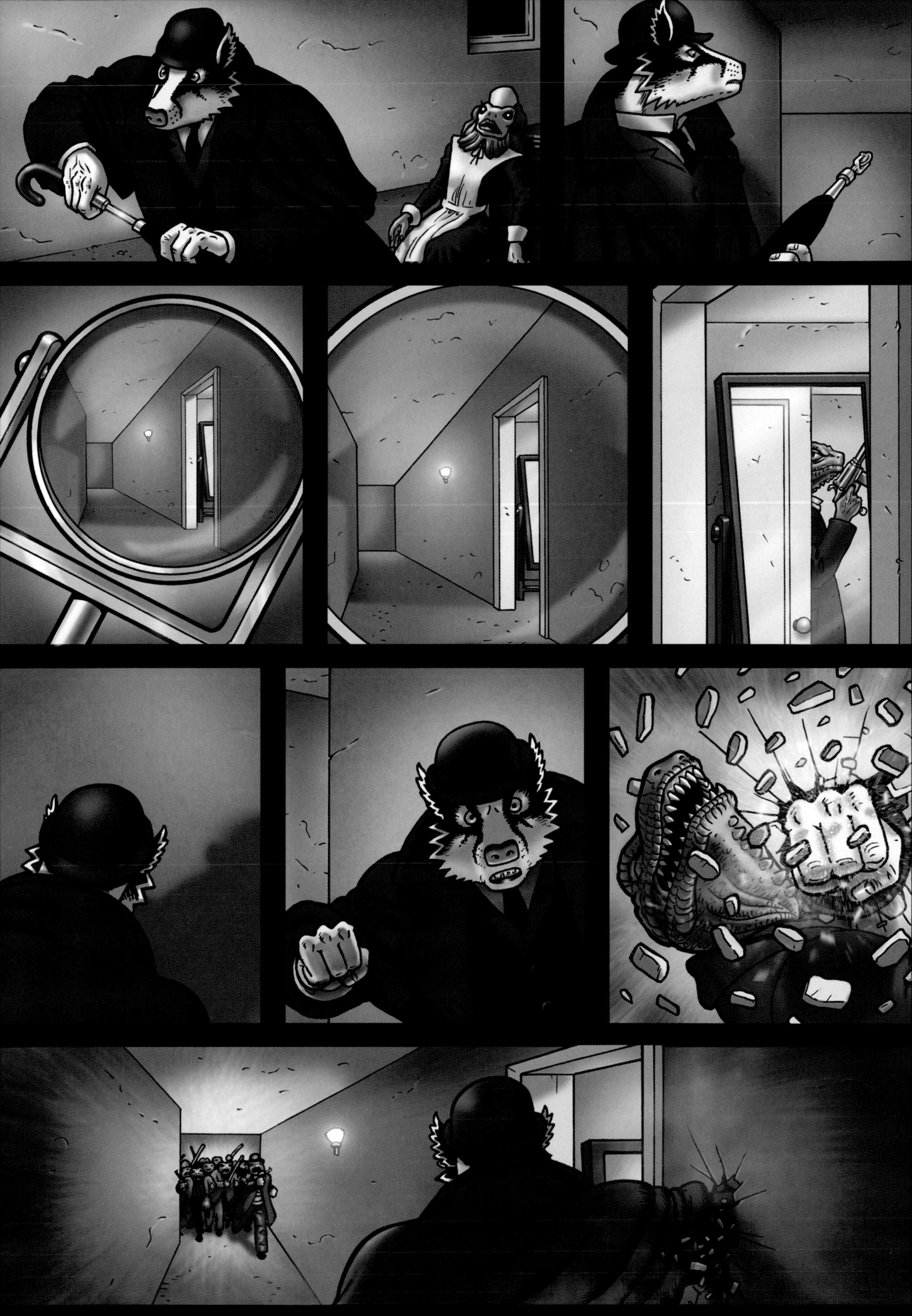

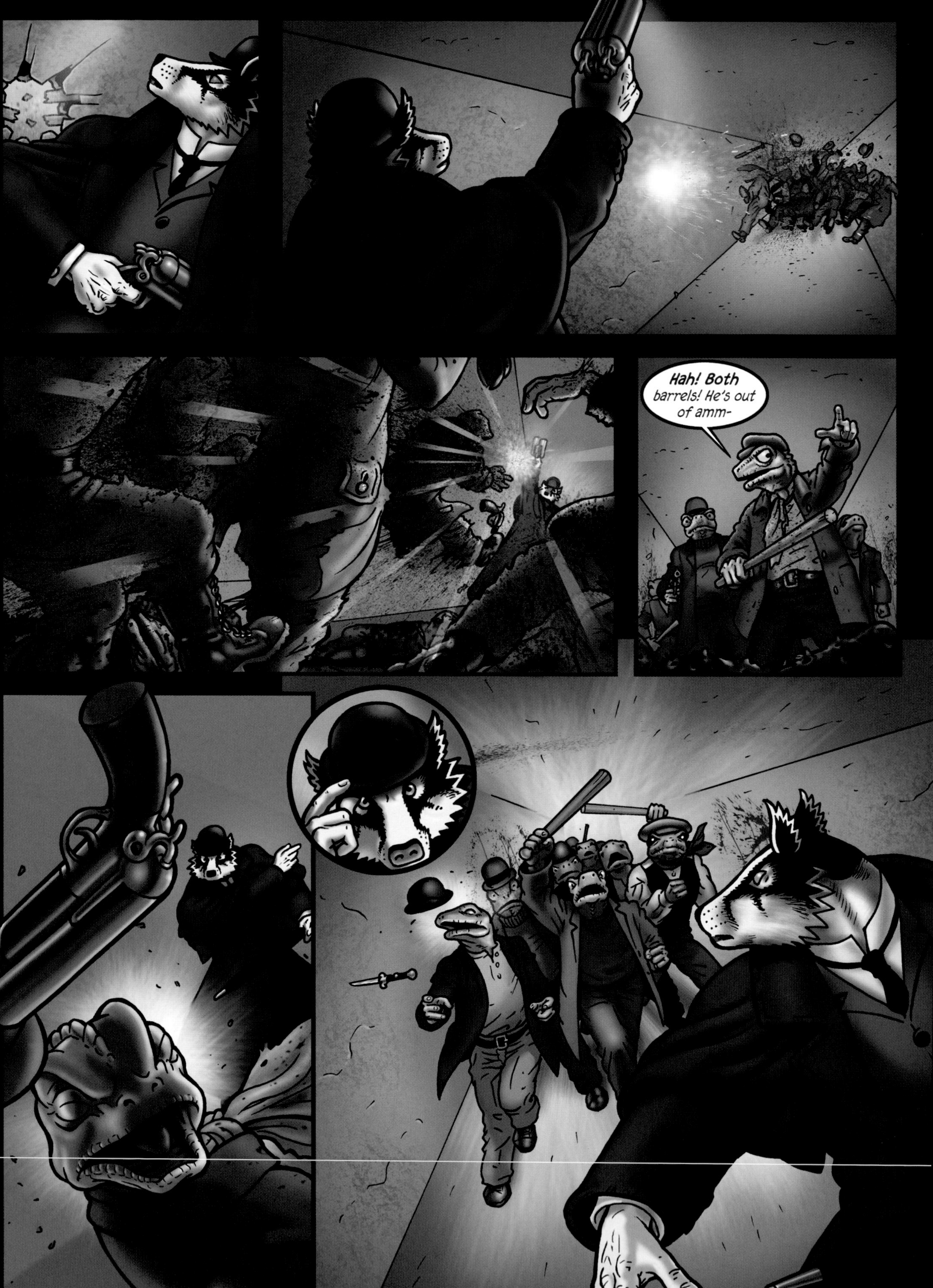
Hah! Both barrels! He's out of amm-

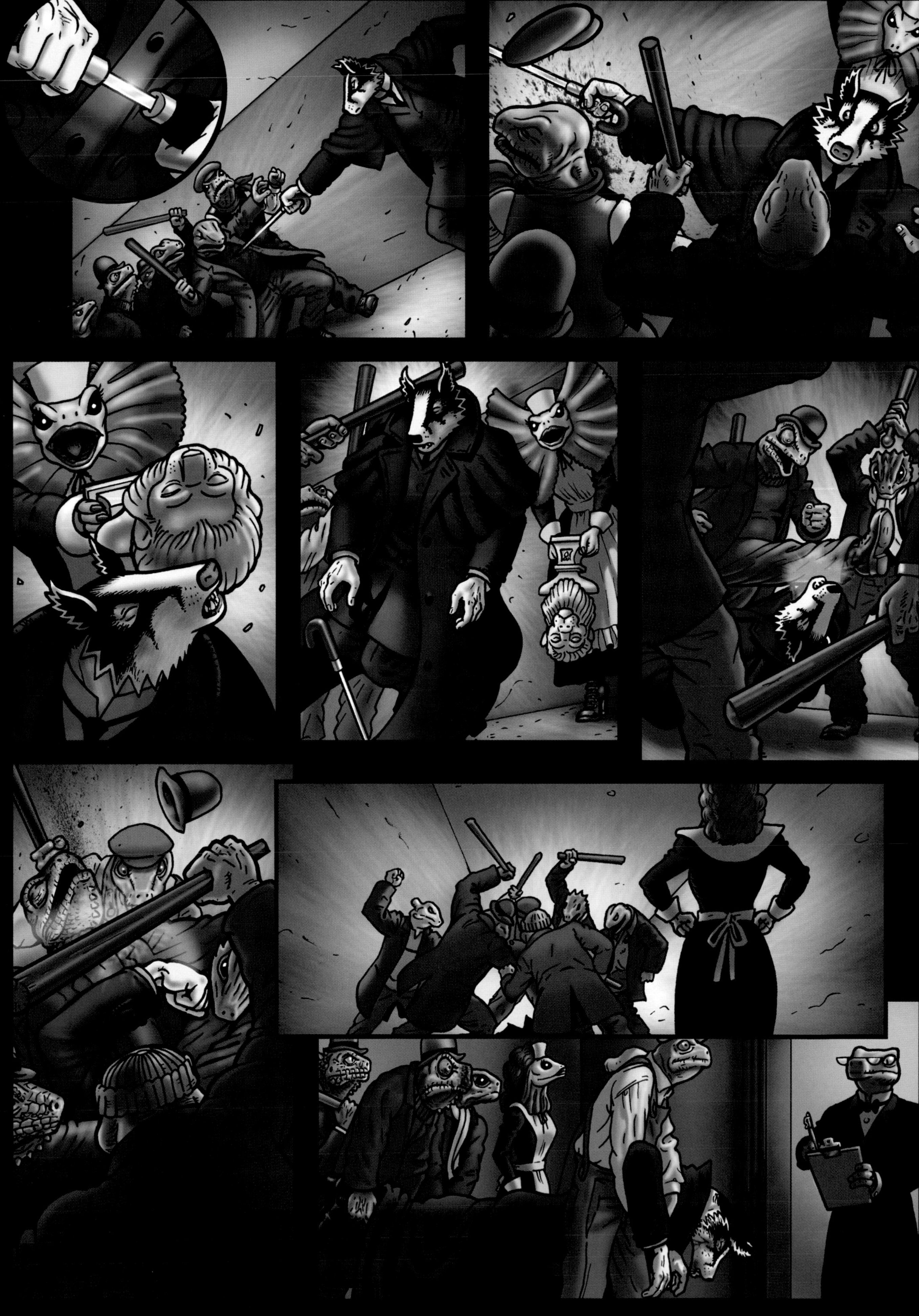

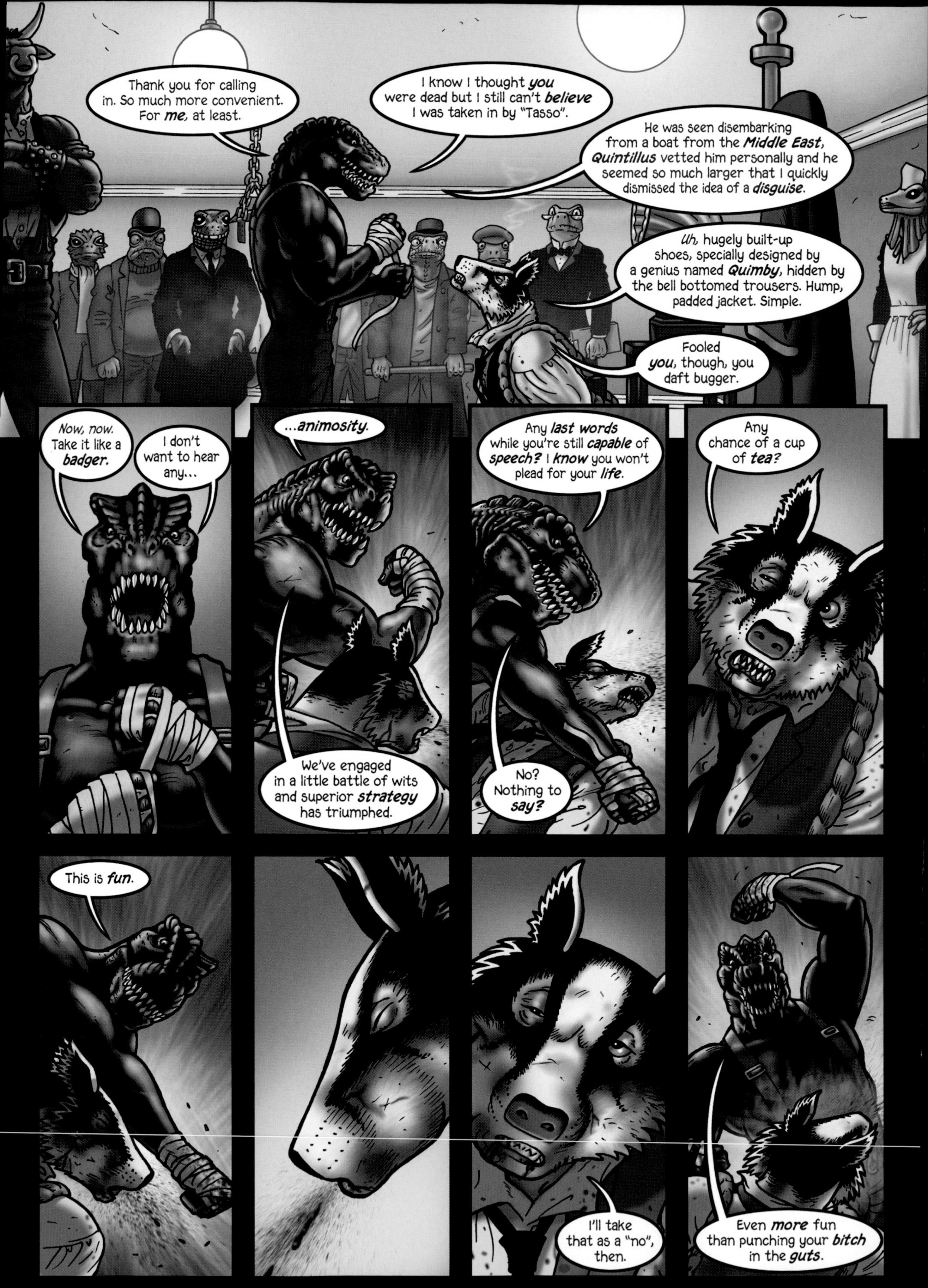

Thank you for calling in. So much more convenient. For *me*, at least.
I know I thought *you* were dead but I still can't *believe* I was taken in by "Tasso".
He was seen disembarking from a boat from the *Middle East*, *Quintillus* vetted him personally and he seemed so much larger that I quickly dismissed the idea of a *disguise*.
Uh, hugely built-up shoes, specially designed by a genius named *Quimby*, hidden by the bell bottomed trousers. Hump, padded jacket. Simple.
Fooled *you*, though, you daft bugger.
Now, now. Take it like a *badger.*
I don't want to hear any...
...*animosity*.
We've engaged in a little battle of wits and superior *strategy* has triumphed.
Any *last words* while you're still *capable* of *speech?* I *know* you won't plead for your *life*.
No? Nothing to *say?*
Any chance of a cup of *tea?*
This is *fun*.
I'll take that as a "no", then.
Even *more* fun than punching your *bitch* in the *guts*.

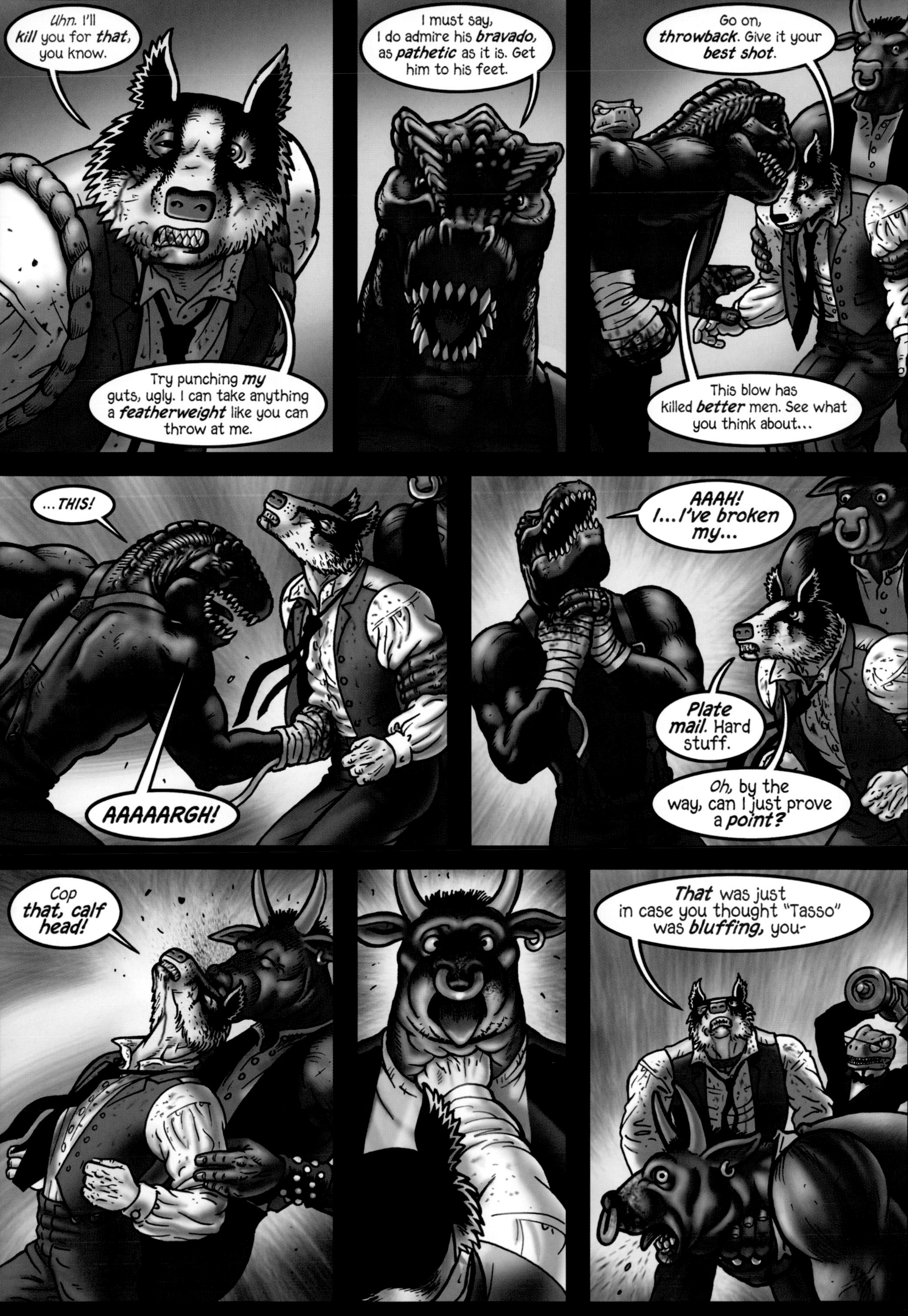
Uhn. I'll kill you for that, you know.
Try punching my guts, ugly. I can take anything a featherweight like you can throw at me.
I must say, I do admire his bravado, as pathetic as it is. Get him to his feet.
Go on, throwback. Give it your best shot.
This blow has killed better men. See what you think about…
…THIS!
AAAAARGH!
AAAH! I…I've broken my…
Plate mail. Hard stuff.
Oh, by the way, can I just prove a point?
Cop that, calf head!
That was just in case you thought "Tasso" was bluffing, you-

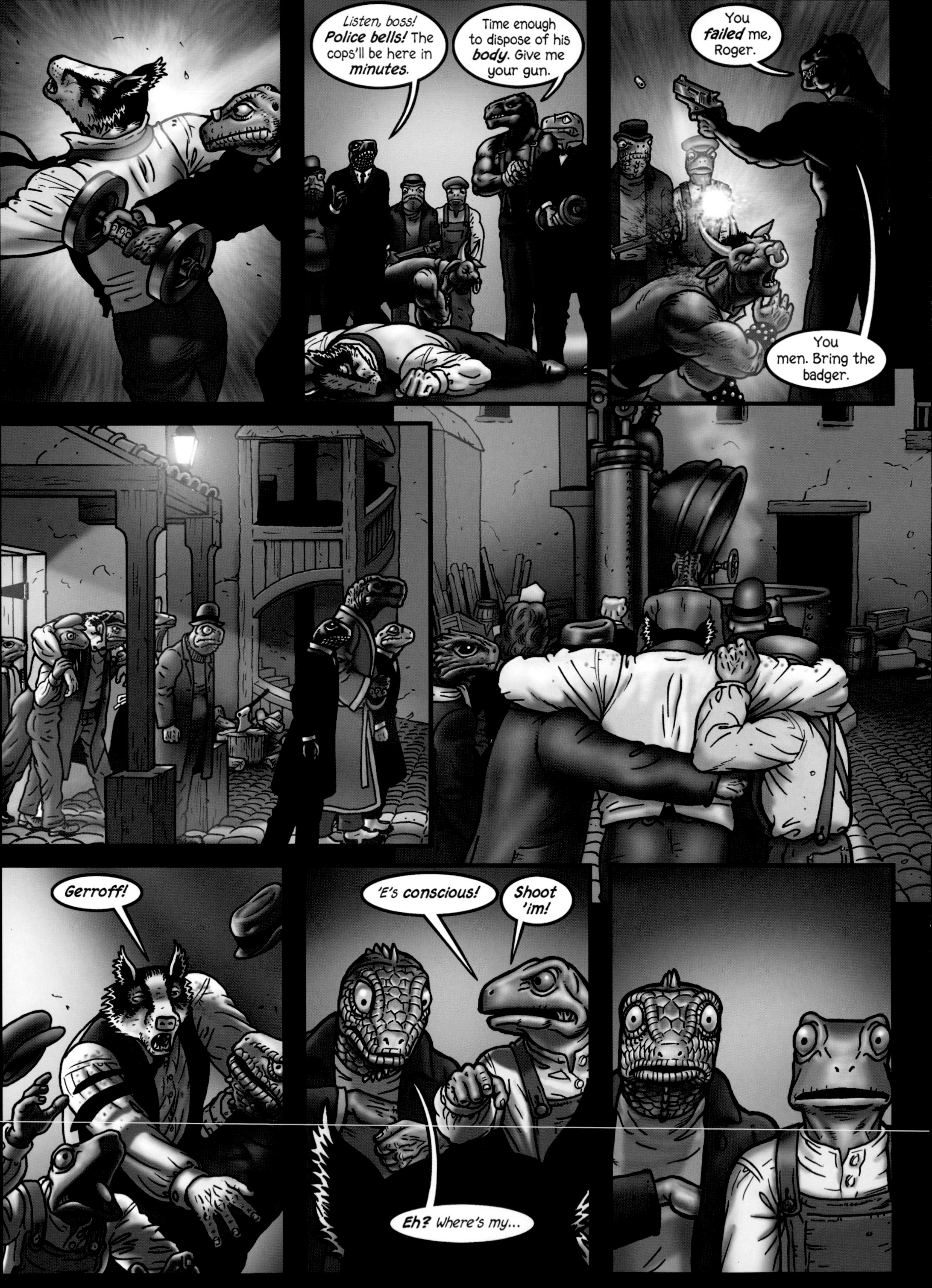
Listen, boss! Police bells! The cops'll be here in minutes.
Time enough to dispose of his body. Give me your gun.
You failed me, Roger.
You men. Bring the badger.
Gerroff!
'E's conscious!
Shoot 'im!
Eh? Where's my...

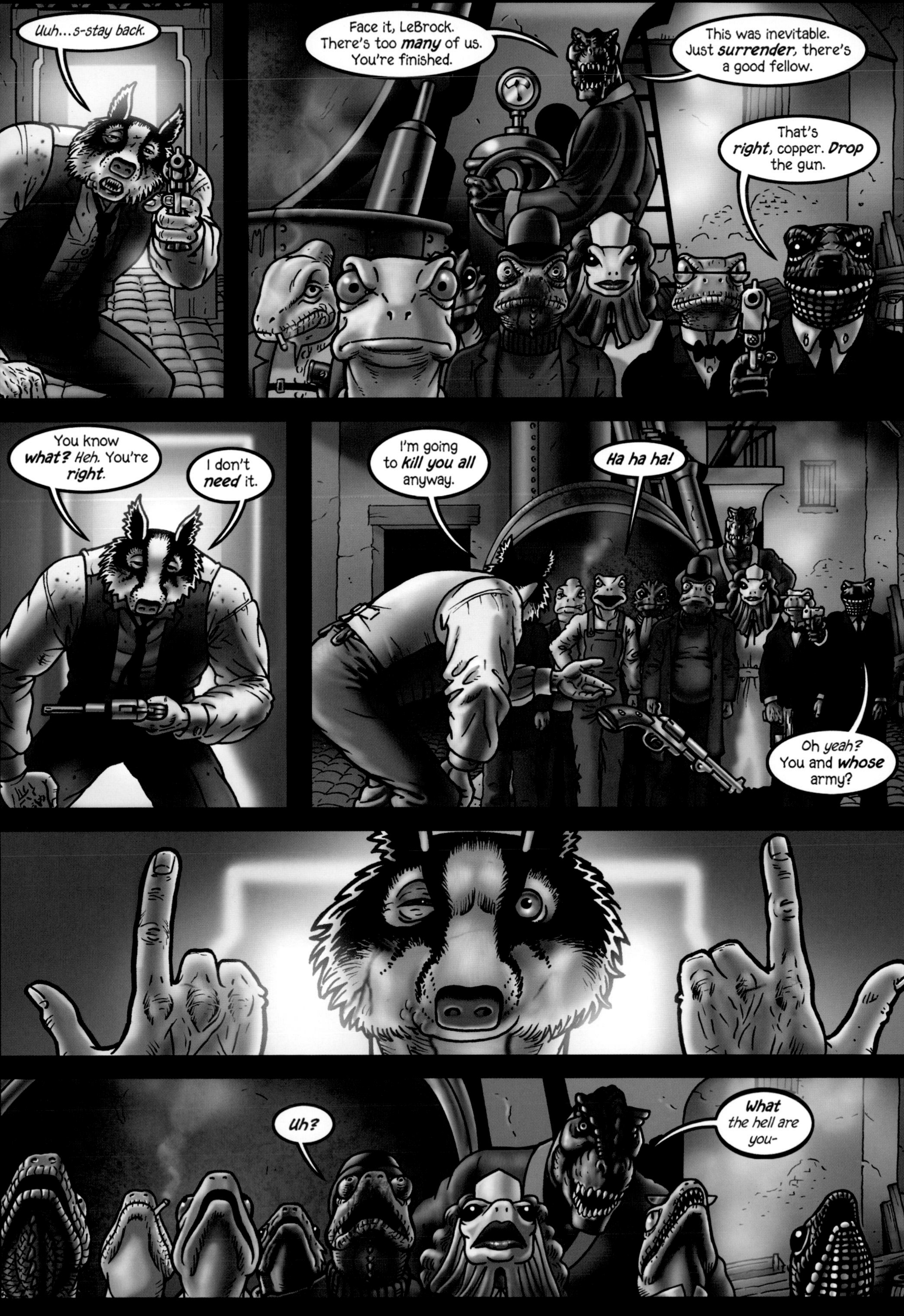

Uuh...s-stay back.
Face it, LeBrock. There's too many of us. You're finished.
This was inevitable. Just surrender, there's a good fellow.
That's right, copper. Drop the gun.
You know what? Heh. You're right.
I don't need it.
I'm going to kill you all anyway.
Ha ha ha!
Oh yeah? You and whose army?
Uh?
What the hell are you-

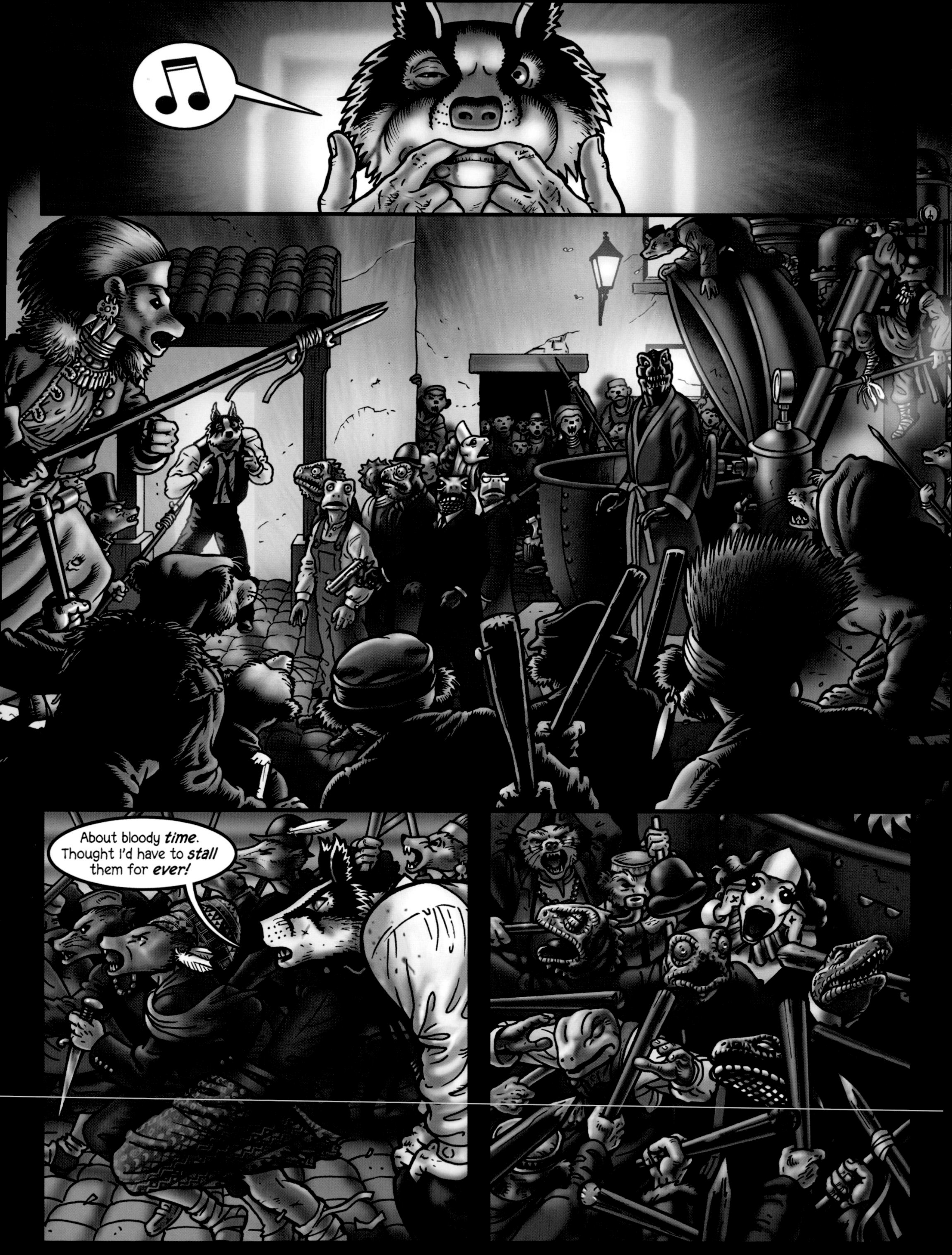
♫
About bloody *time*. Thought I'd have to *stall* them for *ever!*

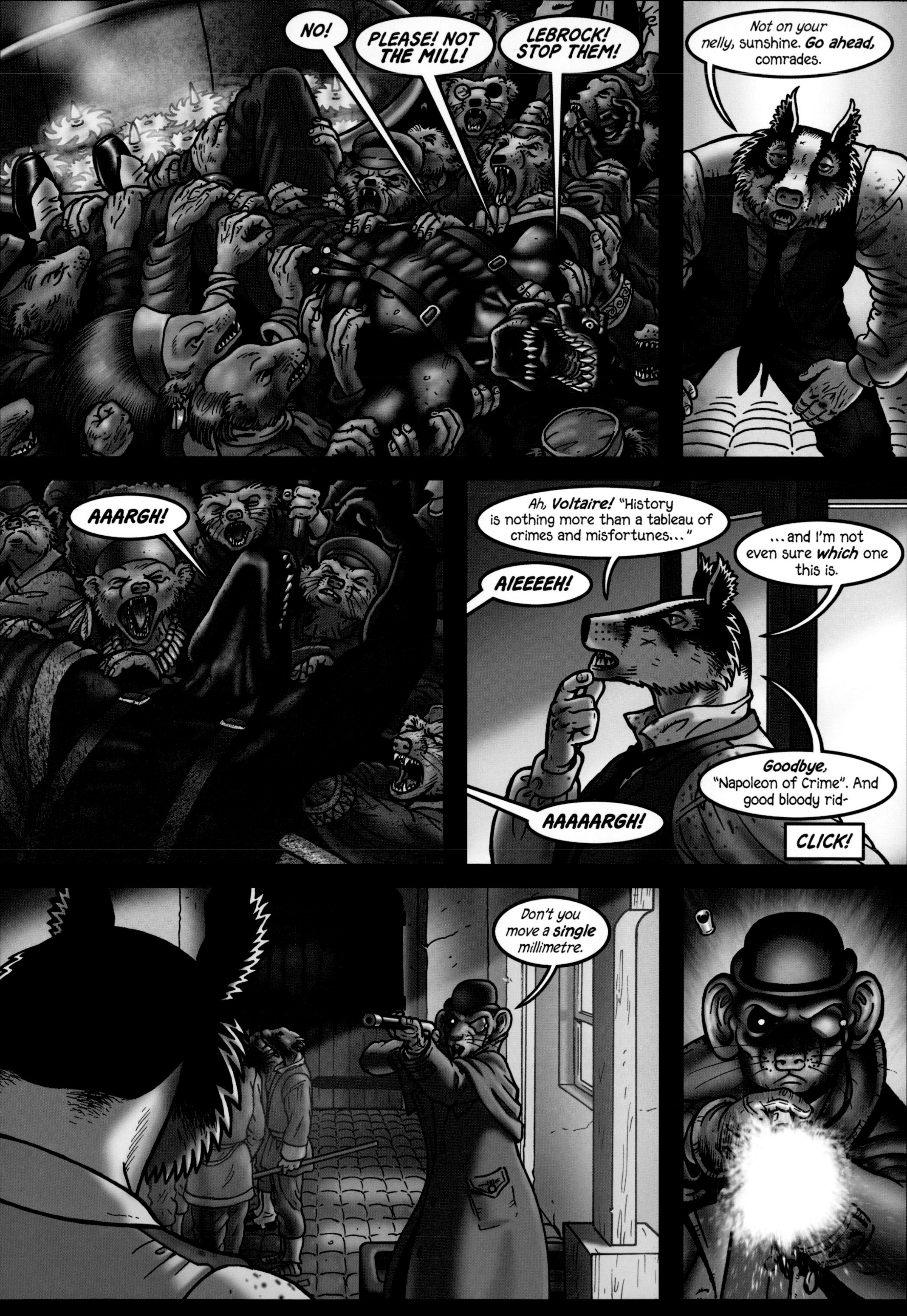

NO!
PLEASE! NOT THE MILL!
LEBROCK! STOP THEM!
Not on your nelly, sunshine. Go ahead, comrades.
AAARGH!
Ah, Voltaire! "History is nothing more than a tableau of crimes and misfortunes..."
AIEEEEH!
...and I'm not even sure which one this is.
Goodbye, "Napoleon of Crime". And good bloody rid-
AAAAARGH!
CLICK!
Don't you move a single millimetre.

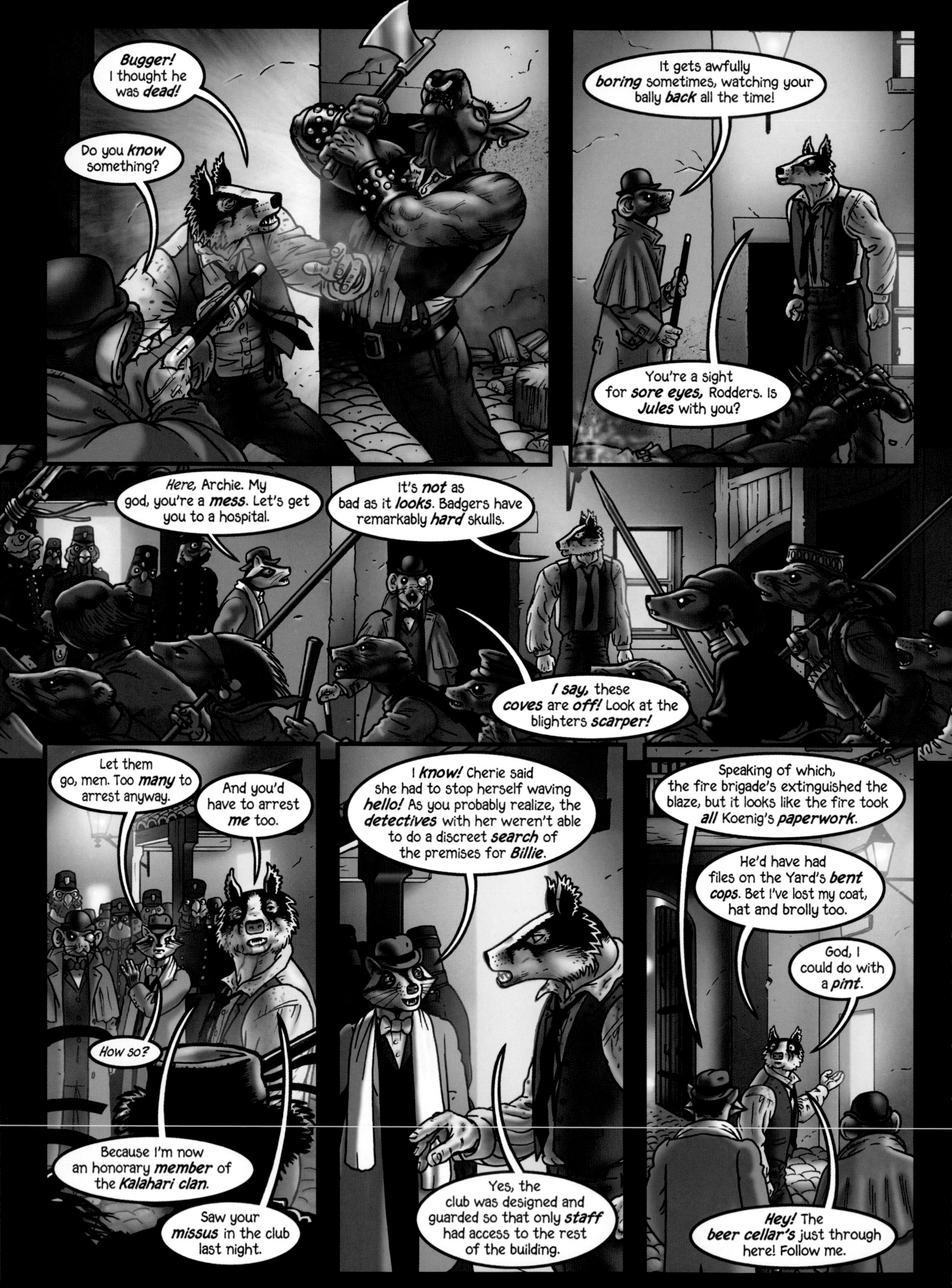

Bugger! I thought he was dead!
Do you know something?
It gets awfully boring sometimes, watching your bally back all the time!
You're a sight for sore eyes, Rodders. Is Jules with you?
Here, Archie. My god, you're a mess. Let's get you to a hospital.
It's not as bad as it looks. Badgers have remarkably hard skulls.
I say, these coves are off! Look at the blighters scarper!
Let them go, men. Too many to arrest anyway.
And you'd have to arrest me too.
How so?
Because I'm now an honorary member of the Kalahari clan.
Saw your missus in the club last night.
I know! Cherie said she had to stop herself waving hello! As you probably realize, the detectives with her weren't able to do a discreet search of the premises for Billie.
Yes, the club was designed and guarded so that only staff had access to the rest of the building.
Speaking of which, the fire brigade's extinguished the blaze, but it looks like the fire took all Koenig's paperwork.
He'd have had files on the Yard's bent cops. Bet I've lost my coat, hat and brolly too.
God, I could do with a pint.
Hey! The beer cellar's just through here! Follow me.

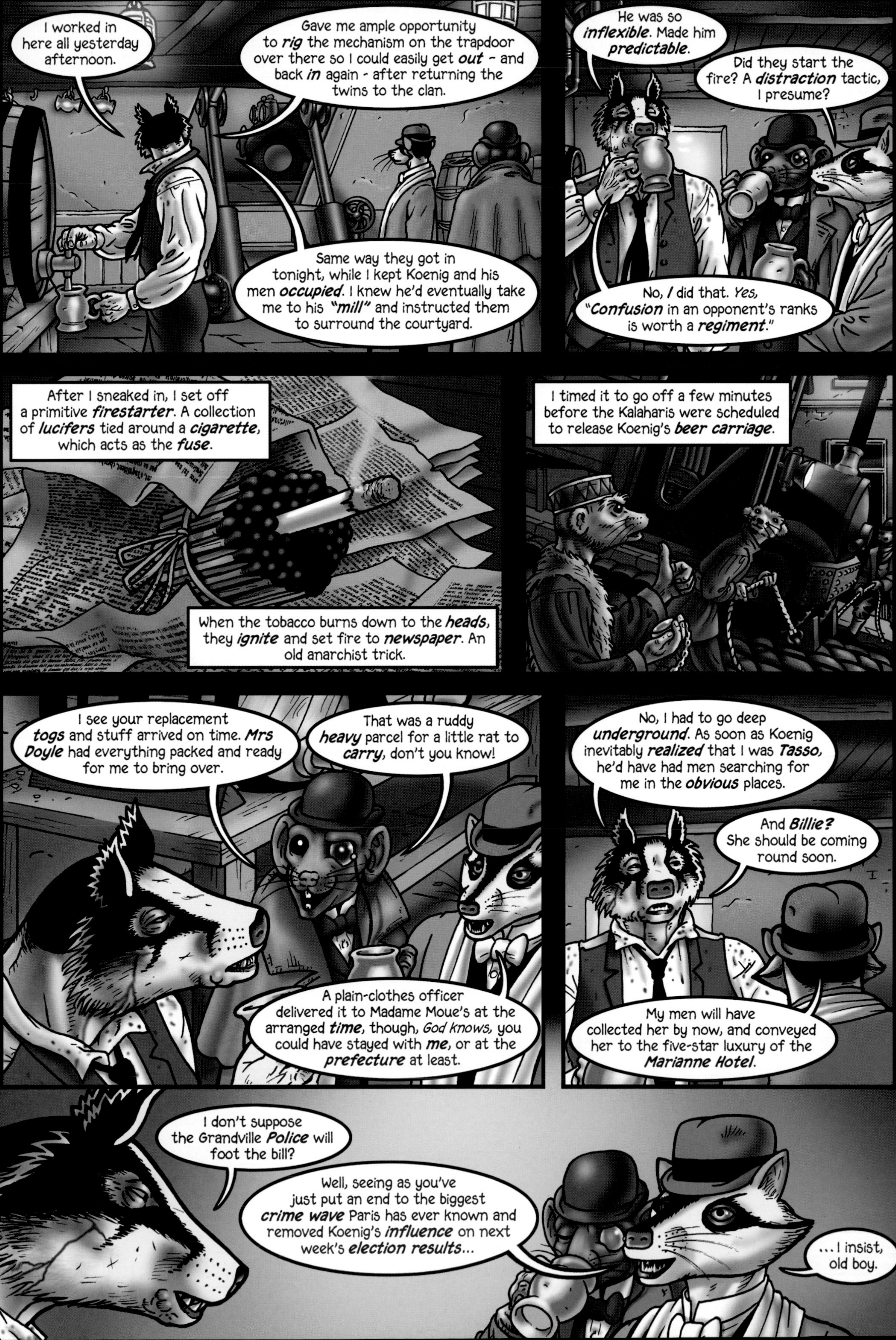
I worked in here all yesterday afternoon.
Gave me ample opportunity to rig the mechanism on the trapdoor over there so I could easily get out - and back in again - after returning the twins to the clan.
Same way they got in tonight, while I kept Koenig and his men occupied. I knew he'd eventually take me to his "mill" and instructed them to surround the courtyard.
He was so inflexible. Made him predictable.
Did they start the fire? A distraction tactic, I presume?
No, I did that. Yes, "Confusion in an opponent's ranks is worth a regiment."
After I sneaked in, I set off a primitive firestarter. A collection of lucifers tied around a cigarette, which acts as the fuse.
When the tobacco burns down to the heads, they ignite and set fire to newspaper. An old anarchist trick.
I timed it to go off a few minutes before the Kalaharis were scheduled to release Koenig's beer carriage.
I see your replacement togs and stuff arrived on time. Mrs Doyle had everything packed and ready for me to bring over.
That was a ruddy heavy parcel for a little rat to carry, don't you know!
A plain-clothes officer delivered it to Madame Moue's at the arranged time, though, God knows, you could have stayed with me, or at the prefecture at least.
No, I had to go deep underground. As soon as Koenig inevitably realized that I was Tasso, he'd have had men searching for me in the obvious places.
And Billie? She should be coming round soon.
My men will have collected her by now, and conveyed her to the five-star luxury of the Marianne Hotel.
I don't suppose the Grandville Police will foot the bill?
Well, seeing as you've just put an end to the biggest crime wave Paris has ever known and removed Koenig's influence on next week's election results...
...I insist, old boy.

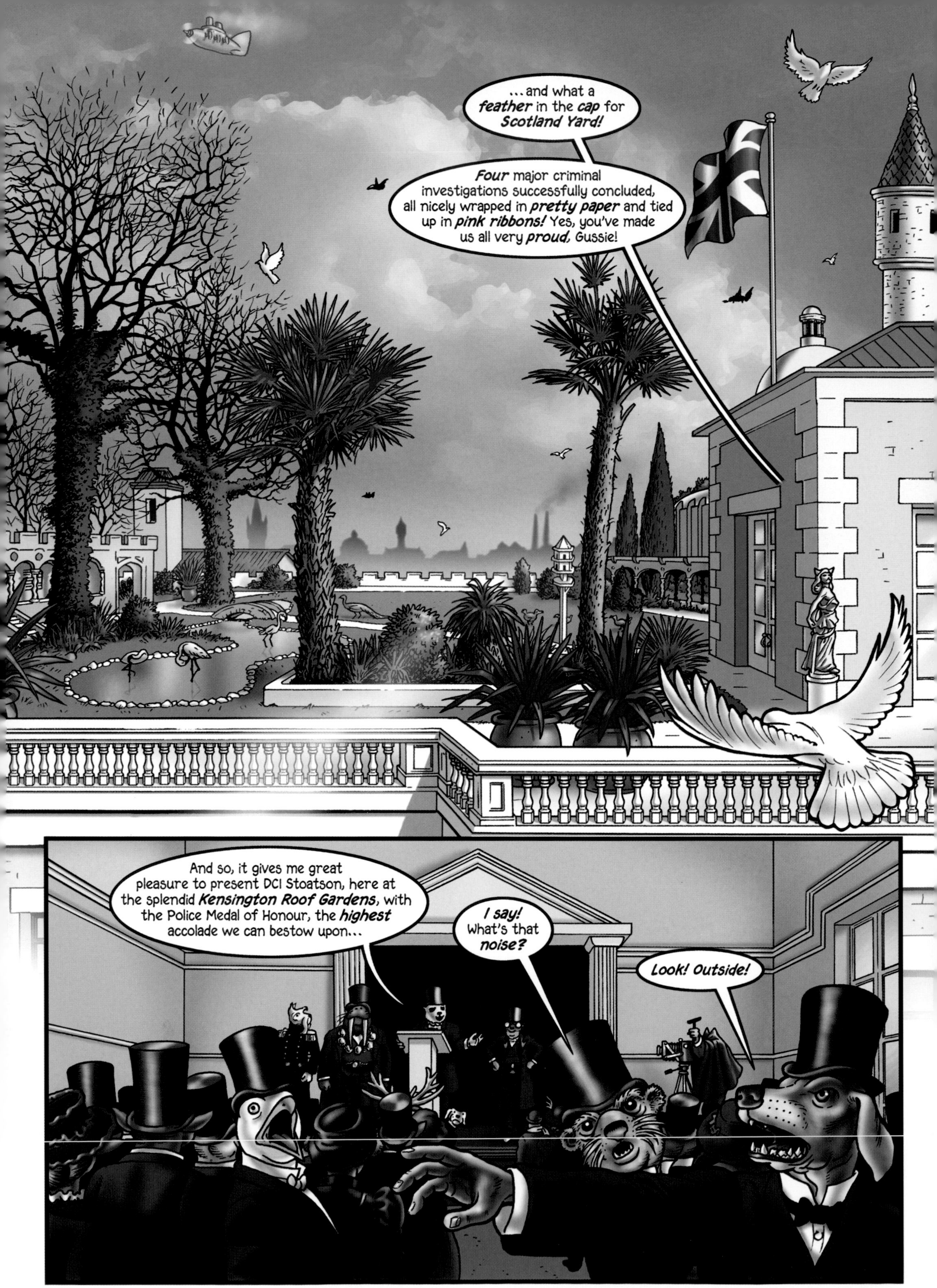
...and what a feather in the cap for Scotland Yard!
Four major criminal investigations successfully concluded, all nicely wrapped in pretty paper and tied up in pink ribbons! Yes, you've made us all very proud, Gussie!
And so, it gives me great pleasure to present DCI Stoatson, here at the splendid Kensington Roof Gardens, with the Police Medal of Honour, the highest accolade we can bestow upon...
I say! What's that noise?
Look! Outside!

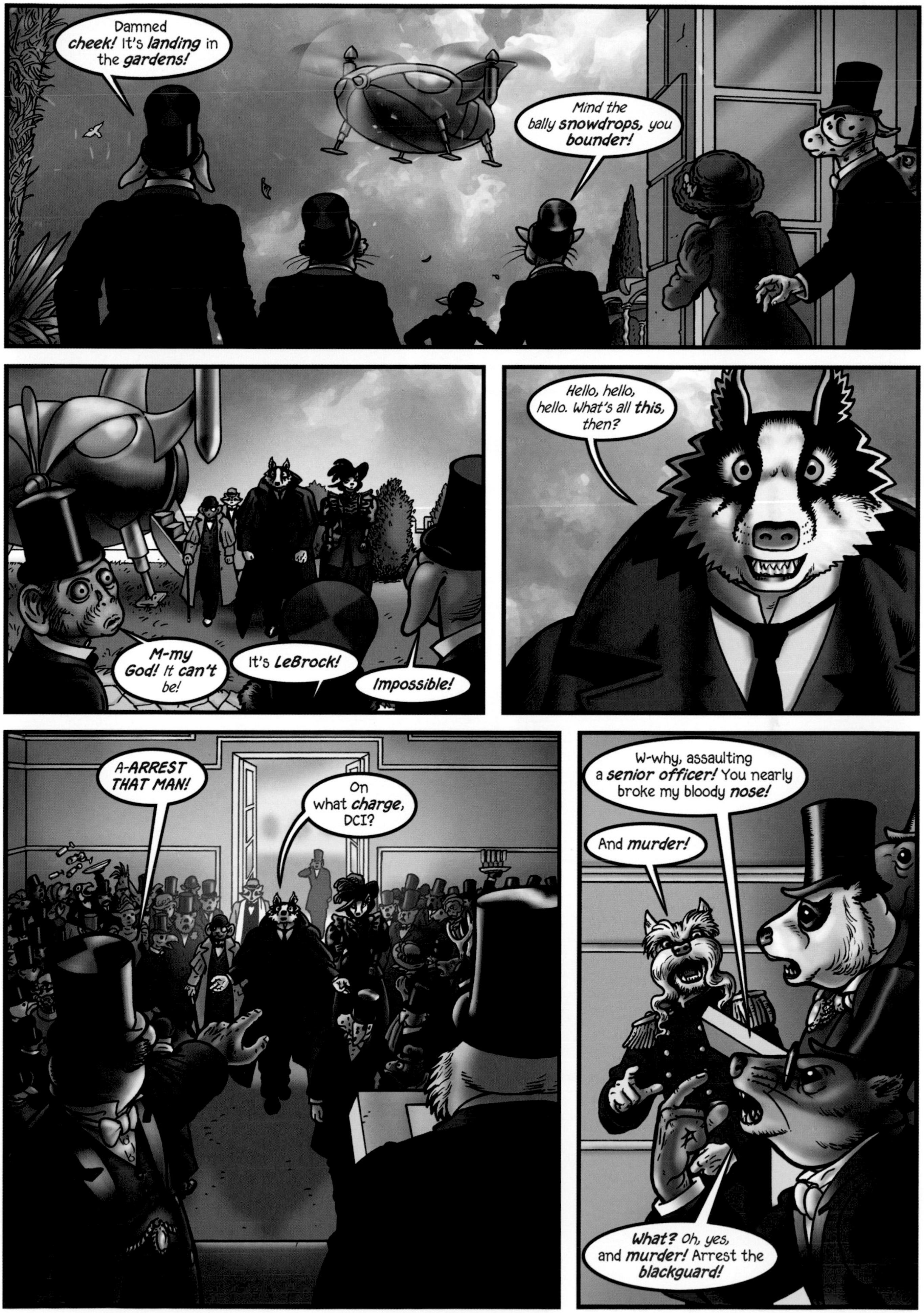

Damned cheek! It's landing in the gardens!
Mind the bally snowdrops, you bounder!
M-my God! It can't be!
It's LeBrock!
Impossible!
Hello, hello, hello. What's all this, then?
A-ARREST THAT MAN!
On what charge, DCI?
W-why, assaulting a senior officer! You nearly broke my bloody nose!
And murder!
What? Oh, yes, and murder! Arrest the blackguard!

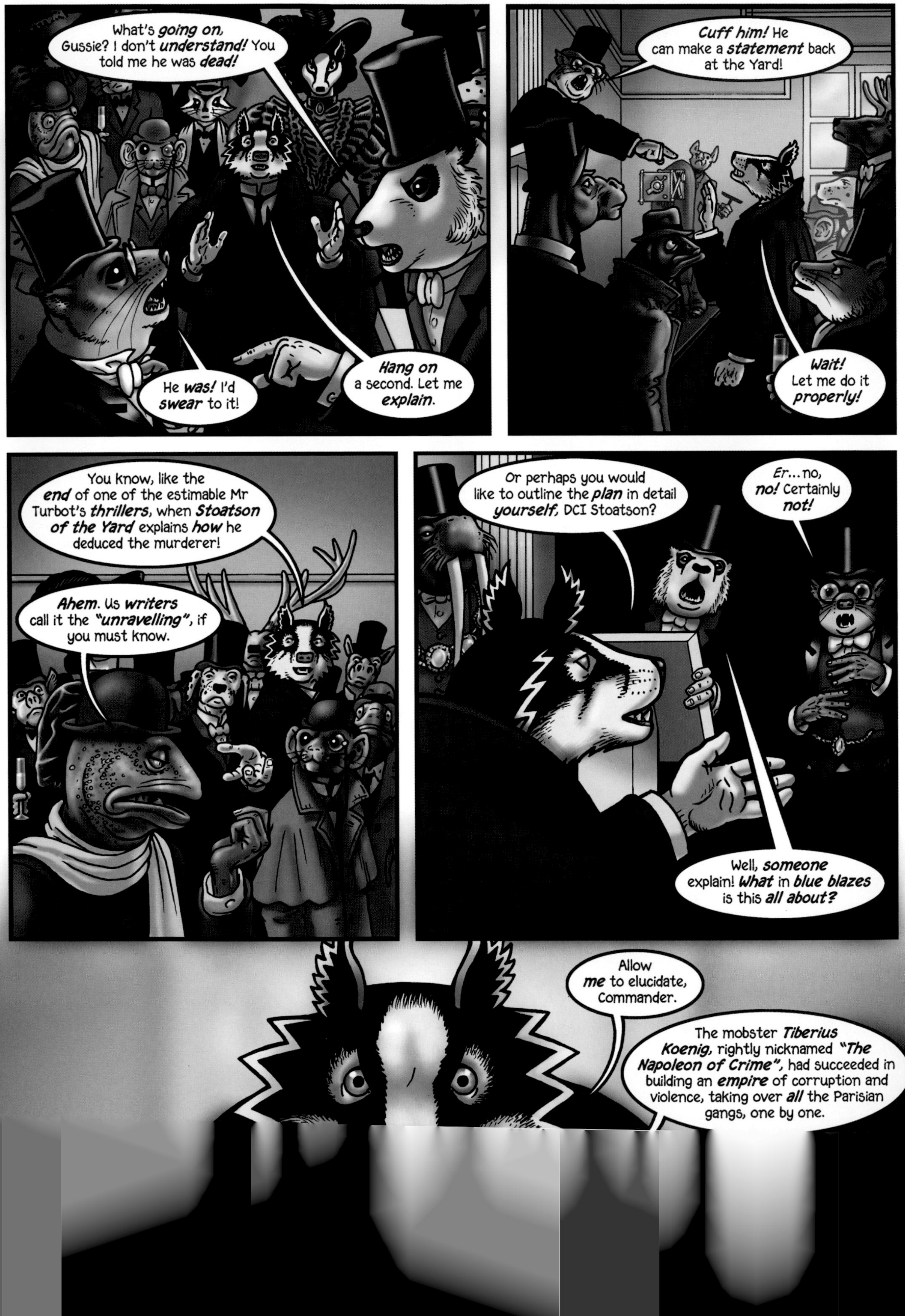
What's going on, Gussie? I don't understand! You told me he was dead!
He was! I'd swear to it!
Hang on a second. Let me explain.
Cuff him! He can make a statement back at the Yard!
Wait! Let me do it properly!
You know, like the end of one of the estimable Mr Turbot's thrillers, when Stoatson of the Yard explains how he deduced the murderer!
Ahem. Us writers call it the "unravelling", if you must know.
Or perhaps you would like to outline the plan in detail yourself, DCI Stoatson?
Er... no, no! Certainly not!
Well, someone explain! What in blue blazes is this all about?
Allow me to elucidate, Commander.
The mobster Tiberius Koenig, rightly nicknamed "The Napoleon of Crime", had succeeded in building an empire of corruption and violence, taking over all the Parisian gangs, one by one.

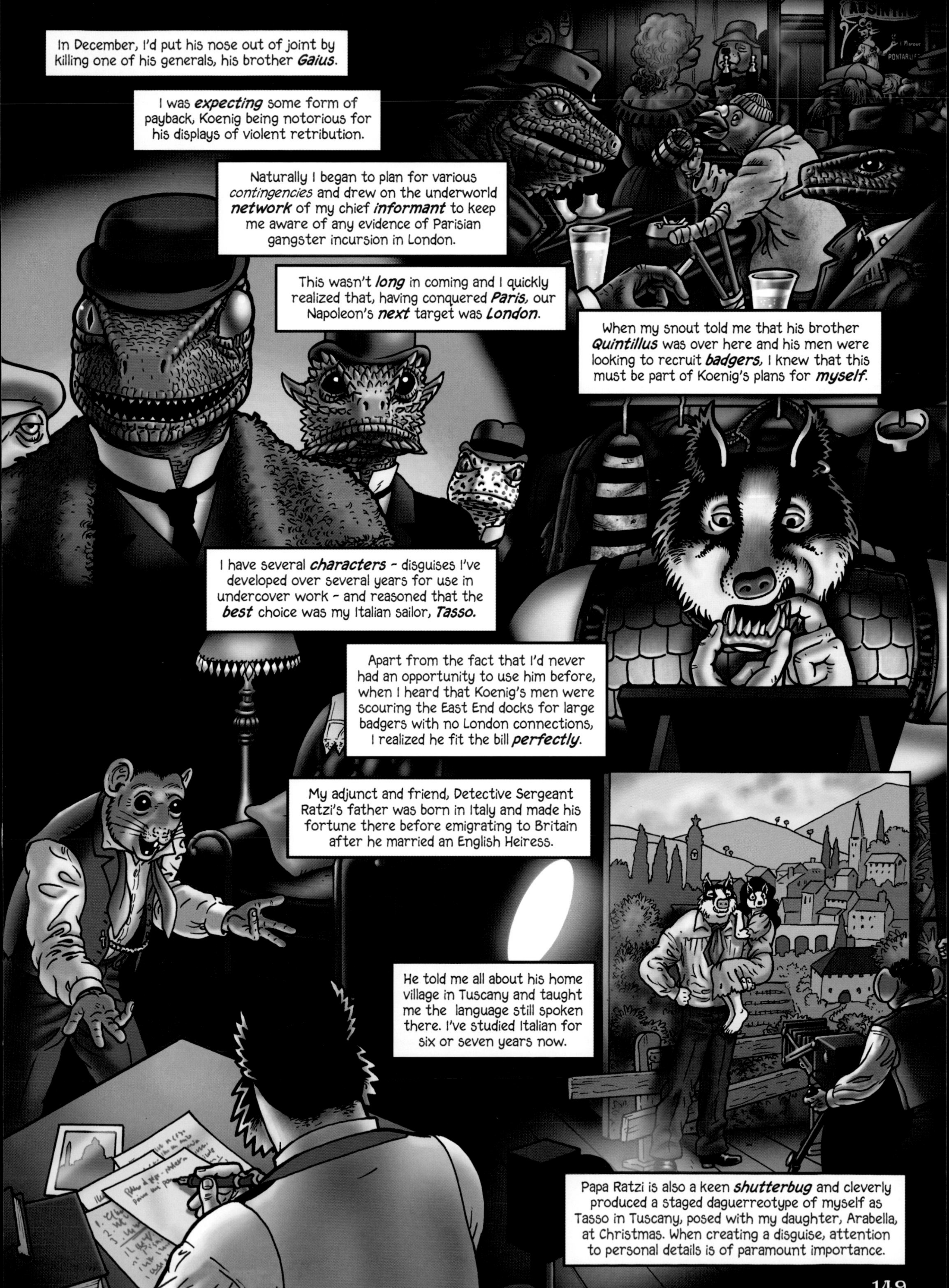
In December, I'd put his nose out of joint by killing one of his generals, his brother Gaius.
I was expecting some form of payback, Koenig being notorious for his displays of violent retribution.
Naturally I began to plan for various contingencies and drew on the underworld network of my chief informant to keep me aware of any evidence of Parisian gangster incursion in London.
This wasn't long in coming and I quickly realized that, having conquered Paris, our Napoleon's next target was London.
When my snout told me that his brother Quintillus was over here and his men were looking to recruit badgers, I knew that this must be part of Koenig's plans for myself.
I have several characters - disguises I've developed over several years for use in undercover work - and reasoned that the best choice was my Italian sailor, Tasso.
Apart from the fact that I'd never had an opportunity to use him before, when I heard that Koenig's men were scouring the East End docks for large badgers with no London connections, I realized he fit the bill perfectly.
My adjunct and friend, Detective Sergeant Ratzi's father was born in Italy and made his fortune there before emigrating to Britain after he married an English Heiress.
He told me all about his home village in Tuscany and taught me the language still spoken there. I've studied Italian for six or seven years now.
Papa Ratzi is also a keen shutterbug and cleverly produced a staged daguerreotype of myself as Tasso in Tuscany, posed with my daughter, Arabella, at Christmas. When creating a disguise, attention to personal details is of paramount importance.

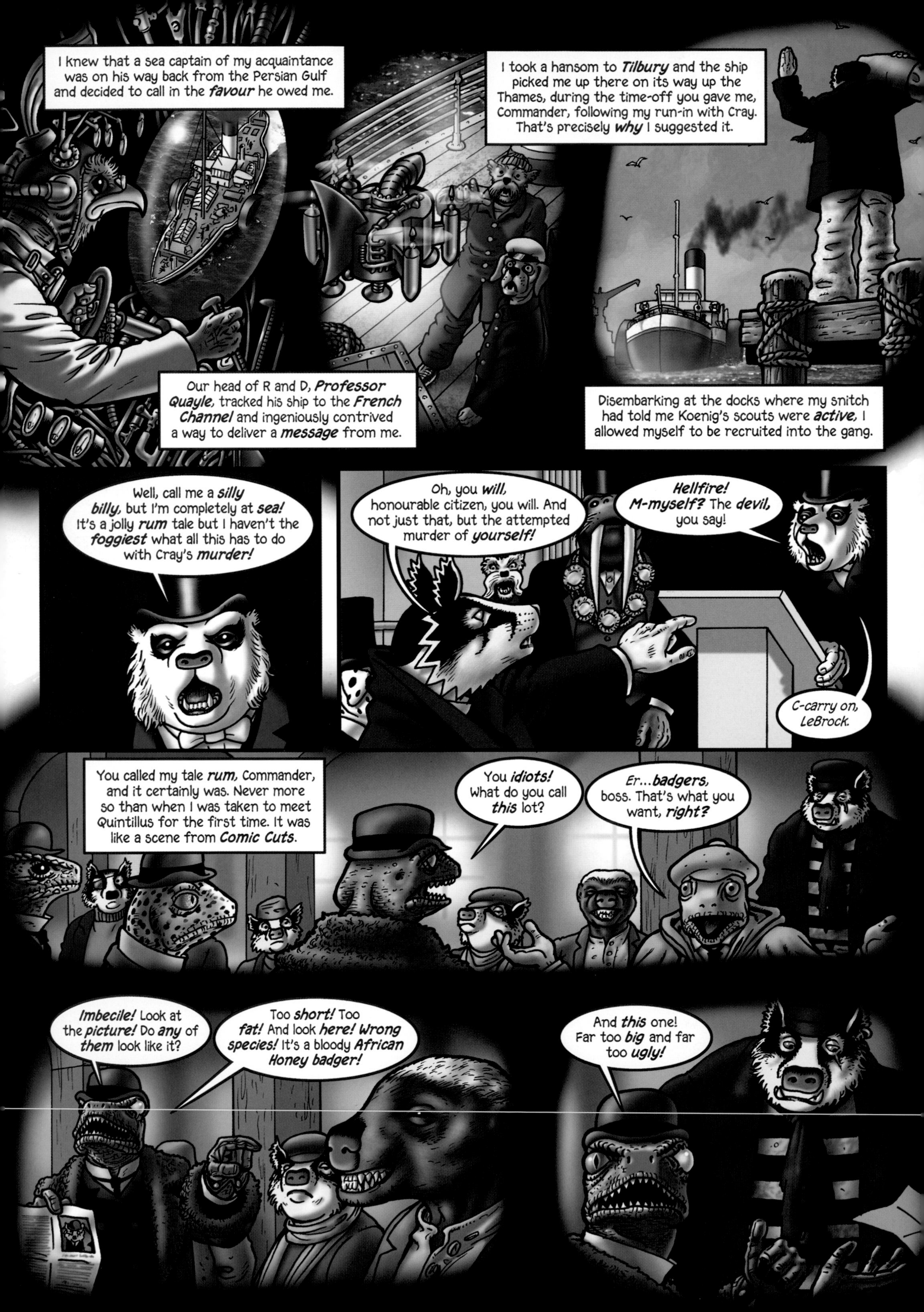

I knew that a sea captain of my acquaintance was on his way back from the Persian Gulf and decided to call in the *favour* he owed me.
I took a hansom to *Tilbury* and the ship picked me up there on its way up the Thames, during the time-off you gave me, Commander, following my run-in with Cray. That's precisely *why* I suggested it.
Our head of R and D, *Professor Quayle*, tracked his ship to the *French Channel* and ingeniously contrived a way to deliver a *message* from me.
Disembarking at the docks where my snitch had told me Koenig's scouts were *active*, I allowed myself to be recruited into the gang.
Well, call me a *silly billy*, but I'm completely at *sea!* It's a jolly *rum* tale but I haven't the *foggiest* what all this has to do with Cray's *murder!*
Oh, you *will*, honourable citizen, you will. And not just that, but the attempted murder of *yourself!*
Hellfire! M-myself? The *devil,* you say!
C-carry on, LeBrock.
You called my tale *rum*, Commander, and it certainly was. Never more so than when I was taken to meet Quintillus for the first time. It was like a scene from *Comic Cuts*.
You *idiots!* What do you call *this* lot?
Er...*badgers*, boss. That's what you want, *right?*
Imbecile! Look at the *picture!* Do *any* of *them* look like it?
Too *short!* Too *fat!* And look *here! Wrong species!* It's a bloody *African Honey badger!*
And *this* one! Far too *big* and far too *ugly!*

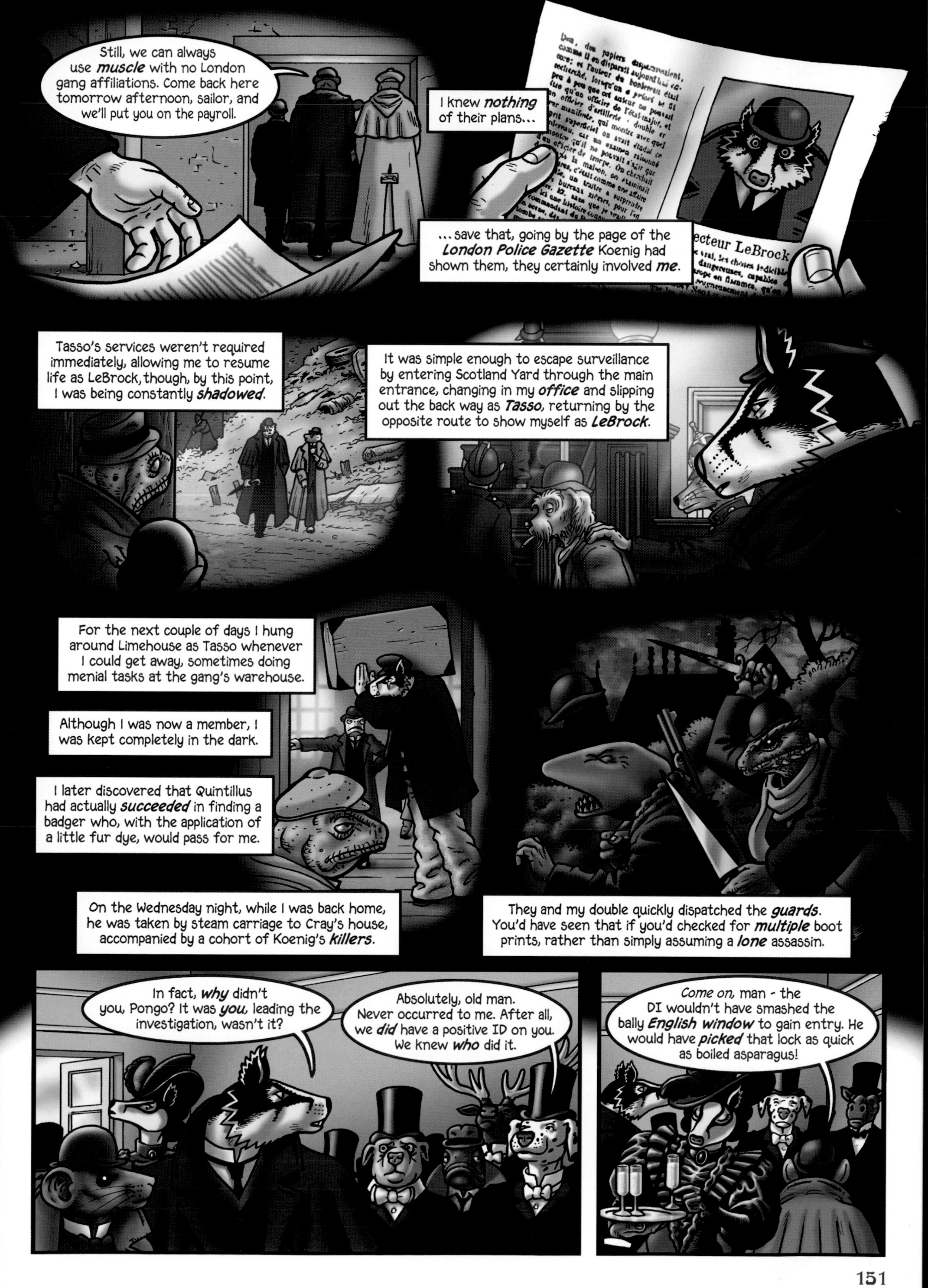
Still, we can always use *muscle* with no London gang affiliations. Come back here tomorrow afternoon, sailor, and we'll put you on the payroll.
I knew *nothing* of their plans...
...save that, going by the page of the *London Police Gazette* Koenig had shown them, they certainly involved *me*.
Tasso's services weren't required immediately, allowing me to resume life as LeBrock, though, by this point, I was being constantly *shadowed*.
It was simple enough to escape surveillance by entering Scotland Yard through the main entrance, changing in my *office* and slipping out the back way as *Tasso*, returning by the opposite route to show myself as *LeBrock*.
For the next couple of days I hung around Limehouse as Tasso whenever I could get away, sometimes doing menial tasks at the gang's warehouse.
Although I was now a member, I was kept completely in the dark.
I later discovered that Quintillus had actually *succeeded* in finding a badger who, with the application of a little fur dye, would pass for me.
On the Wednesday night, while I was back home, he was taken by steam carriage to Cray's house, accompanied by a cohort of Koenig's *killers*.
They and my double quickly dispatched the *guards*. You'd have seen that if you'd checked for *multiple* boot prints, rather than simply assuming a *lone* assassin.
In fact, *why* didn't you, Pongo? It was *you*, leading the investigation, wasn't it?
Absolutely, old man. Never occurred to me. After all, we *did* have a positive ID on you. We knew *who* did it.
Come on, man - the DI wouldn't have smashed the bally *English window* to gain entry. He would have *picked* that lock as quick as boiled asparagus!

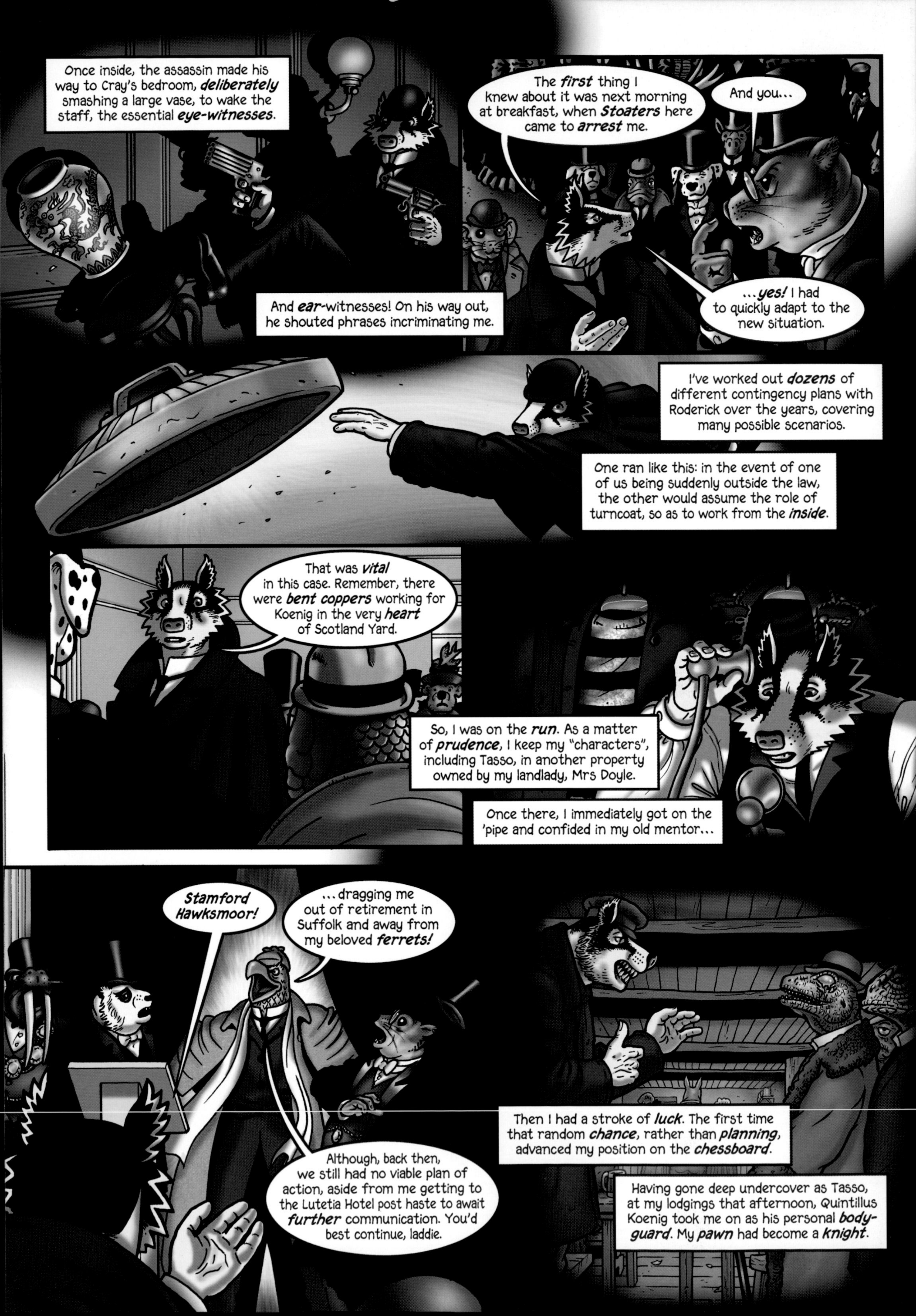
Once inside, the assassin made his way to Cray's bedroom, *deliberately* smashing a large vase, to wake the staff, the essential *eye-witnesses*.
And *ear*-witnesses! On his way out, he shouted phrases incriminating me.
The *first* thing I knew about it was next morning at breakfast, when *Stoaters* here came to *arrest* me.
And you...
...*yes!* I had to quickly adapt to the new situation.
I've worked out *dozens* of different contingency plans with Roderick over the years, covering many possible scenarios.
One ran like this: in the event of one of us being suddenly outside the law, the other would assume the role of turncoat, so as to work from the *inside*.
That was *vital* in this case. Remember, there were *bent coppers* working for Koenig in the very *heart* of Scotland Yard.
So, I was on the *run*. As a matter of *prudence*, I keep my "characters", including Tasso, in another property owned by my landlady, Mrs Doyle.
Once there, I immediately got on the 'pipe and confided in my old mentor...
Stamford Hawksmoor!
...dragging me out of retirement in Suffolk and away from my beloved *ferrets!*
Although, back then, we still had no viable plan of action, aside from me getting to the Lutetia Hotel post haste to await *further* communication. You'd best continue, laddie.
Then I had a stroke of *luck*. The first time that random *chance*, rather than *planning*, advanced my position on the *chessboard*.
Having gone deep undercover as Tasso, at my lodgings that afternoon, Quintillus Koenig took me on as his personal *body-guard*. My *pawn* had become a *knight*.

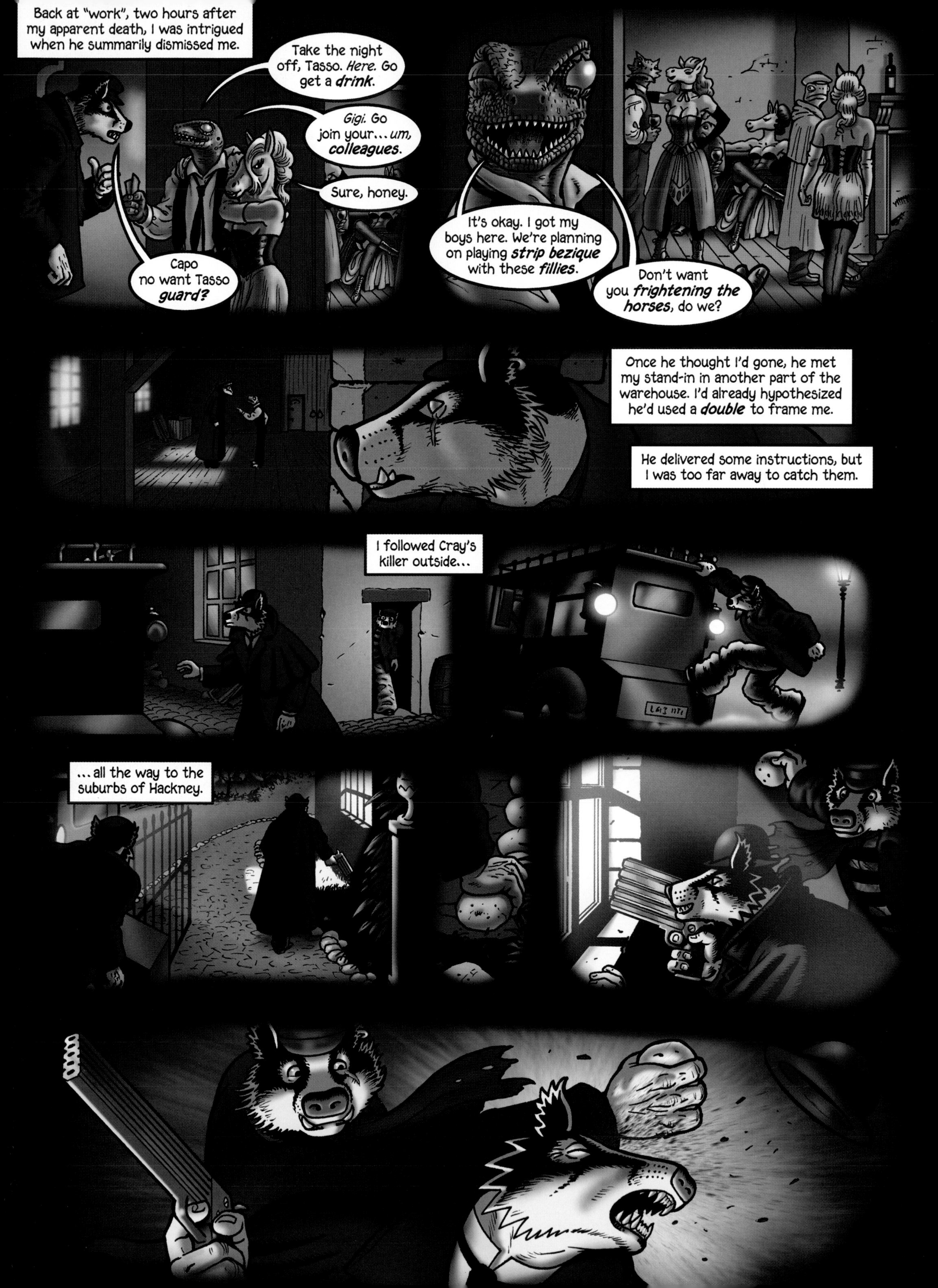

Back at "work", two hours after my apparent death, I was intrigued when he summarily dismissed me.
Take the night off, Tasso. *Here.* Go get a ***drink***.
Gigi. Go join your... *um,* ***colleagues***.
Sure, honey.
Capo no want Tasso ***guard?***
It's okay. I got my boys here. We're planning on playing ***strip bezique*** with these ***fillies***.
Don't want you ***frightening the horses***, do we?
Once he thought I'd gone, he met my stand-in in another part of the warehouse. I'd already hypothesized he'd used a ***double*** to frame me.
He delivered some instructions, but I was too far away to catch them.
I followed Cray's killer outside...
...all the way to the suburbs of Hackney.

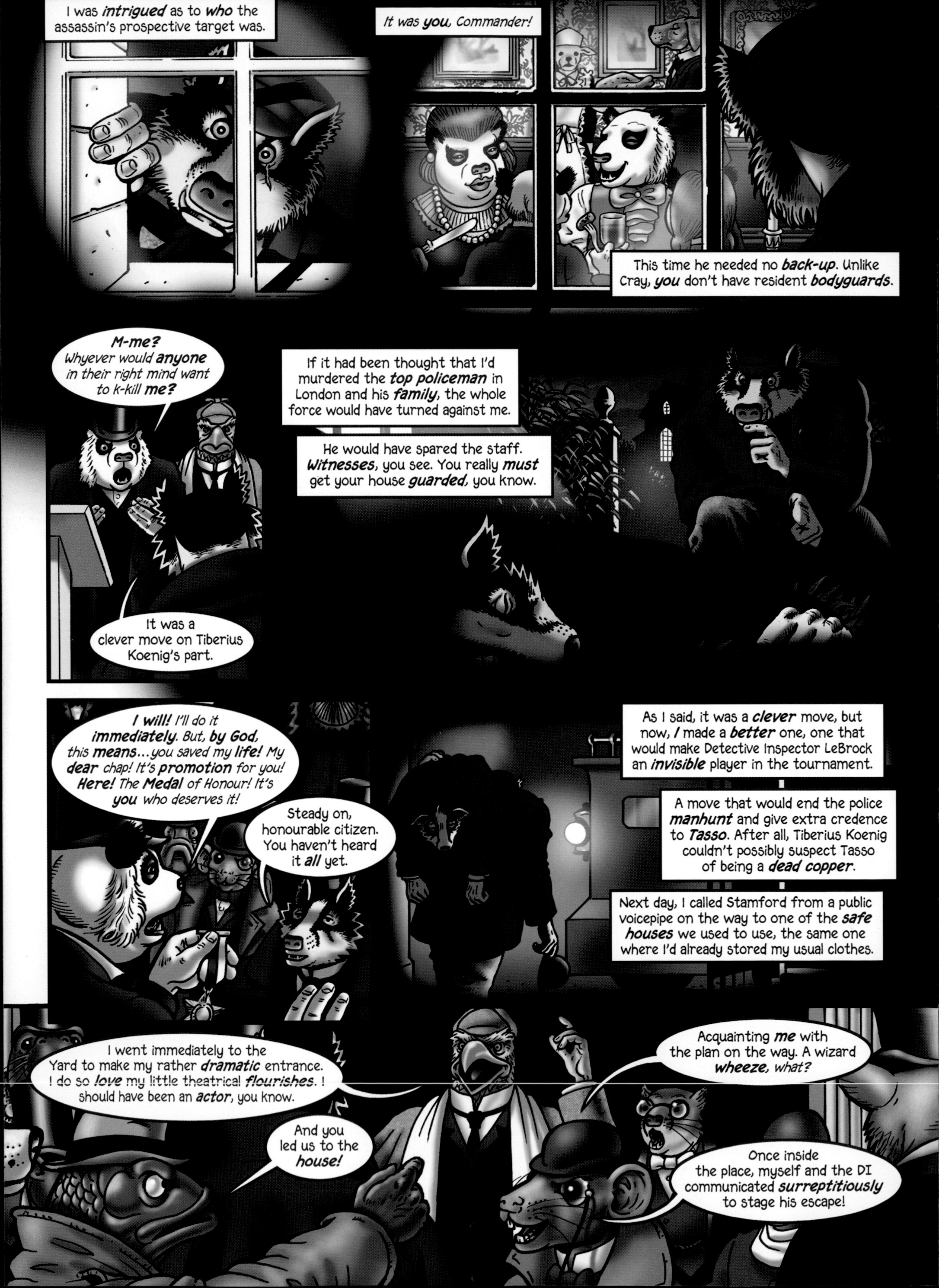

I was *intrigued* as to *who* the assassin's prospective target was.
*It was **you**, Commander!*
This time he needed no ***back-up***. Unlike Cray, ***you*** don't have resident ***bodyguards***.
M-me? *Whyever would **anyone** in their right mind want to k-kill **me?***
If it had been thought that I'd murdered the ***top policeman*** in London and his ***family***, the whole force would have turned against me.
He would have spared the staff. ***Witnesses***, you see. You really ***must*** get your house ***guarded***, you know.
It was a clever move on Tiberius Koenig's part.
I will! *I'll do it **immediately**. But, **by God**, this **means**... you saved my **life**! My **dear** chap! It's **promotion** for you! **Here!** The **Medal** of Honour! It's **you** who deserves it!*
Steady on, honourable citizen. You haven't heard it ***all*** yet.
As I said, it was a ***clever*** move, but now, ***I*** made a ***better*** one, one that would make Detective Inspector LeBrock an ***invisible*** player in the tournament.
A move that would end the police ***manhunt*** and give extra credence to ***Tasso***. After all, Tiberius Koenig couldn't possibly suspect Tasso of being a ***dead copper***.
Next day, I called Stamford from a public voicepipe on the way to one of the ***safe houses*** we used to use, the same one where I'd already stored my usual clothes.
I went immediately to the Yard to make my rather ***dramatic*** entrance. I do so ***love*** my little theatrical ***flourishes***. I should have been an ***actor***, you know.
Acquainting ***me*** with the plan on the way. A wizard ***wheeze***, *what?*
And you led us to the ***house!***
Once inside the place, myself and the DI communicated ***surreptitiously*** to stage his escape!

Eh? *"Communicated surreptitiously"?* What the *deuce* are you blathering about?

It's awfully *clever*, DCI. The DI invented a *code* consisting of minute *facial movements*, each corresponding to a precise instruction or piece of information.

For example, a double backwards *twitch* of the left ear means...

Damn and blast! I don't care if it means *"Your maiden aunt canoodles* with a *duck-billed platypus!"* *Get on* with it, man!

Roderick made sure he gave me at least ten seconds before lobbing in the grenade.

That was *more* than enough. I'd *already* picked the back door lock, swapped coats with the assassin and positioned him so an explosion would leave wreckage *beneath* the body.

If the floor had been *clear* beneath him, it would have been obvious he was lying there even before the blast.

Picking the lock *shut* from the outside, I made good my escape before the explosion, observed by Stamford here and two hand-picked coppers who were known to be *loyal* to me.

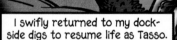

I swifly returned to my dock-side digs to resume life as Tasso.

But...but...your mother *identified* your body and even knew about a birthmark *hidden* from her view!

Easily *arranged*, but let me continue.

By gum! This is *cracking* stuff!

I can use all this in *your* stories, Chief Inspector!

Next morning, a quick call by my *stool pigeon* ensured the warehouse was *raided*. I needed Quintillus Koenig to flee back to his *brother*.

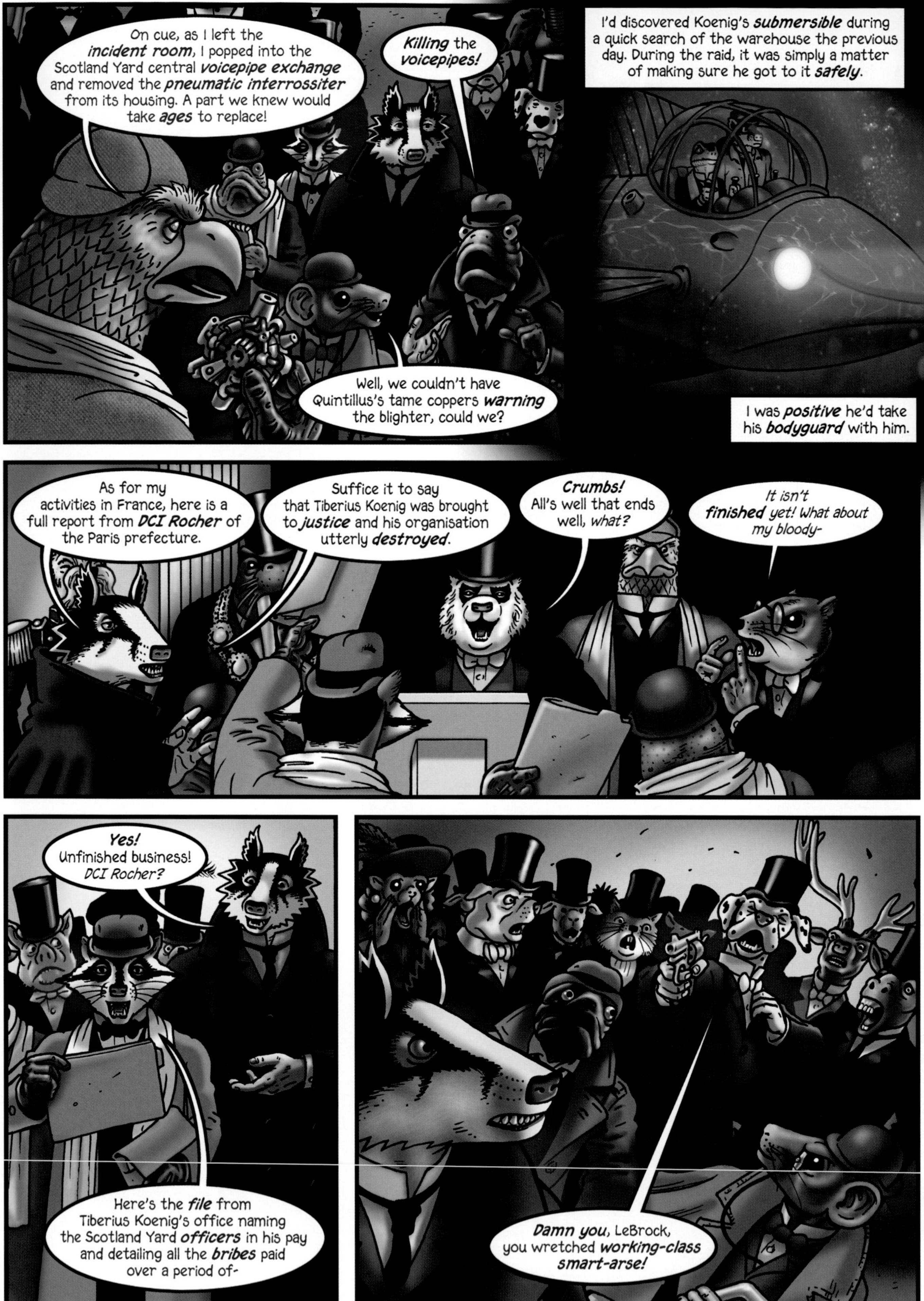
On cue, as I left the incident room, I popped into the Scotland Yard central voicepipe exchange and removed the pneumatic interrossiter from its housing. A part we knew would take ages to replace!
Killing the voicepipes!
Well, we couldn't have Quintillus's tame coppers warning the blighter, could we?
I'd discovered Koenig's submersible during a quick search of the warehouse the previous day. During the raid, it was simply a matter of making sure he got to it safely.
I was positive he'd take his bodyguard with him.
As for my activities in France, here is a full report from DCI Rocher of the Paris prefecture.
Suffice it to say that Tiberius Koenig was brought to justice and his organisation utterly destroyed.
Crumbs! All's well that ends well, what?
It isn't finished yet! What about my bloody-
Yes! Unfinished business! DCI Rocher?
Here's the file from Tiberius Koenig's office naming the Scotland Yard officers in his pay and detailing all the bribes paid over a period of-
Damn you, LeBrock, you wretched working-class smart-arse!

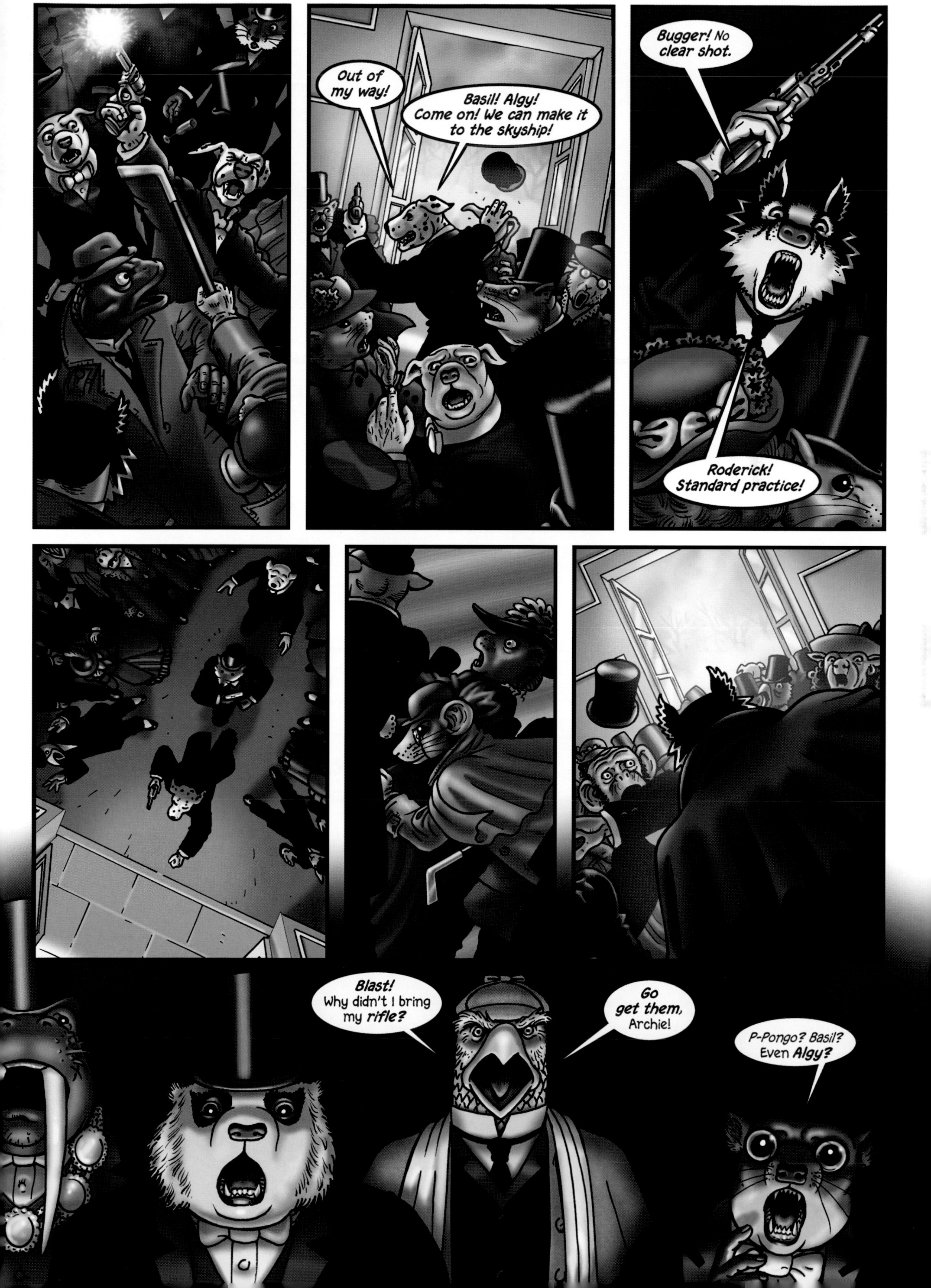

Out of my way!
Basil! Algy! Come on! We can make it to the skyship!
Bugger! No clear shot.
Roderick! Standard practice!
Blast! Why didn't I bring my rifle?
Go get them, Archie!
P-Pongo? Basil? Even Algy?

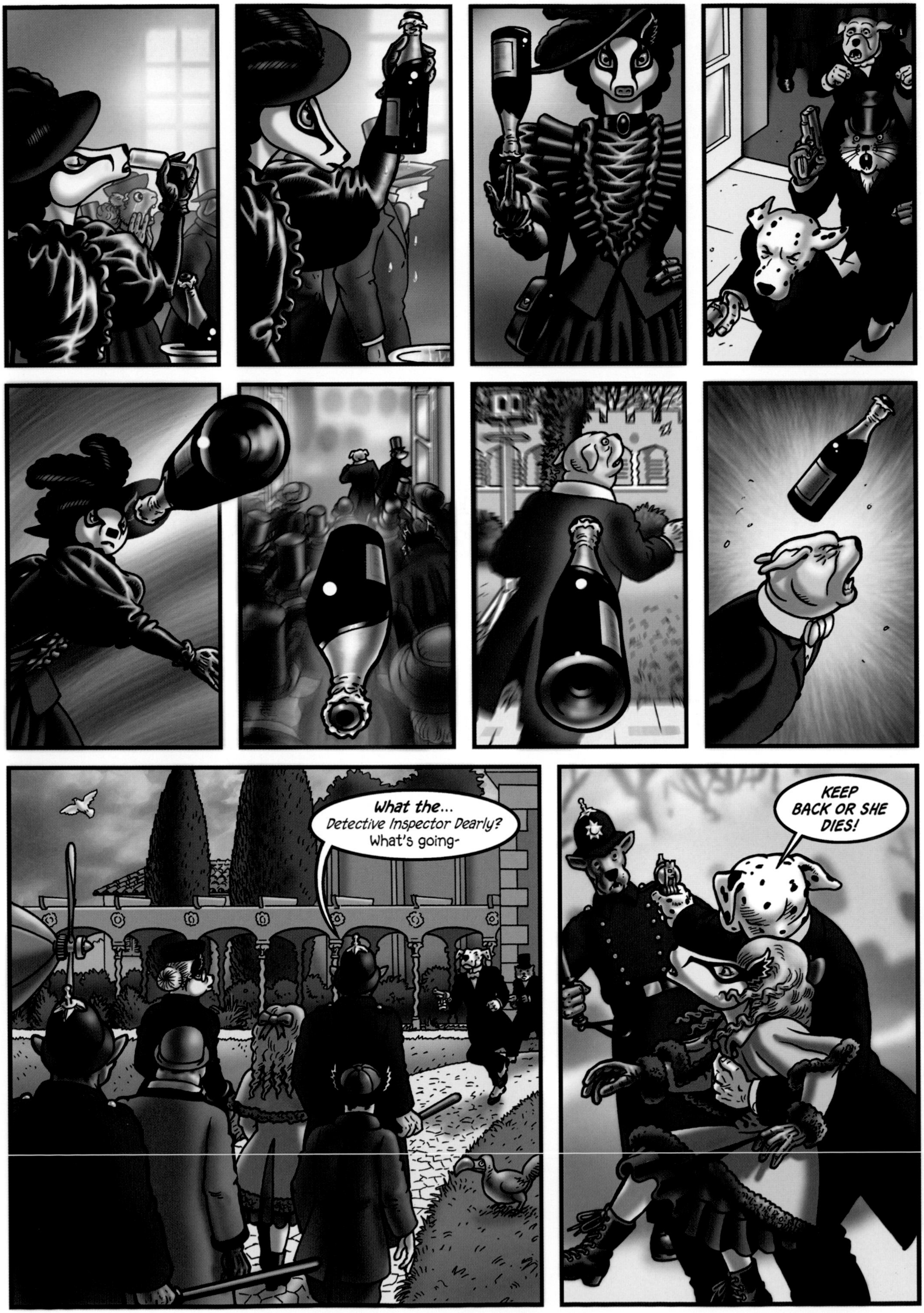

What the...
Detective Inspector Dearly?
What's going-
KEEP BACK OR SHE DIES!

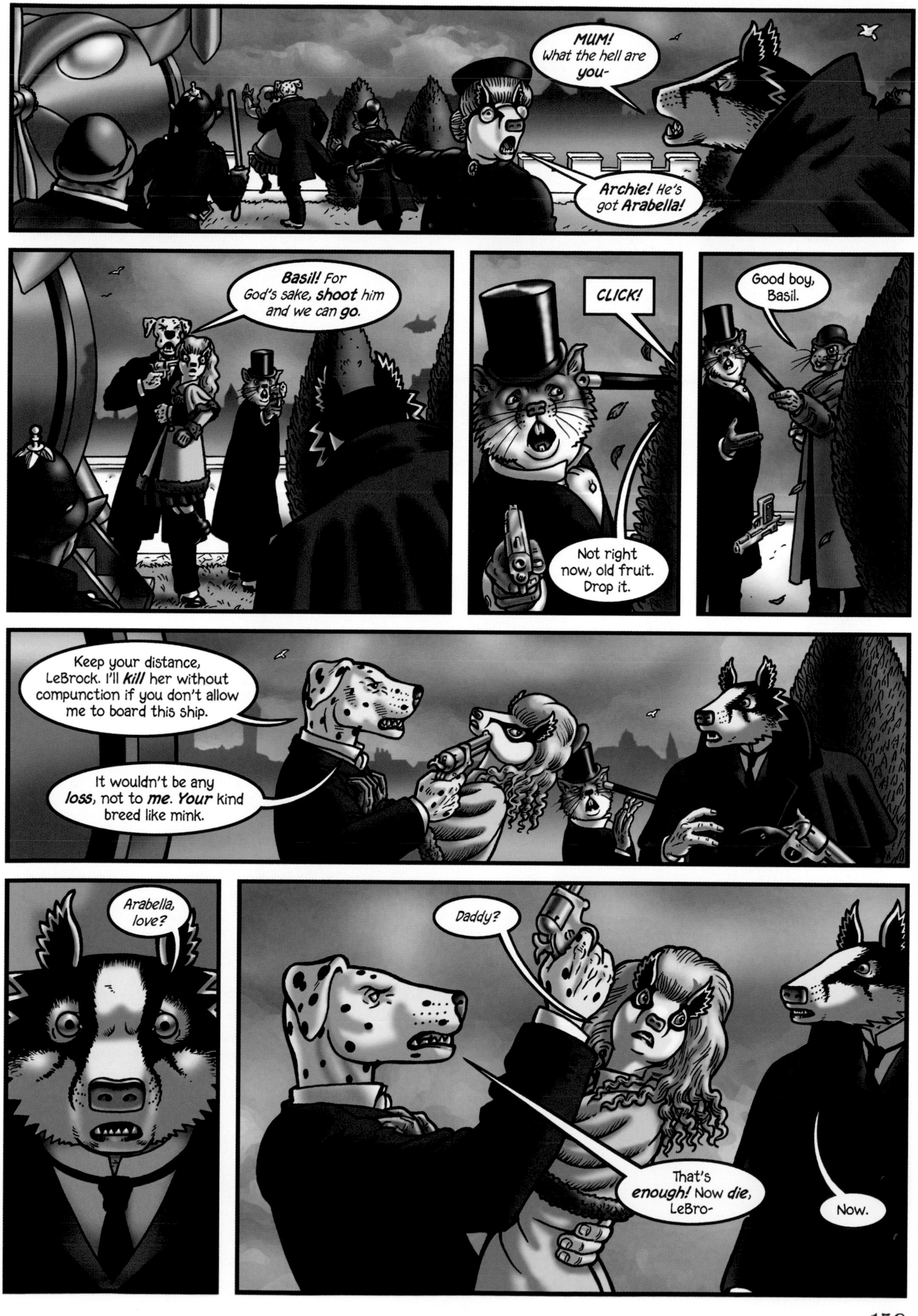
MUM! What the hell are you-
Archie! He's got Arabella!
Basil! For God's sake, shoot him and we can go.
CLICK!
Not right now, old fruit. Drop it.
Good boy, Basil.
Keep your distance, LeBrock. I'll kill her without compunction if you don't allow me to board this ship.
It wouldn't be any loss, not to me. Your kind breed like mink.
Arabella, love?
Daddy?
That's enough! Now die, LeBro-
Now.

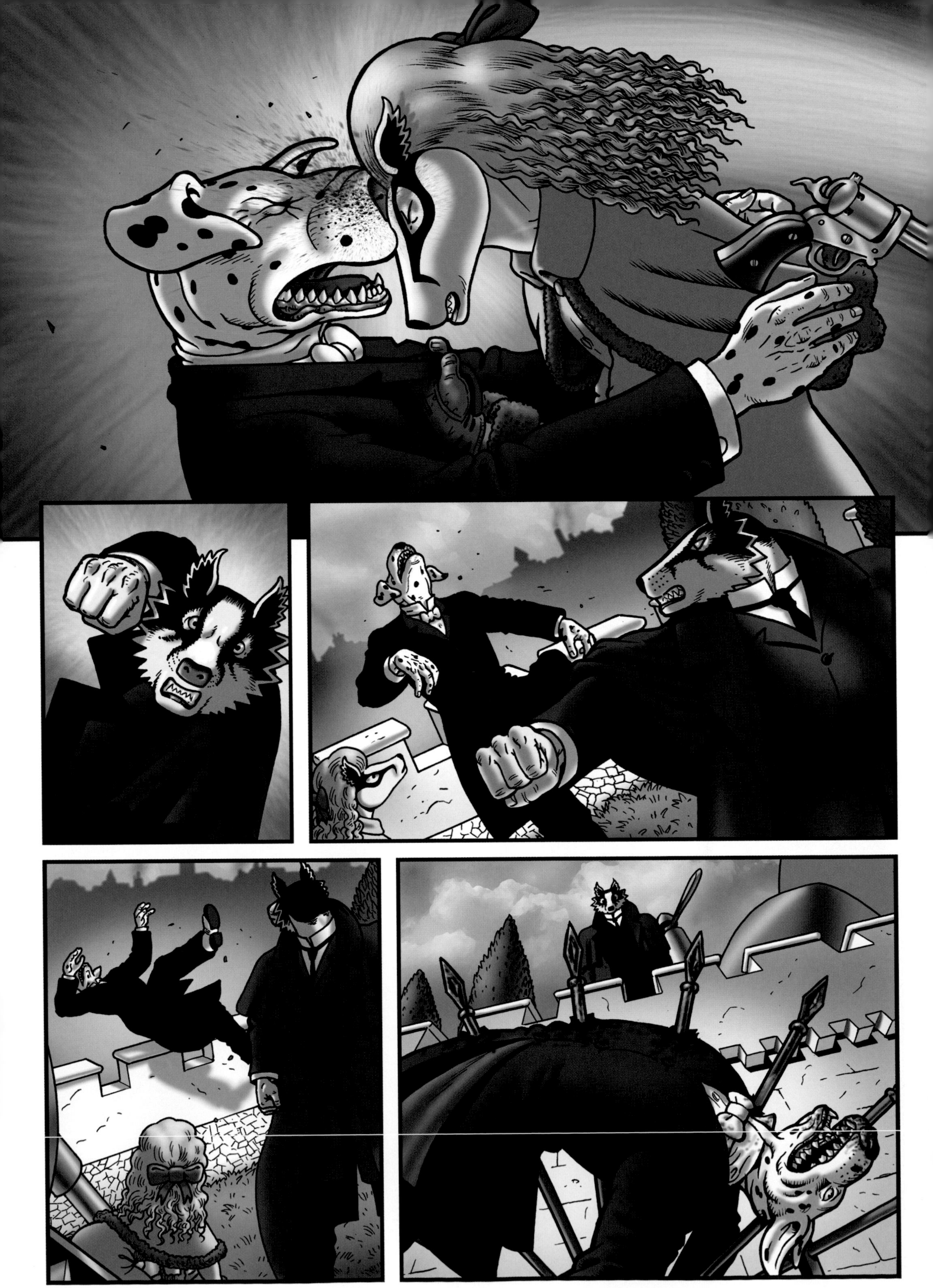

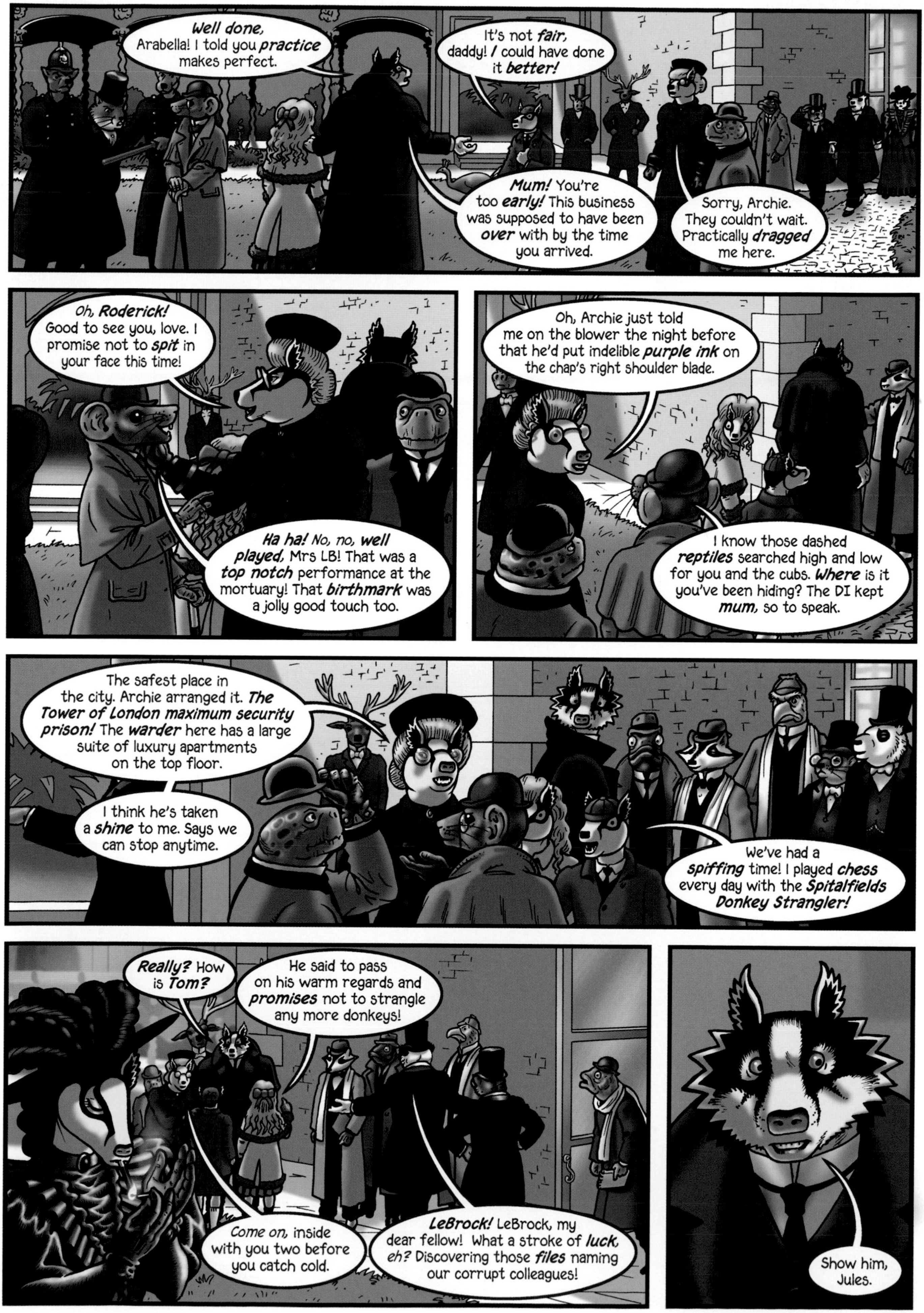

Well done, Arabella! I told you practice makes perfect.
It's not fair, daddy! I could have done it better!
Mum! You're too early! This business was supposed to have been over with by the time you arrived.
Sorry, Archie. They couldn't wait. Practically dragged me here.
Oh, Roderick! Good to see you, love. I promise not to spit in your face this time!
Ha ha! No, no, well played, Mrs LB! That was a top notch performance at the mortuary! That birthmark was a jolly good touch too.
Oh, Archie just told me on the blower the night before that he'd put indelible purple ink on the chap's right shoulder blade.
I know those dashed reptiles searched high and low for you and the cubs. Where is it you've been hiding? The DI kept mum, so to speak.
The safest place in the city. Archie arranged it. The Tower of London maximum security prison! The warder here has a large suite of luxury apartments on the top floor.
I think he's taken a shine to me. Says we can stop anytime.
We've had a spiffing time! I played chess every day with the Spitalfields Donkey Strangler!
Really? How is Tom?
He said to pass on his warm regards and promises not to strangle any more donkeys!
Come on, inside with you two before you catch cold.
LeBrock! LeBrock, my dear fellow! What a stroke of luck, eh? Discovering those files naming our corrupt colleagues!
Show him, Jules.

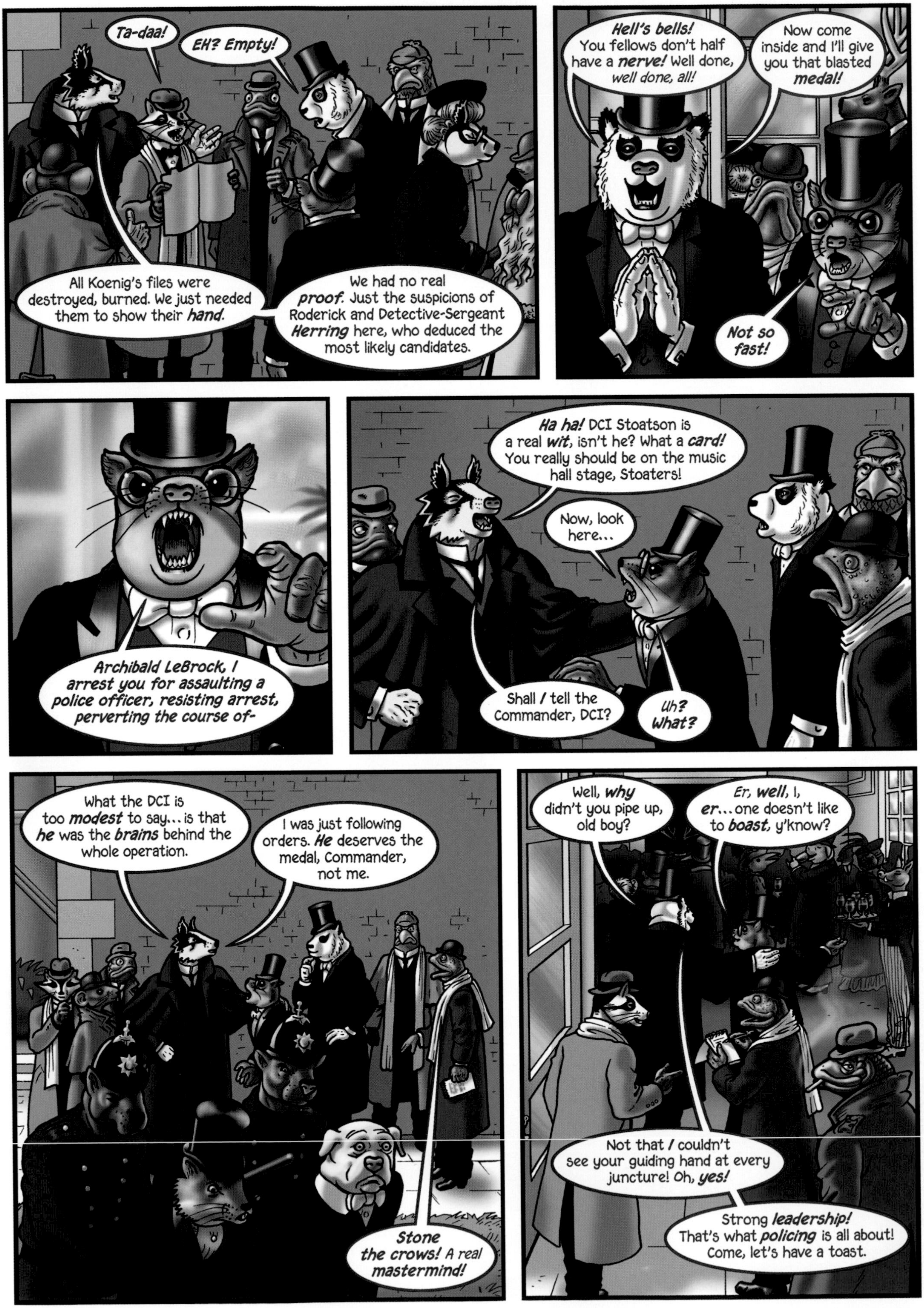
Ta-daa!
EH? Empty!
All Koenig's files were destroyed, burned. We just needed them to show their hand.
We had no real proof. Just the suspicions of Roderick and Detective-Sergeant Herring here, who deduced the most likely candidates.
Hell's bells! You fellows don't half have a nerve! Well done, well done, all!
Now come inside and I'll give you that blasted medal!
Not so fast!
Archibald LeBrock, I arrest you for assaulting a police officer, resisting arrest, perverting the course of-
Ha ha! DCI Stoatson is a real wit, isn't he? What a card! You really should be on the music hall stage, Stoaters!
Now, look here...
Shall I tell the Commander, DCI?
Uh? What?
What the DCI is too modest to say... is that he was the brains behind the whole operation.
I was just following orders. He deserves the medal, Commander, not me.
Stone the crows! A real mastermind!
Well, why didn't you pipe up, old boy?
Er, well, I, er... one doesn't like to boast, y'know?
Not that I couldn't see your guiding hand at every juncture! Oh, yes!
Strong leadership! That's what policing is all about! Come, let's have a toast.

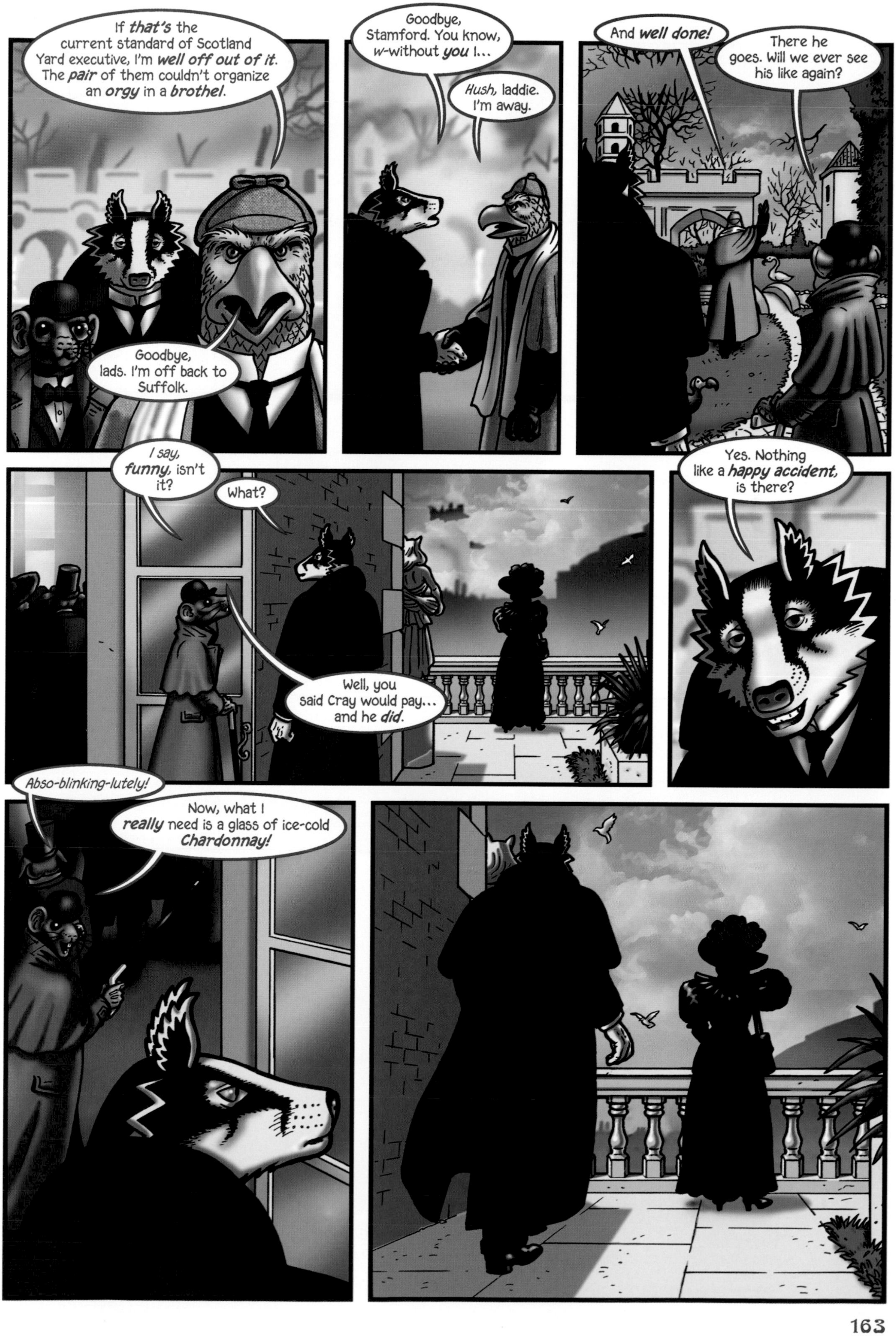

If *that's* the current standard of Scotland Yard executive, I'm ***well off out of it.*** The ***pair*** of them couldn't organize an ***orgy*** in a ***brothel.***
Goodbye, lads. I'm off back to Suffolk.
Goodbye, Stamford. You know, *w*-without ***you*** I...
Hush, laddie. I'm away.
And ***well done!***
There he goes. Will we ever see his like again?
I say, ***funny,*** isn't it?
What?
Well, you said Cray would pay... and he ***did.***
Yes. Nothing like a ***happy accident,*** is there?
Abso-blinking-lutely!
Now, what I ***really*** need is a glass of ice-cold ***Chardonnay!***

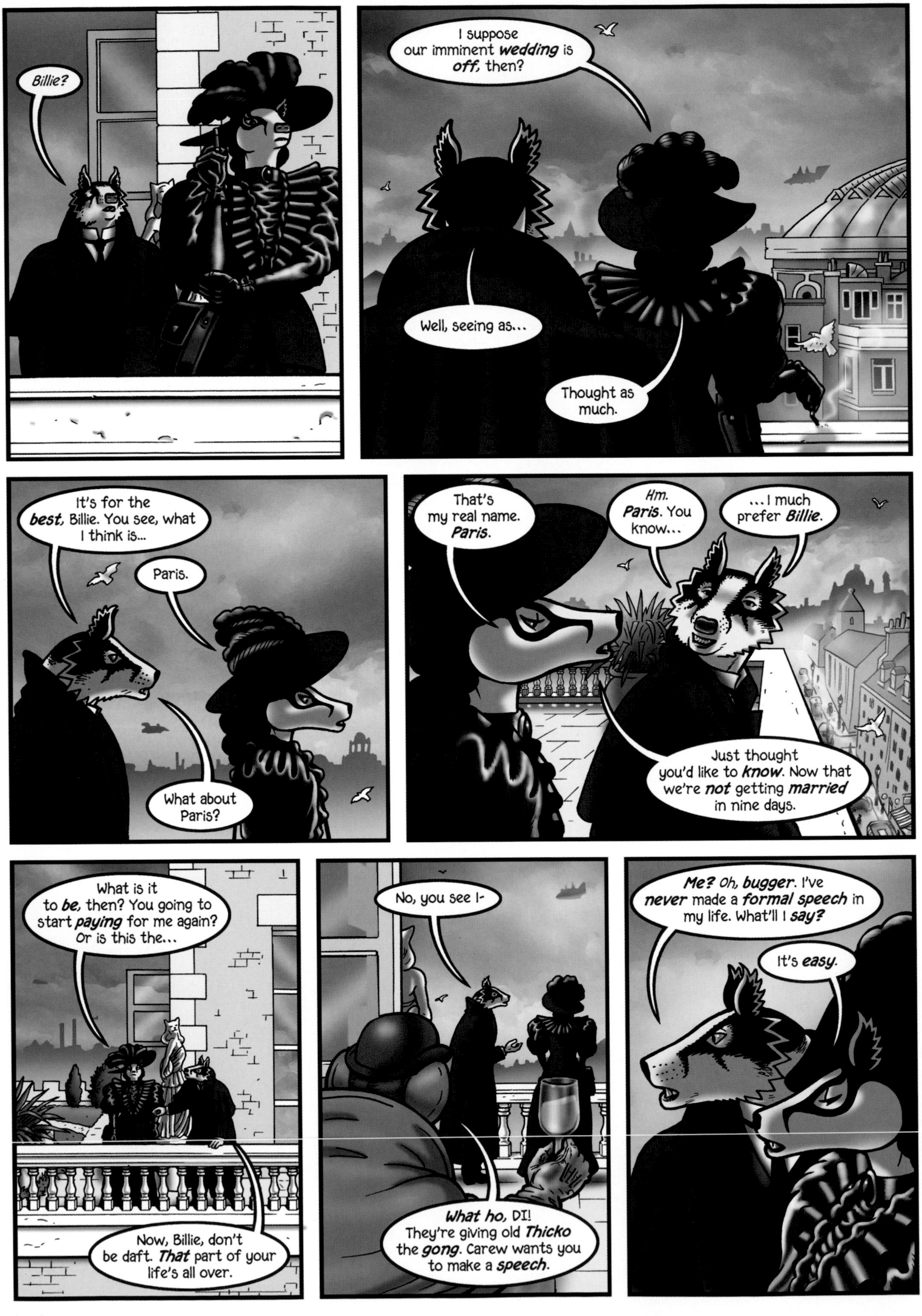
Billie?
I suppose our imminent wedding is off, then?
Well, seeing as...
Thought as much.
It's for the best, Billie. You see, what I think is...
Paris.
What about Paris?
That's my real name. Paris.
Hm. Paris. You know...
...I much prefer Billie.
Just thought you'd like to know. Now that we're not getting married in nine days.
What is it to be, then? You going to start paying for me again? Or is this the...
Now, Billie, don't be daft. That part of your life's all over.
No, you see I-
What ho, DI! They're giving old Thicko the gong. Carew wants you to make a speech.
Me? Oh, bugger. I've never made a formal speech in my life. What'll I say?
It's easy.

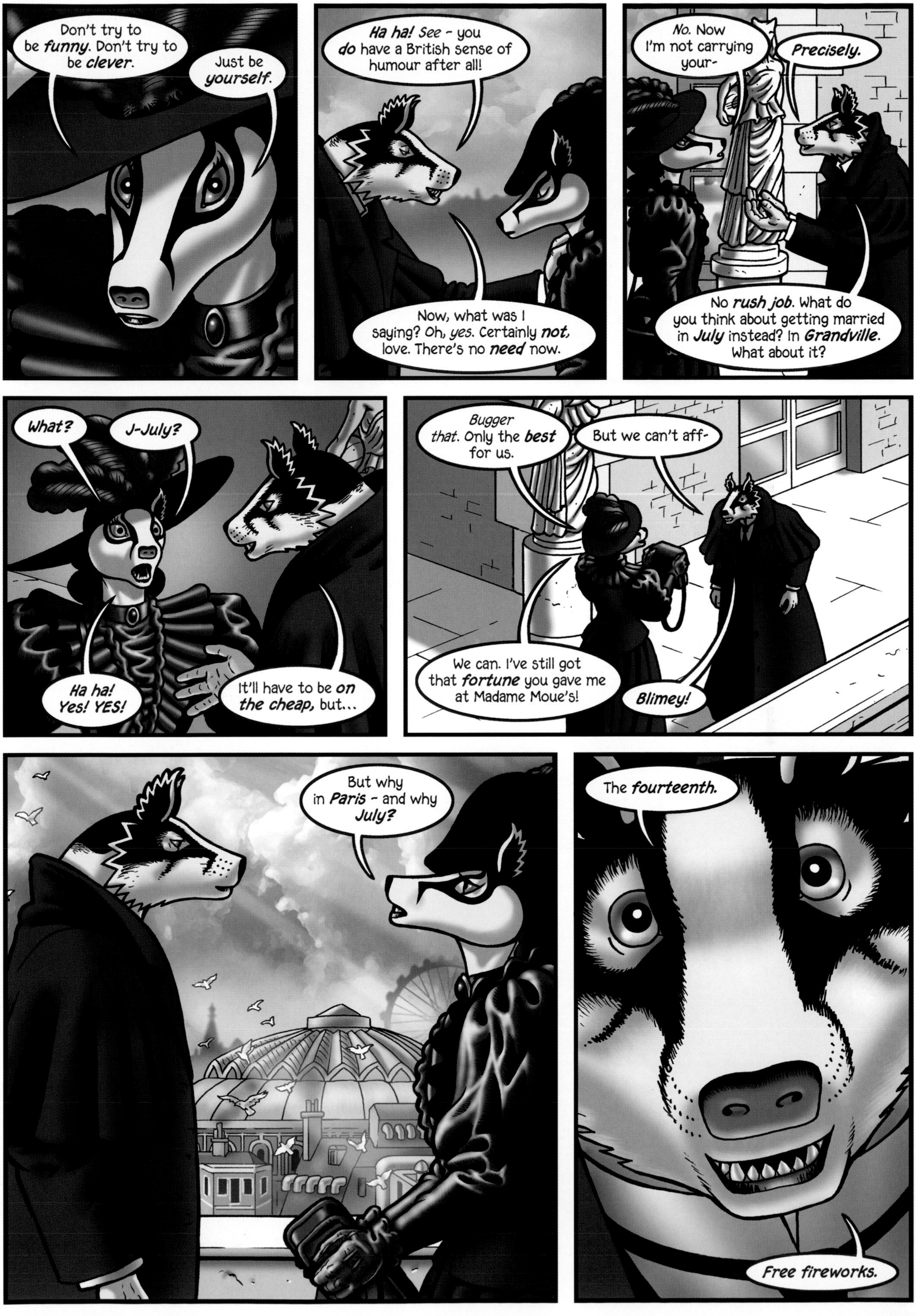
Don't try to be *funny*. Don't try to be *clever*.
Just be *yourself*.
Ha ha! See - you *do* have a British sense of humour after all!
Now, what was I saying? Oh, *yes*. Certainly *not*, love. There's no *need* now.
No. Now I'm not carrying your-
Precisely.
No *rush job*. What do you think about getting married in *July* instead? In *Grandville*. What about it?
What?
J-July?
Ha ha! Yes! YES!
It'll have to be *on the cheap*, but...
Bugger that. Only the *best* for us.
But we can't aff-
We can. I've still got that *fortune* you gave me at Madame Moue's!
Blimey!
But why in *Paris* - and why *July?*
The *fourteenth*.
Free fireworks.

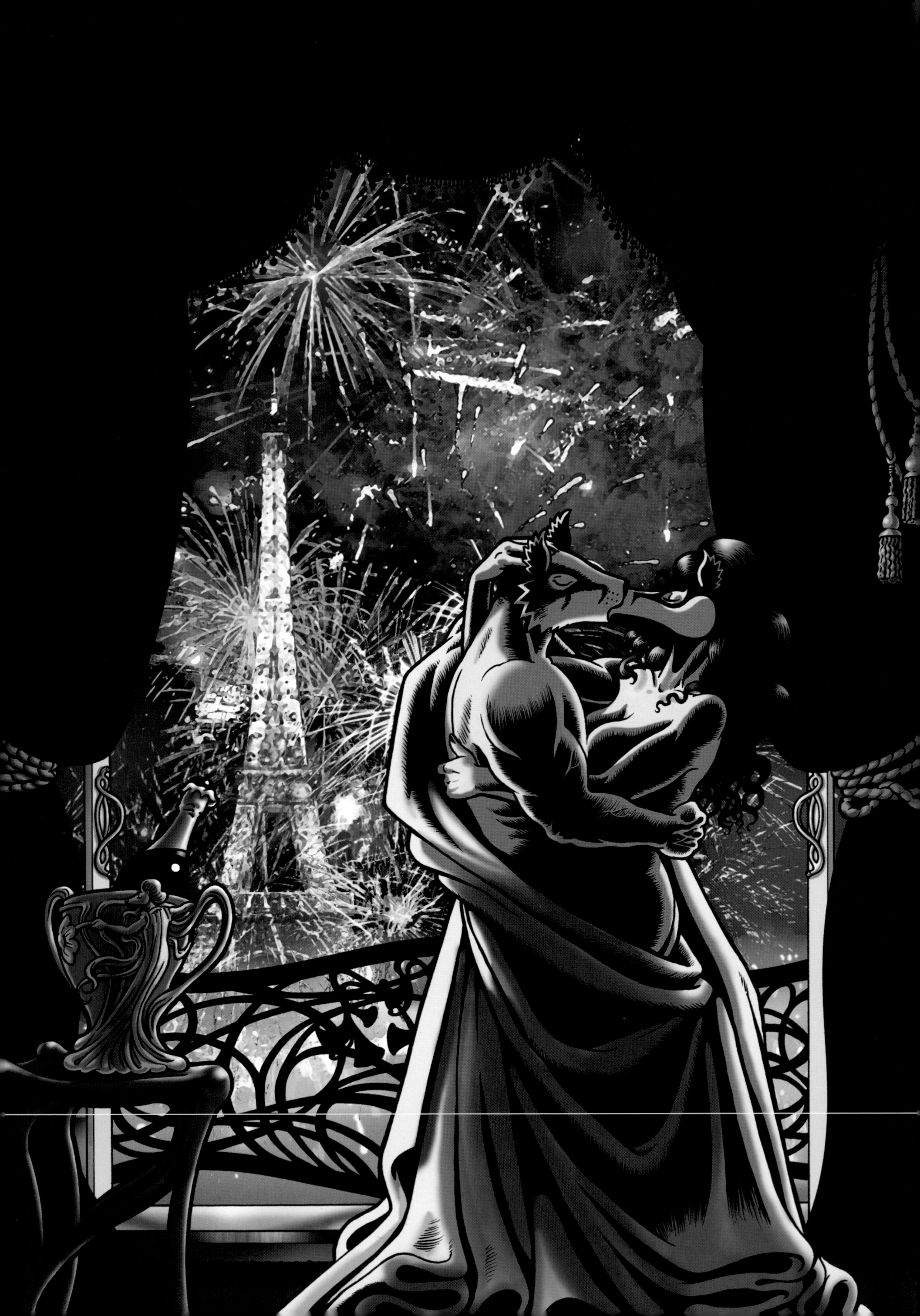

Grandville™
Force Majeure

Fin

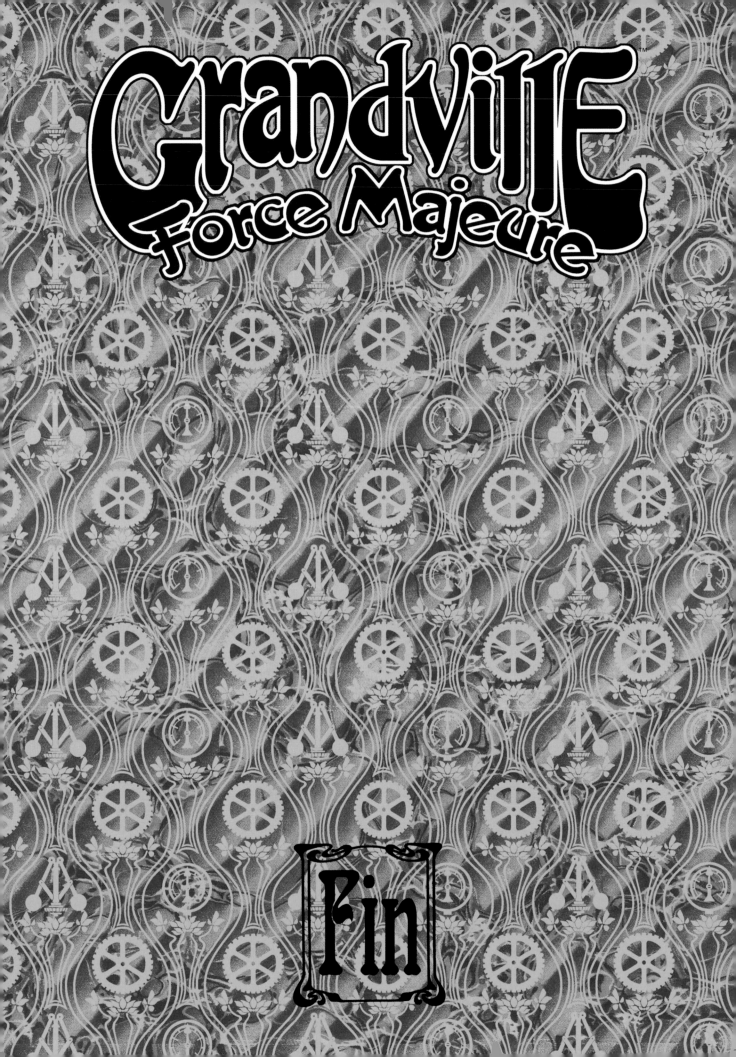

publication design
BRYAN TALBOT

president and publisher
MIKE RICHARDSON

U.S. editor
CHRIS WARNER

digital art technician
BRENNAN THOME

GRANDVILLE FORCE MAJEURE

Dark Horse Books
A division of Dark Horse Comics, Inc.
10956 SE Main Street
Milwaukie OR 97222

darkhorse.com

To find a comics shop in your area, call the Comic Shop Locator Service toll-free at 1-888-266-4226

First edition: October 2017
ISBN 978-1-50670-380-0

10 9 8 7 6 5 4 3 2 1

Printed in China

A la Recherche du Temps Perdu

I always felt exceptionally close to my maternal grandmother. A working class, self-sufficient, hard-working woman, she was as hard as nails, and very fond of proverbs such as "Waste not, want not" and "What the eye does not see, the heart does not grieve." More relevant, as regards the *Grandville* stories, was "You can't go wrong with a badger with guns."

That's a joke.

There's nothing new about stories with anthropomorphic characters. They've been around ever since people have been telling stories, evidenced by Palaeolithic cave painting and sculpture, such as the lion-headed *Löwenmensch* figurine. Carved from a woolly mammoth tusk, discovered in Germany's Hohlenstein-Stadel caves and aged around forty thousand years, it is the oldest example of figurative art in the world. Anthropomorphic characters feature in all the world's mythologies and religions, some more than others, the Bible famously containing a talking snake in the first chapter of Genesis. Passing through the centuries via the fables of Aesop, in the oral tradition of folklore and fairy tales, appearing in medieval illuminated manuscripts and carved into the stone of medieval cathedrals, anthropomorphic (or, more precisely, zoomorphic) creatures have persistently haunted our collective consciousness and popular culture.

Much of *Grandville* is, for me, a return to childhood pleasures, transmogrified to appeal to my adult self. My first comic reading material, courtesy of my parents, was the nursery weekly *Jack and Jill*, which featured a wealth of anthropomorphic strips, such as *Harold Hare*, *Freddy Frog* and the frankly disturbing *Jerry, Don and Snooker* by HM Talintyre. My dad's Christmas presents to me for many years were the *Rupert the Bear* annuals, written and drawn by Alfred E Bestall, with their beautiful watercolour endpapers, something I referenced with *The Tale of One Bad Rat*'s endpapers. In the first *Grandville* volume, the murder at the beginning of the story takes place in Rupert's village of Nutwood.

Meanwhile, on the tiny screen of the TV that was my babysitter, I was fascinated by the reruns of the *Sherlock Holmes* film series starring Basil Rathbone and Nigel Bruce. Another favourite was the supposedly real-life detective series *Scotland Yard*, introduced by Edgar Lustgarten. Back then, I wanted to be a private detective when I grew up. In fact, the first comics that I wrote and drew (as an only child, I had to make my own amusements) from age eight onwards were comedy detective adventures, inspired by the strip *Send for Kelly* in the weekly children's comic *The Topper*, one of dozens published by Dundee's DC Thomson.

You may have noticed that this volume is dedicated to the memory of Leo Baxendale. In the 1950s, exactly the time I was reading them, Leo, along with Ken Reid and Davey Law, reinvented the British children's comic. Their protagonists were out-and-out anarchists. Figures of authority—policemen, teachers, park keepers, even parents—became, not only figures of fun, but sworn enemies. Leo's *Bash Street Kids* and The *Banana Bunch* had pitched battles in the street with the massed ranks of the police force. His Minnie the Minx would use weapons of mass destruction when confronted with boy gangs. Even though DC Thomson forbade the use of artists' credits (with the notable exception of the legendary DW Watkins), each of the gang of three's styles was distinctively recognizable. In the early Sixties, after Leo left the DC Thomson empire and produced, almost single-handedly, the weekly comic *Wham!* for Odham's Press, featuring genius creations *Eagle Eye, Junior Spy* and the terminally creepy *Grimly Fiendish* (I still have the first issue), for the first time, we could see the signature of their creator.

I was awed to briefly meet Leo at a small comics pro con in London in the late Seventies when I was a struggling underground comix artist. Around four years later, at the afternoon opening of a small exhibition of my comic artwork at the Harris Library and Museum in my then hometown of Preston, Lancashire, I was staggered to turn around to find that I was standing right next to one of my comics heroes. It turned out that, although then resident in the south of England, Leo was originally from Preston and frequently journeyed the couple of hundred miles north to visit his mother. To be brief, we became the best of friends and, for the next fifteen years or so, whenever Leo came to see his mum, he stayed with Mary and me, and we shared many a dinner, a movie, and bottle of wine together. We had two touring comic art exhibitions with *Guardian* cartoonist Steve Bell. We even hosted in Preston, as committee members of the Preston Speculative Fiction Group, the official Bash Street Kids 40th Birthday party, complete with alternative comics creator Ben (*Vogarth*) Hunt's indie rock group with Sonia on keyboards dressed as Minnie the Minx.

We only saw Leo occasionally after his mother died, though we did stay in touch and we'd always send each other our latest books. Leo self-published a whole series of prose memoirs, but his short-lived *Baby Basil* for *The Guardian* in 1992 was the last strip he drew. His last published comics work was the one-page strip that he spontaneously and very generously penned for my graphic novel *Alice in Sunderland* (2007), which featured both of us as characters, and which I drew in a mixture of our styles. Attending the Bristol Comics Expo sometime around 2012, I made an excursion to nearby Stroud and spent a pleasant evening with him and his wife, Peggy. Despite having had various health escapades, they both seemed unaffected by them and happy in themselves.

Leo died in April this year aged 86. In panel 2, page 26, you can see my homage to Leo in the form of characters from his anthropomorphic strips *The Gobbles* and *The Three Bears*, something I'd scripted when I wrote this book around five years ago. The page was penciled and inked in 2015.

Leo's work was very much part of my childhood and a big influence—especially his sense of composition and love of detail. Although I was limited to two weekly comics, *The Topper* and *The Beezer*, I caught up with his strips in *The Beano* and *The Dandy* every time I visited a schoolfriend who did get them, so much so that his dad nicknamed me "The Comics Kid," as I stayed in their living room to read through his pile of back issues while my mate went out to play football with his local chums. Both comics had anthropomorphic characters on their covers, *Biffo the Bear* on the former and *Korky the Cat* on the latter. You may spot Korky several times in this book.

In fact, there are many such nods to the comics and TV series of my youth throughout all the *Grandville* books. In this one, these include two characters from the children's TV show *Tuesday Rendezvous*: *Ollie Beak*, standing next to *Fred Barker* on page 28, *Muffin the Mule* on the same page, and *Top Cat* on page 22. Roderick is named after the rat in *Tales of the Riverbank* and Billie after Rupert's friend Bill the badger.

Although I've been enjoying this second childhood, I'm afraid to say that this will be the final volume. Not only do I want to quit while I'm ahead (and I do think that this is the best story and artwork so far), but the *Grandville* art style is far too time-consuming. Each page takes three to four ten-hour days to complete, not counting the scripting. The pages are drawn and inked on the drawing board, then scanned in and coloured and lettered on computer. The best thing about digital painting is that everything's infinitely changeable. The worst about digital painting is that everything's infinitely changeable. This is a nightmare to a perfectionist. Using other art styles, I can produce one or two pages per day, for the same money.

But *Grandville* may go on to have a life of its own. There are already metal figurines of the characters on sale, and a role-playing game is in the works. At the time of writing, the TV and film rights have been optioned by a very big production company, a top TV writer has produced the script for the pilot episode and the structure for the first eight-part series, and they are currently trying to secure a director. It is envisaged as live-action/ CGI fusion, which sounds ideal. Though I'm not holding my breath. I've been here before with *The Adventures of Luther Arkwright*, and more than once at that, so I'll believe it when I see it.

If it does actually get made, I'm sure that my grandmother would have enjoyed it immensely. LeBrock is very much like her: working class, hard as nails, tenacious and enterprising, and she liked cop TV shows. And, like him, saying "bugger" was as natural to her as breathing.

Bryan Talbot
Sunderland, July 2017

Eisner and Eagle award-winner Bryan Talbot has produced underground and alternative comics, notably *Brainstorm!*, science fiction and superhero stories such as *Judge Dredd*, *Nemesis the Warlock*, *Teknophage*, *The Nazz* and *Batman: Legends of the Dark Knight*. He's worked on DC Vertigo titles including *Hellblazer*, *Sandman*, *The Dreaming* and *Fables* and has written and drawn the graphic novels for which he is best known, including *The Adventures of Luther Arkwright*, *Heart of Empire*, *The Tale of One Bad Rat* and *Alice in Sunderland*. He is published in over fifteen countries and is a frequent guest at international comic festivals. He was awarded an honorary Doctorate in Arts by Sunderland University in 2009 and a Doctorate in Letters by Northumbria University in 2012. The *Grandville* series has been twice nominated for a Hugo Award and the French edition of *Grandville Mon Amour* won the Prix SNCF for best graphic novel in 2012. *Dotter of Her Father's Eyes*, a collaboration with his wife Mary Talbot, was the first British graphic novel to win a major literary prize, the Costa Biography Award.

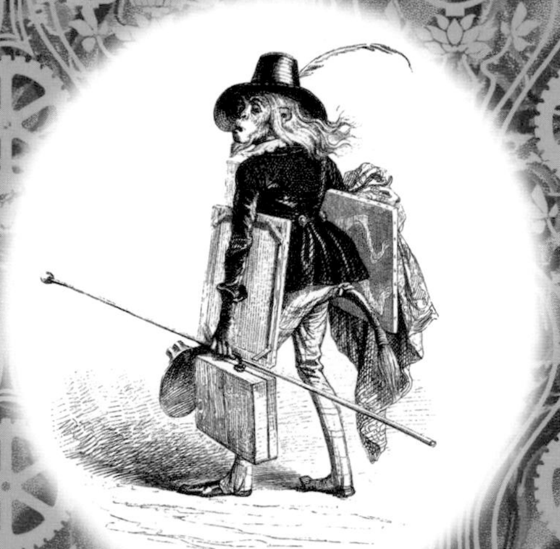

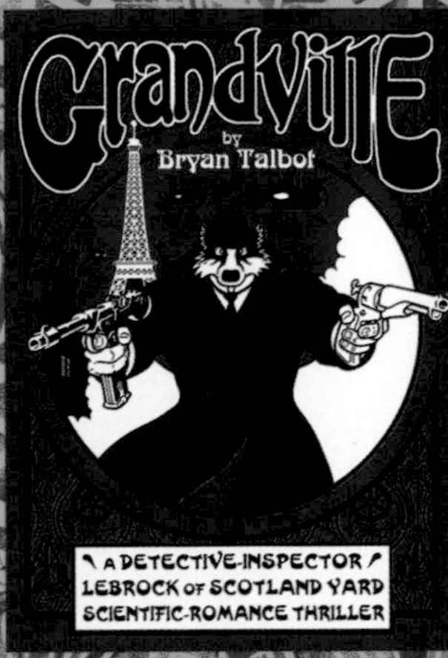
Grandville
by
Bryan Talbot
A DETECTIVE-INSPECTOR
LEBROCK OF SCOTLAND YARD
SCIENTIFIC-ROMANCE THRILLER

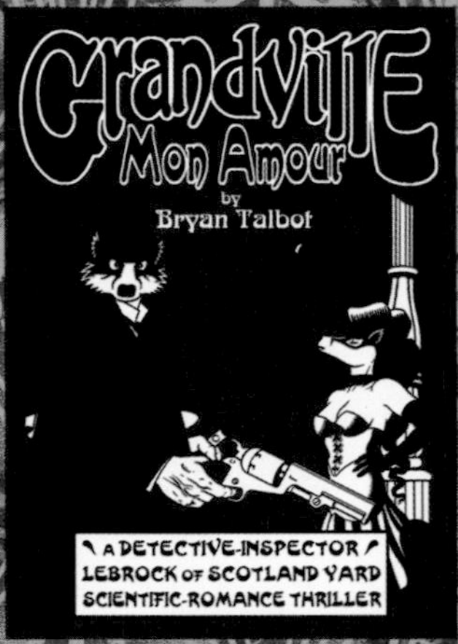
Grandville
Mon Amour
by
Bryan Talbot
A DETECTIVE-INSPECTOR
LEBROCK OF SCOTLAND YARD
SCIENTIFIC-ROMANCE THRILLER

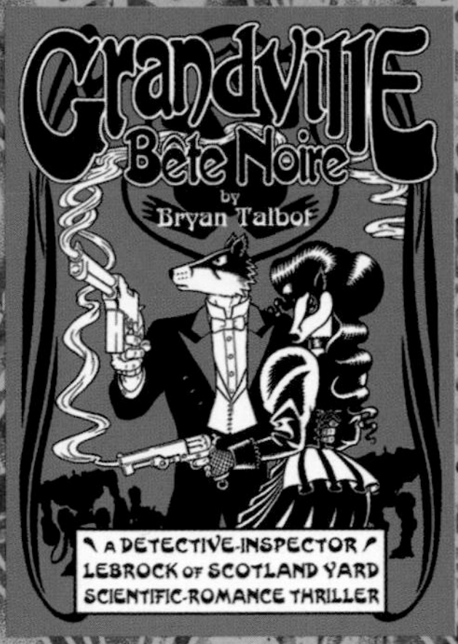
Grandville
Bête Noire
by
Bryan Talbot
A DETECTIVE-INSPECTOR
LEBROCK OF SCOTLAND YARD
SCIENTIFIC-ROMANCE THRILLER

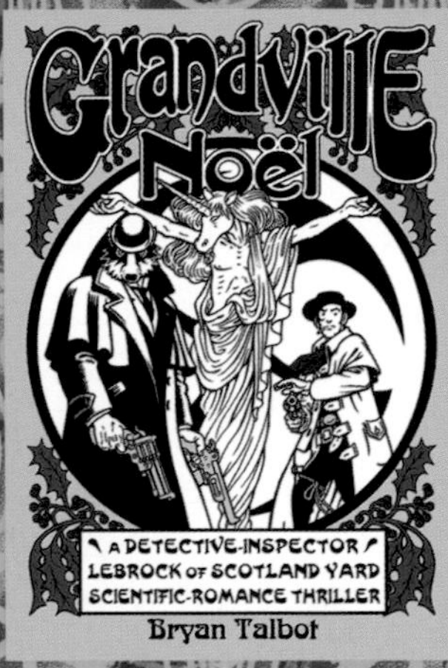
Grandville
Noël
A DETECTIVE-INSPECTOR
LEBROCK OF SCOTLAND YARD
SCIENTIFIC-ROMANCE THRILLER
Bryan Talbot

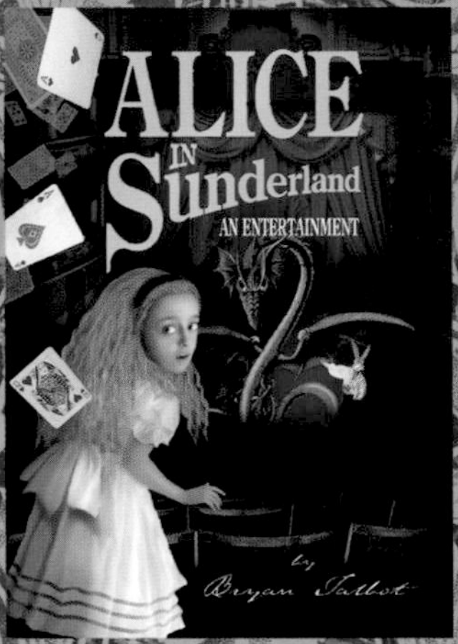
ALICE
IN
Sunderland
AN ENTERTAINMENT
by
Bryan Talbot

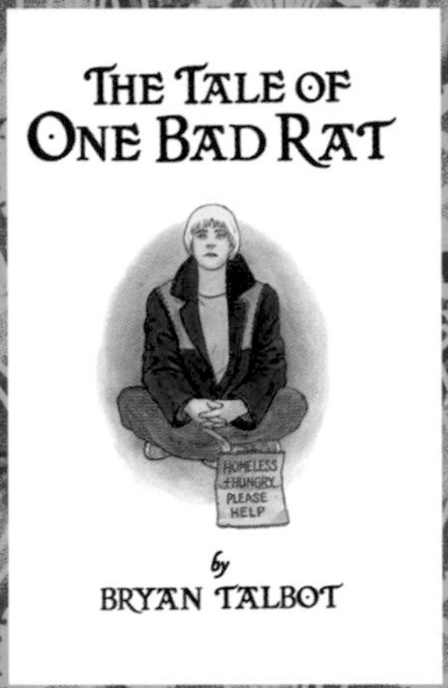
THE TALE OF
ONE BAD RAT
HOMELESS & HUNGRY PLEASE HELP
by
BRYAN TALBOT

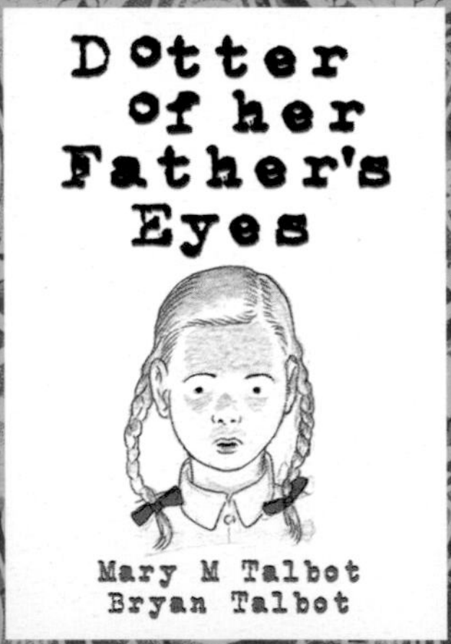
Dotter
of her
Father's
Eyes
Mary M Talbot
Bryan Talbot

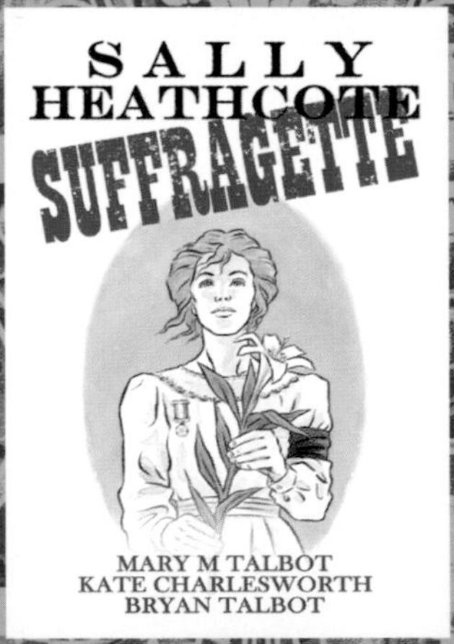
SALLY
HEATHCOTE
SUFFRAGETTE
MARY M TALBOT
KATE CHARLESWORTH
BRYAN TALBOT

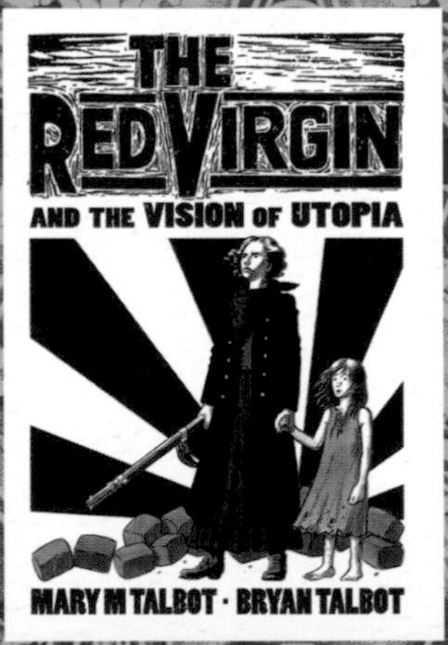
THE
RED VIRGIN
AND THE VISION OF UTOPIA
MARY M TALBOT · BRYAN TALBOT

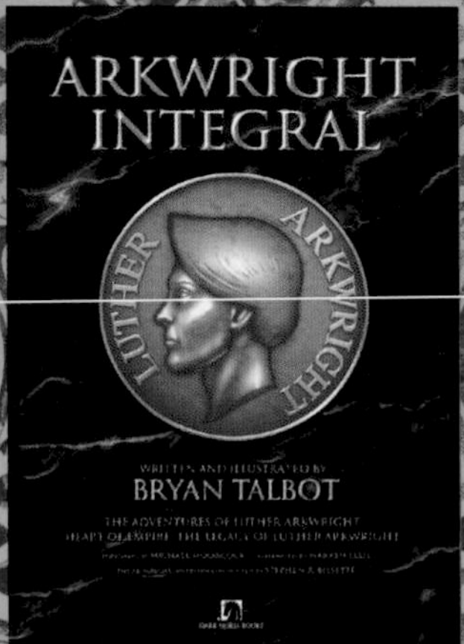
ARKWRIGHT
INTEGRAL
LUTHER ARKWRIGHT
WRITTEN AND ILLUSTRATED BY
BRYAN TALBOT

DARK
HORSE
BOOKS

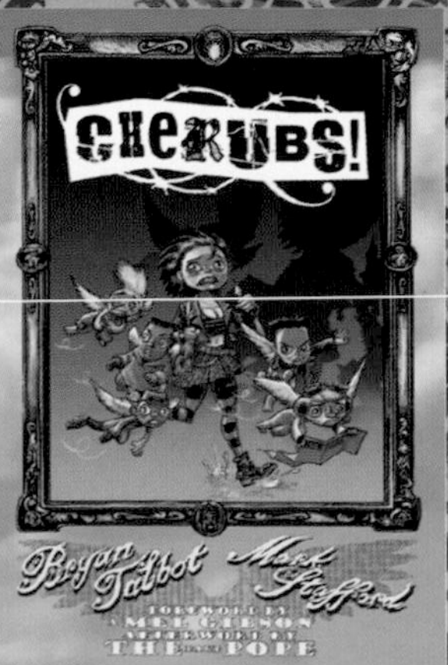
CHERUBS!
Bryan Talbot
Mark Stafford

Other books by Bryan Talbot

Brainstorm!

The Adventures of Luther Arkwright

Heart of Empire

The Tale of One Bad Rat

Alice in Sunderland

The Art of Bryan Talbot

The Naked Artist (Prose)

Grandville

Grandville Mon Amour

Grandville Bête Noire

Grandville Noël

Metronome
(Writing as Veronique Tanaka)

Cherubs!
(With Mark Stafford)

Nemesis the Warlock Vols 1 & 2
(With Pat Mills)

Sandman: Fables and Reflections
(With Neil Gaiman, Stan Woch & Mark Buckingham)

The Dead Boy Detectives and

the Secret of Immortality
(With Ed Brubaker & Steve Leialoha)

Dotter of Her Father's Eyes
(With Mary M Talbot)

Sally Heathcote: Suffragette
(With Mary M Talbot & Kate Charlesworth)

The Red Virgin and the Vision of Utopia
(With Mary M Talbot)

www.bryan-talbot.com

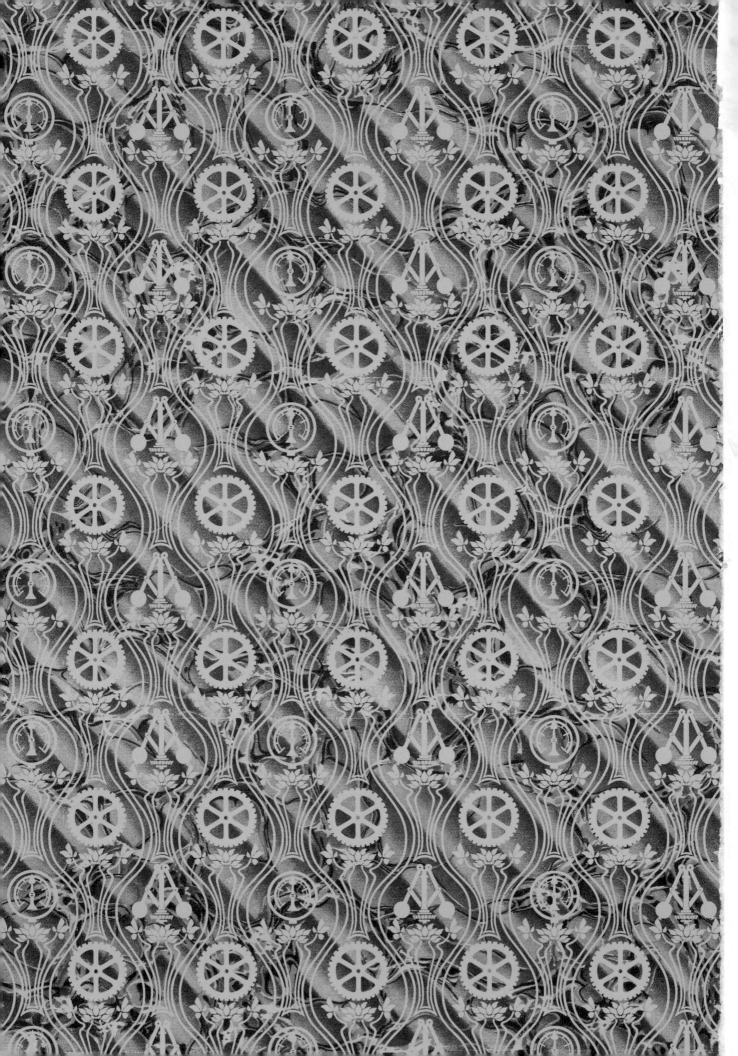